THE FIRST AMENDMENT

THE FREE EXERCISE OF RELIGION CLAUSE

D1260309

BILL OF RIGHTS SERIES

THE FIRST AMENDMENT
THE FREE EXERCISE OF RELIGION CLAUSE

Its Constitutional History and the Contemporary Debate

EDITED BY THOMAS C. BERG

 Prometheus Books

59 John Glenn Drive
Amherst, New York 14228-2119

Published 2008 by Prometheus Books

Inquiries should be addressed to
Prometheus Books
59 John Glenn Drive
Amherst, New York 14228–2119
VOICE: 716–691–0133, ext. 210
FAX: 716–691–0137
WWW.PROMETHEUSBOOKS.COM

12 11 10 09 08   5 4 3 2 1

Library of Congress Cataloging-in-Publication Data

Berg, Thomas C., 1960–
    The First Amendment : the free exercise of religion clause / Thomas C. Berg. — 1st American pbk. ed.
        p. cm.
    Includes bibliographical references.
    ISBN 978–1–59102–518–4
    1. Freedom of religion—United States. 2. Church and state—United States. I. Title.

KF4783.B44 2007
342.7308'52—dc22

2007022224

Printed in the United States of America on acid-free paper

CONTENTS

APPENDICES

BILL OF RIGHTS
SERIES EDITOR'S PREFACE

Abortion; the death penalty; school prayer; the pledge of allegiance; torture; surveillance; tort reform; jury trials; preventative detention; firearm registration; censorship; privacy; police misconduct; birth control; school vouchers; prison crowding; taking property by public domain. These issues, torn from the headlines, cover many, if not most, of the major public disputes arising today, in the dawn of the twenty-first century. Yet they are resolved by our courts based on a document fewer than five hundred words long, drafted in the eighteenth century, and regarded by many at the time of its drafting as unnecessary. The Bill of Rights, the name we give the second ten amendments to the United States Constitution, is our basic source of law for resolving these issues. This series of books, of which this is the second volume, is intended to help us improve our understanding of the debates that gave rise to these rights, and of the continuing controversy about their meaning today.

When our Constitution was drafted, the framers were concerned with defining the structure and powers of our new federal government and balancing its three branches. They did not initially focus on the question of individual rights. The drafters organized the Constitution into seven sections, termed "Articles," each concerned with a specific area of federal authority. Article I sets forth the legislative powers of the Congress; Article II the executive powers of the President; and Article III the judicial power of the federal

11

courts. Article V governs the process for amending the Constitution. Article VI declares the supremacy of federal law on those subjects under federal jurisdiction, while Article VII provides the process for ratification. Only Article IV is concerned with individual rights, and only in a single sentence requiring states to give citizens of other states the same rights they provide to their own citizens. (Article IV also provides for the return of runaway slaves, a provision repealed in 1865 by the Thirteenth Amendment).

When the Constitutional convention completed its work in 1787, it sent the Constitution to the states for adoption. The opponents of ratification, known as the "Anti-Federalists" because they opposed the strong federal government envisioned in the Constitution, argued that without a Bill of Rights the federal government would be a danger to liberty. The "Federalists," principally Alexander Hamilton, James Madison, and John Jay, responded in a series of anonymous newspaper articles now known as the "Federalist Papers." The Federalists initially argued that there was no need for a federal Bill of Rights, because most states (seven) had a state Bill of Rights, and because the proposed Constitution limited the power of the federal government to only those areas specifically enumerated, leaving all remaining powers to the states or the people. But in time, Madison would become the great proponent and drafter of the Bill of Rights.

The proposed Constitution was sent to the states for ratification on September 17, 1787. Delaware was the first State to assent, followed rapidly by Pennsylvania, New Jersey, Georgia, and Connecticut. But when the Massachusetts Legislature met in January 1788 to debate ratification, several vocal members took up the objection that without a Bill of Rights the proposed Constitution endangered individual liberty. A compromise was brokered, with the Federalists agreeing to support amending the Constitution to add a Bill of Rights following ratification. The Anti-Federalists, led by John Adams and John Hancock, agreed, and Massachusetts ratified. When Maryland, South Carolina, and New Hampshire followed, the requisite nine states had signed on. Virginia and New York quickly followed, with North Carolina ratifying in 1789 and Rhode Island in 1790. In addition to Massachusetts, New Hampshire's, Virginia's, and New York's ratifying conventions conditioned their acceptance on the understanding that a Bill of Rights would be added.

The first Congress met in New York City in March 1789 and, among its first acts, began debating and drafting the Bill of Rights. Federalist Congressman James Madison took responsibility for drafting the bill, having by then concluded it would strengthen the legitimacy of the new government. He relied heavily on the state constitutions, especially the Virginia Declaration of Rights, in setting out those individual rights that should be protected from federal interference.

Madison steered seventeen proposed amendments through the House, of which the Senate agreed to twelve. On September 2, 1789, President Washington sent them to the states for ratification. Of the twelve, two, concerning Congressional representation and Congressional pay, failed to achieve ratification by over three-quarters of the states. (The Congressional Pay Amendment was finally ratified in 1992.) The remaining ten were ratified and, with the vote of Virginia on December 15, 1791, became the first ten amendments to the Constitution, or the "Bill of Rights."

The Bill of Rights as originally adopted only applied to the federal government. Its purpose was to restrict Congress from interfering with rights reserved to the people. Thus, under the First Amendment the Congress could not establish a national religion, but the states could establish state support for selected religions, as seven states to some extent did (Connecticut, Georgia, Maryland, Massachusetts, New Hampshire, South Carolina, and Vermont). Madison had proposed that the states also be bound by the Bill of Rights, and the House agreed, but the Senate rejected the proposal.

Although the Declaration of Independence provided that "We hold these truths to be self-evident, that all men are created equal," the Constitution and Bill of Rights are conspicuously silent on the question of equality, because the agreement that made the Constitution possible was the North/South compromise permitting the continuation of slavery. Thus, today's issues like affirmative action, race and sex discrimination, school segregation, and same-sex marriage cannot be resolved through application of the Bill of Rights. This omission of a guarantee of equality led to the Civil War, and in turn to the post-Civil War Fourteenth Amendment that made the newly-freed slaves US and state citizens and prohibited the states from denying equal protection of the laws or due process of law to any citizen. In light of this Amendment, the Supreme Court began developing the "incorporation doctrine," holding that the Fourteenth Amendment extended the Bill of Rights so that it applied to all government action. By applying the Bill of Rights so expansively, the legal and social landscape of America was fundamentally changed.

In the aftermath of the Civil War and with the ratification of the Fourteenth Amendment, the Supreme Court slowly began applying the Bill of

Rights to state and local governments. The result has been that the debates of 1787–1791 have become more and more important to modern life. Could a high school principal begin a graduation ceremony by asking a minister (or a student leader) to say a prayer? Could a state require a girl under the age of sixteen to secure her parent's permission to have an abortion? Could a prison warden deny a pain medication to a prisoner between midnight and 7:00 a.m.? Could a college president censor an article in a student newspaper? These questions required the courts to examine the debates of the eighteenth century to determine what the framers intended when they drafted the Bill of Rights. They also raised the related and hotly disputed question of whether the intent of the framers was even relevant, or whether a "living" Constitution required solely contemporary, not historical, analysis.

Hence this series. Our intent is to select the very best essays from law and history and the most important judicial opinions and to edit them, making the leading views of the framers' intentions and of how we should interpret the Bill of Rights accessible to today's reader. If you find yourself passionately agreeing with some of the views expressed, angrily disagreeing with others, and appreciating how the essays selected have examined these questions with depth and lucidity, we will have succeeded.

David B. Oppenheimer
Professor of Law and Associate Dean for Faculty Development
Golden Gate University School of Law
San Francisco

Part I.
INTRODUCTION

INTRODUCTORY ESSAY
Thomas C. Berg

A. Free Exercise of Religion: Historic Development and Modern Controversy

One of America's greatest achievements has to been to secure freedom of religion as both a constitutional guarantee and a significant social reality. The founding era was only a few generations removed from major religious persecutions and conflicts—Protestants versus Catholics, Puritans versus traditional Anglicans, majority churches versus dissenting sects—in England and continental Europe. America's founders knew very well that, in James Madison's words, "[t]orrents of blood have been spilt in the Old World, by the vain attempt of the secular arm to extinguish religious discord, by proscribing all differences of opinion in religion."[1]

Americans of the colonial and founding periods little by little addressed this problem in their individual states, eventually removing many of their own significant restrictions on religious dissenters (though many states kept restrictions like laws forbidding blasphemy or requiring officeholders to swear belief in God). When the federal government came into being in 1789, Americans feared its possible interference in religious matters enough to ratify the language in the First Amendment: "Congress shall make no law respecting an establishment of religion, or prohibiting the free exercise thereof." As far as the federal Constitution was concerned, this left most matters of church-state relations to the various states. But the Fourteenth Amendment, enacted in 1868, later became the vehicle for extending the religion provisions, like most of the Bill of Rights, to limit state and local government actions as well.

Of the First Amendment's two religion clauses, the Free Exercise Clause seemingly ought to be the easier to interpret. The Establishment Clause poses special challenges, because while government usually can adopt and advance whatever ideas and messages it chooses, the non-establishment principle limits government's power to do so with respect to ideas concerning religion. How far this unique limit on government expression can extend in a society that is religiously pluralistic, but also quite devout, is a deeply contested question that has left the Court still fumbling for a consistent standard to decide Establishment Clause cases.

By contrast, the Free Exercise Clause seems a familiar civil liberties provision, declaring that government may not improperly restrict people's religious exercise just as it may not improperly restrict their speech, political association, or intimate private conduct, or their rights of dignity and fair treatment in criminal or civil proceedings. Of course, the limits of religious freedom have to be defined as against the rights of others and the interests of society; no one can be permitted to sacrifice unwilling victims to his god. But that task seems at first no different in nature than with any other constitutional liberty, such as deciding whether free speech encompasses flag-burning or freedom from unreasonable searches protects the contents of one's automobile.

That free exercise of religion is a simpler concept than non-establishment is shown by the fact that free exercise historically came first. Many of the American colonies at first punished religious dissenters: New England's Puritan government banished Quakers, for example, and hanged some who insisted on returning to preach. But by the early 1790s every one of the new states had written some guarantee of free exercise of religion into its constitution—even the New England states that maintained minimal establishments in the form of tax assessments to support clergy.

America has had significant episodes of religious persecution, of course. In the mid-1800s, Catholic children received whippings in public schools for refusing to participate in Protestant-style prayers and Bible readings; in the 1920s, the Ku Klux Klan secured a law in Oregon shutting down Catholic schools before the U.S. Supreme Court intervened in *Pierce v. Society of Sisters,*

268 U.S. 510 (1925). The federal government's campaign against Mormon polygamy began with a defensible law banning polygamy in general, but escalated into acts confiscating the Mormon Church's property and disqualifying voters simply for being Church members.

By the mid-20th century, however, consensus developed that religious exercise was among an American's constitutionally preferred freedoms. When towns around the country restricted Jehovah's Witnesses's street-corner preaching and door-to-door solicitation, the Supreme Court issued more than a dozen rulings in their favor from 1938 through 1953. Later the Court stated explicitly that governments had to offer "compelling" reasons "of the highest order" to justify substantial restrictions on religious practices, and under this standard it protected Seventh-Day Adventists who objected to Saturday work (*Sherbert v. Verner*, 374 U.S. 398 [1963]) and Amish who objected to compulsory schooling of their teenagers (*Wisconsin v. Yoder*, 406 U.S. 205 [1972]).

And yet in the last twenty years the Free Exercise Clause has provoked a loud and long-running dispute, pitting not only sects or individuals against the government, and religious against secular advocacy groups, but also Congress against the Supreme Court. The battle centers on whether and when religiously motivated conduct should be exempted from facially neutral laws that apply generally to the population but would severely restrict religious freedom in particular applications.

The Supreme Court fired the opening salvo in 1990 in *Employment Division v. Smith*, 494 U.S. 872 (1990), holding that government could punish the consumption of the peyote drug at a Native American Church worship service simply because peyote use was prohibited by a "neutral law of general applicability." This was so, the Court said, regardless of how seriously the law burdened religion (taking peyote is the central act of the ceremony) or how important the social interest it served (is peyote use dangerous in the limited circumstances of a religious ritual?). *Smith* reaffirmed protections for religious belief and speech and against laws aimed solely at religiously motivated conduct. But by exposing religious conduct to generally applicable laws, it seemed to threaten core religious exercise in countless situations, such as (to take just two examples) male-only clergy rules that conflict with general laws against sex discrimination, or religious dress requirements that conflict with general rules of public schools or government employers. *Smith* also appeared to reverse the twenty-five years of precedents applying the compelling interest standard to substantial burdens on religious conduct.

Fearing *Smith*'s implications, a broad coalition of religious and civil-liberties groups formed to persuade Congress to restore the compelling interest standard by means of a statute. Passed by nearly unanimous votes in both houses, the Religious Freedom Restoration Act of 1993 (RFRA) provided that federal, state, and local governments could not substantially burden religious exercise unless the burden was justified as the least restrictive means of achieving a compelling governmental interest.[2] Congress, which must base every law on one of its constitutionally enumerated powers, premised RFRA—as applied to state and local laws—on its power to enforce rights guaranteed in the Fourteenth Amendment,[3] including the incorporated right of free exercise of religion. But RFRA was set on a collision course with the Supreme Court, because in the statute Congress was interpreting free exercise more broadly than the justices had in *Smith*. In *City of Boerne v. Flores*, 521 U.S. 507 (1997), the Court by a six to three vote partially invalidated RFRA on the ground that Congress's power to override state and local laws was limited to enforcing the general constitutional standard that the Court (in *Smith*) had delineated. In claiming for itself the final power to define the maximum constitutional obligations that Congress could enforce against states, the Court hearkened all the way back to *Marbury v. Madison*, 5 U.S. 137 (1803), the foundational decision by Chief Justice John Marshall asserting the power of judicial review.

This remarkable face-off between Congress and the Court did not end the legal skirmishing over religious freedom and generally applicable laws. Congress first considered reenacting much of RFRA under its powers to regulate interstate commerce and place conditions on federal spending—powers it had used in the 1960s civil rights statutes because it feared Fourteenth Amendment powers would be inadequate.[4] New federal legislation that ultimately passed in 2000 covered only religious rights against state land-use (especially zoning) laws and prison regulations;[5] but RFRA remained in operation against federal laws and regulations, and a dozen states passed "mini-RFRAs" subjecting their own laws to the compelling interest requirement.

Meanwhile, over the same decade, a lively and deep scholarly debate developed concerning the conflicts between religious conduct and the law. The debate covered a rich set of themes explored in this book, touching on not only constitutional law, but also history, theology, and political science. Briefly, they include:

1. Should religion have special constitutional protection and why?

Exemptions for religious conduct from general laws rest on the premise that religion is different from many other ideas and activities in a way that justifies heightened constitutional protection. The very existence of two First Amendment provisions addressing religion seems to confirm this; and yet the matter is controversial. Pro-exemptions commentators rest the distinctive importance of religious freedom on the ultimate nature of religion's subject matter, on its importance to individuals, and on other grounds. Critics counter that in a society where many people ground their deep commitments on nonreligious beliefs, it is unfair to give unique value and protection to actions (or refusals to act) based on religious reasons.

Some critics say that religious exemptions not only are not required by the Free Exercise Clause, but are (often) forbidden by the Establishment Clause, so that legislative efforts to accommodate religion—broadly as in RFRA, or in particular contexts—are invalid. Because of these challenges to the accommodation of free exercise, this book on the Free Exercise Clause must necessarily address Establishment Clause matters as well. As Chapter 9 discusses, the Supreme Court has in fact struck down some statutory exemptions as establishments, although it has approved others and indicated in *Smith* that exemptions were permitted although not required.

2. History and its current implications.

Conflicts between religious conscience and American law date back to the colonial period—Mennonites objecting to militia service and Quakers objecting to oath-taking in court—but they were relatively rare. Conflicts have multiplied in the 20th century because of the great increase both in the variety of religious practices and in the number and scope of secular laws and regulations. We might expect a modern nation tolerant of varying religions to be committed to accommodating religious differences. But the rise of secular value systems as competitors to religion, especially among elites, has led many to criticize exemptions limited to religiously motivated practices.

3. Can principled lines be drawn between protected and unprotected conduct?

Outward conduct, unlike inward belief, cannot be absolutely immune from law. As a result, lines must be drawn between protected and unprotected conduct. But *Employment Division v. Smith* rested heavily on the notion that no principled constitutional lines exist for balancing the importance of religious practice against the importance of conflicting laws. The Court argued that the importance of a practice is a theological matter, subjective to individual believers, that judges cannot second-guess; and that the importance of a law is a policy question also beyond a judge's competence to assess. Defenders of exemptions under the Free Exercise Clause and RFRA have responded that this problem is overstated and have offered principles defining the proper scope of protection.

4. The relative roles of courts and legislatures.

Primarily because of the line-drawing problems just discussed, *Smith* said that exempting religious conduct from general laws should be left to legislatures and administrative bodies. This raises a number of questions. Can majority-elected legislatures be trusted to be aware of minority religions and value their needs? Do legislatures do better than courts, and possess more legitimacy, in the task of drawing lines between religious freedom and other interests? If legislatures do make provision for religious freedom, should they do so "wholesale"—that is, announce a general standard like that of RFRA, essentially returning cases to the courts to apply the standard—or "retail"—that is, address instances of conflict with the law one by one through specific, tailored provisions? The debate over *Smith*, RFRA, and subsequent religious freedom legislation is rich in issues concerning the relative institutional competency and legitimacy of courts and legislatures in protecting fundamental rights.

B. Chapters and Excerpts

The four issues just discussed recur throughout the articles excerpted in this book. Part I sets out introductory themes, with a significant emphasis on the historical background of America's religious freedom tradition and particularly of the Free Exercise Clause. John Witte's "The Essential Rights and Liberties of Religion in the American Constitutional Experiment" describes the strands of religious and political thought—Puritanism, evangelical Protestantism, Enlightenment rationalism, and civic republicanism—that coalesced in favor of free religious exercise even though they disagreed on other questions concerning church-state relations. Witte summarizes the "interlocking" religious rights—liberty of conscience, free exercise, pluralism, equality, church-state separation, and disestablishment of religion—that "remain at the heart of the American experiment today." Stephen Pepper, in "Taking the Free Exercise Clause Seriously," adds a twist in discussing history, suggesting that the Clause gives a nod to a theistic worldview that was important in the founders time, but today has been largely eclipsed by secular rationalism. This change, he argues, explains how the absolute language of free exercise has come to "mean so little" to the modern Court, even as the Establishment Clause has grown in potency. One can question some of Pepper's premises: traditional religion has proven quite vigorous in the last twenty years, and the free exercise and non-establishment provisions can easily work together rather than conflict. But his excerpt identifies several problems that have plagued free exercise jurisprudence.

Part II examines the central question whether the Free Exercise Clause offers religious behavior constitutional protection from formally religion-neutral, general laws. Chapter 2 begins with excerpts from three leading Supreme Court opinions: *Reynolds v. United States* (1879), which (in upholding anti-polygamy laws) confined free exercise protection to religious belief rather than conduct; *Wisconsin v. Yoder* (1972), the high-water mark of protection for religious conduct against generally applicable laws; and finally *Employment Division v. Smith* itself. Next, two articles discussing *Smith* introduce the scholarly debate. Professor (now Judge) Michael McConnell, in "Free Exercise Revisionism and the *Smith* Decision," criticizes the Court's central argument that deferring to majoritarian laws is preferable to having judges weigh religious against governmental interests. Two of McConnell's arguments stand out: that constitutional exemptions preserve religious neutrality in substance by giving minority religions consideration that larger bodies already receive in the political process, and that through the Free Exercise Clause government acknowledged that it is not an ultimate authority and citizens may have higher duties to what Madison called "the governour of the universe." In response, William Marshall's article, "In Defense of *Smith* and Free Exercise Revisionism," argues that although exemptions may increase equality among religions in practice, they do so at the unacceptable cost of explicitly "privileging" religious above nonreligious conscientious motives for acting. Marshall makes the fundamental argument of opponents of religious exemptions: "religious belief cannot be qualitatively distinguished from other belief systems in a way that justifies special constitutional consideration."

Chapter 3 returns to historical materials, now specifically on whether the Free Exercise Clause was intended to mandate exemptions from general laws. Evidence of original meaning or understanding provides an important source for constitutional interpretation, although the Court seldom treats it as conclusive. Michael McConnell's "The Origins and Historical Understanding of Free Exercise of Religion" argues that constitutional exemptions coincide more with the founding-era arguments supporting the clause—especially those of Madison and Protestant evangelicals—with state constitutional provisions that limited free exercise only to preserve "peace" or "safety," and with widespread 18th-century exemptions from militia service, oath-taking, and other duties. Philip Hamburger, in "A Constitutional Right of Religious Exemptions: An Historical Perspective," disputes these claims. The public "peace" that limited religious freedom, he argues, referred to all general secular laws, and the exemptions for objectors were matters of legislative grace (as *Smith* holds today) rather than constitutional right. Hamburger adds that founding-era religious-liberty advocates from dissenting groups typically disavowed any right to exemption from civil laws and simply sought "equal civil rights" with others.

The relevant historical events for free exercise interpretation may also include the passage of the Fourteenth Amendment. In "The Second Adoption of the Free Exercise Clause," Kurt Lash argues that although founders like Madison and Jefferson believed religion and government would both have limited spheres and thus seldom conflict, matters changed dramatically with a series of 19th-century revivals—the Second Great Awakening—that produced a socially activist Christianity concerned with slavery among other wrongs. When Southern states restricted both slave religion and abolitionist preaching, general laws collided with religious conscience and, Lash argues, the Fourteenth Amendment aimed among other things to protect such acts of conscience.

Chapter 4 offers four perspectives on the fundamental question of whether and why religion should receive constitutional protection not given to other conscientious reasons for acting. The excerpts fall into two pairs. John Garvey's "An Anti-Liberal Argument for Religious Freedom" offers a religious justification for religious freedom, grounded in the believer's perspective: the law protects religious freedom because it "thinks religion is a good thing" (if adopted voluntarily). Exemptions, he says, avoid the special suffering people feel when their eternal status is threatened or they must violate duties to a higher power. Garvey also criticizes other arguments for religious freedom—that it promotes personal autonomy or civil peace—as inadequate. Alan Brownstein, in "The Right Not to Be John Garvey," answers that free exercise rights do reside in personal autonomy, a right to determine those matters that define one's basic identity. Brownstein insists that justifying free exercise by the value or truth of religion will not motivate people to support freedom for those religions they are certain are wrong. With his emphasis on broader autonomy, Brownstein sees free exercise exemptions as an advantage for religion, but one countered by the Establishment Clause's special limits on promotion of religion.

Douglas Laycock, in "Religious Liberty as Liberty," agrees that religious freedom must rest on non-theological considerations such as the simple importance to individuals of their decisions on religion. Laycock explains his influential thesis (similar to McConnell's) that religious exemptions avoid government discouragement of religion and thus serve the Religion Clauses's overarching goal of "substantive neutrality": leaving religion "as wholly to private choice and private commitment as anything can be." In contrast, Christopher Eisgruber and Lawrence Sager, in "The Vulnerability of Conscience: The Constitutional Basis for Protecting Religious Conduct," criticize all theories that rest on keeping religion free from government influence. Such ideals of "unimpaired flourishing," they say, unjustifiably privilege religion and invite religious oppression. They propose an alternative rule of "equal regard," under which minority religious concerns must receive "the same regard as that enjoyed by the deep concerns of citizens generally"—for example, they must be exempted whenever comparable secular concerns are exempted.

Uneasiness about differential treatment of religious and secular moral views might be calmed by defining "religion" very broadly, an issue explored in Chapter 5. In two Vietnam War–era cases (*United States v. Seeger* and *Welsh v. United States*), the Supreme Court extended the statutory protection for religious objectors to include deeply held nonreligious views. In another excerpt from "Religious Liberty as Liberty," Douglas Laycock defends this broad concept as necessary to maintain government neutrality on one of our era's great religious divides, that between theists and nontheists. In contrast, Michael

Paulsen relies on John Garvey's account of religious freedom (see Chapter 4) to defend the narrower, theistic definition of religion ("God is Great, Garvey is Good: Making Sense of Religious Freedom").

Chapter 6 turns from theory to doctrine, exploring the possibilities for protection of religious exercise under the Supreme Court's current rules. In "Free Exercise is Dead, Long Live Free Exercise! *Smith, Lukumi*, and the General Applicability Requirement," Richard Duncan parallels Eisgruber and Sager in proposing that when (as is frequently the case) a law contains exemptions accommodating secular concerns, religious concerns must also be exempted. Even one comparable secular exception, Duncan argues, renders the law non-general under *Smith* and thus subject to strict review, likely requiring a religious exemption. At the other end of the spectrum, some commentators, such as William Marshall and Steven Gey (see Chapters 2 and 9), would essentially eliminate any independent role for the Free Exercise Clause, protecting religious behavior only when it takes the form of expression protected by the Free Speech Clause. In contrast, Frederick Gedicks, in "Towards a Defensible Free Exercise Doctrine," looks to speech law not to confine protection to religious speech, but to find models for protecting religious conduct as well. Under analogies to established free speech rules, he argues, religious conduct could be protected against laws that give officials discretionary power to decide where churches can locate, or that fail to allow adherents alternative means for practicing their faith.

Although *Smith* rejects judicial weighing of religious claims against governmental interests, that approach survives under the compelling-interest test of RFRA as applied to federal law, and in those states with "mini-RFRAs." Chapter 7's excerpts address the challenges involved in that analysis. Ira Lupu's article, "Where Rights Begin: The Problem of Burdens on the Free Exercise of Religion," written before *Smith*, remains relevant because RFRA claimants still must show that their religious exercise has been "substantially burdened" to trigger the government's obligation of demonstrating a compelling interest. As Lupu shows, courts often try to avoid imposing that demand on the government, but it is hard to second-guess the sincerity or religiosity of a claimant's conscientious objection, and easier—too easy, Lupu warns—to dismiss the burden on the religious practice as insubstantial. The other excerpts examine the governmental-interest side of the ledger. Both Steven Pepper, in another excerpt from "Taking the Free Exercise Clause Seriously," and Thomas Berg, in "The New Attacks on Religious Freedom

Legislation and Why They Are Wrong," suggest that as a matter of logic and history, the Free Exercise Clause gives no right to invade directly the life, liberty, or property interests of another individual—for example, to trespass on her land in order to conduct a religious ceremony—but does offer significant protection when the government's interests are more attenuated or spread across the general population. In "A Common-Law Model for Religious Exemptions," Eugene Volokh responds that the "rights of other individuals" are mostly defined not by logic but by legislative declaration, as for example when New Deal laws created new rights for workers to unionize and be paid above-minimum wages. Because of this complexity, Volokh argues, courts should ultimately defer to legislatures on when another interest will override religious freedom, just as they ultimately bowed to New Deal legislation. But, he adds, courts can take the lead in defining the boundaries of religious freedom if they leave legislatures the final word, as is the case with statutes like state RFRAs.

Volokh's argument transitions neatly to Part III, "Legislative Protection of Religious Freedom," which explores the respective roles of courts and legislatures in defining religious rights. Chapter 8 covers RFRA and the conflict between the Court and Congress over the meaning of free exercise. Thomas Berg's short excerpt describes RFRA's political dynamics, explaining why the statute emerged as a simple "restoration" of the (somewhat unclear) standard existing before *Smith*. Two excerpts follow from RFRA's leading academic proponent and opponent, who argued the two sides before the Supreme Court in *City of Boerne v. Flores*. In "RFRA, Congress, and the Ratchet," written before *Boerne*, Douglas Laycock defends Congress's use of Fourteenth Amendment powers to expand free exercise rights beyond the *Smith* Court's conception. Of special interest are Laycock's argument against judicial exclusivity in protecting constitutional rights—the legacy, he notes, of the Court's otherwise admirable role in combating racial segregation in the 1950s and 60s—and his argument that the Reconstruction Congress would not have left the Fourteenth Amendment's primary enforcement to the very institution, the Supreme Court, that only a few years earlier had negated African Americans' rights in the hated *Dred Scott* ruling. But Laycock's side lost the *Boerne* decision, and Marci Hamilton, whose side prevailed, recaps her arguments against RFRA in "*City of Boerne v. Flores*: A Landmark for Structural Analysis." She argues that RFRA violates principles not only of federalism, by overriding state laws, but also of judicial power going back to *Marbury v. Madison*, by rejecting the Court's definition of a constitutional right and legislating a different standard. Hamilton sees RFRA as invalid as applied to federal as well as state laws, but on that question she has not prevailed.

Chapter 9 deals broadly with legislative exemptions, the roles of courts and legislatures, and whether such exemptions violate the Establishment Clause by "favoring" or "promoting" religion. Again, the articles sort into pairs. Marci Hamilton, in "Religious Institutions, the Public Good, and the No-Harm Doctrine," continues her attack on RFRA-type statutes by arguing that courts, unlike legislatures, lack institutional devices to assess the effect of a religious exemption on the public good: thus the legislature is the sole entity that can define proper exemptions for specific situations. In contrast, Ira Lupu, in "The Trouble with Accommodation," argues that religious exemptions should be declared solely by judges under the rubric of the Free Exercise Clause—in large part because accommodations by legislators or regulators are assertedly likely to favor politically powerful sects over others and over individuals. Then Steven Gey presents the full-bore anti-accommodationist position—that all religious exemptions violate the Establishment Clause—in "Why Is Religion Special? Reconsidering the Accommodation of Religion under the Religion Clauses." Gey argues that religious exemptions unfairly favor religion over other belief systems, but his excerpt adds the argument that religion conflicts with principles of rationality and skepticism that are crucial to democracy, and therefore government cannot defer to a religious assertion even in the sense of removing a coercive legal burden from the religious adherent. To this Michael McConnell responds, in "Accommodation of Religion: An Update and a Response to the Critics," that exemptions—whether by constitutional ruling or legislative act—do not endorse or promote a believer's view but merely refrain from imposing on it, and that the claim that "religion undermines the democratic spirit" is unsupportable both historically and today.

Part IV examines two further free exercise issues that remain hotly contested. Chapter 10 explores the freedom of religious organizations, which may raise different considerations than the individual claims involved in cases like *Smith*, *Sherbert*, *Yoder*, and *Seeger*. The notion of religious institutional autonomy appears in more than a century of Supreme Court decisions limiting the grounds on which civil courts can intervene in disputes within churches over who owns church property or can exercise ecclesiastical authority. The last twenty-five years, however, have seen debate whether any principles of autonomy should protect religious organizations from regulatory statutes, especially those concerning employee unions and employment discrimination. Douglas Laycock, again an early and powerful proponent of free exercise rights, argued in 1981—in an article excerpted here—for a broad right of "church autonomy" extending to most decisions of religious organizations concerning hiring, firing, and bargaining with workers. In response, Ira Lupu in "Free Exercise and Religious Institutions: The Case of Employment Discrimination" (excerpted next) attacked organizational autonomy claims on the grounds that only individuals could display the sincerity of belief and experience the suffering for conscience that free exercise exemptions were meant to address.[6]

Two recent articles revisit the rights of religious organizations in light of the rejection of individual religious exemptions in *Employment Division v. Smith*. Kathleen Brady finds "surprising lessons" in the *Smith* opinion: the freedom of belief it reaffirms necessitates protection of religious organizational autonomy, because religious beliefs are formed and developed in communities, and a wide-ranging freedom for such communities will both promote the democratic virtues on which *Smith* relies and keep government officials from second-guessing the importance of a particular activity in a group's theology. In response, Laura Underkuffler warns of "darker realities" implicated in many church autonomy claims—for example, that legal immunity may harm the beliefs of dissenting members or employees or the interests of societies— and suggests that institutional autonomy presents "far more dangers of oppression, coercion, and the assumption of governmental power than does individual free exercise."

Finally, Chapter 11 examines the effect of the Free Exercise Clause on government funding of religiously grounded education and social services— an issue that the Supreme Court for many years addressed only in terms of whether the Establishment Clause prohibited funding. As the Court relaxed establishment prohibitions on funding and emphasized that the essence of free exercise is neutral, nondiscriminatory treatment of religion, free exercise issues arose because of state policies barring religious entities from general funding programs. Such policies that invoke the value of church-state separation, but it can be argued that they unconstitutionally condition their funding on a recipient's willingness to forego his right of religious education. But somewhat surprisingly, the Court in its first case on the issue, *Locke v. Davey*, 512 U.S. 740 (2004), allowed a state that offered college scholarships for a wide range of majors at public and private institutions to single out for exclusion those students majoring in theology taught from a "devotional" perspective. Thomas Berg and Douglas Laycock criticize *Locke v. Davey* for approving a state policy that violated the lodestar of "substantive neutrality"—distorting students's choices in religious matters by withdrawing funding for their choice of a theology major—and assess how the decision might affect the controversial outstanding issue of whether to include religious elementary schools in programs of private school "vouchers." In contrast, Steven Green defends the result in *Locke v. Davey*, arguing that an approach of neutrality—"substantive" or "formal"—toward religion is inappropriate for government funding decisions because of the need to maintain a public sphere favoring "rational secular values."

This book therefore ends on themes that have been prominent throughout. Some say the Religion Clauses, including the free exercise portion, call for a distinctive constitutional freedom of choice in religious matters; others say the only requirement is nondiscrimination among religions and between religious and secular commitments. Some say that strong protection for religious exercise endangers a democratic order that must be secular and rational; others say that strong protection places a wholesome, even indispensable, limit on government's power to reach into matters of ultimate importance.

C. Editor's Notes

A book such as this requires certain clarifications and caveats. To begin with, the articles here are often heavily edited. To present contrasting points of view on multiple issues required multiple articles, which had to be cut significantly to keep the book a manageable length. Like Alan Brownstein, the editor of this series's first volume (*The Establishment Clause*), "I have tried to maintain the integrity of the author's arguments, but in doing so I have often had to eliminate examples and tangential discussions that added considerably to the persuasiveness and value of their work."[7] Readers interested in the arguments in their entirety should consult the original articles.

In keeping with the guidelines of this series, I have minimized endnotes, using them only for citations to named cases and for quotations (and not even all of the latter). Again, readers who wish may consult the original articles to find and evaluate the authorities cited for arguments in the texts. I also edited and modified some endnotes for purposes of clarity and continuity (for example, turning a second-reference citation form into a first reference where the note with the first reference is omitted). Most notes have been conformed to Chicago Style as per the desire of the publisher, but references to court cases appear in their traditional legal style.

In selecting articles, I tried to include a balanced range of perspectives, and the anthology includes thirty excerpts by twenty-one different scholars. Several writers have multiple articles or excerpts included. Sometimes this is because their work seemed to fit best with others: the topics discussed were the same, or one article actually referred to another. Sometimes the selection reflects the quantity, quality, and prominence of the person's work in the field. As a final thought on the selection of articles, I again can do no better than to adapt Professor Brownstein's words from his volume: "Needless to say, there are many excellent articles by distinguished scholars that I could not include in this volume because of page limitations. The content of the cutting room floor from this book could have easily provided materials for another volume of comparable size and quality. The wealth of valuable scholarship on the meaning of the [Free Exercise] Clause made the task of compiling this anthology a formidable challenge and a humbling experience."[8]

NOTES

1. James Madison, *Memorial and Remonstrance Against Religious Assessments* (1785), reprinted in Robert A. Rutland and William M. E. Rachal, eds., *The Papers of James Madison*, vol. 8 (1973), p. 11.

2. 42 U.S.C. § 2000bb-1.

3. See U.S. Constitution, amend. XIV, § 5 (giving Congress power to "enforce the provisions" of the Amendment "by appropriate legislation").

4. See, e.g., *Katzenbach v. McClung*, 379 U.S. 294 (1964) (upholding application of Civil Rights Act of 1964 to restaurants and other businesses based on Commerce Power); *Civil Rights Cases*, 109 U.S. 3 (1883) (striking down earlier antidiscrimination laws on ground that Fourteenth Amendment did not reach private businesses).

5. Religious Land Use and Institutionalized Persons Act, 42 U.S.C. § 2000cc.

6. Lupu has since become more hospitable to church autonomy claims, defending a limited but important set of them. See, e.g., Ira C. Lupu and Robert W. Tuttle, "Sexual Misconduct and Ecclesiastical Immunity," *Brigham Young University Law Review* (2004): 1789.

7. Alan Brownstein, Introduction, in *The Establishment Clause* (Buffalo: Prometheus, 2007).

8. Ibid.

Chapter 1

INTRODUCTORY THEMES

Religious Freedom at the Founding and Today

THE ESSENTIAL RIGHTS AND LIBERTIES OF RELIGION IN THE AMERICAN CONSTITUTIONAL EXPERIMENT

JOHN WITTE JR.

A. Four Perspectives on Religious Rights and Liberties

[T]wo theological perspectives on religious liberties and rights were critical to [the development of the First Amendment and state constitutional provisions]: those of congregational Puritans and of free church evangelicals. Two contemporaneous political perspectives were equally influential: those of enlightenment thinkers and civic republicans. Exponents of these four perspectives often found common cause and used common language, particularly during the Constitutional Convention and ratification debates. Yet each group cast its views in a distinctive ensemble, with its own emphases and its own applications. . . .

John Witte Jr., "The Essential Rights and Liberties of Religion in the American Constitutional Experiment," *Notre Dame Law Review* 71 (1996): 371, 377–400.

1. Puritan Views

The New England Puritans were the direct heirs of the theology of religious liberty taught by European Calvinists. They had revised and refined this European legacy through the efforts of John Winthrop, John Cotton, Cotton Mather, Jonathan Edwards, Charles Chauncy, Jonathan Mayhew, and a host of other eminent writers. Since the 1630s, the Puritans had dominated the New England colonies and thus had ample occasion to cast their theological and political principles into constitutional practice.

The Puritans who wrote on religious liberties and rights were concerned principally with the nature of the church, of the state, and of the relationship between them. They conceived of the church and the state as two separate covenantal associations, two seats of Godly authority in the community. Each institution, they believed, was vested with a distinct polity and calling. The church was to be governed by pastoral, pedagogical, and diaconal authorities who were called to preach the word, administer the sacraments, teach the young, [and] care for the poor and the needy. The state was to be governed by executive, legislative, and judicial authorities who were called to enforce law, punish crime, cultivate virtue, and protect peace and order.

In the New England communities where their views prevailed, the Puritans adopted a variety of safeguards to ensure the basic separation of the institutions of church and state. Church officials were prohibited from holding political office, serving on juries, interfering in governmental affairs, endorsing political candidates, or censuring the official conduct of a statesman. Political officials, in turn, were prohibited from holding ministerial office, interfering in internal ecclesiastical government, performing sacerdotal functions of clergy, or censuring the official conduct of a cleric. To permit any such officiousness on the part of church or state officials, Governor John Winthrop averred, "would confound those Jurisdictions, which Christ hath made distinct."[1]

Although church and state were not to be confounded, however, they were still to be "close and compact." For, to the Puritans, these two institutions were inextricably linked in nature and in function. Each was an instrument of Godly authority. Each did its part to establish and maintain the community. As one mid-eighteenth century writer put it, "I look upon this as a little model of the Gloriou[s] Kingdome of Christ on earth. Christ Reigns among us in the Common wealth as well as in the Church, and hath his glorious Interest involved and wrapt up in the good of both Societies respectively."[2] The Puritans, therefore, readily countenanced the coordination and cooperation of church and state.

State officials provided various forms of material aid to churches and their officials [and church officials provided various forms of material and moral support to the state]....

Puritan leaders of colonial New England left little room for individual religious experimentation. Despite their adherence to a basic separation of the institutions of church and state, the New England authorities insisted on general adherence to the creeds and canons of Puritan Calvinism. Already in the 1630s, dissidents from this faith, such as Anne Hutchinson and Roger Williams, were summarily dismissed from the colony. Immigration restrictions in Massachusetts Bay throughout the seventeenth century left little room to Quakers, Catholics, Jews, "Familists, Antinomians, and other Enthusiasts." Although in the eighteenth century, religious dissidents of many kinds came to be tolerated in the New England colonies, they enjoyed only limited political rights and social opportunities and were subject to a variety of special governmental restrictions, taxes, and other encumbrances.

2. Evangelical Views

Though the evangelical tradition of religious liberty is sometimes traced to the seventeenth century—particularly to Roger Williams, the founder of colonial Rhode Island, and William Penn, the founder of Pennsylvania—it did not emerge as a strong political force until after the Great Awakening circa 1720–1780. Numerous spokesmen for the evangelical cause rose up in the course of the later eighteenth century all along the Atlantic seaboard—Isaac Backus, John Leland, John Wesley, and a host of other pastors and pamphleteers. Though the evangelicals had enjoyed fewer opportunities than the Puritans to institutionalize their views, they nonetheless had a formidable influence on the early American constitutional experiment.

Like the Puritans, the evangelicals advanced a theological theory of religious rights and liberties. They likewise advocated the institutional separation of church and state—the construction of a "wall of Separation between the Garden of the Church and the Wilderness of the world," to quote Roger Williams.[3] The evangelicals went beyond the Puritans, however, both in their definition of individual and institutional religious rights and in their agitation for a fuller separation of the institutions of church and state. The evangelicals sought to protect the liberty of conscience of every individual and the freedom of association of every religious group. Their solution was thus to prohibit all legal establishments of religion, and, indeed, all admixtures of religion and politics....

[R]eligious voluntarism lay at the heart of the evangelical view. Every individual, they argued, must be given the liberty of conscience to choose or to change his or her faith. "[N]othing can be true religion but a voluntary obedience unto [God's] revealed will," declared the Baptist Isaac Backus.[4] State coercion or control of this choice—either directly through persecution and forced collection of tithes and services, or indirectly through withholding civil rights and benefits from religious minorities—was an offense both to the individual and to God. A plurality of religions should coexist in the community, and it was for God, not the state, to decide which of these religions should flourish and which should fade. "Religious liberty is a divine right," wrote the evangelical preacher Israel Evans, "immediately derived from the Supreme Being, without the intervention of any created authority.... [T]he all-wise Creator invested [no] order of men with the right of judging for their fellow-creatures in the great concerns of religion."[5]

Every religious body was likewise to be free from state control of their assembly and worship, state regulations of their property and polity, state incorporation of their society and clergy, state interference in their discipline and government. Every religious body was also to be free from state emoluments like tax exemptions, civil immunities, property donations, and other forms of state support for the church that were readily countenanced by Puritan and other leaders. The evangelicals feared state benevolence towards religion and religious bodies almost as much as they feared state repression. For those religious bodies that received state benefits would invariably become beholden to the state and distracted from their divine mandates. "[I]f civil Rulers go so far out of their Sphere as to take the Care and Management of religious affairs upon them," reads a 1776 Baptist Declaration, "Yea... Farewel to 'the free exercise of Religion.'"[6]

The chief concern of the evangelicals was theological, not political. Having suffered for more than a century as a religious minority in colonial America, and even longer in Europe, they sought a constitutional means to free all religion from the fetters of the law, to relieve the church from the restrictions of the state....

3. Enlightenment Views

Exponents of the Enlightenment tradition in America provided a political theory that complemented the religious rights theology of the evangelicals. Though American exponents of the Enlightenment claimed early European visionaries such as John Locke and David Hume, they did not emerge as a significant political voice until the mid-eighteenth century.... [Enlightenment spokesmen included] Thomas Jefferson, Benjamin Franklin, and others.

The primary purpose of Enlightenment writers was political, not theological. They sought not only to free religion and the church from the interference of politics and the state, as did the evangelicals, but, more importantly, to free politics and the state from the intrusion of religion and the church. Exponents of the enlightenment movement taught that the state should give no special aid, support, privilege, or protection to organized religion in the form of tax exemptions, special criminal protections, administrative subsidies, or the incorporation of religious bodies. Nor should the state predicate its laws or policies on explicitly religious grounds or religious arguments, or draw on the services of religious officials or bodies to discharge state functions. As Madison put it in 1822: "[A] perfect separation between ecclesiastical and civil matters" is the best course, for "religion & Gov. will both exist in greater purity, the less they are mixed together."[7] ...

Such views were based on a profound skepticism about organized religion and a profound fear of an autocratic state. To allow church and state to be unrestricted, it was thought, would be to invite arbitrariness and abuse. To allow them to combine would be to their mutual disadvantage—to produce, in Thomas Paine's words, "a sort of mule-animal, capable only of destroying, and not of breeding up."[8] Such views were also based on the belief that a person is fundamentally an individual being and that religion is primarily a matter of private reason and conscience and only secondarily a matter of communal association and corporate confession. Every person, James Madison wrote, has the right to form a rational opinion about the duty he owes the Creator and the manner in which that duty is to be discharged.[9] Whether that religious duty is to be discharged individually or corporately is of secondary importance. Such views were also based on a contractarian political philosophy that called for the state to ensure the maximum liberty of citizens and their associations and to intervene only where one party's exercise of liberty intruded on that of the other.

Post-revolutionary Virginia proved to be fertile ground for political exponents of the enlightenment tradition to cultivate these views. . . .

4. Civic Republican Views

The "civic republicans," as they have come to be called in recent histories, were an eclectic group of politicians, preachers, and pamphleteers who strove to cultivate a set of common values and beliefs for the new nation. Their principal spokesmen were John Adams, Samuel Adams, Oliver Ellsworth, George Washington, James Wilson, and other leaders. . . .

[T]he civic republicans shared much common ground with evangelical and enlightenment exponents. They, too, advocated liberty of conscience for all and state support for a plurality of religions in the community. They, too, opposed religious intrusions on politics that rose to the level of political theocracy and political intrusions on religion that rose to the level of religious establishment. But, contrary to evangelical and enlightenment views and consistent with Puritan views, civic republicans sought to imbue the public square with a common religious ethic and ethos—albeit one less denominationally specific and rigorous than that countenanced by the Puritans.

"Religion and Morality are the essential pillars of Civil society," George Washington declared.[10] "[W]e have no government," John Adams echoed, "armed with power capable of contending with human passions unbridled by morality and religion."[11] "Religion and liberty are the meat and the drink of the body politic," wrote Yale President Timothy Dwight.[12] According to the civic republicans, society needs a fund of religious values and beliefs, a body of civic ideas and ideals that are enforceable both through the common law and through communal suasion. This was what Benjamin Franklin had called the "Publick Religion" (and what is now called the "civil religion") of America, which undergirded the plurality of sectarian religions. This "Publick Religion" taught a creed of honesty, diligence, devotion, public spiritedness, patriotism, obedience, love of God, neighbor, and self, and other ethical commonplaces taught by various religious traditions at the time of the founding. Its icons were the Bible, the Declaration of Independence, the bells of liberty, and the Constitution. Its clergy were public-spirited Christian ministers and religiously devout politicians. Its liturgy was the proclamations of prayers, songs, sermons, and Thanksgiving Day offerings by statesmen and churchmen. Its policy was government appointment of legislative and military chaplains, government sponsorship of general religious education and organization, and government enforcement of a religiously based morality through positive law....

Post-revolutionary Massachusetts proved to be fertile ground for the cultivation of these civic republican views. [They] also found favor in the Continental Congress, which authorized the appointment of tax-supported chaplains to the military, tax appropriations for religious schools and missionaries, diplomatic ties to the Vatican, and recitations of prayer at its opening sessions and during the day of Thanksgiving. The Continental Congress also passed the Northwest Ordinance in 1787, which provided, in part: "Religion, morality, and knowledge, being necessary to good government and the happiness of mankind, schools and the means of education shall forever be encouraged."[13]

B. The Essential Rights and Liberties of Religion

Despite the tensions among them, exponents of these four groups generally agreed upon what New England Puritan jurist and theologian Elisha Williams called, "the essential rights and liberties of [religion]." To be sure, these "essential rights and liberties" never won uniform articulation or universal assent in the young republic. But a number of enduring and interlocking principles found widespread support, many of which were included in state and federal constitutional discussions. These principles included liberty of conscience, free exercise of religion, pluralism, equality, separationism, and disestablishment of religion. Such principles remain at the heart of the American experiment today.

The common goal of these principles was to replace the inherited tradition of religious establishment with a new experiment that rendered religious rights and liberties the "first freedom" of the constitutional order. To be sure, a number of writers were reluctant to extend religious liberty to Catholics and Jews, let alone to Muslims and Indians—and these prejudices are sometimes betrayed in the earliest drafts of the state constitutions. For many eighteenth century writers, the term "religion" was synonymous with Christianity (or even Protestantism), and the discussion of "religious liberty" was often in terms of the "liberty or rights of Christians." And, to be sure, some Puritans and civic republicans continued to support what John Adams called a "slender" form of congregationalist establishment in some of the New England states—consisting principally of tax collections and preferences for the congregational churches and schools. But such "compromises" do not deprive the early American experiment, and the sentiments that inspired it, of their validity or ongoing utility. By eighteenth-century European standards, this experiment was remarkably advanced, and calculated to benefit the vast majority of the population. Many provisions on religious rights and liberties were cast in broad terms, and those that were more denominationally specific could easily be extended to other religious groups, as later state courts repeatedly demonstrated. The "slender" New England establishments, which ended in 1833, were a far cry from the repressive, bloody regimes of the American colonies and of post-Reformation Europe. The maintenance of such soft establishments was not seen as inconsistent with guarantees of essential religious rights and liberties of all citizens within the state.

Virtually all eighteenth century writers embraced religious liberty as the "first liberty" and the "first freedom." ... At the same time, virtually all writers denounced the bloody religious establishments of previous eras....

1. Liberty of Conscience

Liberty of conscience was the general solvent used in the early American experiment in religious liberty. It was universally embraced in the young republic—even by the most churlish of establishmentarians....

First, liberty of conscience protected voluntarism—"the right of private judgment in matters of religion," the unencumbered ability to choose and to change one's religious beliefs and adherences.[14] The Puritan jurist Elisha Williams put this matter very strongly for Christians in 1744[:]

> Every man has an equal right to follow the dictates of his own conscience in the affairs of religion. Every one is under an indispensable obligation to search the Scriptures for himself... and to make the best use of it he can for his own information in the will of God, the nature and duties of Christianity. As every Christian is so bound; so he has an unalienable right to judge of the sense and meaning of it, and to follow his judgment wherever it leads him; even an equal right with any rulers be they civil or ecclesiastical.[15]

James Madison wrote more generically in 1785: "The Religion then of every man must be left to the conviction and conscience of every man; and it is the right of every man to exercise it as these may dictate."[16] The evangelical leader John Leland echoed these sentiments in 1791:

Every man must give an account of himself to God and therefore every man ought to be at liberty to serve God in that way that he can be reconcile it to his conscience.... It would be sinful for a man to surrender to man which is to be kept sacred for God. A man's mind should be always open to conviction, and an honest man will receive that doctrine which appears the best demonstrated; and what is more common for the best of men to change their minds?[17]

Puritan, Enlightenment philosophe, and evangelical alike could agree on this core meaning of liberty of conscience.

Second, and closely related, liberty of conscience prohibited religiously based discrimination against individuals. Persons could not be penalized for the religious choices they made, nor swayed to make certain choices because of the civil advantages attached to them. Liberty of conscience, Ezra Stiles opined, permits "no bloody tribunals, no cardinals inquisitors-general, to bend the human mind, forceably to control the understanding, and put out the light of reason, the candle of the Lord in man."[18] Liberty of conscience also prohibits more subtle forms of discrimination, prejudice, and cajolery by state, church, or even other citizens. "[N]o part of the community shall be permitted to perplex or harass the other for any supposed heresy," wrote a Massachusetts pamphleteer, "... each individual shall be allowed to have and enjoy, profess and maintain his own system of religion."[19]

Third, in the view of some eighteenth-century writers, liberty of conscience guaranteed "a freedom and exemption from human impositions, and legal restraints, in matters of religion and conscience."[20] Persons of faith were to be "exempt from all those penal, sanguinary laws, that generate vice instead of virtue."[21] Such laws not only included the onerous criminal rules that traditionally encumbered and discriminated against religious nonconformists, and led to fines, whippings, banishments, and occasional executions of dissenting colonists. They also included more facially benign laws that worked injustice to certain religious believers—conscription laws that required religious pacifists to participate in the military, oath-swearing laws that ran afoul of the religious scruples of certain believers, tithing and taxing laws that forced believers to support churches, schools, and other causes that they found religiously odious....

[According to these writers, where] general laws and policies did intrude on the religious scruples of an individual or group, liberty of conscience demanded protection of religious minorities and exemption. Whether such exemptions should be accorded by the legislature or by the judiciary, and whether they were per se a constitutional right or simply a rule of equity—the principal bones of contention among recent commentators[22]—the eighteenth century sources at my disposal simply do not clearly say.

All the early state constitutions include a guarantee of liberty of conscience for all. The Delaware Constitution provides typical language:

> That all men have a natural and inalienable right to worship Almighty God according to the dictates of their own consciences and understandings; and that no man ought or of right can be compelled to attend any religious worship or maintain any religious ministry contrary to or against his own free will and consent, and that no authority can or ought to be vested in, or assumed by any power whatever that shall in any case interfere with, or in any manner controul [*sic*] the right of conscience and free exercise of religious worship.[23] . . .

The principle of liberty of conscience also informed some of the federal constitutional debates on religion. Article VI [section 3] of the Constitution explicitly provides: "[N]o religious Test [oath] shall ever be required as a Qualification" for public office, thereby, inter alia, protecting the religiously scrupulous against oath-swearing. Early versions of the First Amendment religion clauses included such phrases as: "That any person religiously scrupulous of bearing arms ought to be exempted, upon payment of an equivalent to employ another to bear arms in his stead"; "The civil rights of none shall be abridged on account of religious belief or worship . . . nor shall the full and equal rights of conscience be in any manner, or on any pretext, infringed"; "Congress shall make no law . . . to infringe the rights of conscience." Such phrases were ultimately abandoned (though not argued against in the extant records) for the more pregnant language: "Congress shall make no law . . . prohibiting the free exercise [of religion]." This language does not leave conscience unprotected, but more protected. Since Congress cannot "prohibit" the free exercise, the public manifestation, of religion, a fortiori Congress cannot "prohibit" a person's private liberty of conscience, and the precepts embraced therein.

Liberty of conscience was the cardinal principle for the new experiment in religious liberty. Several other "essential rights and liberties of religion" built directly on this core principle.

2. Free Exercise

Liberty of conscience was inextricably linked to free exercise of religion. Liberty of conscience was a guarantee to be left alone to choose, to entertain, and to change one's religious beliefs. Free exercise of religion was the right to act publicly on the choices of conscience once made, without intruding on or obstructing the rights of others or the general peace of the community. Already in 1670, the Quaker leader William Penn had linked these two guarantees, insisting that religious liberty entails "not only a mere liberty of the mind, in believing or disbelieving...but [also] the exercise of ourselves in a visible way of worship."[24] By the next century, this organic linkage was commonly accepted. Religion, Madison wrote, "must be left to the convictions and conscience of every man; and it is the right of every man to exercise it as these may dictate." For most eighteenth-century writers, religious belief and religious action went hand-in-hand, and each deserved legal protection.

Though eighteenth-century writers, or dictionaries, offered no universal definition of "free exercise," the phrase generally connoted various forms of free public religious action—religious speech, religious worship, religious assembly, religious publication, religious education, among others. Free exercise of religion also embraced the right of the individual to join with like-minded believers in religious societies, which religious societies were free to devise their own modes of worship, articles of faith, standards of discipline, and patterns of ritual. Eighteenth-century writers did not speak unequivocally of what we now call group rights, or corporate free exercise rights, but they did regularly call for "ecclesiastical liberty," "the equal liberty of one sect ...with another," and the right "to have the full enjoyment and free exercise of those spiritual powers...which, being derived only from CHRIST and His Apostles, are to be maintained, independent of every foreign, or other, jurisdiction, so far as may be consistent with the civil rights of society."[25]

Virtually all of the early state constitutions guaranteed "free exercise" rights—adding the familiar caveat that such exercise not violate the public peace or the private rights of others. Most states limited their guarantee to "the free exercise of religious worship" or the "free exercise of religious profession"—thereby leaving the protection of other noncultic forms of religious expression and action to other constitutional guarantees. A few states provided more generic free exercise guarantees. Virginia, for example, guaranteed "the free exercise of religion, according to the dictates of conscience"[26]

—expanding constitutional protection to cultic and noncultic religious expression and action, provided it was mandated by conscience. The Georgia constitution provided even more flatly: "All persons whatever shall have the free exercise of their religion; provided it be not repugnant to the peace and safety of the State."[27] The First Amendment drafters chose equally embracive language of "the free exercise" of religion. Rather than using the categorical language preferred by state drafters, however, the First Amendment drafters guaranteed protection only against Congressional laws "prohibiting" the free exercise of religion. Whether Congress could make laws "infringing" or "abridging" the free exercise of religion—as earlier drafts sought to outlaw— was left open to subsequent interpretation.

3. Pluralism

Eighteenth-century writers regarded "multiplicity," "diversity," or "plurality," as an equally essential dimension of religious rights and liberties....

Evangelical and enlightenment writers urged the protection of confessional pluralism—the maintenance and accommodation of a plurality of forms of religious expression and organization in the community. Evangelical writers advanced a theological argument for this principle, emphasizing that it was for God, not the state, to decide which forms of religion should flourish and which should fade. "God always claimed it as his sole prerogative to determine by his own laws what his worship shall be, who shall minister in it, and how they shall be supported," Isaac Backus wrote. "God's truth is great, and in the end He will allow it to prevail."[28] Confessional pluralism served to respect and reflect this divine prerogative. Enlightenment writers advanced a rational argument. "Difference of opinion is advantageous in religion," Thomas Jefferson wrote:

> The several sects perform the office of a Censor morum over each other. Is uniformity attainable? Millions of innocent men, women, and children, since the introduction of Christianity, have been burnt, tortured, fined, imprisoned; yet we have not advanced one inch towards uniformity.... Reason and persuasion are the only practicable instruments.[29]

Pluralism was thus not just a sociological fact for several eighteenth-century writers; it was a constitutional condition for the guarantee of true religious rights and liberties. This was a species and application of Madison's argument about pluralism in Federalist Paper No. 10—that the best protection against political tyranny is the guarantee of a multiplicity of interests, each contending for public endorsement and political expression in a federalist republic.

4. Equality

The efficacy of liberty of conscience, free exercise of religion, and confessional pluralism depended on a guarantee of equality of all peaceable religions before the law. For the state to single out one pious person or one form of faith for either preferential benefits or discriminatory burdens would skew the choice of conscience, encumber the exercise of religion, and upset the natural plurality of faiths. Many eighteenth-century writers therefore inveighed against the state's unequal treatment of religion. Madison captured the prevailing sentiment: "A just Government... will be best supported by protecting every Citizen in the enjoyment of his Religion with the same equal hand which protects his person and property; by neither invading the equal rights of any Sect, nor suffering any Sect to invade those of another."[30]

This principle of equality of all peaceable religious persons and bodies before the law found its way into a number of early state constitutions. [For example,] Delaware guaranteed Christians "equal rights and privileges"—a guarantee soon extended to all religions.[31]...Even Massachusetts, which maintained a "slender" establishment, nonetheless guaranteed that "all religious sects and denominations, demeaning themselves peaceably, and as good citizens of the commonwealth, shall be equally under the protection of the law; and no subordination of any one sect or denomination to another shall ever be established by law."[32]

The principle of equality also found its place in early drafts of the First Amendment religion clauses, yielding such phrases as: "nor shall the full and equal rights of conscience be in any manner, or on any pretext, infringed." ...

5. Separationism

The principle of separationism was designed primarily to protect religious bodies and religious believers in their inherent rights.

On the one hand, separationism guaranteed the independence and integrity of the internal processes of religious bodies. Elisha Williams spoke for many churchmen when he wrote: "[E]very church has [the] Right to judge in what manner God is to be worshipped by them, and what Form of Discipline ought to be observed by them, and the Right also of electing their own Officers." In the mind of most eighteenth-century writers, the principle of separation of church and state mandated neither the separation of religion and politics nor the secularization of civil society. No eighteenth-century writer would countenance the preclusion of religion altogether from the public square or the political process. The principle of separationism was directed to the institutions of church and state, not to religion and culture.

On the other hand, the principle of separationism also protected the liberty of conscience of the religious believer. President Thomas Jefferson, for example, in his famous 1802 Letter to the Danbury Baptist Association, tied the principle of separationism directly to the principle of liberty of conscience:

> Believing with you that religion is a matter which lies solely between man and his God, that he owes account to none other for his faith or his worship, that the legislative powers of government reach actions only, and not opinions, I contemplate with sovereign reverence that act of the whole American people which declared that their legislature should "make no law respecting an establishment of religion, or prohibiting the free exercise thereof," thus building a wall of separation between church and State. Adhering to this expression of the supreme will of the nation in behalf of the rights of conscience, I shall see with sincere satisfaction the progress of those sentiments which tend to restore to man all his natural rights, convinced he has no natural right in opposition to his social duties.[33]

Separatism thus assured individuals of their natural, inalienable right of conscience, which could be exercised freely and fully to the point of breaching the peace or shirking social duties. . . .

The principles of pluralism, equality, and separationism—separately and together —served to protect religious bodies, both from each other and from the state. It was an open question, however, whether such principles precluded governmental-financial and other forms of support of religion altogether. Evangelical and enlightenment writers sometimes viewed such principles as a firm bar on state support, particularly financial support, of religious beliefs, believers, and bodies. . . . Puritan and republican writers often viewed such principles only as a prohibition against direct financial support for the religious worship or exercise of one particular religious group.

NOTES

As a result of editing, the notes for this essay have been renumbered. The note number from the original essay or article is shown in parentheses at the end of each citation.

1. Quoted in T. H. Breen, *The Character of the Good Ruler, 1630-1730* (1970), p. 42 n.24. (35)

2. Urian Oakes, *New-England pleaded with and pressed to consider the things which concern her peace at least in this her day* (1673). (37)

3. Roger Williams, *Mr. Cotton's Letter Lately Printed, Examined and Answered* (1644), reprinted in *The Complete Writings of Roger Williams* 1 (1963), p. 392. (46)

4. Isaac Backus, *Draft for a Bill of Rights for the Massachusetts Constitution* (1779), in William G. McLoughlin, ed., *Isaac Backus on Church, State, and Calvinism: Pamphlets, 1754-1789* (1968), p. 487. (49)

5. Israel Evans, "A Sermon Delivered at Concord, Before the Hon. General Court of the State of New Hampshire at the Annual Election" (1791), in Ellis Sandez, ed., *Political Sermons of the American Founding Era, 1730-1805* (1991), p. 1062–63 [hereafter Political Sermons]. (50)

6. "Declaration of the Virginia Association of Baptists" (December 25, 1776), in Julian Boyd, ed., *The Papers of Thomas Jefferson*, vol. 1 (1950), p. 660–61. (51)

7. "Letter from James Madison to Edward Livingston" (July 10, 1822), in Gaillard Hunt, ed., *The Writings of James Madison*, vol. 9 (1910), p. 102. (53)

8. Philip S. Foner, ed., *The Complete Writings of Thomas Paine*, vol. 1 (1945), p. 292. (55)

9. James Madison, *Memorial and Remonstrance Against Religious Assessments* (1785), reprinted in Robert A. Rutland and William M. E. Rachal, eds., *The Papers of James Madison*, vol. 8 (1973), p. 298. (56)

10. "Letter from George Washington to the Clergy of Different Denominations Residing In and Near the City of Philadelphia" (March 3, 1797), in John C. Fitzpatrick, ed., *The Writings of George Washington, 1745–1799*, vol. 36 (1931), p. 416. (64)

11. "Letter from John Adams to the Officers of the First Brigade of the Third Division of the Militia of Massachusetts" (1798), in *Life and Works of John Adams*, vol. 9 (1854), p. 229. (65)

12. Timothy Dwight, "The Duty of Americans, at the Present Crisis, Illustrated in a Discourse, Preached on the Fourth of July, 1798" (1798), in Sandez, ed., *Political Sermons*, pp. 1365 n.6, 1380. (66)

13. *Northwest Territory Ordinance of 1787*, 1 Stat. 50, 52 (1789), ch. 8, art. III. (77)

14. Elisha Williams, *The Essential Rights and Liberties of Protestants: A Seasonable Plea for The Liberty of Conscience, and the Right of Private Judgment in Matters of Religion, Without any Controul from Human Authority* (1744), p. 42. (90)

15. Ibid., p. 7–8. (91)

16. Madison, *Memorial and Remonstrance Against Religious Assessments*, par. 1.

17. John Leland, *The Rights of Conscience Inalienable* (1791), reprinted in Sandez, ed., *Political Sermons*, p. 1079. (92)

18. Ezra Stiles, *The United States Elevated to Glory and Honor* (1793), p. 56. (94)

19. Worcestriensis, *Number IV* (1776), reprinted in Charles Hyneman and Donald S. Lutz, eds., *American Political Writing During the Founding Era, 1760–1805*, vol. 1 (1983), p. 449. (95)

20. John Mellen, *The Great and Happy Doctrine of Liberty* (1795), p. 17. (96)

21. Ibid., p. 20. (97)

22. [Ed. Note: See part II of this book.] (104)

23. *Delaware Declaration of Rights of 1776*, § 2. (106)

24. William Penn, *The Great Case of Liberty of Conscience* (1670), reprinted in *A Collection of the Works of William Penn*, vol. 1 (1726), pp. 443, 447. (115)

25. Levi Hart, *Liberty Described and Recommended* (1775), p. 14. (120)

26. *Virginia Constitution of 1776*, § 16. (121)

27. *Georgia Constitution of 1777*, art. LVI. (122)

28. Backus, *Church, State, and Calvinism*, p. 317; Isaac Backus, *Truth is Great and Will Prevail* (1781), p. 3. (124)

29. Thomas Jefferson, "Notes on the State of Virginia," query 17, in Philip Kurland and Ralph Lerner, eds., *The Founders' Constitution*, vol. 5 (1987), pp. 79, 80. (125)

30. Madison, *Memorial and Remonstrance*, par. 8. (131)

31. *Declaration of Rights and Fundamental Rules of the Delaware Senate* (1776), § 3. (133)

32. *Massachusetts Constitution of 1780*, amend. XI. Originally, the guarantee applied only to "every denomination of Christians." Ibid., art III. (137)

33. "Letter from Thomas Jefferson to Danbury Baptist Association" (January 1, 1802), in H. A. Washington, ed., *The Writings of Thomas Jefferson*, vol. 8 (1854), p. 113. (143)

TAKING THE FREE EXERCISE CLAUSE SERIOUSLY

STEPHEN PEPPER

CAN IT MEAN SO MUCH? CAN IT MEAN SO LITTLE?

The text of the Free Exercise Clause is singularly absolute: "Congress shall make no law...prohibiting the free exercise [of religion]." Other provisions in the Bill of Rights have buffering language: security against "unreasonable searches and seizures," "due process of law," "excessive bail," and "cruel and unusual punishments." The other First Amendment freedoms of speech and press share with religion this absoluteness. But freedom of speech and press are inherently limited because they protect only communication, while the term "exercise" denotes action. Religious conduct is not inherently limited to communication, nor to worship, but can extend into all facets of human life. That the protection is unusually limited is clear within the text of the first amendment itself. Assembly for redress of grievances (a sort of speech plus

Stephen Pepper, "Taking the Free Exercise Clause Seriously," *Brigham Young University Law Review* (1986): 299, 300–308.

conduct), is only protected if it is "peaceable." No similar limit is placed upon exercise of religion.

Thus, the language of the Free Exercise Clause seems to provide greater freedom from governmental interference and regulation than any segment of the Constitution. The natural contemporary reaction to this is disbelief. Why would the Constitution grant such extraordinary protection only to religious conduct? This reaction suggests that the free exercise clause may be an anachronism. Can that degree of favoritism for religion suggested by a textual approach be justified from the perspectives of history or political theory? One can, of course, read too much into language. But in this case there is some historical and conceptual support for what appears to be the plain meaning.

It is probable that those who framed and adopted the free exercise clause did not have a common point of view or intention. It is now well known that there were at least two quite different streams of thought supporting freedom of religion and separation of church and state. The radical protestant view perceived government, both its support as well as its possible hostility, as a threat to religion. In the vivid image of Roger Williams, this stance wished to separate the "garden of religion" from the "wilderness of civil government."[1]

Even though history cannot provide us with one answer, it is worth noting that the record does provide some support for concluding that the surprisingly absolute language of the free exercise clause was not inadvertent. It is particularly significant that part of this support comes from James Madison. No one had a more important role in framing the first amendment. Madison's initial proposal—which eventually, in somewhat different language, became the Free Exercise Clause—would have bound the states as well as the federal government. Moreover, Madison belonged to the Enlightenment-deist-rationalist stance, which perceived religion as a threat. Madison's educational background, however, was far more intricately connected to the Christian intellectual tradition than Jefferson's, and his "Enlightenment" approach was not as hostile to religion as Jefferson's. Madison's final tutor at home in Virginia, who had a significant, lasting impact on him, was a graduate of Princeton (then called the College of New Jersey). Perhaps as a result, Madison, although from a patrician, Anglican family, attended, graduated from, and did post-graduate work at Princeton, and this appears to have influenced him greatly. Princeton was then "a kind of West Point for dissenting Presbyterianism, opposed to ecclesiastical and political authority,"[2] and Madison was educated in a vibrant, politically active brand of dissenting protestantism. To the extent one can attribute the language of the free exercise clause to Madison, its absoluteness is consistent with a major strand of his intellectual background.

Madison manifested his position early in his career. George Mason drafted the original version of the religion clause of the 1776 *Virginia Declaration of Rights*, a portion of the newly independent state's constitution. That version stated in part: "[A]ll men should enjoy the fullest toleration in the exercise of religion, according to the dictates of conscience, unpunished and unrestrained by the magistrate, unless under color of religion any man disturb the peace, the happiness, or safety of society...."[3] This version contained plenty of buffering language. But Madison objected, and his proposed language was quite different:

> [A]ll men are equally entitled to the full and free exercise of [religion], according to the dictates of conscience; and therefore that no man or class of men ought on account of religion to be...subjected to any penalties or disabilities, unless under color of religion the preservation of equal liberty and the existence of the State be manifestly endangered.

Madison's version provided far broader protection for religious conduct— only the similar liberty of others, or the existence of the state, justify governmental interference.

Madison's most complete declaration upon freedom of religion expresses a similar view. In the first substantive paragraph of his influential Memorial and Remonstrance he asserts that religious duties are "precedent, both in order of time and degree of obligation, to the claims of Civil Society." He concludes "that in matters of Religion, no man's right is abridged by the institution of Civil Society, and that Religion is wholly exempt from its cognizance."[4] The absolute language of the free exercise clause is thus perfectly consistent both with Madison's earlier assertions on the subject and with the fabric of his intellectual background....

There is a conceptual point of view, consistent with the intellectual history of the period, from which such an expansive freedom of religion provision makes sense. It is fair to characterize the Constitution as essentially an Enlightenment document. Enlightenment thought was skeptical, rational, and scientific. Such a stance toward the world was made possible by secularization and was the cause of further secularization in western society. The American

Constitution as a product of this point of view is rational, mechanistic, and extremely secular. No significant reference to religion or to God is in the document. Yet, Enlightenment thought was hardly pervasive in the Colonies; we have already mentioned the radical Protestants, and many states still had an established or quasi-established church or religion. At the time of the framing of the Constitution and the Bill of Rights, the secular Enlightenment approach to the world was relatively new and still struggling with the preceding, dominant, underlying intellectual paradigm—a religious worldview based on faith, authority and the pervasive presence of a supernatural power and authority. The Constitution is designed according to the new secular paradigm, but through the mechanism of the free exercise clause it defers to the prior religious understanding. The brief but absolute words of the clause are a substantial accommodation to a powerful religious view.

Looking at the clause in this way, as a mediation between a secular Enlightenment vision of government and a religious worldview, its absoluteness is coherent. Social contract imagery is apt: in matters of religion no consent was given to be governed by the mechanisms of the new Constitution; in the area of religion there was no consent to majority rule. This seems consonant with the radical Protestant view of religion and government—the wilderness must be kept from the garden—and with Madison's view, which recognized the primacy of religious authority over that of civil government.

This concession may be hard to understand from the Enlightenment-deist-rationalist view—until it is coupled with the establishment clause. The quid pro quo for the extraordinary shelter of the free exercise clause is a balancing guaranty that the secular government created by the Constitution will remain secular. Religious conduct is privileged, but it must use private means to reach its goals; it cannot use the government.

If there is a border between the garden and the wilderness, if the line between religion and the state can be discerned, the functioning of such a scheme is conceivable, but religion mandates conduct in this world, and the state's rules govern conduct in this world. The first major Supreme Court case dealt with a religious mandate to have plural wives, while the state ruled that only one was permissible.[5] More than a century later, a recent Supreme Court free exercise decision dealt with a state requirement that drivers' licenses bear the photograph of the licensee, as applied to one whose religious beliefs prohibit use of a photograph.[6] Is it an impingement on the free exercise of religion to enforce such rules on believers? Or, is it contrary to establishment clause principles to demand that the state apply different rules to religious believers?

These questions suggest the well-recognized fact that the logic of the two clauses is in conflict. If the establishment clause focuses on the protection of government from the encroachment of the church (and is thus emblematic of the Enlightenment stream of thought), while the free exercise clause reflects more the radical Protestant view of protecting religion from the state, then the subsequent dominance of the establishment clause view will come as no surprise. Secularization has continued apace in the intervening two centuries, and the struggle for predominance between a fundamentally religious and a fundamentally secular worldview is long since over in western intellectual, political, and legal thought. From a secular perspective, religion is not perceived as inherently valuable, vulnerable, or worthy of special protection or cultivation. From a modern Constitutional perspective, religion is more likely to be perceived as akin to race: of no intrinsic importance, but subject historically to abuse and persecution and therefore "inherently suspect" as a basis for governmental classification. This point of view is comfortably concordant with both the dominant modern social-scientific stance toward religion and the modern intellectual discomfort with the root irrationality of much religious thought and many religious movements. For those who perceive in religion more of a threat than a promise (irrationality en masse), it is easy to emphasize the constraints of the Establishment Clause to the point of leaving little effective content for the Free Exercise Clause.

Until 1963 this was, in effect, the Supreme Court's religion clause doctrine. In the first polygamy case the Court turned to Jefferson's dichotomy between belief and action, holding the Free Exercise Clause to protect only belief. And in the Jehovah's Witnesses cases it was never clear that the free exercise clause granted anything beyond the shelter for non-religious conduct provided by the speech, press, and assembly clauses of the First Amendment.[7] In dicta it was clear that laws intentionally discriminating against religion would violate the free exercise clause. As the analysis implied above suggests, including religion with race as suspect classifications under the equal protection clause has the same effect under modern doctrine as does such a limited interpretation of the Free Exercise Clause. But this would help neither the religious polygamist nor the believer opposed to pictures on drivers' licenses, because neither law is religiously discriminatory on its face or in its intent. Intentionally discriminating in favor of religion, or among religions, is prohibited by the Establishment Clause. Thus, congruent with a secular age, the Establishment Clause is a strong barrier to religious domination of the government, while the free exercise clause is reduced to a vestigial anachronism. But is this justifiable? Can the Free Exercise Clause mean so little?

NOTES

As a result of editing, the notes for this essay have been renumbered. The note number from the original essay or article is shown in parentheses at the end of each citation.

1. See generally M. Howe, *The Garden and the Wilderness* (1965). (8)

2. W. Miller, *The First Liberty* (1985), p. 88. (15)

3. Hunt, "James Madison and Religious Liberty" *American Historical Association Annual Report* (1902): 165–66. (16)

4. James Madison, *Memorial and Remonstrance Against Religious Assessments* (1785), para. 1. (18)

5. *Reynolds v. United States*, 98 U.S. 145 (1879) [p. 57 of this book]. (31)

6. *Jensen v. Quaring*, 472 U.S. 478 (1985). (32)

7. Pepper, "Reynolds, Yoder, and Beyond: Alternatives for the Free Exercise Clause," *Utah Law Review* (1981): 309. (39)

Part II.

ARE RELIGIOUS EXEMPTIONS FROM GENERAL LAWS CONSTITUTIONALLY REQUIRED?

Chapter 2

THE BASIC QUESTION
OF EXEMPTIONS

EDITOR'S INTRODUCTION:
THE US SUPREME COURT'S POSITIONS

The Supreme Court has nearly always affirmed that religious belief may not be the basis for government punishment or sanctions. It also has given strong protection to speech with religious content or religious motivation, as much because of the Free Speech Clause as the Free Exercise Clause. But the Court has made dramatic shifts in positions on the protection of religiously motivated conduct. The most common question has been whether the Free Exercise Clause ever protects religious conduct from a coercive burden imposed by a formally religion-neutral law applicable generally to the population. The following three excerpts from major decisions show the Court's shifting positions on whether the Constitution ever requires an exemption from the law in such a case.

1. Protection for Belief Only, Not Action:
  Reynolds v. United States, *98 U.S. 145 (1879)*

The early members of the Mormon Church believed in the practice of polygamy as a religious duty, at least for the male leaders of the church. George Reynolds, an elder in the

church, was prosecuted under a federal law making polygamy a crime within the territo-
ries of the United States. He raised the Free Exercise Clause in defense. The Supreme
Court first looked for guidance to the Virginia Bill for the Establishment of Religious
Freedom, drafted by Thomas Jefferson in 1777 and finally enacted in Virginia in 1786:

In the preamble of this act religious freedom is defined; and after a recital
"that to suffer the civil magistrate to intrude his powers into the field of opinion,
and to restrain the profession or propagation of principles on supposition of
their ill tendency, is a dangerous fallacy which at once destroys all religious liberty," it is declared "that it is time enough for the rightful purposes of civil government for its officers to interfere when principles break out into overt acts
against peace and good order." In these two sentences is found the true distinction between what properly belongs to the church and what to the State.

In a little more than a year after the passage of this statute the convention
met which prepared the Constitution of the United States. Of this convention
Mr. Jefferson was not a member, he being then absent as minister to France.
As soon as he saw the draft of the Constitution proposed for adoption, he, in
a letter to a friend, expressed his disappointment at the absence of an express
declaration insuring the freedom of religion. [And] at the first session of the
first Congress the amendment now under consideration was proposed with
others by Mr. Madison. It met the views of the advocates of religious freedom,
and was adopted. Mr. Jefferson afterwards, in reply to an address to him by a
committee of the Danbury Baptist Association, took occasion to say:

> Believing with you that religion is a matter which lies solely between man
> and his God; that he owes account to none other for his faith or his worship;
> that the legislative powers of the government reach actions only, and not
> opinions—I contemplate with sovereign reverence that act of the whole
> American people which declared that their legislature should "make no law
> respecting an establishment of religion or prohibiting the free exercise
> thereof," thus building a wall of separation between church and State.
> Adhering to this expression of the supreme will of the nation in behalf of
> the rights of conscience, I shall see with sincere satisfaction the progress of
> those sentiments which tend to restore man to all his natural rights, con-
> vinced he has no natural right in opposition to his social duties.

Coming as this does from an acknowledged leader of the advocates of the
measure, it may be accepted almost as an authoritative declaration of the
scope and effect of the amendment thus secured. Congress was deprived of all

legislative power over mere opinion, but was left free to reach actions which were in violation of social duties or subversive of good order....

In our opinion, the statute immediately under consideration is within the legislative power of Congress. [T]he only question which remains is, whether those who make polygamy a part of their religion are excepted from the operation of the statute. If they are, then those who do not make polygamy a part of their religious belief may be found guilty and punished, while those who do, must be acquitted and go free. This would be introducing a new element into criminal law. Laws are made for the government of actions, and while they cannot interfere with mere religious belief and opinions, they may with practices. Suppose one believed that human sacrifices were a necessary part of religious worship, would it be seriously contended that the civil government under which he lived could not interfere to prevent a sacrifice? Or if a wife religiously believed it was her duty to burn herself upon the funeral pile of her dead husband, would it be beyond the power of the civil government to prevent her carrying her belief into practice?

So here, as a law of the organization of society under the exclusive dominion of the United States, it is provided that plural marriages shall not be allowed. Can a man excuse his practices to the contrary because of his religious belief? To permit this would be to make the professed doctrines of religious belief superior to the law of the land, and in effect to permit every citizen to become a law unto himself. Government could exist only in name under such circumstances.

2. Protection Against Generally Applicable Laws:
Wisconsin v. Yoder, 406 U.S. 205 (1972)

Members of the Old Order Amish religion reject, on religious grounds, many aspects of the modern world. Three Amish families in rural Wisconsin refused to send their children, ages fourteen and fifteen, to school and were fined five dollars apiece for violating the state law requiring attendance at a public or private school until age sixteen. The Amish argued that the secondary school would "expos[e] their children to a 'worldly' influence"—including an emphasis on intellectualism, competitiveness, success, and conformity with peers—"in conflict with their beliefs." Instead, the parents sought to give their children the traditional, informal Amish training for work as farmers, carpenters, or other artisans. The Supreme Court ruled that punishing the parents violated the Free Exercise Clause:

There is no doubt as to the power of a State, having a high responsibility for education of its citizens, to impose reasonable regulations for the control and duration of basic education. See, e.g., *Pierce v. Society of Sisters*, 268 U.S. 510 (1925). Providing public schools ranks at the very apex of the function of a State. Yet even this paramount responsibility was, in *Pierce*, made to yield to the right of parents to provide an equivalent education in a privately operated system.... Thus, a State's interest in universal education, however highly we rank it, is not totally free from a balancing process when it impinges on fundamental rights and interests, such as those specifically protected by the Free Exercise Clause of the First Amendment, and the traditional interest of parents with respect to the religious upbringing of their children....

The essence of all that has been said and written on the subject is that only those interests of the highest order and those not otherwise served can overbalance legitimate claims to the free exercise of religion....

Wisconsin concedes that under the Religion Clauses religious beliefs are absolutely free from the State's control, but it argues that "actions," even though religiously grounded, are outside the protection of the First Amendment. But our decisions have rejected the idea that religiously grounded conduct is always outside the protection of the Free Exercise Clause. It is true that activities of individuals, even when religiously based, are often subject to regulation by the States in the exercise of their undoubted power to promote the health, safety, and general welfare, or the Federal Government in the exercise of its delegated powers. But to agree that religiously grounded conduct must often be subject to the broad police power of the State is not to deny that there are areas of conduct protected by the Free Exercise Clause of the First Amendment and thus beyond the power of the State to control, even under regulations of general applicability. This case, therefore, does not become easier because respondents were convicted for their "actions" in refusing to send their children to the public high school; in this context belief and action cannot be neatly confined in logic-tight compartments.

Nor can this case be disposed of on the grounds that Wisconsin's requirement for school attendance to age sixteen applies uniformly to all citizens of the State and does not, on its face, discriminate against religions or a particular religion, or that it is motivated by legitimate secular concerns. A regulation neutral on its face may, in its application, nonetheless offend the constitutional requirement for governmental neutrality if it unduly burdens the free exercise of religion. *Sherbert v. Verner*, 374 U.S. 398 (1963). The Court must not ignore the danger that an exception from a general obligation of citizenship on religious grounds may run afoul of the Establishment Clause, but that danger cannot be allowed to prevent any exception no matter how vital it may be to the protection of values promoted by the right of free exercise....

We turn, then, to the State's broader contention that its interest in its system of compulsory education is so compelling that even the established religious practices of the Amish must give way. Where fundamental claims of religious freedom are at stake, however, we cannot accept such a sweeping claim; despite its admitted validity in the generality of cases, we must searchingly examine the interests that the State seeks to promote by its requirement for compulsory education to age sixteen, and the impediment to those objectives that would flow from recognizing the claimed Amish exemption.

[The Court rejected the claim that forcing Amish teenagers to attend school was necessary to prepare them "to be self-reliant and self-sufficient participants in society":] Whatever their idiosyncracies as seen by the majority, this record shows that the Amish community has been a highly successful social unit within our society, even if apart from the conventional "mainstream." Its members are productive and very law-abiding members of society; they reject public welfare in any of its usual forms....

There is nothing in this record to suggest that the Amish qualities of reliability, self-reliance, and dedication to work would fail to find ready markets in today's society. Absent some contrary evidence supporting the State's position, we are unwilling to assume that persons possessing such valuable vocational skills and habits are doomed to become burdens on society should they determine to leave the Amish faith, nor is there any basis in the record to warrant a finding that an additional one or two years of formal school education beyond the eighth grade would serve to eliminate any such problem that might exist.

Insofar as the State's claim rests on the view that a brief additional period of formal education is imperative to enable the Amish to participate effectively and intelligently in our democratic process, it must fail. The Amish alternative to formal secondary education has enabled them to function effectively in their day-to-day life under self-imposed limitations on relations with the world, and to survive and prosper in contemporary society as a separate, sharply identifiable and highly self-sufficient community for more than two hundred years in this country.... Indeed, the Amish communities singularly parallel and reflect many of the virtues of Jefferson's ideal of the "sturdy yeoman" who would form the basis of what he considered as the ideal of a democratic society.

3. No Protection Against Generally Applicable Laws:
Employment Division v. Smith, 494 U.S. 872 (1990)

Oregon law makes it a criminal felony to possess peyote, a hallucinogenic drug extracted from cactus plants. Members of the Native American Church ingest peyote as the central sacramental act of their worship services. Smith and Black were fired from their jobs with a private drug rehabilitation organization because they ingested peyote at a church service. They requested unemployment benefits from the state but were denied because they had been fired for work-related "misconduct." They sued, claiming the denial of benefits violated their free exercise rights, but the U.S. Supreme Court ultimately ruled against them:

[T]he "exercise of religion" often involves not only belief and profession but the performance of (or abstention from) physical acts: assembling with others for a worship service, participating in sacramental use of bread and wine, proselytizing, abstaining from certain foods or certain modes of transportation. It would be true, we think (though no case of ours has involved the point), that a State would be "prohibiting the free exercise [of religion]" if it sought to ban such acts or abstentions only when they are engaged in for religious reasons, or only because of the religious belief that they display. It would doubtless be unconstitutional, for example, to ban the casting of "statues that are to be used for worship purposes," or to prohibit bowing down before a golden calf.

Respondents in the present case, however, seek to carry the meaning of "prohibiting the free exercise [of religion]" one large step further. They contend that their religious motivation for using peyote places them beyond the reach of a criminal law that is not specifically directed at their religious practice, and that is concededly constitutional as applied to those who use the drug for other reasons. They assert, in other words, that "prohibiting the free exercise [of religion]" includes requiring any individual to observe a generally applicable law that requires (or forbids) the performance of an act that his religious belief forbids (or requires)....

[But w]e have never held that an individual's religious beliefs excuse him from compliance with an otherwise valid law prohibiting conduct that the State is free to regulate. On the contrary, the record of more than a century of our free exercise jurisprudence contradicts that proposition. As described succinctly by Justice Frankfurter in *Minersville School Dist. v. Gobitis*, 310 U.S. 586 (1940): "Conscientious scruples have not, in the course of the long struggle for religious toleration, relieved the individual from obedience to a general law not aimed at the promotion or restriction of religious beliefs." [I]n *Reynolds v. United States,* ... we rejected the claim that criminal laws against polygamy could not be constitutionally applied to those whose religion commanded the practice. ...

Subsequent decisions have consistently held that the right of free exercise does not relieve an individual of the obligation to comply with a "valid and neutral law of general applicability on the ground that the law proscribes (or prescribes) conduct that his religion prescribes (or proscribes)." ...

The only decisions in which we have held that the First Amendment bars application of a neutral, generally applicable law to religiously motivated action have involved not the Free Exercise Clause alone, but the Free Exercise Clause in conjunction with other constitutional protections, such as freedom of speech and of the press, or the right of parents to direct the education of their children, see *Wisconsin v. Yoder.* ...

The present case does not present such a hybrid situation, but a free exercise claim unconnected with any communicative activity or parental right. Respondents urge us to hold, quite simply, that when otherwise prohibitable conduct is accompanied by religious convictions, not only the convictions but the conduct itself must be free from governmental regulation. We have never held that, and decline to do so now. There being no contention that Oregon's drug law represents an attempt to regulate religious beliefs, the communication of religious beliefs, or the raising of one's children in those beliefs, the rule to which we have adhered ever since *Reynolds* plainly controls. ...

Respondents argue that even though exemption from generally applicable criminal laws need not automatically be extended to religiously motivated actors, at least the claim for a religious exemption must be evaluated under the balancing test set forth in *Sherbert v. Verner* [and *Wisconsin v. Yoder*]. Under the *Sherbert* test, governmental actions that substantially burden a religious practice must be justified by a compelling governmental interest. ...

[But the compelling interest test should not apply to] an across-the-board criminal prohibition on a particular form of conduct. ... The government's ability to enforce generally applicable prohibitions of socially harmful conduct, like its ability to carry out other aspects of public policy, "cannot depend on measuring the effects of a governmental action on a religious objector's spiritual development." To make an individual's obligation to obey such a law contingent upon the law's coincidence with his religious beliefs, except where the State's interest is "compelling"—permitting him, by virtue of his beliefs, "to become a law unto himself," *Reynolds v. United States*—contradicts both constitutional tradition and common sense....

Nor is it possible to limit the impact of respondents' proposal by requiring a "compelling state interest" only when the conduct prohibited is "central" to the individual's religion. It is no more appropriate for judges to determine the "centrality" of religious beliefs before applying a "compelling interest" test in the free exercise field, than it would be for them to determine the "importance" of ideas before applying the "compelling interest" test in the free speech field. What principle of law or logic can be brought to bear to contradict a believer's assertion that a particular act is "central" to his personal faith? Judging the centrality of different religious practices is akin to the unacceptable "business of evaluating the relative merits of differing religious claims." ...

If the "compelling interest" test is to be applied at all, then, it must be applied across the board, to all actions thought to be religiously commanded. Moreover, if "compelling interest" really means what it says (and watering it down here would subvert its rigor in the other fields where it is applied), many laws will not meet the test. Any society adopting such a system would be courting anarchy, but that danger increases in direct proportion to the society's diversity of religious beliefs, and its determination to coerce or suppress none of them. Precisely because "we are a cosmopolitan nation made up of people of almost every conceivable religious preference," and precisely because we value and protect that religious divergence, we cannot afford the luxury of deeming presumptively invalid, as applied to the religious objector, every regulation of conduct that does not protect an interest of the highest order. The rule respondents favor would open the prospect of constitutionally required religious exemptions from civic obligations of almost every conceivable kind—ranging from compulsory military service, to the payment of taxes, to health and safety regulation such as manslaughter and child neglect laws, compulsory vaccination laws, drug laws, and traffic laws; to social welfare legislation such as minimum wage laws, child labor laws, animal cruelty laws, and laws providing for equality of opportunity for the races. The First Amendment's protection of religious liberty does not require this.

Values that are protected against government interference through enshrinement in the Bill of Rights are not thereby banished from the political process. Just as a society that believes in the negative protection accorded to the press by the First Amendment is likely to enact laws that affirmatively foster the dissemination of the printed word, so also a society that believes in the negative protection accorded to religious belief can be expected to be solicitous of that value in its legislation as well. It is therefore not surprising that a number of States have made an exception to their drug laws for sacramental peyote use. But to say that a nondiscriminatory religious-practice exemption is permitted, or even that it is desirable, is not to say that it is constitutionally required, and that the appropriate occasions for its creation can be discerned by the courts. It may fairly be said that leaving accommodation to the political process will place at a relative disadvantage those religious practices that are not widely engaged in; but that unavoidable consequence of democratic government must be preferred to a system in which each conscience is a law unto itself or in which judges weigh the social importance of all laws against the centrality of all religious beliefs.

FREE EXERCISE REVISIONISM
AND THE *SMITH* DECISION

MICHAEL W. MCCONNELL

THE THEORETICAL ARGUMENT [OF *SMITH*]

Virtually the entire theoretical argument of the *Smith* opinion is packed into this one sentence:

> It may fairly be said that leaving accommodation to the political process will place at a relative disadvantage those religious practices that are not widely engaged in; but that unavoidable consequence of democratic government must be preferred to a system in which each conscience is a law unto itself or in which judges weigh the social importance of all laws against the centrality of all religious beliefs.[1]

Michael W. McConnell, "Free Exercise Revisionism and the *Smith* Decision," *University of Chicago Law Review* 57 (1990): 37, 44, 52, 1109, 1129, 1139, 1149.

... The Court's argument has a certain unity, but for purposes of analysis I propose to break it up into five separate but related ideas expressed in this sentence and a few other key passages in the opinion. The first idea is an implied devaluation of the importance of denominational neutrality under the Religion Clauses. Second is the assumption that free exercise exemptions are a form of special preference for religion and that generally applicable laws written from the perspective of the majority are necessarily and by definition neutral. Third is the claim that exceptions under the Free Exercise Clause are a constitutional anomaly. Fourth is that decisions regarding free exercise exemptions are inherently subjective and therefore legislative in character; in other words, courts have no non-arbitrary way to adjudicate conflicts between religious conscience and law. Fifth, and most important, is that it is contrary to the rule of law—it would be "courting anarchy"—for individual conscience to take precedence over law.

A. Denominational Neutrality

The *Smith* opinion does not specifically address how one should weigh the evils of disadvantaging religious minorities against those of arbitrary judging and lawlessness. The outcome of the case, however, implicitly suggests that denominational neutrality is of secondary importance. The opinion characterizes the doctrine of free exercise exemptions as a "luxury," suggesting that its purposes, while worthy, are distinctly subordinate. Had this proposition been raised explicitly, the Court would have found much in our constitutional history bearing on the question and might have found it more difficult to reach the balance it struck.

In *Larson v. Valente*, the Court noted that the "clearest command of the Establishment Clause is that one religious denomination cannot be officially preferred over another."[2] This conclusion is confirmed repeatedly in both statements and constitutional enactments of the founding period.... The twelve state constitutional free exercise provisions extant in 1789 were different in many respects, but all contained language referring to denominational equality (though in two states this equality was extended only to Christian denominations)....

Against this background, it seems the Supreme Court should have given more serious attention to the problem of "plac[ing] at a relative disadvantage those religious practices that are not widely engaged in" before concluding that this consideration is outweighed by other principles less firmly rooted in our constitutional scheme....

B. Special Privileges or Neutrality in the Face of Differences?

Throughout the *Smith* opinion, generally applicable laws are treated as presumptively neutral, with religious accommodations a form of special preference, akin to affirmative action. The opinion describes religious accommodations as laws that "affirmatively foster" the "value" of "religious belief." In *Sherbert v. Verner*, by contrast, Justice Brennan's majority opinion characterized a religious exemption as "reflect[ing] nothing more than the governmental obligation of neutrality in the face of religious differences."[3] In a sense, then, both *Smith* and *Sherbert* are about neutrality toward religion. But which has the correct understanding of neutrality?

To examine this question, I will use the facts of *Stansbury v. Marks*, the first recorded case raising free exercise issues after adoption of the First Amendment. The case arose in the Pennsylvania courts and was decided under state law. The Reporter's summary of the holding of the case was: "A Jew may be fined for refusing to testify on his Sabbath." The entire report of the case is as follows:

> In this cause (which was tried on Saturday, the 5th of April), the defendant offered Jonas Phillips, a Jew, as a witness; but he refused to be sworn, because it was his Sabbath. The court, therefore, fined him £10; but the defendant, afterwards, waiving the benefit of his testimony, he was discharged from the fine.[4]

We can assume that, in those days of the six-day work week, the courts of Pennsylvania were routinely open for business on Saturday. The decision to operate on Saturday, we may assume, was not aimed at members of the Jewish faith, but was simply a matter of convenience. Nor was the law allowing parties to civil suits to compel witnesses to attend court proceedings, on pain of paying a fine, instituted for the purpose of restricting religious exercise. This is an example of a generally applicable, otherwise valid, law. Is it neutral toward religion?

No, it is not. The courts were closed on Sundays, the day on which the Christian majority of Pennsylvania observed the Sabbath. The effect of the six-day calendar was to impose a burden on Saturday Sabbath observers (mostly Jews) that is not imposed on others (mostly Christians). It is anything but neutral—not because the burden happened to fall disproportionately on Jews, but because the burden was attached to a practice that, among others, defines what it means to be a faithful Jew.

What would neutrality require? Surely it is not necessary to conduct court business on Sunday. Since the vast majority of Pennsylvanians were Christians and observed Sunday as the day of Sabbath, that would create needless conflict and administrative costs. It would be more neutral to close on both Saturday and Sunday, the modern solution, but that has significant costs in an era of a six-day work week. And if there were other religious minorities in the Commonwealth who observed the Sabbath on other days, Moslems perhaps, then this solution would not work at all. The best, least costly, and most neutral solution is to exempt Saturday Sabbath observers from the obligation of testifying on Saturday. Thus, an exemption is not "affirmative fostering" of religion; it is more like *Sherbert*'s neutrality in the face of differences.

It may be objected that this example is loaded because the selection of days of rest is fraught with religious significance. The selection of Sunday as the day on which the courts would not operate was itself a religious choice, almost an establishment of the Christian religion. It might be said that an exemption is required in that case only to equalize a situation in which Christians had already been granted a benefit on account of religious practice.

But this objection presupposes that there are decisions that are not fraught with religious significance. And perhaps there are—but those decisions will not give rise to free exercise claims. All free exercise claims involve government decisions that are fraught with religious significance, at least from the point of view of the religious minority. In this respect, *Stansbury v. Marks* cannot be distinguished from *Smith*. In *Smith*, the generally applicable law was the prohibition on the use of hallucinogenic drugs. The Native American Church uses peyote as its sacrament. Application of the anti-drug laws to the sacramental use of peyote effectively destroys the practice of the Native American Church. Is this neutral?

No, it is not. Christians and Jews use wine as part of their sacrament, and wine is not illegal. Even when wine was illegal during Prohibition, Congress exempted the sacramental use of wine from the proscription. The effect of laws prohibiting hallucinogenic drugs but not alcohol, or of allowing exemptions from one law but not the other, is to impose a burden on the practice of the Native American Church that is not imposed on Christians or Jews. It is no more neutral than operating courts on Saturday and not on Sunday....

It should be apparent why a mere absence of attention to religious consequences on the part of the legislature cannot prove that legislation is neutral. In a world in which some beliefs are more prominent than others, the political branches will inevitably be selectively sensitive toward religious injuries. Laws that impinge upon the religious practices of larger or more prominent faiths will be noticed and remedied. When the laws impinge upon the practice of smaller groups, legislators will not even notice, and may not care even if they do notice. If believers of all creeds are to be protected in the "full and equal rights of conscience," then selective sensitivity is not enough. The courts offer a forum in which the particular infringements of small religions can be brought to the attention of the authorities and (assuming the judges perform their duties impartially) be given the same sort of hearing that more prominent religions already receive from the political process.

C. CONSTITUTIONAL ANOMALIES

Closely related to the preceding point is the *Smith* Court's claim that the compelling interest test in free exercise exemption cases is "a constitutional anomaly."...

[For example, the opinion] draws an analogy to "race-neutral laws that have the effect of disproportionately disadvantaging a particular racial group," noting that such laws "do not thereby become subject to compelling-interest analysis under the Equal Protection Clause."[5] This is true, but the difference in doctrinal analysis is rooted in the nature of the underlying constitutional principles.

At the risk of oversimplification, it can be said that the ideal of racial nondiscrimination is that individuals are fundamentally equal and must be treated as such; differences based on race are irrelevant and must be overcome. The ideal of free exercise of religion, by contrast, is that people of different religious convictions are different and that those differences are precious and must not be disturbed. The ideal of racial justice is assimilationist and integrationist. The ideal of free exercise is counter-assimilationist; it strives to allow individuals of different religious faiths to maintain their differences in the face of powerful pressures to conform.

A better analogy can be drawn between free exercise theory and the theory of handicap discrimination, which is quite different from race discrimination. The theory of handicap discrimination recognizes that individuals with a handicap are different in a way that cannot be changed but can only be accommodated. Failure to install a low-cost ramp for access to a building, for example, is a core violation of the norms of handicap discrimination theory—even though a rampless building was presumably not constructed for the purpose of exclusion. Religion is more like handicap than it is like race. A person who cannot work on Saturday is not merely disproportionately disadvantaged by a requirement that he accept "suitable" work (where "suitable" is defined in secular terms); he is excluded precisely on account of his "difference," as surely as the wheelchair-bound person is from a rampless building. By contrast, the black job applicant in *Washington v. Davis* was not excluded on account of his "difference," but on account of a factor that under the ideal vision of racial justice is wholly unrelated to his "difference." If the paradigmatic instance of race discrimination is treating people who are fundamentally the same as if they were different, the paradigmatic instance of free exercise violations or handicap discrimination is treating people who are fundamentally different as if they were the same....

D. The Judicial Role

A major theme of the *Smith* opinion is that the compelling interest test forces the courts to engage in judgments that cannot be made on a nonarbitrary basis. The Court commented that "it is horrible to contemplate that federal judges will regularly balance against the importance of general laws the significance of religious practice." It is better that minority religions will be at "a relative disadvantage," the Court said, than that judges have to "weigh the social importance of all laws against the centrality of all religious beliefs."

The Court illustrated this concern with what it playfully admitted to be a "parade of horribles"—claims for free exercise exemptions from such laws as compulsory military service, health and safety regulation, compulsory vaccination laws, traffic laws, and social welfare legislation including minimum wage, child labor, and animal cruelty laws.... [But] this parade is almost risible in its one-sidedness. For every claim that would, if granted, produce a horrible result, there is a claim that ought to be granted but will not be after the *Smith* decision.

Consider the fact that employment discrimination laws could force the

Roman Catholic Church to hire female priests, if there are no free exercise exemptions from generally applicable laws. Or that historic preservation laws could prevent churches from making theologically significant alterations to their structures. Or that prisons will not have to serve kosher or hallel food to Jewish or Moslem prisoners. Or that Jewish high school athletes may be forbidden to wear yarmulkes and thus excluded from interscholastic sports. Or that churches with a religious objection to unrepentant homosexuality will be required to retain an openly gay individual as church organist, parochial school teacher, or even a pastor. Or that public school students will be forced to attend sex education classes contrary to their faith. Or that religious sermons on issues of political significance could lead to revocation of tax exemptions. Or that Catholic doctors in public hospitals could be fired if they refuse to perform abortions. Or that Orthodox Jews could be required to cease and desist from sexual segregation of their places of worship.

If the Court wishes to consider a parade of horribles, it should parade the horribles on both sides. But while the two parades may be of the same length, they are of very different quality. The judicial system is able to reject claims that would be horrible if granted; believers are helpless to deal with infringements on religious freedom that the courts refuse to remedy.

Challenged by Justice O'Connor's rejoinder that the parade of horribles only "demonstrates . . . that courts have been quite capable of . . . strik[ing] sensible balances between religious liberty and competing state interests," the Court retreated to the proposition that "the purpose of our parade . . . is not to suggest that courts would necessarily permit harmful exemptions from these laws (though they might), but to suggest that courts would constantly be in the business of determining whether the 'severe impact' of various laws on religious practice . . . suffices to permit us to confer an exemption."

The Court's evident hostility to subjective judicial second-guessing of legislative judgments is generally salutary, at least if not taken to extremes. But it raises the question: why is the Free Exercise Clause a particular target? The author of the *Smith* opinion, Justice Scalia, is reasonably consistent regarding the undesirability of judicial discretion. In most areas of constitutional law, however, the majority of the Court does not hesitate to weigh the social importance of laws against their impact on constitutional rights. There is no particular reason to believe that judgments under the Free Exercise Clause are any more discretionary or prone to judicial abuse than judgments under the Commerce Clause, the Due Process Clause, or the Free Speech

Clause, to take a few examples from the current catalog of compelling interest or balancing tests. Unless *Smith* is the harbinger of a wholesale retreat from judicial discretion across the range of constitutional law, there should be some explanation of why the problem in this field is more acute than it is elsewhere.

The *Smith* opinion suggests that the problem with the compelling interest test is that it requires inquiry into whether religious beliefs are "central" to the claimant's religion, which is "akin to the unacceptable 'business of evaluating the relative merits of differing religious claims.'" But is this true? In such cases, the court is not judging the "merits" of religious claims but solely trying to determine what they are. To be sure, the court may get it wrong, but what is the grave injury from that (other than the impact on the case itself)? The court does not purport to be resolving issues of religious interpretation for any purpose other than understanding the nature of the plaintiff's claim, and its misinterpretation carries no weight beyond the courtroom. I agree that courts must be sensitive to the impropriety of second-guessing religious doctrine, but I cannot agree that the possibility of error warrants abandonment of the enterprise....

E. The Rule of Law

The deepest and most important theme of the *Smith* opinion is its perception of a conflict between free exercise exemptions and the rule of law. The Court refers to exemptions as "a private right to ignore generally applicable laws." Elsewhere, it states that to apply the compelling interest test rigorously "would be courting anarchy" and warns against making "each conscience ... a law unto itself." These fears are an unconscious echo of John Locke, who wrote in his *Letter Concerning Toleration* [(1690)] that "the private judgment of any person concerning a law enacted in political matters, for the public good, does not take away the obligation of that law, nor deserve a dispensation."

Viewed through the lens of legal positivism, this concern is wholly out of place in the context of a written constitution with a provision that, by hypothesis, authorizes exemptions. The Court itself concedes that there is nothing inappropriate or "anomalous" about legislation that makes exceptions for religious conflicts. Presumably, legislation of this sort is valid whether it is specific (like laws exempting the Native American Church from the ban on consumption of peyote) or general (like laws requiring employers to make reasonable accommodations of their employees' religious needs). Although the judicial role is broader when the legislation is general, the Court would not say that such legislation is therefore improper or unconstitutional. Why, then, is it problematic for the People to enact a similar provision into constitutional law? From the perspective of legal positivism there is no difference between statutes and constitutional amendments. Both are commands of the sovereign.

If there is nothing wrong with statutory commands of the sovereign that make exceptions from generally applicable laws in cases of conflict with religious conscience, then there should be nothing wrong with constitutional commands of the same sort. To Locke, the right to claim exemptions was tantamount to the right to rebellion, since there was no written constitution expressing the sovereign will in a form superior to legislation, and no institution of judicial review to mediate claims of exemption. To the modern Supreme Court, the claim to exemptions is a routine matter of invoking the supreme law of the land. There is nothing lawless or anarchic about it.

From the perspective of legal positivism, free exercise exemptions do not make each conscience "a law unto itself." An arm of the government, the court, decides in each instance what the reach of the law will be. The Free Exercise Clause draws a boundary between the powers of the government and the freedom of the individual, but that boundary is defined and enforced by the government. The significance of the Free Exercise Clause is that the definition and enforcement of the boundary is entrusted to the arm of the government most likely to perform the function dispassionately and best equipped to consider the specifics of the case. The individual believer is not judge in his own case.

From a natural rights perspective, the Court's concerns about the rule of law are more substantial. According to eighteenth-century legal thought, freedom of religious conscience was not a product of the sovereign's will but a natural and inalienable right. The New Hampshire Constitution of 1784, for example, declared: "Among the natural rights, some are in their very nature unalienable, because no equivalent can be given or received for them. Of this kind are the RIGHTS OF CONSCIENCE."[6] George Washington addressed the Hebrew Congregation of Newport, Rhode Island, in these words: "It is now no more that toleration is spoken of, as if it was by the indulgence of one class of people, that another enjoyed the exercise of their inherent natural rights."[7] The reason the rights of conscience were deemed inalienable is that they represented duties to God as opposed to privileges of the individual. Thus, the Free Exercise Clause is not an expression of the will of the sovereign but a declaration that the right to practice religion is jurisdiction-ally beyond the scope of civil authority. This, then, is an anarchic idea: that duties to God, perceived in the conscience of the individual, are superior to the law of the land.

That the idea may be anarchic does not mean that we should dismiss it, for there is reason to believe that this inalienable rights understanding is the genuine theory of the Religion Clauses of the First Amendment. One of the leading expositions of the thinking of the day about government and religion, James Madison's *Memorial and Remonstrance Against Religious Assessments*, makes the point in this way:

> Before any man can be considered as a member of Civil Society, he must be considered as a subject of the Governor of the Universe: And if a member of Civil Society, who enters into any subordinate Association, must always do it with a reservation of his duty to the general authority; much more must every man who becomes a member of any particular Civil Society, do it with a saving of his allegiance to the Universal Sovereign.[8]

Note the contrast between the *Smith* opinion and Madison's *Memorial and Remonstrance*. *Smith* insists that conscience must be subordinate to civil law; Madison insists that civil law must be subordinate to conscience.

At its very core, the Free Exercise Clause, understood as Madison understood it, reflected a theological position: that God is sovereign. It also reflected a political theory: that government is a subordinate association. The theological and political positions are connected. To recognize the sovereignty of God is to recognize a plurality of authorities and to impress upon government the need for humility and restraint. To deny that the government has an obligation to defer, where possible, to the dictates of religious conscience is to deny that there could be anything like "God" that could have a superior claim on the allegiance of the citizens—to assert that government is, in principle, the ultimate authority. Those are propositions that few Americans, today or in 1789, could accept.

NOTES

As a result of editing, the notes for this essay have been renumbered. The note number from the original essay or article is shown in parentheses at the end of each citation.

1. *Employment Division v. Smith*, 494 U.S. 872, 890 (1990). (94)

2. 456 U.S. 228, 244 (1982). (98)

3. 374 U.S. 398, 409 (1963). (110)

4. 2 U.S. 213 (1793). (112)

5. [494 U.S., p. 884 n.3 (citing *Washington v. Davis*, 426 U.S. 229 (1976), which held that Equal Protection Clause was not violated by facially neutral test for police-department employment that black applicants failed at three times the rate of whites).] (130)

6. Ben Perley Poore, ed., *Federal and State Constitutions, Colonial Charters, and Other Organic Laws of the United States 1280-81*, vol. 1, 2d ed. (GPO, 1878). (179)

7. John C. Fitzpatrick, ed., *The Writings of George Washington*, vol. 31 (GPO, 1939), pp. 93–94 n.65. (180)

8. James Madison, *Memorial and Remonstrance Against Religious Assessments* (1785), par. 1. (183)

IN DEFENSE OF *SMITH* AND FREE EXERCISE REVISIONISM

WILLIAM P. MARSHALL

In *Smith*, the Supreme Court held that the Free Exercise Clause does not compel courts to grant exemptions from generally applicable criminal laws to individuals whose religious beliefs conflict with those laws.... In [defending the *Smith* result,] I concentrate on the two critical theoretical concerns: (1) the cogency of exemption analysis; and (2) the role of equality in free exercise theory. Both concerns lead to a rejection of the free exercise exemption claim.

I. THE TROUBLE WITH EXEMPTIONS

A. The Inherent Difficulties

[A] particular analysis should be rejected when it undermines the constitutional values it purports to protect, is inherently arbitrary, forces courts to

William P. Marshall, "In Defense of *Smith* and Free Exercise Revisionism," *University of Chicago Law Review* 58 (1991): 308, 309–12, 317–22, 324–27.

engage in a balancing process that systematically underestimates the state interest, and threatens other constitutional values. Such is the case with free exercise exemption analysis.

First, exemption analysis threatens free exercise values because it requires courts to consider the legitimacy of the religious claim of the party seeking the exemption. Under the exemption analysis, the court must first determine, at a definitional level, whether the belief at issue is "religious." Then it must determine whether the belief is sincerely held. [B]oth inquiries are not only awkward and counterproductive; they also threaten the values of religious freedom. Moreover, the judicial definition of religion does more than simply limit religion; it places an official imprimatur on certain types of belief systems to the exclusion of others. At the very least, as Justice Stevens has argued, this power of approval or disapproval raises Establishment Clause problems....

Minority belief systems—not majority belief systems—will bear the brunt of the definition and the sincerity inquiries. A court is more likely to find against a claimant on definitional grounds when the religion is bizarre, relative to the cultural norm, and is more likely to find that a religious belief is insincere when the belief in question is, by cultural norms, incredulous. The religious claims most likely to be recognized, therefore, are those that closely parallel or directly relate to the culture's predominant religious traditions. To put it in concrete terms, Mrs. Sherbert's claim that she is forbidden to work on Saturdays is likely to be accepted as legitimate; Mr. Hodges's claim that he must dress like a chicken when going to court is not.

Second, the exemption analysis requires courts to engage in a highly problematic form of constitutional balancing. In other doctrinal areas, the Court balances the state interest in the regulation at issue against the interests of the regulated class taken as a whole. Exemption analysis, however, requires a court to weigh the state interest against the interest of the narrower class comprised only of those seeking exemption. This leads to both unpredictability in the process and potential inconsistency in result as each regulation may be subject to limitless challenges based upon the peculiar identity of the challenger.

Third, the exemption balancing process necessarily leads to underestimating the strength of the countervailing state interest. The state interest in a challenged regulation will seldom be seriously threatened if only a few persons seek exemption from it. A legitimate state interest is often "compelling" only in relation to cumulative concerns. If, for example, one factory is exempt from anti-pollution requirements, the state's interest in protecting air quality will not be seriously disturbed. When many factories pollute, on the other hand, the state interest is seriously threatened. Weighing the state interest against a narrow class seeking exemption is similar to asking whether this particular straw is the one that breaks the camel's back.

Finally, in some circumstances, free exercise exemption analysis may result in a troublesome interplay with the Speech Clause that threatens both speech and free exercise interests. Many activities that raise only speech concerns when undertaken by a secular group—literature distribution, for example—will raise both speech and free exercise concerns when undertaken by a religious group. The problem is that allowing only free exercise exemptions from governmental restrictions on those activities would mean that only religious groups could engage in the expressive activity. Such a result offends the central Speech Clause principle of content neutrality; it creates, in effect, a content-based distinction in favor of religious expression....

II. Exemptions and the Two Faces of Equality

A. Denominational Equality

[The critics'] most sympathetic argument is that the denial of exemptions would have a disproportionate impact on minority groups. [They are] correct in noting that neutral restrictions have disproportionate impacts.... [C]ultural traditions and social mores generally reflect majoritarian religious beliefs. Legislators are more likely to be aware of majoritarian religious practices (their own) when they fashion general regulations, and thus are unlikely to place disabilities on those practices. Similarly, they are less likely to be concerned with religious practices outside their religious tradition and accordingly are more likely to place burdens on those practices inadvertently. [The critics] thus plausibly argu[e] that concerns of denominational neutrality might support allowing exemptions in those cases where the challenged regulation results in de facto inequality for a minority religious practice.

On the other hand, the free exercise exemption "cure" is arguably worse than the "disease"—i.e., the harm to religious exercise created by neutral laws. After all, even without the free exercise exemption, the constitutional protection for religion is extensive and stringent. The Free Exercise Clause itself prohibits any direct attempt to single out religion for adverse treatment, and the Free Speech Clause includes the protection of prayer, proselytizing, preaching, and aspects of religious conscience in its ambit. Moreover, the incidental de facto inequality created by neutral laws is just that—incidental. It occurs only randomly and haphazardly. Some minority religious beliefs will be aligned with majority beliefs, while other minority beliefs will not. The Amish, unlike Jews, are not disadvantaged by Sunday closing laws. In other circumstances this pattern will be reversed. Jews, unlike the Amish, are not disadvantaged by social security laws. One need not fully accept Professor Mark Tushnet's claim that in a complex society "the overall distribution of burdens and benefits is likely to be reasonably fair"[1] to acknowledge that minority religions will be on both sides of neutral laws.

B. Equality of Belief

The free exercise exemption, however, raises another serious concern. Granting exemptions only to religious claimants promotes its own form of inequality: a constitutional preference for religious over non-religious belief systems.

Case law readily illustrates this problem. In *Wisconsin v. Yoder*,[2] the Court explicitly stated that constitutional exemption from compulsory education requirements was available only to the Amish on religious grounds and would not be available to a non-religious group seeking exemption because of adherence to, for example, the philosophical precepts of Henry David Thoreau. Similarly, in *Thomas v. Review Board*,[3] the Court held that exemption from unemployment insurance requirements would be available to an individual whose religious tenets prevent him from working in an armaments factory, but would not be available to one whose claim was based upon "personal philosophical choice."

This favoritism for religious belief over other beliefs itself raises serious constitutional concerns. Most obviously, a constitutional preference for religious belief cuts at the heart of the central principle of the Free Speech Clause—that every idea is of equal dignity and status in the marketplace of ideas.

The free exercise exemption also offends Establishment Clause principles. Special treatment for religion connotes sponsorship and endorsement; providing relative benefits for religion over non-religion may have the impermissible effect of advancing religion. In fact, the type of discrimination created by the free exercise exemption is arguably worse than the de facto inequality purportedly redressed by the exemption analysis because it is intentional, a matter of critical concern in equal protection analysis. The explicit assertion in the free exercise claim that religious belief is uniquely entitled to constitutional protection is also troublesome from another equal protection vantage. As the Court has noted, explicit endorsement of inequality is particularly egregious because it sends a clear message of second-class status. Thus, the explicit inequality required by the free exercise exemption analysis more directly and powerfully harms equality interests than does the inadvertent de facto discrimination caused by generally applicable laws.

Importantly, religious belief cannot be qualitatively distinguished from other belief systems in a way that justifies special constitutional consideration. For example, bonds of ethnicity, interpersonal relationships, and social and political relationships as well as religion may be, and are, integral to an individual's self-identity. Similarly, both non-religious and religious groups further the values of pluralism by fostering diversity within society and forming "intermediate communities" that shield the individual from the state.

McConnell argues that religious belief is uniquely entitled to exemption because it involves a duty to God—a transcendent sovereign. This contention, however, is neither persuasive nor fully accurate. First, to the extent that it depends on a notion that special suffering attaches to violations of extra-temporal obligations, the argument is extraordinarily overbroad. The violation of deeply held moral or political principles may cause as much psychic harm to the believer as would a violation of a religious tenet, even if the latter is believed to have extra-temporal effect.

Second, not all religions are theistic—Buddhism and Taoism are but two examples. Moreover, even with respect to theistic religions, some religious exercise is based upon religious custom rather than divine obligation. Belief in an external sovereign, therefore, does not distinguish religious belief from all other forms of belief. McConnell then may not rely upon any purported special significance of extra-temporal belief as justifying special treatment for religious exercise because not all religious exercise is premised upon extra-temporal obligation.

Perhaps the most significant evidence of the constitutional equivalency between religious and non-religious belief systems, however, is the critical role they share in the social and political process. Religion is not insular. It is a powerful social and political force that competes with other forms of belief in the shaping of the mores and values of the society which, in turn, become part of the society's political landscape. Thomas's claim that it is wrong to engage in armaments work or Bob Jones University's claim that racial discrimination is divinely based are morally and politically laden and, if accepted by enough persons, would dramatically influence social and political reactions to those issues. Religious views on the sanctity of life form a part of the social and moral background from which political issues as diverse as capital punishment, abortion, animal rights, the environment, and foreign policy will be resolved....

C. McConnell's Response

...In the last section of his article, [McConnell] candidly asserts that the free exercise exemption reflects a constitutional recognition of the theological position "that God is sovereign" and the commensurate political position "that government is a subordinate association."

Obviously, if the Free Exercise Clause endorses religious belief in this manner, it would support the contention that the favoritism of religiously based belief systems over non-religiously based systems is not constitutionally suspect (although it would perhaps support special deference only to theistic religious claims). This position, however, is more revisionist than *Smith*. At least since 1944, the Court has rejected the claim that the Constitution prefers one particular mode of belief....

McConnell's proposed change in constitutional understanding would require fundamental changes in other doctrinal areas.... McConnell's proposition suggests that laws that favor religion over non-religion should be readily upheld —establishment, equal protection, and speech principles notwithstanding....

[T]he Establishment Clause suggests that the framers did not see religion as the beneficent force that McConnell assumes. Instead, the Establishment Clause uniquely singles out government advancement of religion as a matter to be avoided. Because there is no comparable limitation on other types of belief systems, the claim that religion is preferred is not persuasive.

The non-establishment point is particularly critical given the role of religion in politics and society. As noted previously, religion is a primary force in the development of cultural mores and values. To suggest that religion receive added vitality in this role by either directly aiding its dissemination or insulating it from other social forces wholly distorts the non-establishment principle.

NOTES

As a result of editing, the notes for this essay have been renumbered. The note number from the original essay or article is shown in parentheses at the end of each citation.

1. Mark Tushnet, "The Emerging Principle of Accommodation of Religion (Dubitante)," *Georgetown Law Journal* 76 (1988): 1691, 1700. (56)

2. 406 U.S. 205 (1972) [Ed. Note: see p. 59 of this book]. (58)

3. 450 U.S. 707, 713 (1981). (59)

Chapter 3

THE DEBATE OVER EXEMPTIONS AND CONSTITUTIONAL HISTORY

A. THE FOUNDING-ERA UNDERSTANDING

THE ORIGINS AND HISTORICAL UNDERSTANDING OF FREE EXERCISE OF RELIGION

MICHAEL W. MCCONNELL

FREE EXERCISE BEFORE THE CONSTITUTION

Although often linked with Jefferson's "Enlightenment-deist-rationalist" stance toward religious freedom, Madison's views on the religion-state question should be distinguished from those of his fellow Virginian, and hence from [John] Locke.... Madison advocated a jurisdictional division between religion and government based on the demands of religion rather than solely on the interests of society. In his *Memorial and Remonstrance*, he wrote:

Michael W. McConnell, "The Origins and Historical Understanding of Free Exercise of Religion," *Harvard Law Review* 103 (1990): 1409.

The Religion then of every man must be left to the conviction and conscience of every man; and it is the right of every man to exercise it as these
may dictate....It is the duty of every man to render to the Creator such
homage, and such only, as he believes to be acceptable to him.

Moreover, Madison claimed that this duty to the Creator is "precedent both
in order of time and degree of obligation, to the claims of Civil Society," and
"therefore that in matters of Religion, no man's right is abridged by the institution of Civil Society."

This striking passage illuminates the radical foundations of Madison's
writings on religious liberty. While it does not prove that Madison supported
free exercise exemptions, it suggests an approach toward religious liberty consonant with them. If the scope of religious liberty is defined by religious duty
(man must render to God "such homage...as he believes to be acceptable to
him"), and if the claims of civil society are subordinate to the claims of religious freedom, it would seem to follow that the dictates of religious faith must
take precedence over the laws of the state, even if they are secular and generally applicable....

[Washington, too, expressed support for religious accommodations,
writing to a group of Quakers in 1789:

[I]n my opinion the conscientious scruples of all men should be treated with
great delicacy and tenderness; and it is my wish and desire, that the laws may
always be as extensively accommodated to them, as a due regard to the protection and essential interests of the nation may justify and permit....]

Legal Protections after Independence

The Revolution inspired a wave of constitution-writing in the new states.
Eleven of the thirteen states (plus Vermont) adopted new constitutions
between 1776 and 1780. Of those eleven, six (plus Vermont) included an
explicit bill of rights; three more states adopted a bill of rights between 1781
and 1790. With the exception of Connecticut, every state, with or without an
establishment, had a constitutional provision protecting religious freedom by
1789, although two states confined their protections to Christians and five
other states confined their protections to theists. There was no discernible difference between the free exercise provisions adopted by the states with an
establishment and those without.... Freedom of religion was universally said

to be an unalienable right; the status of other rights commonly found in state bills of rights, such as property or trial by jury, was more disputed and often considered derivative of civil society.

These state constitutions provide the most direct evidence of the original understanding, for it is reasonable to infer that those who drafted and adopted the first amendment assumed the term "free exercise of religion" meant what it had meant in their states. The wording of the state provisions thus casts light on the meaning of the first amendment.

New York's 1777 Constitution was typical:

> [T]he free exercise and enjoyment of religious profession and worship, without discrimination or preference, shall forever hereafter be allowed, within this State, to all mankind: Provided, That the liberty of conscience, hereby granted, shall not be so construed as to excuse acts of licentiousness, or justify practices inconsistent with the peace or safety of this State.[1]

Likewise, New Hampshire's provision stated:

> Every individual has a natural and unalienable right to worship GOD according to the dictates of his own conscience, and reason; and no subject shall be hurt, molested, or restrained in his person, liberty or estate for worshipping GOD, in the manner and season most agreeable to the dictates of his own conscience, ... provided he doth not disturb the public peace, or disturb others, in their religious worship.[2]

... Other state provisions were similar....

While differing in their particulars, these constitutional provisions [were similar] both in the scope of the liberty and in its limitations. Each of these elements warrants attention.

1. *Scope of the Liberty.*—Each of the state constitutions first defined the scope of the free exercise right in terms of the conscience of the individual believer and the actions that flow from that conscience. None of the provisions confined the protection to beliefs and opinions, as did Jefferson [in the passage quoted in *Reynolds* (p. 57) above], nor to expression of beliefs and opinions, as some recent scholars have suggested. Indeed, the language appears to have been drafted precisely to refute those interpretations. Maryland, for example, prohibited punishment of any person "on account of his religious persuasion or profession, or for his religious practice." Opinion,

expression of opinion, and practice were all expressly protected. The key word "exercise," found in six of the constitutions, was defined in dictionaries of the day to mean "action." Two of the other constitutions used terms as broad or broader—Maryland referred to religious "practice," Rhode Island to matters of "religious concernment."...

2. *Limits on the Liberty.*—The second common element in state free exercise provisions is that the provisions limit the right by particular, defined state interests. Nine of the states limited the free exercise right to actions that were "peaceable" or that would not disturb the "peace" or "safety" of the state. Four of these also expressly disallowed acts of licentiousness or immorality; two forbade acts that would interfere with the religious practices of others; one forbade the "civil injury or outward disturbance of others"; one added acts contrary to "good order"; and one disallowed acts contrary to the "happiness," as well as the peace and safety of society.

These provisos are the most revealing and important feature of the state constitutions. They...make sense only if free exercise envisions religiously compelled exemptions from at least some generally applicable laws. Since even according to the Lockean no-exemptions view religious persons cannot be prohibited from engaging in otherwise legal activities, the provisos would only have effect if religiously motivated conduct violated the general laws in some way. The "peace and safety" clauses identify a narrower subcategory of the general laws; the free exercise provisions would exempt religiously motivated conduct from these laws up to the point that such conduct breached public peace or safety.

The language of these provisos cannot be dismissed as boilerplate, synonymous with "an assertion of interest on the part of the public." The debates surrounding the drafting of these provisos suggest that they served as independent criteria for evaluating assertions of legislative power. The debate over the free exercise provision of the Virginia Bill of Rights of 1776 most clearly demonstrates the understanding of the states that passed these provisos. [As the Pepper excerpt (p. 49) recounts, Madison criticized George Mason's proposal that that all religious exercise be fully tolerated unless it "disturb[ed] the peace, the happiness, or safety of society."] Madison proposed instead that free exercise be protected "unless under color of religion the preservation of equal liberty and the existence of the State are manifestly endangered."[3] This is obviously a much narrower state interest exception than Mason's. While "peace" and "safety" refer to the fundamental peacekeeping functions of government, "happiness" is a term as compendious as all of public policy. The "peace, happiness, or safety of society" is therefore a standard that would encompass virtually all legitimate forms of legislation. The "preservation of equal liberty" and "manifest endangerment of the existence of the State," on the other hand, is a standard that only the most critical acts of government can satisfy.

The Virginia legislature ultimately passed a religious liberty guarantee that did not spell out the nature of the state interest that could outweigh a free exercise claim. Apparently, the legislature could not decide between the Mason and Madison formulations and compromised through silence.... In any event, the dispute between Madison and Mason would not have mattered if the proviso were of no legal significance, and the proviso would have been of no legal significance if the "full and free exercise of religion" did not include the right of exemption from generally applicable laws that conflict with religious conscience.

The wording of the state constitutions also provides some guidance regarding when the government's interest is sufficiently strong to override an admitted free exercise claim. The modern Supreme Court has stated only that the government's interest must be "compelling," "of the highest order," "overriding," or "unusually important."[4] These formulations are unnecessarily open-ended, leading to grudging and inconsistent results. The historical sources suggest that the government's interest can be more precisely delimited in a few specific areas, although other cases will remain difficult to resolve.

The most common feature of the state provisions was the government's right to protect public peace and safety. As Madison expressed it late in life, the free exercise right should prevail "in every case where it does not trespass on private rights or the public peace."[5] This indicates that a believer has no license to invade the private rights of others or to disturb public peace and order, no matter how conscientious the belief or how trivial the private right on the other side. There is no free exercise right to kidnap another person for the purpose of proselytizing, or to trespass on private property—whether it be an abortion clinic or a defense contracting plant—to protest immoral activity. Conduct on public property must be peaceable and orderly, so that the rights of others are not disturbed.

Where the rights of others are not involved, however, the free exercise right prevails. The state constitutional provisions give no warrant to paternalistic legislation touching on religious concerns. They protect the "public" peace and safety but respect the right of the believer to weigh spiritual costs

without governmental interference. Thus, some modern free exercise controversies, such as the refusal by Jehovah's Witnesses to receive blood transfu-
sions or the enforcement of minimum wage laws in a religious community,
should be easy to resolve and require no subjective judicial judgments about
the importance of public policy. Moreover, the early free exercise clauses
seem to allow churches and other religious institutions to define their own
doctrine, membership, organization, and internal requirements without state
interference. As Jefferson wrote to the Reverend Samuel Miller, "the government of the United States [is] interdicted by the Constitution from intermed-
dling with religious institutions, their doctrines, discipline, or exercises."[6]
That their internal practices may seem unjust or repugnant to the majority
should be of no moment. Only a handful of states allowed laws against "licentiousness" or immorality to override free exercise claims, and those provisions
may well have referred to public displays of immoral behavior....

Actual Free Exercise Controversies

An examination of actual free exercise controversies in the preconstitutional
period bears out these conclusions. To be sure, the issue of exemptions did
not often arise. The American colonies were peopled almost entirely by
adherents of various strains of Protestant Christianity. The Protestant moral
code and mode of worship was, for the most part, harmonious with the mores
of the larger society. Even denominations like the Quakers, whose theology
and religious practice differed sharply from the others, entertained similar
beliefs about public decorum. Moreover, the governments of that era were far
less intrusive than the governments of today. Thus, the occasions when religious conscience came into conflict with generally applicable secular legislation were few.

Nonetheless, the issue of exemptions did arise, primarily centered around
three issues: oath requirements, military conscription, and religious assessments. The resolution of these conflicts suggests that exemptions were seen as
a natural and legitimate response to the tension between law and religious
convictions.

1. *Oaths.*—By far the most common source of friction was the issue of
oaths. The oath requirement was the principal means of ensuring honest
testimony and of solemnizing obligations. At a time when perjury prosecutions
were unusual, extratemporal sanctions for telling falsehoods or reneging on

commitments were thought indispensable to civil society. Quakers and certain other Protestant sects, however, conscientiously refused to take oaths, producing more serious consequences than it might at first seem. A regime requiring oaths prior to court testimony effectively precluded these groups from using the court system to protect themselves and left them vulnerable to their adversaries, "who could sue them for property and never doubt the result." There are three possible responses. First, the government could eliminate the oath-taking requirement for everyone, making oath-taking purely voluntary. Second, the government could continue to insist on the oath requirement, making it impossible for dissenters to give evidence in court or participate in any civic activity involving an oath. Third, the government could continue the oath requirement for the majority, allowing those with religious scruples to comply by an alternative procedure. According to the no-exemption view, only the first two possibilities are available. But the first possibility is disruptive of the entire judicial system and the second is unnecessarily harsh to the dissenters.

The third alternative—to create a religious exception to the oath requirement—was in fact adopted in most of the colonies. As early as the seventeenth century the proprietors of the Carolina colony permitted Quakers to enter pledges in a book in lieu of swearing an oath. Similarly, New York passed a law in 1691 permitting Quakers to testify by affirmation in civil cases, and in 1734 passed a law permitting Quakers to qualify for the vote by affirmation instead of oath. Jews in Georgia received dispensation to omit the words "on the faith of a Christian" from the naturalization oath required in 1740. In 1743, Massachusetts, one of the states with a strong established church tradition, substituted an affirmation requirement for "'Quakers [who] profess to be in their consciences scrupulous of taking oaths.'"[7] By 1789, virtually all of the states had enacted oath exemptions.

2. *Military Conscription.*—The exemption issue also arose in connection with military conscription. Exemption from conscription provides a particularly telling example due to the entirely secular nature of conscription, its importance to preservation of the state in times of war, and the high costs the granting of exemptions imposes on others. Several denominations in colonial America, most prominently the Quakers and Mennonites, refused on religious grounds to bear arms. As early as 1670–80, Quakers in several states asserted that liberty of conscience exempted them from bearing arms. Rhode Island, North Carolina, and Maryland granted the exemptions; New York refused. It is presumably not coincidental that Rhode Island, North Carolina, and

Maryland had explicit free exercise or liberty of conscience clauses in the seventeenth century, while New York did not.

In Georgia, the Moravians claimed a right to be exempt from military service during the troubles with Spanish Florida, and when they were denied, the entire Moravian community departed Georgia between 1737 and 1740 and moved to Pennsylvania. Pennsylvania, where Quakers were most numerous and influential, went without a militia until 1755, when one was organized on a voluntary basis. The issue arose in New York again in 1734, and again the Quakers were denied exemption from penalties imposed for refusal to train for military service. The colony finally relented in 1755, provided the objector would pay a commutation fee or send a substitute. Massachusetts and Virginia soon adopted similar policies. New Hampshire exempted Quakers from conscription in 1759. Later, the Continental Congress was to grant exemptions in these words:

> As there are some people, who, from religious principles, cannot bear arms in any case, this Congress intend no violence to their consciences, but earnestly recommend it to them, to contribute liberally in this time of universal calamity, to the relief of their distressed brethren in the several colonies, and to do all other services to their oppressed Country, which they can consistently with their religious principles.[8]

The language as well as the substance of this policy is particularly significant, since it recognizes the superior claim of religious "conscience" over civil obligation, even at a time of "universal calamity," and leaves the appropriate accommodation to the judgment of the religious objectors.

3. *Religious Assessments.*—A third example of a religious exception recognized under the preconstitutional free exercise provisions is found only in states with established churches. Such states often required the citizens to make payments for the support of ministers either of the established church or of their own denomination. Not uncommonly, however, these states accommodated the objection of members of sects conscientiously opposed to compelled tithes. For example, from 1727 on, Massachusetts and Connecticut exempted Baptists and Quakers from ministerial taxes. This exception was expressly, if grudgingly, made in recognition of the "alleged scruple of conscience" of these sects....

4. *Other Religious Exemptions.*—Other colonies and states responded to

particular conflicts between religious convictions and generally applicable laws by exempting those faced with the conflict. The Trustees of Georgia, for example, allowed certain groups of Protestant refugees from the European Continent virtual rights of self-government, a form of wholesale exemption that enabled these dissenters from the Church of England to organize themselves in accordance with their own faith. A group from Salzburg formed the town of Ebenezer, described by one historian as "a state within a state, a sort of theocracy under the direction of their ministers with daily conferences of the entire congregation in which God's guidance was invoked at the beginning and end."[9] In 1764, the colonial legislature of Rhode Island passed a statute waiving the laws governing marriage ceremonies for "any persons possessing [professing] the Jewish religion who may be joined in marriage, according to their own usages and rites."[10] In 1798, the state legislature exempted Jewish residents from the operation of state incest law, "within the degrees of affinity or consanguinity allowed by their religion."[11] This was important because Jewish law was understood to encourage the marriage between uncle and niece, a relationship illegal under Rhode Island law.

Similarly, both North Carolina and Maryland exempted Quakers from the requirement of removing their hats in court, which they considered a form of obeisance to secular authority forbidden by their religion. This exemption may seem trivial today, but it was an issue of historical and emotional importance to the Quakers of that day. One of the most notorious courtroom cases of religious intolerance in England involved William Penn's refusal to remove his hat when he appeared in court to face an indictment for speaking to an unlawful assembly.... Although acquitted on the charge on which he was tried, Penn was held in contempt and imprisoned for refusing to doff his hat.[12] This case became a cause celebre in America, and the North Carolina and Maryland exemptions were no doubt passed as a result.

The history of oath requirements, military conscription, religious assessments, and other sources of conflict between religious convictions and general legislation demonstrates that religion-specific exemptions were familiar and accepted means of accommodating these conflicts. Rather than make oaths, military service, and tithes voluntary for everyone, which would undercut important public programs and objectives, and rather than coerce the consciences of otherwise loyal and law-abiding citizens who were bound by religious duty not to comply, the colonies and states wrote special exemptions into their laws....

THE FEDERAL FREE EXERCISE CLAUSE

Framing and Ratifying the Free Exercise Clause

[After the passage of the original Constitution,] Madison admitted that the lack of a provision protecting the rights of conscience had "alarmed many respectable Citizens," and he pledged to work for "the most satisfactory provisions for all essential rights, particularly the rights of Conscience in the fullest latitude, the freedom of the press, trials by jury, security against general warrants...."[13] Lawmakers in other states responded to the same popular pressure. Seven states drafted proposals for amendments, and five of them (plus the minority report in Pennsylvania) urged protection for religious freedom....

The recorded debates in the House over these proposals cast little light on the meaning of the free exercise clause. Indeed, the main controversy during these debates centered on establishment.... Thus, we must rely primarily on the successive drafts of the clause during its passage through the First Congress.

Madison undertook an initial draft of the Bill of Rights, to be proposed to the House of Representatives. His draft free exercise clause did not follow the language of the state proposals. Rather, he suggested the following formulation: "The civil rights of none shall be abridged on account of religious belief or worship, [n]or shall any national religion be established, nor shall the full and equal rights of conscience be in any manner, nor on any pretext, infringed."[14] ...

After [a couple of other formulations], the House adopted a formulation proposed by Fisher Ames of Massachusetts: "Congress shall make no law establishing religion, or to prevent the free exercise thereof, or to infringe the rights of conscience."[15] ...

More strikingly, the Ames version introduced a new term into the debate: "free exercise of religion." "Free exercise" had been part of most of the state proposals but had not appeared in the [proposals by Madison or others] previously debated in the House, all of which had used the alternative formulation "rights of conscience." ...

The House of Representatives approved the amendment as proposed by Ames without recorded debate or discussion. Both the House and the Senate journals record that the House passed and sent to the Senate a proposed amendment slightly different from the Ames proposal: "Congress shall make no law establishing Religion, or prohibiting the free exercise thereof, nor shall the rights of conscience be infringed." ...

In the Senate, the debate was not recorded, but various versions of the religion clauses were adopted and rejected in succession. The versions adopted, in order, were as follows:

(1) "Congress shall make no law establishing one religious sect or society in preference to others, nor shall the rights of conscience be infringed."

(2) "Congress shall make no law establishing religion, or prohibiting the free exercise thereof."

(3) "Congress shall make no law establishing articles of faith or a mode of worship, or prohibiting the free exercise of religion...."[16]

[T]he third version passed the Senate and was transmitted to the House, which rejected it, presumably because of its narrow provision on establishment. A conference committee, on which Madison served, proposed the version of the religion clauses that was ultimately ratified. The free exercise clause itself was unchanged from the final Senate bill....

(b) The Substitution of "Free Exercise of Religion" for the "Rights of Conscience." ... [Madison did not use the term "free exercise of religion"] in his draft, using instead the term "rights of conscience," a term also used by the Select Committee and New Hampshire drafts debated on the floor of the House of Representatives. The term "free exercise of religion" reappeared after the close of recorded debate, in the Ames version, which protected both "free exercise of religion" and the "rights of conscience," and which the House [approved]. The Senate first voted to protect "rights of conscience" and then settled upon protecting the "free exercise of religion" alone, a formulation that ultimately carried the day....

[The difference between "rights of conscience" and "free exercise of religion" may have some significance.] The least ambiguous difference is that the term "free exercise" makes clear that the clause protects religiously motivated conduct as well as belief. This point merits emphasis, because in 1879 [in *Reynolds* (p. 57)] the Supreme Court, relying on Jefferson, explicitly rejected this reading.

[Another] difference between the "free exercise of religion" and the "rights of conscience" is that the latter might seem to extend to claims of conscience based on something other than religion—to belief systems based on science, history, economics, political ideology, or secular moral philosophy. By deleting references to "conscience," the final version of the first amendment singles out religion for special treatment. And so the Supreme Court has held [in *Yoder* (p. 59)]: "A way of life, however virtuous and admirable, may not be interposed as a barrier to reasonable state regulation ... if it is based on purely secular considerations; to have the protection of the Religion Clauses, the claims must be rooted in religious belief."

This distinction between religion and other belief systems has come under substantial attack in academic circles. Religion is understood to be a product of individual choice, and protected as such. It is said to be arbitrary (and even unconstitutional) to differentiate between belief systems, all of which are the product of individual judgment, on the ground that some are "religious" and some are not.

David A. J. Richards has presented the most sustained and thoughtful exposition of this position.[17] Professor Richards' conception of free exercise is rooted in liberal individualism. He views religious freedom as an aspect of the "equal respect" that must be shown "for the capacity to exercise our twin moral powers of rationality and reasonableness." It is ultimately based on "respect for the person as an independent source of value." ...

Under this view, religious claims have no higher status than non-religious claims—and maybe even lower status, to the extent that modern moral philosophy elevates "rationality and reasonableness" over the characteristic religious claims of revelation, tradition, and spirit-filled inspiration. And if the distinction between religious and nonreligious conscience is arbitrary, then it amounts to an indefensible preference—an establishment of religion—to accommodate religious and not nonreligious claims of comparable magnitude.

The question is therefore whether the principle of free exercise, as enacted by the framers and ratifiers of the first amendment, was a specific instantiation of a wider liberty of conscience encompassing individual moral judgments rooted in nonreligious as well as religious sources, or whether religious conscience is different in some fundamental respect from other forms of individual judgment, in which case the free exercise clause would provide no warrant for protecting a broader class of claims. The question is all the more significant for the practical reason that if the exercise of religion extends to "everything and anything," the interference with ordinary operations of government would be so extreme that the free exercise clause would fall of its own weight. To protect everything is to protect nothing.

The historical materials uniformly equate "religion" with belief in God or in gods, though this can be extended without distortion to transcendent extrapersonal authorities not envisioned in traditionally theistic terms. By contrast, Noah Webster's Dictionary of the English Language, the first comprehensive American dictionary (published in 1807), defined "conscience" as: "natural knowledge, or the faculty that decides on the right or wrong of actions in regard to one's self." Similarly, James' Buchanan's 1757 dictionary, *Linguae Britannicae Vera Pronunciatio*, defined "conscience" as "the testimony of one's own mind." And Samuel Johnson's great Dictionary of the English Language gave as the first definition: "The knowledge or faculty by which we judge of the goodness or wickedness of ourselves." In none of these definitions was there specific reference to religion, although about half of the literary examples Johnson gave in the four volume edition had a religious context.

On the other hand, outside of dictionaries, the vast preponderance of references to "liberty of conscience" in America were either expressly or impliedly limited to religious conscience. A few examples suffice to make the point; dozens of others would do as well. St. George Tucker's 1803 commentary on American constitutional law divided "the right of personal opinion" into two subcategories: "Liberty of conscience in all matters relative to religion" and "liberty of speech and of discussion in all speculative matters, whether religious, philosophical, or political."[18] Madison himself used the terms "free exercise of religion" and "liberty of conscience" interchangeably when explaining the meaning of the first amendment. The laws of at least ten of the states expressly linked "liberty of conscience" to religion....

In any event, it does not matter [whether "conscience" was equated with or narrower than "religion,"] for under either explanation, nonreligious "conscience" is not included within the free exercise clause. If "the rights of conscience" were dropped because they were redundant, "conscience" must have been used in its narrow, religious, sense. If the omission was a substantive change, then the framers deliberately confined the clause to religious claims. Neither explanation supports the view that free exercise exemptions must be extended to secular moral conflicts.

The textual insistence on the special status of "religion" is, moreover, rooted in the prevailing understandings, both religious and philosophical, of the difference between religious faith and other forms of human judgment. Not until the second third of the nineteenth century did the notion that the opinions of individuals have precedence over the decisions of civil society gain currency in American thought. In 1789, most would have agreed with

Locke that "the private judgment of any person concerning a law enacted in political matters, for the public good, does not take away the obligation of that law, nor deserve a dispensation."[19]

Religious convictions were of a different order. Conflicts arising from religious convictions were conceived not as a clash between the judgment of the individual and of the state, but as a conflict between earthly and spiritual sovereigns. The believer was not seen as the instigator of the conflict; the believer was simply caught between the inconsistent demands of two rightful authorities, through no fault of his own. This understanding was grounded in the Protestant doctrine of "two kingdoms," taught by both Calvin and Luther, and had still older roots in Augustinian thought.

NOTES

As a result of editing, the notes for this essay have been renumbered. The note number from the original essay or article is shown in parentheses at the end of each citation.

1. New York Constitution of 1777, art. XXXVIII. (239)

2. New Hampshire Constitution of 1784, part I, art. V. (240)

3. Ibid. (267)

4. See *Goldman v. Weinberger*, 475 U.S. 503, 529–30 (1986) (O'Connor, J., dissenting) (summarizing free exercise tests from earlier cases). (269)

5. "Letter from James Madison to Edward Livingston" (July 10, 1822), in Gaillard Hunt, ed., *The Writings of James Madison* 9 (1910), pp. 98, 100. (271)

6. "Letter from Thomas Jefferson to the Rev. Samuel Miller" (January 23, 1808), in in Julian Boyd, ed., *Papers of Thomas Jefferson*, vol. 2 (1950), p. 7. (274)

7. Curry, *The First Freedom* (1986), p. 90 (citing 1 Massachusetts Acts and Resolves 305; and ibid., p. 494–95). (287)

8. See Resolution of July 18, 1775, reprinted in W. Ford, ed., *Journals of the Continental Congress, 1774–1789*, vol. 2 (1905), pp. 187, 189. (299)

9. See R. Strickland, *Religion and State in Georgia in the Eighteenth Century* (1939), p. 72. (313)

10. Hartogensis, "Rhode Island and Consanguineous Jewish Marriages," Publication of the American Jewish Historical Society 20 (1911): 137, 144. (314)

11. "An Act Regulating Marriage and Divorce," 1798 Rhode Island Publication of Laws, § 7. (315)

12. An excellent summary of the case may be found in I. Brant, *The Bill of Rights* (1965), pp. 62–67. (319)

13. "Letter from James Madison to the Rev. George Eve" (January 2, 1789), in *Madison Papers*, vol. 11, pp. 404–05. (358)

14. See J. Gales, ed., *Annals of Congress* (1834), p. 451 (proposal of James Madison, June 8, 1789). (365)

15. Ibid., p. 796 (proposal of Fisher Ames, August 20, 1789). (369)

16. L. De Pauw, ed., *Documentary History of the First Federal Congress of the United States of America* (1972), p. 166. (376)

17. David A. J. Richards, *Toleration and the Constitution* (1986), pp. 136–46. (422)

18. St. George Tucker, *Blackstone's Commentaries*, reprinted in Kurland and Lerner, eds., *The Founders' Constitution*, vol. 5 (1987), pp. 96–97. (436)

19. Locke, *A Letter Concerning Toleration* (1690), p. 43. (450)

A CONSTITUTIONAL RIGHT OF RELIGIOUS EXEMPTION: AN HISTORICAL PERSPECTIVE

PHILIP A. HAMBURGER

Did late eighteenth-century Americans understand the Free Exercise Clause of the United States Constitution to provide individuals a right of exemption from civil laws to which they had religious objections? Claims of exemption based on the Free Exercise Clause have prompted some of the Supreme Court's most prominent free exercise decisions, and therefore this historical inquiry about a right of exemption may have implications for our constitutional jurisprudence....

In fact, late eighteenth-century Americans tended to assume that the Free Exercise Clause did not provide a constitutional right of religious exemption from civil laws. The first part of this article examines and calls into question McConnell's arguments that the Free Exercise Clause may have created such a right. The second part of this article then considers more generally the

Philip A. Hamburger, "A Constitutional Right of Religious Exemption: An Historical Perspective," *George Washington Law Review* 60 (1992): 915.

history of a right of religious exemption and shows the extent to which Americans did not seek and even rejected such a right. Among other things, the second part also suggests how Americans reconciled their distaste for a right of exemption with their support for religious freedom. Of course, many Americans sympathized with their neighbors who had pious scruples about oaths, military service, and a few other legal requirements, and, therefore, in various statutes and even state constitutions, Americans expressly granted religious exemptions from some specified civil obligations. Americans did not, however, authorize or acknowledge a general constitutional right of religious exemption from civil laws.

I. McConnell's Evidence

Eighteenth-century Americans spoke and wrote extensively about religious freedom and about government. Yet Professor McConnell apparently cites no instance in which a late eighteenth-century American explicitly and unambiguously said that an individual's right to the free exercise of religion included a general right of peaceable, religious exemption from civil laws— that is, from the otherwise secular laws of secular government. . . .

State Constitutions

McConnell finds support for his position in the religion clauses of certain state constitutions . . . that acknowledged an individual's right to the free exercise of religion or to freedom of worship but that added a caveat, such as, "provided he doth not disturb the public peace." According to McConnell, these caveats indicate that the right of free exercise was understood to include a right of exemption from religiously objectionable civil laws, except with regard to nonpeaceable behavior. . . .

[However, t]he behavior described by the caveats included more than just nonpeaceful behavior. A caveat that required persons to avoid disturbing the "good order," "safety," or "happiness" of society or of the state appears to have demanded a greater degree of obedience than just peaceful behavior. Indeed, in Maryland, the caveat expressly mentioned persons who "shall infringe the laws of morality, or injure others in their natural, civil or religious rights," and, in New York and South Carolina, the caveats dealt with, among other things, "acts of licentiousness."[1] Even those caveats that mentioned only disturbances of the peace did not exclusively concern acts of violence or force. According to long tradition, the criminal offenses over which common law courts had jurisdiction were said to be "contra pacem." Consequently, the phrase "contra pacem" became associated with the notion of violation of law. Whereas McConnell assumes that a disturbance of the peace was simply nonpeaceful behavior, eighteenth-century lawyers made clear that "every breach of law is against the peace."[2] Thus, the disturb-the-peace caveats apparently permitted government to deny religious freedom, not merely in the event of violence or force, but, more generally, upon the occurrence of illegal actions....

Exemptions from Particular Civil Obligations

Both before and after the adoption of constitutions guaranteeing the free exercise of religion, legislative and constitutional documents (including charters) granted exemptions from particular obligations, such as oaths, conscription, and assessments. McConnell suggests that when legislatures and other bodies created these exemptions they were attempting to reflect a free exercise right of exemption. Yet legislators equally may have been showing their sympathy for Quakers and others whose piety prevented their conformity to law. As McConnell concedes, the issue whether an individual was understood to have a general constitutional right of religious exemption from civil laws is hardly the same issue as whether statutes or, occasionally, constitutions granted exemptions with respect to a few specific matters....

II. A CONSTITUTIONAL RIGHT OF RELIGIOUS EXEMPTION IN THE EIGHTEENTH CENTURY?

A review of McConnell's evidence has suggested reasons to doubt whether Americans thought the First Amendment provided a constitutional right of religious exemption from civil laws. It remains necessary, however, to examine more generally Americans' attitudes toward such a right. Although Americans frequently said religious freedom was based on an authority higher than the civil government and that the exercise of religion could not be submitted to civil authority, does this mean that they sought a religious or constitutional right of exemption from civil laws?... [The evidence] suggest[s], first, that the free exercise of religion tended not to be considered a particularly extensive or radical claim of religious liberty—indeed, it was a freedom espoused not only by dissenters but also by establishments. Second, when advocating religious freedom—even a religious freedom broader than mere free exercise—dissenters who were politically active and influential in lobbying for expanded religious liberty did not seek a constitutional right of exemption from objectionable civil laws. Third, a right of exemption may have been considered a "law respecting religion" and may have been understood to create "unequal civil rights"—precisely what many dissenters considered attributes of establishment and sought to abolish....

Exemption

Whether claiming free exercise or a broader religious liberty, dissenters—particularly politically active and influential dissenters—tended not to ask for a right of exemption from religiously objectionable civil laws. Just as establishment writers could acknowledge that religion was based on an authority higher than the civil government, so too dissenters typically could admit that natural liberty was protected only through submission to civil government and its laws. According to vast numbers of Americans, individuals in the state of nature had a liberty that was free from civil restraints but was insecure; therefore, said these Americans, individuals sought protection for their natural liberty by establishing civil government. Liberty could only be obtained by submission to the civil laws of civil government.

One reason late eighteenth-century ideas about religious freedom did not seem to require a general religious exemption is that the jurisdiction of civil government and the authority of religion were frequently considered distinguishable. It should not be assumed that late eighteenth-century Americans viewed religion as being necessarily in tension with civil authority. In fact, many Americans, especially dissenters seeking an expansion of religious liberty, repeatedly spoke of civil authority as if it could be differentiated from the scope of religion or religious freedom. This assumption is apparent in the language of the First Amendment, which begins, "Congress shall make no law." Rather than suppose that civil laws will in some respects prohibit the free exercise of religion and that exemptions will be necessary, the First Amendment assumes Congress can avoid enacting laws that prohibit free exercise. So too, it assumes Congress can avoid making laws respecting the establishment of religion.

In explaining the difference between religious and civil matters, Americans of the last half of the eighteenth century employed several different formulations. Locke had argued that individuals entrusted civil government with the security of "temporal goods" and "the things of this life" but that "the care of each man's soul, and the things of heaven...is left entirely to every man's self."[3] Similarly, many Americans differentiated between the temporal and the spiritual, between "this world" and "the Kingdom of Christ." Americans also sometimes listed the things that civil authority could not establish or determine. Typically, they mentioned religious belief and doctrine—what Locke had called "speculative opinions." Occasionally, they also specified the internal governance of a sect and its mode or form of worship....

The assumption that religious liberty would not, or at least should not, affect civil authority over civil matters was so widely held that a general right of religious exemption rarely became the basis for serious controversy. Of course, some dissenters did broadly claim religious exemption from objectionable civil laws, on grounds of freedom of conscience or even divine command. Their claims, however, illustrate the marginal character of the support for a general right of religious exemption. For example, John Bolles—a Rogerene [member of a small New England Baptist sect]—apparently claimed some religious exemption from civil laws. In defense of two Quaker women who "went naked...one into a Meeting, the other...through the Streets of Salem," Bolles wrote that "they did it in Submission to a divine Power...as a Sign."[4] For precedent, he cited the Bible, saying simply: "Isaiah went Naked." This was not, however, the sort of analysis that most late eighteenth-century Americans found persuasive with respect to constitutional law.

Although other dissenters, less extreme than Bolles, did seek exemption from civil laws, they typically asked, not for a general right of exemption, but merely for exemptions from a small number of specified civil obligations. Of these limited exemptions, moreover, only those relating to military service frequently were granted in constitutions. Even constitutional military exemptions, however, often appear to have been given largely for reasons of compassion and politics.

Indeed, the idea that individuals had a general right to be exempted from civil laws contrary to their consciences was so unpopular that establishment writers attempted to use it to smear their opponents. By citing lurid stories about the sixteenth-century Anabaptists of Munster and by attributing the enthusiasms of extremists to dissenters as a whole, establishment writers could accuse dissenters of attempting to subvert all civil liberty. For example, in support of Connecticut's religious establishment, Elihu Hall said that persons objecting to that establishment on grounds of conscience were making arguments that would justify nonpayment of civil taxes or breach of contract: "Thus a man may plead Conscience for the support or excuse of all the moral Dishonesty and Promise & Covenant-breaking in the World. But men have no Right to be their own Judges in their own Case in moral Matters, and where their neighbors Interest is equally concerned with their own."[5]

To defend themselves from such accusations, dissenters who sought an expanded religious liberty disavowed a right of exemption from civil laws. Writing against the Connecticut establishment, Ebenezer Frothingham argued that no "hurt" would be done to "any man's civil interest, by different sects worshipping God in different places in the same town."[6] Eight different sects might live together in one community, but none, he observed, would be exempt: "If any person of… these professions breaks the law, he lies open to punishment, equally so, as if there was but one profession in the town." Frothingham was not alone. Other influential dissenters also rejected a right of exemption.[7] …

Although some dissenters asked for grants of exemption from a few specified civil obligations, such as military service, dissenters typically did not demand a general exemption from objectionable civil laws, let alone a constitutional right to such an exemption. If the myriad and voluble dissenters who sought an expansion of religious freedom were advocating a general constitutional right of religious exemption from civil laws, it is remarkable that they tended not to claim such a right and that some of their leading publicists disavowed it.

Establishment

In the late eighteenth century, the overwhelming majority of dissenters sought not a constitutional right of exemption, but an end to establishments. …In the last half of the eighteenth century, many Americans had unequal civil rights on account of their religious opinions; others had equal civil rights but thought this equality precarious. Therefore, many of these Americans wanted guarantees of equal civil rights. Of course, some wanted equality only for Protestants or Christians. Yet a form of equal civil rights was, increasingly, the minimum dissenters believed was theirs by right and what they believed they could get. Indeed, some—anxious that religion not be dependent upon civil government—demanded that government avoid legislating with respect to religion. If civil government was established for exclusively civil purposes, they argued, then it had no authority to make any law concerning religion. These anti-establishment claims—and, to a lesser degree, the grants of exemption from a few, specified obligations—were the goals pursued by large numbers of dissenters. For these Americans, the possibility of a general right of exemption was, at most, a distraction from the real issues at stake.

What dissenters said about establishments, moreover, had implications for exemption. Of course, the anti-establishment demands for equal civil rights and for the absence of laws respecting religion were made in response to legislative or constitutional provisions that benefited particular denominations or, more broadly, a particular religion rather than in response to claims of exemption for the religiously scrupulous. Nonetheless, the dissenters' positions on establishment were suggestive of their position on exemption. A right of exemption for the religiously scrupulous could be considered a law respecting religion. It even could create unequal civil rights; in the words of the Virginia Act for Establishing Religious Freedom [(1786)], men's "opinions in matters of religion" shall "in no wise diminish, enlarge, or affect their civil capacities." The sweeping language with which so many Americans attacked establishments was not the language of persons seeking a constitutional right of exemption.

NOTES

As a result of editing, the notes for this essay have been renumbered. The note number from the original essay or article is shown in parentheses at the end of each citation.

1. Maryland Declaration of Rights of 1776, art. 33; New York Constitution of 1777, art. XXXVIII; South Carolina Constitution of 1790, art. VIII, § 1. (14)

2. Incidentally, this definition of a breach of the peace was recognized by Baptists, who pleaded for an expanded religious freedom. Dissenting ministers who opposed most legislation with respect to religion and who insisted that individuals not be treated differently on account of their religions frequently were accused of opposing the regulation of morality. In responding to such charges, dissenters pointed out that the state could punish immoralities—peaceful and nonpeaceful—as breaches of the peace. For example, after setting forth his strong stand on religious freedom, a Baptist, Caleb Blood, explained:

This however, by no means prohibits the civil magistrate from enacting those laws that shall enforce the observance of those precepts in the christian religion, the violation of which is a breach of the civil peace; viz. such as forbid murder, theft, adultery, false witness, and injuring our neighbor, either in person, name, or estate....

3. John Locke, *A Letter Concerning Toleration*, 2nd ed. (Bobbs-Merrill, 1955), pp. 48, 49. (92)

4. John Bolles, *To Worship God in Spirit* (1756), pp. 116–17. (101)

5. Elihu Hall, *The Present Way of the Country* (1749), p. 59. (107)

6. Ebenezer Frothingham, *A Key to Unlock the Door* (1767), p. 154. (109)

7. [John] Leland, [leader of Virginia's Baptists,] explicitly opposed exemptions from civil laws. Although Baptists had religious objections to contracts between a minister and his flock, Leland nonetheless argued that such contracts, if made, were enforceable. Moreover, "To indulge [ministers] with an exemption from taxes and bearing arms is a tempting emolument. The law should be silent about them; protect them as citizens, not as sacred officers, for the civil law knows no sacred religious officers." ... (111)

B. THE FOURTEENTH AMENDMENT

THE SECOND ADOPTION OF THE
FREE EXERCISE CLAUSE: RELIGIOUS EXEMPTIONS
AND THE FOURTEENTH AMENDMENT

KURT T. LASH

INTRODUCTION

[T]he available evidence supports the view that the Founders did not anticipate the need for religious exemptions from generally applicable laws....

[However, this] Article explores the proposition that the Free Exercise
Clause was adopted a second time through its incorporation into the Privileges or Immunities Clause of the Fourteenth Amendment [in 1868,] and that

Kurt T. Lash, "The Second Adoption of the Free Exercise Clause: Religious Exemptions and the Fourteenth Amendment," *Northwestern University Law Review* 88 (1994):
1106, 1111–17, 1131–37, 1140–41, 1146–56.

the scope of the new Free Exercise Clause was intended to include protections un-anticipated at the Founding. Contrary to Jeffersonian notions of "separate spheres [between religion and government]," the nation by the time of Reconstruction had experienced decades of clashes resulting from the overlapping concerns of religion and government. In particular, the suppression of slave religion called into question the government's power to interfere, even indirectly, with legitimate religious exercise. Accordingly, the Privileges or Immunities Clause incorporated a conception of religious liberty vastly different from that intended in 1791 and constitutes a constitutional modification of the original "rights of conscience." Religious exemptions from generally applicable laws, considered unnecessary and improbable at the Founding, now became necessary and proper....

I. THE RELIGION CLAUSES AND THE FOUNDERS: FEDERALISM AND SEPARATIONISM

The Federalist First Amendment

The [First] Amendment begins by stating that "Congress shall make no law." By referring at the outset to Congress, the First Amendment begins a theme that runs as a leitmotif throughout the original Bill of Rights, that of federalism. When read in conjunction with other provisions, in particular the Tenth Amendment, the First Amendment signals an intention to give Congress no enumerated power over matters such as religion and speech, reserving the same "to the States respectively, or to the people."[1] ...

To our ears, the Bill of Rights in general, and the First Amendment in particular, sound in terms of libertarianism—the protection of individual rights against unwarranted intrusion by the government. However,... the First Amendment was originally understood to protect the rights of popular [especially local] majorities against a [distant and] possibly unrepresentative and self-interested Congress....

Given the above background, interpreting the original First Amendment to include religious exemptions is problematic.... [T]he primary concern of the Founders was the right of the majority to representative government, not the needs of minorities (and minority faiths)....

Separationism

[Thomas] Jefferson's advocacy of a "wall" between church and state was based on his assumption that religion and government belonged to separate spheres and that each could and ought to be prevented from intruding upon the other's domain. To Jefferson, this meant not only that government should be prevented from interfering with matters of religious belief, but also that it should stay out of religious matters altogether. The federal government was prohibited from passing any law "respecting religion."

The free exercise of religion had its boundaries as well. Although religion was to be protected in its "doctrines, discipline, or exercises,"[2] it had no right to be excluded from "social duties."[3] Religious faith, moreover, was a personal affair and should be free from interference by priests or proselytizers. In fact, Jefferson was deeply troubled by the "fanatical" religious revivals that swept the country in the initial decades of the nineteenth century. [Madison similarly emphasized strict separation of church and state.]

Jefferson and Madison were both what I call "separationist" republicans by which I mean they believed religion and government could and ought to remain in separate spheres. Although most often invoked in terms of the Establishment Clause, separation of church and state had free exercise implications as well. Jefferson's famous Wall was supported by assumptions regarding the proper roles of religion and government—roles that made the need for religious exemptions highly unlikely.

Supporting one side of the Wall was the belief that republican government could survive without active support of religion. Government therefore had no reason to involve itself in the affairs of religion. Supporting the other side was the assumption that religion is a private matter that need never involve itself with worldly matters—so long as the world refrained from establishing a particular sect. . . .

II. THE NEW REPUBLIC: RELIGIOUS REPUBLICANISM AND THE RISE OF RELIGIOUS SOCIAL ACTIVISM

Expanding the Sphere of Religion:
The Rise of Religious Social Activism

Religion was not immune to the heady individualism that characterized post-Revolutionary America. In the First Great Awakening, "[r]evivalist clergymen urged the people to trust only in 'self-examination' and their own private judgments."[4] The Second Great Awakening, which occurred in the first decades of the nineteenth century, expanded on these same ideas. According to Baptist evangelist Elias Smith, the people were "wholly free to examine for ourselves what is truth, without being bound to a catechism, creed, confession of faith, discipline or any rule excepting the scriptures."[5] ...

This radical individualism led to a massive fragmentation among the denominations. As the influence of denominations waned, evangelists like Lyman Beecher feared that nothing protected "society against depravity within and temptation without" except the force of God's law "written upon the heart of each individual."[6] Only the moral character of individuals remained to hold together an unruly and splintered society. According to Gordon Wood, "to be successful in America, religion had to pre-occupy itself with morality."[7] To the dismay of separationists like Jefferson and Madison, the clergy took their new-found responsibility for society's character to heart and formed societies against, among other things, gambling, drinking, Sabbath-breaking, profanity, and horse racing. Rejecting both separationist and religious republican admonitions that religion remain aloof from political affairs, the religious activists of the nineteenth century invaded the public arena on an unprecedented scale.

Of course, the issue that would occasion the greatest conflict between religion and government was slavery. Here, the separationist belief that the overlap of church and state would be so minor as to involve only "unessential points" became demonstrably untenable. Moreover, the suppression of slave religion would provide the framers of the Fourteenth Amendment with clear examples of why a second adoption of the Free Exercise Clause was necessary.

III. THE ABOLITIONISTS AND THE SUPPRESSION OF SLAVE RELIGION

The Abolitionists

Abolitionism had its roots in the evangelistic movements arising out of the Second Great Awakening. To the religiously inspired abolitionist, slavery was an affront to the laws of God and was "irreconcilable with the manifested will of our Great Creator, and with the imperative declaration of our blessed Savior 'all things whatsoever ye would that men should do to you, do ye even so to them; for this is the law and the prophets.'"[8] ...

Believing God would deny his blessing to a nation that permitted slavery, the abolitionists embarked on a campaign to convert the country. In 1835, antislavery forces sent tracts by the hundreds to southern clergymen and postmasters with the direction that they be distributed in their communities. In New England, the "Conscience Whigs" joined abolitionists in issuing a tract in which clergy were "entreated in the name of God and Christ to pray for the slave; and preach at least one sermon against the admission of Texas as a slave state, as soon as may be."[9] Beginning with the words "in the Name of Almighty God" and bearing the names of 3,050 New England clergymen, a two-hundred-foot-long memorial against the extension of slavery was presented to Congress. Within a few months, 125 separate remonstrances came from the ministers of these New England states. Not only had the Second Great Awakening changed the conception of the proper sphere of religion generally, but it had now become the specific duty of the abolitionists to fight what they believed was an ungodly political institution. Religion was invading the "sphere" of government with a vengeance.

The Southern Suppression of Religious Exercise

Southern governments were not disposed to take the invasion lightly. [Early in the abolitionist campaign,] an event occurred in Virginia that would inspire southern governments to become extremely interested in religious activities. On August 22, 1831, a group of slaves headed by Nat Turner began a bloody rebellion in which seventy whites were killed before Turner and his group were captured. The fact that Turner was a preacher confirmed Southern suspicions that religion, if left unregulated, could be used to dangerously subversive ends. Not only would the religious exercise of blacks in the South have to be closely monitored and controlled, but also religious sentiments flowing in from the North would have to be stanched lest slaves be incited to follow the example of the Reverend Turner. What emerged was a complex and highly regulated system of religious exercise—a system so abhorrent to members of the Thirty-ninth Congress that its abolition was explicitly cited as one of the purposes behind the Fourteenth Amendment.

1. Direct Regulation of Religious Exercise

In response to the Turner uprising, laws were passed that directly impinged upon certain types of religious activities. For instance, in many southern states it was a crime, punishable by death, to "write, print, publish or distribute" abolitionist literature. Persons found with abolitionist pamphlets or books were subject to public lashings, regardless of whether the literature had been distributed. Those who attacked slavery through sermons, speeches, or written documents risked death by law or at the hands of proslavery mobs. The mail, with the assistance of southern federal postmasters, was "cleansed" of letters seeking to convert slaveholders to antislavery Christianity. Congress itself, at the insistence of southern Democrats, instituted "gag rules," whereby antislavery petitions would be received, but immediately rejected.

Direct burdens on free exercise in the South went beyond mere prohibitions of "incendiary" language or literature. Black religious assemblies were heavily regulated with severe punishments authorized for improper religious gatherings. Slaves were not permitted to have their own ministers or to worship without the presence of a white man. Even when a religious gathering received the state's imprimatur, the content of the sermon was dictated by proslavery Christian ideology with the message invariably focused on the biblical admonition that slaves "obey their masters."

2. Indirect Regulation of Religious Exercise

In addition to laws that directly regulated or prohibited certain religious activities, numerous laws were passed that indirectly burdened the most basic religious freedoms. For example, laws prohibiting the assembly of blacks at night for any purpose had an unavoidable impact on black religious assemblies. Of course, the "generally applicable" law having the greatest impact on free exercise in the South was the prohibition against teaching slaves how to read and write. This prevented slaves from reading the Bible....

The Abolitionist Critique

Despite Southern protestations to the contrary, northern abolitionists saw the cumulative effect of laws circumscribing black assemblies, "incendiary language," and the ability to read and write as devastating slaves' ability to exercise their religious faith. Violation of religious freedom was seized upon by abolitionists and proclaimed as one of the greatest evils of the peculiar institution.

It was not simply a matter of equal protection—it would be as unreasonable to the abolitionist to prohibit all from reading the Bible as it was to prohibit only the slave. What was being denied was "access to that heavenly chart, which is laid down by Jehovah as the only safe rule of faith and practice, the liberty of reading and understanding how he may serve God acceptably."[10] Denying access to the Bible was an offense over and above mere political deprivations—it was its own justification for the abolition of slavery.

If the original Free Exercise Clause was intended to prohibit nothing more than laws that targeted religion qua religion, the abolitionists challenged the adequacy of that protection. Laws preventing blacks from learning to read the Bible were no less violations of religious liberty because the abridgement was the result of a religiously neutral law. The abolitionists thus joined a growing chorus of voices calling for a broader interpretation of the original Bill of Rights, one that emphasized the rights of the individual over the prerogatives of state majorities.

IV. REINTERPRETING THE WORDS OF THE RELIGION CLAUSES

Reinterpreting the Federalist First Amendment

In *Barron v. Mayor of Baltimore*,[11] the Supreme Court held that the protection of the Bill of Rights bound only the federal government, not states or municipalities. [Later decisions held the same for the Free Exercise Clause.]

[But during the mid-1800s, states began adopting the language of the First Amendment in their own constitutions.] The language of the First Amendment now appeared, to the letter, in both state and territorial constitutions. Words once intended to signal a reservation of power to state majorities were now invoked to express the rights of citizens against state majorities.... Words that once expressed the rights of states now expressed the rights of individuals....

Reinterpreting the Scope of Religious Liberty:
The Militia Exemptions

The clash between the abolitionists and the southern states dispelled whatever remained of the idea that religion and government had separate and distinct concerns. By the time of the Civil War, it was clear that the spheres of church and state overlapped a great deal. More than just the assumptions underlying the original religion clauses had changed; the words themselves could now be read as declarations of individual rights. These developments created new interpretive possibilities; perhaps religious exemptions rejected at the Founding now could be revisited with different results. This appears to have happened in the case of exemptions for the religiously scrupulous from military service....

[During and after the Civil War, exemptions from military conscription for those conscientiously opposed to war were written both into federal statutes and into state constitutions' declaration of rights.] This was something new under the sun. For the first time, the national government mandated a religious exemption from a generally applicable secular law. Moreover, the law was not based on considerations of political expediency, but on the demands of higher law: the rights of conscience.

V. THE SECOND ADOPTION OF THE FREE EXERCISE CLAUSE

The framers of the Fourteenth Amendment wrote against a specific historical background: (1) Jeffersonian notions of "separate spheres" had become wholly untenable in light of the clash between religion and government over slavery; (2) Congress had recently recognized the threat to the rights of conscience arising from the overlapping interests of church and state; (3) Congress also had recognized that these overlapping interests may require a religious exemption from an otherwise generally applicable law.

However, even if the general conception of religious liberty had broadened since the Founding, *Barron* was still the law of the land. The amendment that would overturn *Barron* and reconstruct the federalist structure of the Bill of Rights had yet to be drafted and adopted. When it was, it incorporated a new declaration of the religious liberty of United States citizens.

Drafting the Fourteenth Amendment

The architects of the Fourteenth Amendment were well aware of how slavery had resulted in the suppression of religious exercise. John Bingham, author of Section One of the Fourteenth Amendment, believed slavery violated basic principles of the Constitution, including the right "to utter, according to conscience."[12] James Wilson, Chair of the House Judiciary Committee and sponsor of the Civil Rights Act of 1866, the provisions of which Section One was designed to embrace, noted slavery's "incessant, unrelenting, aggressive warfare upon... the purity of religion."[13] Lyman Trumbull, Wilson's cosponsor of the Civil Rights Act, reminded the Congress of the oppressive laws that existed under slavery, including provisions which prohibited blacks from "exercising the function of a minister" and made it "a highly penal offense for any person... to teach slaves."[14] Congressman James Ashley noted that "slavery has silenced every free pulpit within its control."[15] According to Senator Henry Wilson, "religion, 'consisting in the performance of all known duties to God and our fellow men,' never has been and never will be allowed free exercise in any community where slavery dwarfs the consciences of men."[16] Senator James Nye believed that, with the fall of slavery, Congress now had the power to protect "freedom in the exercise of religion." Finally, Congressman Roswell Hart believed that the rebel states should not be readmitted until they set up a government where "no law shall be made prohibiting the free exercise of religion."

The vehicle through which the free exercise of religion would be "incorporated" was the [Fourteenth Amendment's] Privileges or Immunities Clause. ... Henry Wilson listed the free exercise of religion as one of the "privileges and immunities" violated by slavery.[17] Senator Jacob Howard, discussing the content of the Privileges or Immunities Clause... listed, among other rights, "the personal rights guaranteed and secured by the first eight amendments to the Constitution."[18] ... In the Forty-second Congress, Henry L. Dawes declared that the Privileges or Immunities Clause had "secured the free exercise of... religious belief." John Sherman declared that the "right to worship God according to the dictates of one's own conscience is not only a right, but a privilege which in a Christian country a man ought to enjoy," and that under the Fourteenth Amendment, "no state shall make or enforce any law which shall abridge the privileges or immunities of citizens of the United States."[19] Finally, the author of the Privileges or Immunities Clause, John Bingham, declared that the free exercise of religion was within the "scope and meaning" of the first section of the Fourteenth Amendment.[20] ...

The Scope of the Second Free Exercise Clause

The framers of the Fourteenth Amendment not only signaled their intent to incorporate the rights of conscience into the Privileges or Immunities Clause, but they also provided clues as to the intended scope of those rights. Specifically, religious exercise was to be protected from majoritarian hostility or indifference; [and] it was to be a substantive right affording more than simply "equal protection[."] Most importantly, by explicitly targeting "religiously neutral" laws as examples of what would become unconstitutional with the passage of the Fourteenth Amendment, men like John Bingham and Lyman Trumbull gave notice that in the future, generally applicable laws might sometimes impermissibly violate an individual's religious liberty.

1. From Federalism to Libertarianism

At the time of the Founding, "liberty" was largely understood as the "public liberty" of democratic self-government; majoritarian liberty rather than liberty against popular majorities. In terms of the First Amendment, the freedoms of speech and press had been linked to religious freedoms for reasons of federalism. However, by the 1860s, libertarianism had replaced federalism as the unifying theme of the First Amendment freedoms. Accordingly, Jacob Howard described the privileges and immunities to be incorporated into the Fourteenth Amendment as including "the personal rights guaranteed and secured by the first eight amendments to the Constitution."

The implications for free exercise were significant.... [T]he new Free Exercise Clause belonged to the individual, not the majority. As such, no longer was a law restricting the free exercise of religion prima facie constitutional merely because it served the needs of the majority. The suppression of religious exercise by the slaveholding states had forever eliminated that interpretation of the Free Exercise Clause. But this is simply to assert that the original prohibitions of the Free Exercise Clause now apply against the states: no law may be passed that prohibits religion qua religion. There is evidence that the framers of the Fourteenth Amendment had a broader view of the rights of conscience.

2. Protecting Religiously Motivated Conduct

> Under the Constitution as it is, not as it was, and by force of the fourteenth amendment, no State hereafter can...ever repeat the example of Georgia and send men to the penitentiary, as did that State, for teaching the Indian to read the lessons of the New Testament....[21]

[T]he activities intended to be protected under the incorporated Free Exercise Clause were vastly different from those anticipated at the Founding.

Although some persisted in limiting the free exercise of religion to worship, others declared that religion "consists in the performance of all known duties to God and our fellow men."[22] The rights of conscience were repeatedly linked with such activities as assisting runaway slaves, teaching literacy, and engaging in religiously motivated political discourse. To the framers of the Fourteenth Amendment, freedom of belief included the freedom to act publicly upon that belief.

Reconstructing the rights of conscience to embrace religiously motivated conduct does more than simply expand the definition of legitimate religious exercise. It evidences a change in the purpose of the Free Exercise Clause. As originally conceived, the religion clauses focused on discriminatory federal legislation; Congress could not pick out one religious belief for special benefits or particular burdens. Nondiscriminatory laws which regulated conduct in the public square were a different matter—this was, after all, the government's turf and no legitimate place for religion. This view made no sense, however, to those who had witnessed the intrusive regulation of the southern states and whose own religion was anything but a private affair. Moved by the events of recent history and guided by their own interpretation of true religion, the framers of the Fourteenth Amendment turned the focus of the Free Exercise Clause away from belief and towards the believer and the impact of generally applicable law.

3. Beyond Direct Regulation of Religious Exercise

Southern laws preventing blacks from reading and writing, as well as those regulating black assembly, were all "religiously neutral." [Yet the Fourteenth Amendment proponents attacked them.] Generally applicable laws in the North were targeted as well; for example, laws preventing anyone from assisting runaway slaves were seen as restrictions on the rights of conscience that would not be permitted under the Fourteenth Amendment:

> Before [the Fourteenth Amendment,] a State, as in the case of the State of Illinois, could make it a crime punishable by fine and imprisonment for any citizen within her limits, in obedience to the injunction of our divine Master, to help a slave who was ready to perish; to give him shelter, or break with him his crust of bread.[23] ...

[Moreover,] the debates criticizing southern prohibitions of assembly and education of blacks revea[l] that the concerns were at least as spiritual as they were political. To Henry Wilson, withholding the Bible violated Free Exercise in that it forced Christianity to surrender "the choicest jewel of its faith."[24] These laws were not mere political handicaps, but prevented the proclamation of the "new evangel, 'The pure in heart shall see God,'"[25] and forced those under their rule to "die without hope."[26] The problem with a law preventing someone from learning to read was not that others were allowed to read, nor was it simply a matter of violating the individual's right to "utter, according to conscience." The problem was that Christians could not preach, and slaves could not hear, the Good News—to the endangerment of the slaves' eternal souls.

In fact, when Reconstruction legislation attempting to effect the goal of equality came into conflict with free exercise principles, free exercise won the day. In 1870, Charles Sumner introduced a Civil Rights Bill that provided:

> That no citizen of the United States shall, by any reason of race, color, or previous condition of servitude, be excepted or excluded from the full and equal enjoyment of any accommodation, advantage, facility, or privilege furnished by innkeepers,... by trustees and officers of church organizations, cemetery associations, and benevolent institutions incorporated by national or State authority.[27]

[Some congressmen] challenged the proposed amendment as an indirect abridgment of the rights of conscience [by forbidding churches from having segregation policies]. Matthew Carpenter, for example, cited the religion clauses of the First Amendment and noted that "without discussing very minutely whether it does or does not violate the letter of the Constitution, I think it is in violation of the spirit of the Constitution in that it disregards the opinions and the motives of those who framed the Constitution, and is in conflict with what they believed they had secured.... It cannot be doubted that they ... intended to, and thought they had, carefully excluded the whole subject of religion from federal control or interference."[28] ...

Carpenter was concerned with the law's effect: interference with the rights of conscience. As we have seen, however, the original Free Exercise Clause served only as a statement of nonenumeration—Congress had no power over religion qua religion, but had significant power to interfere with religious exercise indirectly through other enumerated powers. Sumner [defended his proposal on this ground].

To those who believed in the rights of conscience, however, the fact that it was a political law which interfered with the rights of conscience was irrelevant. According to Senator Henry Anthony:

> I am very anxious indeed to vote to give to the colored people all their legal rights, but I shall not vote to give any person any religious rights, or to take from any person any religious rights. If there are white men so foolish as to believe that it is not right for negroes to worship with them, I pity them, but I shall not vote to deprive them of their undoubted right to worship so.... I shall not vote for any bill that contains any provision which interferes with religious worship, even if it compels me to vote against the amnesty bill, which I should regret very much.[29]

In the end, the church provision was removed and the remainder of Sumner's bill was passed.

The church-regulation debate, as well as the debates surrounding the passage of the Fourteenth Amendment, indicate that many in Congress believed there existed a higher authority that constrained the legitimate reach of secular law.

NOTES

As a result of editing, the notes for this essay have been renumbered. The note number from the original essay or article is shown in parentheses at the end of each citation.

1. United States Constitution, amendment 10. (16)
2. "Letter from Thomas Jefferson to Rev. Samuel Miller" (January 23, 1808), in Merrill D. Peterson, ed., *Thomas Jefferson: Writings* (1984), p. 1186. (36)
3. "Letter from Jefferson to Danbury (CT) Baptist Association" (January 1, 1802), in Peterson, ed., *Jefferson: Writings*, p. 510. (37)
4. Gordon S. Wood, *The Radicalism of the American Revolution* (1992), p. 145. (105)
5. Ibid., p. 332 (quoting Elias Smith, *The Loving Kindness of God Displayed in the Triumph of Republicanism in America* [1809]). (106)
6. Ibid., p. 333 (quoting Lyman Beecher, "The Necessity of Revivals of Religion to the Perpetuity of Our Civil and Religious Institutions," in *The Spirit of the Pilgrims* [1831]). (109)

7. Ibid. (111)

8. *Address to the Citizens of the State of Ohio, Concerning What Are Called The Black Laws* (Issued in Behalf of the Society of Friends of Indiana Yearly Meeting, 1848), reprinted in *Slavery, Race, and the American Legal System, 1700–1872*, Ser. No. 7; Paul Finkelman, ed., *Statutes on Slavery: The Pamphlet Literature*, vol. 2 (1988), p. 101. (117)

9. John T. Noonan Jr., *The Believer and the Powers That Are* (1987), p. 170 (quoting *How to Settle the Texas Question* [1845]). (121)

10. Speech by Charles W. Gardner, delivered at the Broadway Tabernacle, New York, New York, May 9, 1837, in C. Peter Ripley, ed., *The Black Abolitionist Papers*, vol. 3 (1991), p. 206. (143)

11. 32 U.S. (7 Pet.) 243 (1833). (145)

12. *Congressional Globe*, 35th Congress, 2nd Session, p. 985. (181)

13. *Congressional Globe*, 38th Congress, 1st Session (1864), p. 1199. (182)

14. *Congressional Globe*, 39th Congress, 1st Session (1865), p. 474. (183)

15. *Congressional Globe*, 38th Congress, 1st Session (1864), excerpted in Virginia Common on Constitutional Government, ed., *The Reconstruction Amendments' Debates* (1967), p. 81 [hereinafter *Reconstruction Debates*]. (184)

16. Ibid., p. 1202. (185)

17. *Congressional Globe*, 38th Congress, 1st Session (1864), p. 1202. (190)

18. *Congressional Globe*, 39th Congress, 2nd Session (1865), p. 2765. (191)

19. *Congressional Globe*, 42nd Congress, 2nd Session (1872), excerpted in *Reconstruction Debates*, p. 615. (194)

20. *Congressional Globe*, 42nd Congress, 1st Session (1871), p. 84. (195)

21. Ibid. (remarks of John Bingham). (199)

22. *Congressional Globe*, 38th Congress, 1st Session (1864), p. 1202 (remarks of Henry Wilson) (emphasis added). (204)

23. *Congressional Globe*, 42nd Congress, 1st Session (1871), p. 84 (remarks of John Bingham). (208)

24. *Congressional Globe*, 38th Congress, 1st Session (1859), p. 1202 (remarks of Henry Wilson). (210)

25. *Congressional Globe*, 42nd Congress, 1st Session (1871), p. 84 (remarks of John Bingham). (211)

26. *Congressional Globe*, 39th Congress, 1st Session (1865), p. 1090 (remarks of John Bingham). (212)

27. 42nd Cong., 2nd Session (1872), excerpted in *Reconstruction Debates*, p. 600. (213)

28. Ibid. (213)

29. *Congressional Globe*, 42nd Congress, 2nd Session (1872), excerpted in *Reconstruction Debates*, p. 610. (215)

Chapter 4

WHY SHOULD RELIGIOUS FREEDOM HAVE DISTINCTIVE CONSTITUTIONAL PROTECTION?

AN ANTI-LIBERAL ARGUMENT FOR RELIGIOUS FREEDOM

JOHN H. GARVEY

I want to consider why we protect freedom of religion as a constitutional right. The commonsense answer, which I think hits close to the truth, is that we protect it because religion is important. I will try to show that this answer is better than the alternatives which liberal theory offers.

A. The Agnostic Viewpoint

I begin by considering the standard answers given by liberal legal theory (and adopted by courts and commentators) to the question, "Why do we protect freedom of religion?" I deal first with the claim that religious freedom is an aspect of personal autonomy. Then I address the idea that freedom of religion prevents political strife. These claims are designed to protect a variety of

John H. Garvey, "An Anti-Liberal Argument for Religious Freedom," *Journal of Contemporary Legal Issues* 7 (1996): 275.

choices. The autonomy theory and the political theory make no assumptions about the truth or value of religious decisions. They view such questions from an agnostic standpoint.

1.

Some say freedom of religion is important because it is one way (though only one) of exercising our autonomy as human beings interested in making our own choices and shaping our own lives. The religious devotee creates a life for herself around certain kinds of beliefs and values. She will probably join a community of like-minded people (a church). She typically has ideas about her relationship to God that orient her in her daily life. And so on. In doing these things she is protected by what Laurence Tribe calls "rights of religious autonomy."[1]

There is nothing unique about religious autonomy. It is a name for one set of choices people make about how to live, but there are other sets of choices within the field of autonomy: choices about reproduction, risk taking, vocation, travel, education, appearance, and sexual behavior. For Tribe religious autonomy is just one aspect of the larger "rights of privacy and personhood."

Moreover, within the set of religious choices we attach value to the act of choosing, not to particular outcomes. A decision to reject God is entitled to the same protection as a decision to follow him. "[I]ndividual choice in matters of religion should remain free: individual decisions are to be protected whether they operate for or against the validity of any or all religious views. … [T]he individual is freed from … the oppressive effects of government regulation in order to believe or disbelieve as he chooses."[2]

The Supreme Court has given some support to the idea that autonomy is the value underlying religious freedom. It held in *Torcaso v. Watkins* that Maryland had violated religious freedom by requiring state officeholders to declare their belief in God.[3] This suggests that the constitution attaches equal value to belief and disbelief: the important thing is the choice, not the outcome.

This conclusion is hard to square with the language of the first amendment, which protects only the free exercise "of religion." Rejecting religion is an exercise of freedom, but it is not an exercise of religion. (Amputation is not a way of exercising my foot.) The free exercise clause by its terms seems inconsistent with the idea of autonomy. It seems to favor choices for religion over choices against religion.

One way to avoid this textual limitation is to define "religion" very broadly—so broadly that even disbelief is a kind of religion. This is what the Court did in interpreting the draft law. When I was a boy people were exempt from military service if their "religious training and belief" made them oppose war. Federal law defined religious belief as "an individual's belief in a relation to a Supreme Being involving duties superior to those arising from any human relation[.]"[4] The Supreme Court interpreted the law with an eye on the free exercise clause, and said that the question was whether "the claimed belief occup[ies] the same place in the life of the objector as an orthodox belief in God holds in the life of one clearly qualified for exemption."[5] The idea of "God" is "'more of a hindrance than a help.'" We should think of "God not as a projection 'out there' or beyond the skies but as the ground of our very being." And "religion" is nothing more than "'the devotion of man to the highest ideal that he can conceive.'"[6]

The autonomy theory views religious freedom from an agnostic standpoint. This is hardly surprising. It follows rather naturally from the "autonomous" view of human nature. If you scratch a person deep enough, the theory holds, you will find a kind of free-floating self. If you looked at the surface of my life you might say that I was a middle-class Irish Catholic, husband, father of five children, law professor, part-time musician, Celtics fan, and so on. I have naturally inherited a variety of moral convictions (those typical of bourgeois Catholics, or lawyers, etc.). I am also moved by various desires that arise from and act upon the details of my life (I want prestigious publishers for my books, money for my children's education, time with my wife, etc.).

But my essential self is able to rise above these details. It is unencumbered, unsituated. It can step back from my habitual convictions and desires (my first-order preferences), reflect critically on them, and change them to suit its own plan (second-order preferences) for what my life should be like. Exactly where I get my second-order preferences is a matter of some dispute. Some say that I am guided by reason to universally applicable principles. Others say that I just make them up. But everyone agrees that it's up to me— to my unencumbered self—to choose them, however I might find them.

This view of human nature is the basis for a powerful argument in favor of freedom. A just political order has to take account of the way people really are. It must, in other words, respect their freedom to act as unencumbered selves on their second-order preferences. In the case of religion this means that it must view them as persons choosing, from a detached position, a theological orientation. This is what I mean by saying that the autonomy theory assumes the agnostic viewpoint. I might be a Catholic in my daily life, but that is a first-order preference. The real me is able to step back from it, assume an agnostic stance, and make a fresh start. I might then renew my religious commitment, but I might reject it. It does not really matter. The important thing is that the real me should organize my life along lines it freely chooses. The law protects religious freedom to facilitate that choice.

[T]he autonomy theory is in one sense too powerful. It holds that a just society must let its citizens choose how to live their own lives. Some relevant choices are religious, so it follows that the government must not interfere with them. But there is nothing special about religious choices in this argument. They are on a par with promiscuous sex, cigarette smoking, and the practice of optometry. Our instincts and the language of our Constitution tell us, though, that there is a difference. The Bill of Rights protects the free exercise of religion. It says nothing about free love, free trade, or excise taxes on tobacco. What we need is an argument that protects religion while leaving unprotected many other activities that we do not support as strongly.

Having said this much, I will not pursue the point further. I want to turn instead to a second problem with the autonomy theory. It concerns the assumptions about human nature that I outlined above. One is the factual assumption that we can step back from our convictions and desires and reorganize them according to second-order preferences that we freely choose. Another is the more value-laden assumption that we should do this in order to live "authentic" lives. There are those who would dispute both assumptions, and people who want religious freedom are among those most likely to do so.

Consider first the factual assumption. It is inconsistent in several ways with recurring ideas in Christian theology. The notion of original sin is meant to suggest the inherent imperfection of human nature. In the strongest statements of this idea—Augustine is a good example—it entails our inability to master sinful desires and to freely will doing good. In the common phrase, human nature is the slave of sin. The counterpoint to this unhappy view of human nature is the idea of grace. It is a kind of sharing in divine life, a power that enables us to control sinful desire, live good lives, and win salvation. But grace is given to us by God gratuitously. We cannot call it down with a rain dance, and we cannot behave as we should without it. It is out of our control. This aspect of grace, followed to its logical conclusion, leads to the Calvinist notion of predestination: our salvation is entirely in God's hands, and some are not saved.

This view of human nature affects the way many religious people look at the idea of choice. The individual does not have complete control over choosing the religious option. It is God who makes the choice. I might have to accept God's choice and cooperate in carrying it out, but I am cast as a supporting actor. Thus the Jews understand themselves as the chosen people. Their stories tell of people pursued by God and brought back to do his work. Jonah, called by God to be his prophet, tried to escape on a boat for Tarshish but was brought back by miraculous means. In the New Testament Jesus himself set the example by praying before his death, "Father, if it be thy will, take this cup from me. Yet not my will but thine be done."[7] God converted the apostle Paul by striking him to the ground and blinding him....

Those who take this view of human nature will also disagree with the autonomy theory about the value of running our own lives according to our second-order preferences. That is not the basis of real freedom. Augustine claims, for example, that real freedom is freedom from the bondage of sin. "And it is out of the question for free will to realize this freedom through its own power; this it can do only through the grace of God[.]"[8] It sounds paradoxical, but it is accurate to say that Christian freedom consists not in making our own choices but in obeying the law of God.

The autonomy theory, then, bases religious freedom on a view of human nature that many religious people would reject. This need not be a fatal defect. We also justify freedom of speech on grounds that some speakers would reject—we say that it promotes democracy, and yet we grant it to Nazis who do not believe in democracy. But religious believers play a crucial role in free exercise law. They are not like the Nazis. They are like the New England town meeting—the paradigm around which the theory is built. If the theory does not work for them, there probably is something wrong with it....

2.

The second standard argument for freedom of religion is political rather than ethical. The argument is that the denial of freedom causes strife that leaves everyone worse off. We can find both comparative and historical evidence for this conclusion. Lebanon, Iran, India, and the Sudan have recently seen violent struggles for religious supremacy. England and much of Western Europe did so in the sixteenth and seventeenth centuries. The Supreme Court has found parallels in early American history....

Like the autonomy theory, the political theory tries to justify religious freedom from an agnostic viewpoint. It stresses two kinds of harm affecting unbelievers. One is civil war. Even noncombatants get killed in a civil war, and everyone suffers from the collapse of the government and the economy. The other harm is persecution. Unbelievers cannot be prevented from practicing their faith. (They have none.) But if the government wants to compel a particular form of religious observance it might have to "torture, maim and kill... 'atheists' or 'agnostics'" along with nonconforming believers.[9]

This theory, like the autonomy theory, makes freedom universally available. But here the value of freedom is instrumental, not intrinsic. It leads to peace. If it did not, we would take another approach. The autonomy argument, by contrast, said that freedom was intrinsically good for people like us. Of course it had to make some controversial assumptions about what kind of people we were. It is a virtue of the political argument that it dispenses with those assumptions. And there is much else to recommend it. It is realistic and practical, and goes some way toward justifying a special place for religious freedom. It does, though, have some weaknesses. The most important one is that it is incomplete.

Consider first the case of fringe groups. In American society there are, depending on how you count, hundreds or thousands of them. They include small but well-known sects (Hare Krishnas, Moonies) and smaller, little known local cults. For our purposes they also include unchurched believers— religious individualists who seek God in their own way. The political defense of freedom gives no protection to these people. If a group is sufficiently small the government can simply stamp it out without running the risk of civil war. Of course civil war is only one kind of strife. Stamping out fringe groups is persecution, and the political argument is designed to avoid that too. But what is wrong with fining, jailing, medicating, (executing?) religious eccentrics? These forms of punishment and cure are not in themselves objectionable, the way cruel and unusual punishment would be. We routinely apply them to drug offenders and think that we're doing the right thing. The obvious answer is that there is a difference between religious activity and drug dealing: one is good and the other is bad. That is the very argument I will make in the next section. But it takes us beyond our concern with political strife.

So the political strife argument does not protect groups who cannot fight because they are too small. Neither does it protect groups (some of them large) who are unwilling to fight. The Amish on principle flee from controversy and eschew politics. Quakers are well known for their pacifism. Groups that are far larger engage in many practices that they see as desirable but not essential, and that they would not defend with violence. Consider the employment practices of Catholic schools. The political defense of freedom gives no shelter to these groups if they pose no threat to peace.

I think we can state these objections in even more general form. The political explanation tells us that freedom is good because it brings peace. It does not tell us why we should prefer freedom to other means of bringing peace. It gives us no reason to object to the suppression or the establishment of religion, provided the job is done ruthlessly enough to prevent civil war. Religion was an insignificant cause of strife in the Soviet Union from Stalin's time until very recently. There was little freedom, but that is no objection if all that matters is peace. The obvious advantage of freedom is that it respects piety as well as peace. But we need an argument that will tell us why it is good to respect piety.

B. The Believer's Viewpoint

The best reasons for protecting religious freedom rest on the assumption that religion is a good thing. Our Constitution guarantees religious freedom because religious people want to practice their faith. Mark DeWolfe Howe said: "Though it would be possible...that men who were deeply skeptical in religious matters should demand a constitutional prohibition against abridgments of religious liberty, surely it is more probable that the demand should come from those who themselves were believers."[10] I will examine the matter from their point of view....

There are different forms of religious action, and various reasons that believers would give for protecting them. The ones I will mention are not intended to be a scientific taxonomy. They are just clusters of recurring problems that seem to warrant similar treatment.

One such form of distinctively religious action is the performance of ritual acts. These include prayer and other kinds of worship; compliance with sumptuary rules governing dress, diet, the use of property; the observance of sacred times (feasts and holy days) and places (pilgrimages to shrines); rites connected with important events in the believer's life (birth, death, maturity, marriage); and so on....

There is in our traditions a religious argument for religious freedom that is peculiarly associated with ritual acts. It is, simply, that it is futile to coerce people to perform ceremonies (prayer, worship, declarations of belief) they do not believe in. This idea has ancient roots, but it was most fully developed by English Protestants during the seventeenth century. Locke appeals to it in his Letter Concerning Toleration: "[T]rue and saving religion consists in the inward persuasion of the mind, without which nothing can be acceptable to God. And such is the nature of the understanding, that it cannot be compelled to the belief of anything by outward force." Coercion can be worse than futile—it can be counterproductive. In Milton's phrase, to force a ritual performance is "to compell hypocrisie, not to advance religion."[11] ...

Coerced ritual is futile because it cannot put the soul in touch with God. The individual cannot hear God unless he has faith. And faith does not come to people just because they go through the ritual motions. God gives it to whom he wills. It is an idea characteristic of Protestantism that this happens in a very individual way. The most effective medium is scripture, through which God may speak to the pious reader.

This distinctively Protestant "right of private judgment" began as a protest against the Catholic Church's claim to mediate between God and individual souls. But it served equally well as an objection against state mediation. Roger Williams underlines the connection in *The Bloudy Tenent*.[12]

> In vaine have English Parliaments permitted English Bibles in the poorest English houses, and the simplest man or woman to search the Scriptures, if yet against their soules perswasion from the Scripture, they should be forced (as if they lived in Spaine or Rome it selfe without the sight of a Bible) to beleeve as the Church beleeves.

Let me turn now to a second form of religious action, and a different argument for religious freedom. Members of a religious tradition typically want to acquire and spread knowledge about the esoterica of their belief, ritual forms, ceremonial duties, and so on. These special kinds of religious truth are often set down in sacred texts (Bible, Torah, Koran) and elaborated upon in written and oral commentaries (Talmud, Sunna). Believers like to study these texts and commentaries, to discuss them with others, and in some traditions to bring them to the attention of unbelievers.

Those who feel this way sometimes argue that the freedom to acquire and spread religious knowledge leads us to the truth. We inherit this idea, like the last, from seventeenth century English Protestantism. It is the message of Milton's *Areopagitica*.... Milton offered several reasons why unlicensed printing would promote the discovery of religious truth. One was the now familiar claim that truth will prevail over a falsehood in any free encounter. A less familiar but more radical idea was that God's revelation is progressive. This makes free inquiry not only safe but actually desirable. Individual thinkers might wander astray, but the net social effect of freedom is to bring us closer to God....

Let me reemphasize that these two arguments (futility, truth) rest on religious premises (faith is a gift; revelation is progressive). They will convince only religious believers. But within that group they have carried the day. [For example, they have been adopted by] the Catholic Church and the Presbyterian Church—the two chief targets of Puritan polemicists like Milton and Williams....

Let me turn now to a third variety of religious action, and a different argument for religious freedom. Religious believers are often bound by special moral obligations. These come from a moral code that has some supernatural sanction (the law in Judaism, the shari'a in Islam). Such a code often demands forms of behavior that the rest of society views as supererogatory, morally neutral, or even (occasionally) wrong. A violation of the moral code may be seen as something worse than a breach of duty—as a kind of personal harm or insult to the author of the code, which calls for repentance and might be punished or forgiven on a transcendent level.

About these kinds of actions we might say that the government should not force people to violate moral duties if (in their system of belief) they will face transcendent consequences. Otherwise, X might have to choose between violating the law and risking damnation. This is how it was with the early Mormons who were convicted [in *Reynolds* and other cases] for the practice of polygamy. Or X might be forced to forego a great good. An American Indian recently complained that the government's use of a social security number for his daughter would "rob [her] spirit."[13]

Of course the government often causes great harm to unbelievers as well. A religious pacifist fears for his salvation when he is drafted, but the average Marine also suffers at the thought of leaving his family and going into combat. From a religious point of view, though, the cases are not comparable. The harm threatening the believer is more serious (loss of heavenly comforts, not domestic ones) and more lasting (eternal, not temporary). That is what justifies restricting this special kind of freedom to religious claimants alone.

This is a consequentialist argument for freedom (though the consequences it relies on are religious). But we could also make a nonconsequentialist argument. Moral codes impose religious duties, and there is something uniquely wrong with forcing a person to violate a religious duty even if she is not primarily concerned about final rewards and punishments. A strict Calvinist, for example, sees no connection between the performance of religious duties and election to heaven. But she can still demand religious freedom. The focus of her claim is not her own destiny. She is concerned instead with the effect on God, as it were—she has to disappoint him to comply with the law. The individual places great value in keeping faith with such duties, and it is this value that religious liberty protects.

These arguments about suffering and duty differ from the earlier arguments about futility and truth. Claims about suffering and duty focus on the personal interests of religious believers. They are an appeal to rights in the modern sense—a form of protection for people who are losers in the political process. Claims about the futility of coercion and the discovery of truth focus on a larger social interest. "We will all be better off," the believer says, "if we allow religious freedom." (Compare the argument that free speech is a form of self-expression, and the argument that free speech is crucial for self-government.)

Along with this difference in focus is a difference in coverage. The earlier arguments apply universally. Coercion is futile no less for atheists than for Catholics and Jews. God may give them faith or he may not, but the government cannot help him out. So too with the discovery of truth. It's no use letting only right-thinking Christians search, because we're talking about revelation and God can reveal himself to anyone. As the gospel says, "The spirit blows where it wills."[14] The arguments about suffering and duty, by contrast, offer protection only to religious believers. The believer's suffering is special precisely because she believes in heaven, hell, eternal life, and so on. The believer's duties are more compelling just because they arise from God's commands.

This explains what I [have] called the split-level character of free exercise law. In some areas the clause protects everyone. This happens when we are dealing with ritual acts and the pursuit of knowledge. Atheists and Quakers alike can object to laws prescribing forms of faith (test oaths) and worship (school prayers). Anyone can object to a law that forbids inquiry (the teaching of evolution) for religious reasons. Similarly, anybody can object—on free exercise or free speech grounds—when the government tries to limit communication about religiously significant questions. These matters are all covered by the first set of principles: compelled belief is futile; revelation is progressive.

In other areas the free exercise clause protects only religious believers. The cases where this happens are cases about compliance with a moral code. X's faith might require him to leave his job, or school, or the army. The Court used to give serious consideration to all such claims. Today it is harder to get special treatment, but it is still possible. And it remains true now, as before, that "to have the protection of the Religion Clauses, the claims must be rooted in religious belief."[15] This disparity is explained by the second set of principles: believers face a special kind of suffering; they are subject to a higher kind of duty.

The draft cases do not fit in this picture. None of the reasons I have given seems to cover the conscientious objection of nonreligious young men to service in the armed forces. But we should not generalize from these cases, any more than we should make death penalty cases the pattern for rules of criminal procedure. Killing is an extreme act, and the feeling of dread that attends it can give even nonreligious duties an absolute cast.

C. Reprise

I have argued that we should take the believer's viewpoint rather than the agnostic's viewpoint in thinking about religious freedom. But my argument seems incomplete. It relies upon reasons that only some people find convincing. And sometimes it protects freedom only for those who are convinced. How can such a lopsided idea justify one of our basic constitutional rights?....

I began this paper with two arguments for religious freedom (autonomy, political strife) that were designed to appeal to everyone. This is the standard method of justifying social practices in liberal theory. It is, to take a more famous example, the technique used in social contract theory. We need not test a practice against some objective standard of goodness if we can show that everyone would agree to it. The agnostic point of view is a device (like the veil of ignorance[16]) for securing everyone's agreement. It keeps the contracting parties ignorant about certain details of their situation so that they are willing to make concessions. The most important thing to hide from the parties is information about their goals in life. If I know that I will be committed to the ideals of Mao Zedong I will insist on rules (like the dictatorship of the proletariat) that suit me, but that other people will not like. If I am ignorant about my own ends the safe bargain is one that is fair to everybody, because when the veil is lifted I could be anybody. As you might expect, the best way to be fair to everybody is to maximize freedom. That lets each person pursue her own goals.

The standard arguments assume the agnostic point of view, then, because they want a rule of religious freedom that is fair to everyone. Fairness here has two dimensions. One is consent. Universal consent is a good indication that a rule treats everyone fairly. (This is why social contracts are always adopted unanimously.) The agnostic point of view tries to base freedom on principles everyone can agree with. Revelation is out because it is hidden from some people. We are asked to look instead at facts about human nature and our social situation: the autonomy argument refers to the unencumbered self; the political strife argument refers to the causes of war and peace.

The other dimension of fairness is reciprocity. A contract is fair in this sense if the parties share equally in the benefits of the bargain. The autonomy argument satisfies this condition by making religion just one of many protected choices, and by offering equal religious freedom to believers and unbelievers. The political argument says that freedom results in a public good (peace) that everyone enjoys.

The religious defense of free exercise is lopsided because it violates these conditions of fairness. The principles that it relies on to justify freedom—futility, truth, suffering, and duty—all refer in some way to religious beliefs that many people do not hold. This makes it hard for some people to consent. The religious defense also gives special protection to some kinds of religious action. That is, it excuses religious actors from some generally applicable laws when their moral code requires another course of conduct. This violates the condition of reciprocity. Why should we prefer an argument of this kind over arguments that seem to satisfy the canons of fairness?

For several reasons. First, the standard arguments themselves fail the test of fairness. The autonomy theory, like my own, appeals to assumptions about human nature (the unencumbered self, the value of authenticity) that are inconsistent with convictions that many religious people hold about original sin, grace, faith, and revelation. In the real world these people would not consent to a social contract based on autonomy. To avoid this problem the theory asks us to assume the agnostic viewpoint (the veil of ignorance). But why not ask agnostics to assume the religious viewpoint? That too would produce unanimous consent. It would not be consistent with liberal theory, because it commits us to a view of the good before we have resolved the issue of rights. But we cannot assume the correctness of liberal theory. That is the very question we're debating. If my theory will not get universal consent, neither will the autonomy theory.

The political strife theory is flawed in the same way. It asks us to make the empirical assumption that we can only have civil peace through religious freedom. But there are other ways of avoiding strife; repression is one of them. Unless freedom has some other good points, there is no reason to prefer it to repression.

There is reason to doubt, then, that the standard arguments are more fair than mine. My own approach, on the other hand, has some real strengths that they lack. It is the most convincing explanation for why our society adopted the right to religious freedom in the first place. It is possible to imagine a society of skeptics insisting on a free exercise clause, but the idea is far-fetched.

The religious justification is also the reason many—perhaps most—religious believers claim the right to freedom today. It enables them to perform their religious duties, and to avoid religious sanctions. It allows them to pursue the truth, as God gives them to know the truth. And no other course could bring them closer to God.

Finally, the religious justification is the only convincing explanation for the split-level character of free exercise law. Sometimes religious believers and nonbelievers are treated alike, but sometimes the law protects only religious believers. This is not something that we can explain by appeals to consent and fairness. It violates the canon of reciprocity. The only convincing explanation for such a rule is that the law thinks religion is a good thing.

NOTES

As a result of editing, the notes for this essay have been renumbered. The note number from the original essay or article is shown in parentheses at the end of each citation.

1. Laurence H. Tribe, *American Constitutional Law*, 2nd ed. (1988), ch. 14. (1)

2. Gail Merel, "The Protection of Individual Choice: A Consistent Understanding of Religion Under the First Amendment," *University of Chicago Law Review* 45 (1978): 805, 810–11. (3)

3. 367 U.S. 488 (1961). (4)

4. 50 U.S.C. § 456(j) (1958). (5)

5. *United States v. Seeger*, 480 U.S. 163, 184 (1965). (6)

6. Ibid., pp. 180–83. (7)

7. Luke 22:42. (14)

8. Augustine, *Faith, Hope and Charity (Enchiridion)*, trans. Louis A. Arand (1947), ch. 28, § 106. (17)

9. *Zorach v. Clauson*, 343 U.S. 306, 319 (1952) (Black, J., dissenting). (26)

10. Mark DeWolfe Howe, *The Garden and the Wilderness* (1965), p. 15. (29)

11. John Milton, "A Treatise of Civil Power in Ecclesiastical Causes," in C. A. Patrides, ed., *John Milton: Selected Prose* (1985), pp. 289, 311. (32)

12. William Haller, *Liberty and Reformation in the Puritan Revolution* (1955), p. 157. (35)

13. *Roy v. Cohen*, 590 F. Supp. 600, 604 (M.D. Pa. 1984), rev'd, *Bowen v. Roy*, 476 U.S. 693 (1986). (43)

14. John 3:8. (48)

15. *Wisconsin v. Yoder*, 406 U.S. 205, 215–16 (1972). (49)

16. John Rawls, *A Theory of Justice* (1971), § 24. (50)

THE RIGHT NOT TO BE JOHN GARVEY

ALAN BROWNSTEIN

PERSONAL AUTONOMY AND FREEDOM

Garvey's repudiation of personal autonomy as a constitutional value is seriously flawed. Put simply, he underestimates the importance of personal autonomy as a foundation for constitutional rights. Garvey believes that constitutional freedoms can be adequately protected without any reference to autonomy under an alternative framework grounded on moral values. Ultimately, as I argue below, his framework is just not capable of doing the job that Garvey assigns to it.

In part, Garvey's failure to appreciate the value of autonomy for constitutional purposes reflects a misunderstanding of how a respect for personal autonomy structures the relationship between the individual and the state. To Garvey, autonomy refers to the discretion to make choices. From my

Alan Brownstein, "The Right Not to Be John Garvey," *Cornell Law Review* 83 (1998): 767, 770–71, 774–76, 805–12, 814–18.

perspective, autonomy asserts the independence and integrity of the self against the use of state power to define and transform a person against his will. The difference in our understanding of personal autonomy has substantial implications for Garvey's analysis of freedom....

Autonomy and Self-Defining Choices

[My] view of autonomy does not accept the idea [that Garvey sets forth] of an essential self—one that selects and changes preferences the way a person puts on clothes—as the basis for protecting personal autonomy as a moral good and constitutional value. The self is not completely independent from all its choices. When I talk about protected autonomy choices, for example, the decision whether to have children, I am not talking about choices that a person can easily discard and replace. I take the idea of self-defining choices seriously and literally. Once such choices are made, the individual making the decision is no longer the same person in a very basic and important sense. Thus, choices have consequences for the self that makes them.

A therapist I once knew described how one of his patients made an important breakthrough when he stopped saying, "I have a problem," and began saying, "I am a problem." The idea was that the patient could not improve until he recognized that he would have to change in central ways, even in some ways seemingly unrelated to his symptoms. He could not continue to be the person he was and solve his problems. I think of protected autonomy choices in the same way. Speaking personally, I cannot imagine who I would be if I were not Jewish, and I do not believe I am the same person I was before my children were born. In brief, certain autonomy choices can transform, or at least have the potential to transform, a person's self. Those are the kinds of choices that I believe the Constitution protects....

If we [a]ccept the proposition that an individual's personal decisions influence who he or she is, [t]his conclusion will have important ramifications for our understanding of the nature of constitutional rights. If we forthrightly and knowingly refuse to protect self-transforming decisions, we necessarily reject the right to determine one's own identity. If no such rights exist, it would seem that the state is free to engage in activities designed to change a person's identity as long as it does not impede the individual from living a good life in other respects....

As good a person as John Garvey may be, I would like greater assurance that the state cannot attempt to mold me into his image....

What Religious Liberty Is Not For

1. Justifying the Grant of Special Protection to Religion Under an Autonomy Model

I suggest that Garvey overstates the difficulty with grounding religious freedom on an autonomy model and understates the model's explanatory value. His first challenge to the utility of an autonomy model—that, for autonomy purposes, there is nothing special about religion—is the easiest to refute, assuming that one accepts the meaning of autonomy I have described. For serious believers, religion is one of the most self-defining and transformative decisions of human existence. Religious beliefs affect virtually all of the defining decisions of personhood. They influence whom we will marry and what that union represents, the birth of our children, our interactions with family members, the way we deal with death, the ethics of our professional conduct, and many other aspects of our lives. Almost any other individual decision pales in comparison to the serious commitment to religious faith.

But a reader might reply, "Isn't that what Garvey is arguing? Aren't you conceding that religion is special? Moreover, under your analysis, why should we protect the decision to reject religion? All of the examples you have given apply only to religious believers, they do not encompass the autonomy choices of nonbelievers."

These contentions are true to some extent. I do think religion is special. All self-defining decisions are special to the person who makes them. There is a difference, however, between arguing that a decision is special because it is important and arguing that a decision is special because the choice that one has made is good. Religion is important. It is very important to individuals. I do not need to recognize all religious beliefs and practices as good to justify protecting decisions of this importance under an autonomy theory. I leave it to others who are far more capable than I to evaluate the moral worth of the religions of the world.

With respect to the unidirectional nature of religious freedom that Garvey posits, I think he is basically correct. I think there is a split-level character to free exercise rights. The justification for this attribute of religious liberty is more complicated than Garvey suggests, however, and it can be grounded on personal autonomy.

Religious freedom is bilateral in one primary sense. The decision not to be religious, not to adopt a religious persuasion, is fully protected. The state cannot order everyone to join a religion of their choice because the refusal to accept any religion is a profound personal decision. The election to be morally eclectic is obviously self-defining, as is the decision to confront major life events such as marriage, birth, parenthood, and death without the unifying perspective that religious faith provides. The decision to go it alone without G-d or a religious community to provide guidance and support is an autonomy choice of great personal significance.

Once a person makes that essential decision, however, most of the individual choices he makes throughout his life are separate and unrelated. Some may be of sufficient significance that they are independently recognized as a protected personal liberty, such as the right to marry. For many other choices, such as the decision to rest on the Sabbath, a secular individual will view the question of what to do on Saturday as a relatively trivial one, while an orthodox Jew will see this choice as a significant aspect of his religious identity. It is not difficult to understand why we would treat these decisions differently under a system of rights that is grounded on respect for personal autonomy.

I would protect the religious individual more than her secular counterpart for three reasons. First, the text of the Constitution supports such a distinction. Second, protecting religious liberty more than secular acts of conscience is defensible on administrability grounds. It is difficult enough to determine what constitutes a religion for First Amendment purposes. Allowing all sincere acts of conscience some immunity from general regulation would create an unmanageable system that could not survive in any complex society. Finally, and not surprisingly, I think the religious individual has a stronger claim to personal autonomy. For most seriously religious persons, religion provides a center to their identity for which there is no secular counterpart. Political beliefs, for example, are not so central to an individual's identity. They do not determine how one will understand, or relate to, so many important events and aspects of life. Religion addresses our most human concerns—love, marriage, parenthood, birth, and death—far more deeply, profoundly, and comprehensively than secular belief systems do. Therefore, out of respect for the autonomy of the individual, we assign special protection to the development and maintenance of religious beliefs and practices....*

---

*Ed. Note: This paragraph has been relocated from Section III: Political Justifications for Freedom.

It is easy to understand why those who strongly believe in a secular philosophy may feel that the rigorous enforcement of free exercise principles treats them unjustly. They have an argument under both Garvey's "religion is good" model and my "religious liberty as an autonomy right" approach. In either case, the secular believer argues, why should only religious liberty receive protection? Even if my beliefs are not quite as "good" as religious beliefs, they are still worth something from a constitutional value perspective. Similarly, even if decisions grounded on secular beliefs are not as self-defining as religious obligations, my secular moral code and philosophy of life may still be reasonably comprehensive. Surely it deserves some respect as an aspect of my identity. Yet under constitutional doctrine prior to *Employment Division v. Smith*, or pursuant to the Religious Freedom Restoration Act of 1993 [see p. 20], laws abridging religious liberty receive rigorous scrutiny, while laws infringing on secular belief systems receive no serious scrutiny at all, not even some form of intermediate level review. Where is the justice in such an all-or-nothing approach? . . .

The mandates of the Establishment Clause correct (some would say overcorrect) that imbalance. The limitations that the Establishment Clause imposes on governmental support of religion give secular belief systems an edge. There are no restrictions on government's power to endorse or promote secular beliefs that act as a counterpart to Establishment Clause requirements. . . .

Thus, one response to the individual, who holds secular beliefs and receives no constitutional protection for practices associated with them, is that the failure to provide him the same level of constitutional immunity from regulation that a religious person receives is part of the attempt to achieve some degree of balance within the operation of both religion clauses. The relatively unfavorable treatment of the secular believer under Free Exercise Clause doctrine is offset by the relatively unfavorable treatment afforded religious beliefs under the Establishment Clause.

Choosing Between Competing Positions

Suppose we ask this question: How does our understanding of the purpose of a right relate to the likelihood that the right will receive rigorous protection as a matter of constitutional law? If John Garvey and I both agree that the Free Exercise Clause should rigorously and equally protect the beliefs and activities of all the religious faiths practiced in the United States, what purpose of religious freedom best secures this right against challenges that might be brought against it? What meaning of religious freedom provides the best guarantee that the right will be defined broadly and fairly? How do we avoid or mitigate attempts to reduce its scope or the rigor with which it will be enforced?

I think an autonomy model provides a superior answer to these questions. Put simply, I would argue that a model of religious freedom grounded on the moral virtue of religious belief is a model at war with itself that cannot withstand the friction that its own internal contradictions create.

For the most part, religious beliefs are closed systems that identify their own tenets and traditions with religious truth. There is no requirement that religions operate this way. One can easily imagine a religious person who believes that because G-d is divine and infinite in his power, he is also unknowable to humankind. Indeed, one might argue that human limitations so distort the mortal perspective of G-d that, at best, what we claim to know of G-d are viewpoints of an infinite being perceived from such different and limited perspectives that we cannot help but disagree about G-d's nature. Thus, the disagreements among myriad faiths about the nature of G-d are not only understandable, but could not be otherwise. There is no right way to perceive G-d....

[But] I do not believe that [this position] describes the reality of religious belief in the United States, or anywhere else for that matter. Religious people believe in the truth of their faith. To a considerable extent, they believe in the error of competing faiths. They may disagree about the consequences of this error. Not everyone believes that the proponent of a false faith is damned for eternity. But most religious individuals believe in the truth of their convictions and the falsehood of contrary beliefs. The first of the Ten Commandments[1] that Moses brought down from Mount Sinai is meant to be taken seriously.

If I understand Garvey correctly, he argues that we should protect the right to practice religious beliefs that we hold to be false because we recognize that they may be true. We cannot know that they are false. I do not think that his argument accurately describes the reason there is such a strong consensus in support of religious freedom in this country. I also do not believe that his argument accurately describes the reality of religious experience here. Most importantly, I think that telling people that the primary reason we protect the practices of other faiths is the potential truth of religious beliefs that are contrary to their own will create a powerful disincentive against religious freedom.

Let me use a freedom-of-speech ... example to illustrate this point. When the Nazis wanted to march through the streets of Skokie, Illinois,[2] many people who were committed to freedom of speech struggled with the conflict that the situation created. It is not easy to protect the speech we hate, particularly when it is expressed in such a loathsome manner. I believe that the courts were correct in upholding the right of the Nazis to conduct their march. But I can hold that belief under my understanding of First Amendment doctrine without conceding for a moment that the Nazi marchers were anything other than the deceitful purveyors of falsehood and evil that I take them to be.

If I were told that by upholding the claim of the Nazis to march, I was even implicitly recognizing that the racist and anti-Semitic message they were conveying may be truthful, what had been a difficult moral dilemma would become an impossible one. The same argument applies to any other form of hate speech. It is hard enough to ask citizens to protect the right to communicate evil when constitutional theory allows the polity to distance itself completely from the subject matter of the communication. Insisting that freedom of speech for hatemongers presupposes some commitment to the possible truth of their statements may place a burden on the citizenry that no polity can bear.

The same analysis applies to religious freedom....

Ultimately, no constitutional doctrine has intrinsic permanence. As long as the political branches of government control the appointment of judges and justices and people do not live forever, the Constitution over time can mean only what the polity is willing to allow it to mean. Constitutional doctrine eventually depends on political will. I do not think that we can count on the continuing "will" to protect religious freedom if we require people to undermine their commitment to the unique truth of their own religious beliefs. Yet we do just that by insisting that protecting the free exercise of other faiths is grounded on the possibility of the truth of contrary beliefs. Thus, one of the great virtues of grounding constitutional rights on the foundation of personal autonomy is that it allows one person to respect the rights of another without implicitly affirming the moral value of the way the person exercises the right.

An autonomy foundation for religious freedom has other virtues over a model grounded on the moral value of religion. By generalizing the purpose of religious freedom so that it resonates with the purpose of other rights, we create a firmer foundation for a range of rights. Both religious and nonreligious individuals stand to lose valuable protection if the "protecting personal autonomy" purpose of the several rights linked to this objective is challenged. Not only is the security of the right strengthened by linking it to other interests that diverse political groups value, but the justification for the right becomes more persuasive as the principle underlying it is broadened.

In determining whether protecting a right truly furthers the public good, arguments in favor of protecting an interest as a right by the group receiving the benefit from that designation in terms of that group's own well-being are always open to challenge. The self-serving testimony of a witness is always suspect. One can explain and discount the support that religious individuals give to religious freedom as nothing more than self-interested constitutional politics.

A defense of religious freedom that lays the groundwork for also protecting nonreligious self-defining activities is different. Here the costs and benefits of protecting personal autonomy are not so one-sided, and religious believers will bear some of the costs of nonbelievers' autonomous decisions just as nonbelievers will bear some of the costs intrinsic to protecting religious liberty. We trust the results of the political and the constitutional process more when the costs of liberty are spread more broadly.

Finally, we must ask how the judicial and political process will define the scope of religious freedom if we elect to protect religious freedom primarily because religion is good....

I have little difficulty imagining an insensitive majority concluding that various religious practices and belief systems are unnatural, immoral, sinful, or symptomatic of a psychological disorder. We can see arguments of this kind already in public debates about so-called religious cults.[3] Exactly what protection does Garvey's model provide the minority if the majority can isolate particular faiths or rituals that most people do not practice or understand (and of which many people may be more than a little afraid) and conclude that these practices and beliefs are not good, natural, or psychologically normal enough to constitute real religion? This risk also exists with regard to autonomy rights, but it is more pronounced if the foundation of a right represents the moral worth of the activity.

NOTES

As a result of editing, the notes for this essay have been renumbered. The note number from the original essay or article is shown in parentheses at the end of each citation.

1. Exodus 20:3 (Menorah Press, 1960) ("Thou shalt have no other gods before Me"). (158)

2. See *Smith v. Collin*, 439 U.S. 916 (1978) (Blackmun, J., dissenting from denial of certiorari). (161)

3. See, e.g., *Church of Lukumi Babalu Aye v. City of Hialeah*, 508 U.S. 520 (1993) [(Santeria Afro-Caribbean sect)]. (166)

RELIGIOUS LIBERTY AS LIBERTY

Douglas Laycock

WHY RELIGIOUS LIBERTY?

A. The Problem of Reasons

Contemporary scholars have puzzled over why the Constitution would specially protect religious liberty, as distinguished from liberty in other domains. If one views religion as a silly superstition of no importance, or as a dangerous force that requires tight regulation, or as containing one fundamental and binding truth competing with many falsehoods that lead to individual and collective ruin—and if one fails to learn from history—then constitutional guarantees of religious liberty might indeed seem puzzling or even wrongheaded....

Searching for "the reason" has an extra difficulty with respect to religious liberty, because many people support religious liberty for reasons based in

Douglas Laycock, "Religious Liberty as Liberty," *Journal of Contemporary Legal Issues* 7 (1996): 313, 316–20, 350–51.

their views about religion. These conflicting views about religion cannot be imputed to the Constitution without abandoning the widely held intuition that part of the core content of religious liberty is that government may not adopt some religious beliefs and reject others. The Constitution cannot adopt a Baptist or Deist or Episcopal conception of religious liberty, at least not without a deep paradox. Nor can the Constitution adopt a view of religion as idea or religion as identity; religion plainly includes both.

Moreover, explanations of religious liberty based on beliefs about religion cannot possibly persuade persons who do not hold the same religious beliefs, and so these explanations have little ability to explain or maintain support for religious liberty. To those who do not share the relevant religious belief, "because my religion says so," or "because the Founders' religion said so," is even less persuasive than "because the Constitution says so." To explain the Religion Clauses as a Baptist or Deist or Episcopalian capture is to forfeit their credibility.

B. The Religion-Neutral Case for Religious Liberty

An acceptable explanation of the Religion Clauses must make sense of the ratified text. For the reasons just given, the strongest such explanation would make sense of the ratified text without entailing commitments to any proposition about religious belief. On what theory would the Founders single out the domain of religious choice and commitment for a special guarantee of liberty? The answer seems to me obvious, and while it is not at all illogical, it depends far more on history than on logic. Three secular propositions are sufficient to justify a strong commitment to religious liberty.

First, in history that was recent to the American Founders, governmental attempts to suppress disapproved religious views had caused vast human suffering in Europe and in England and similar suffering on a smaller scale in the colonies that became the United States. The conflict had continued for centuries without producing a victor capable of restoring peace by suppressing all opposition. This is prima facie reason to forever ban all such governmental efforts. Madison argued:

> Torrents of blood have been spilt in the old world, by vain attempts of the secular arm to extinguish Religious discord, by proscribing all difference in Religious opinions. Time has at length revealed the true remedy. Every relaxation

of narrow and rigorous policy, wherever it has been tried, has been found to assuage the disease. The American Theatre has exhibited proofs, that equal and complete liberty, if it does not wholly eradicate it, sufficiently destroys its malignant influence on the health and prosperity of the state.[1]

The negative goal is to minimize this conflict; the affirmative goal is to create a regime in which people of fundamentally different views about religion can live together in a peaceful and self-governing society.

Second, beliefs about religion are often of extraordinary importance to the individual—important enough to die for, to suffer for, to rebel for, to emigrate for, to fight to control the government for. This is why governmental efforts to impose religious uniformity had been such bloody failures. But this is also an independent reason to leave religion to the people who care about it most, which is to say, to each individual and to the groups that individuals voluntarily form or join.

Third, beliefs at the heart of religion—beliefs about theology, liturgy, and church governance—are of little importance to the civil government. Failure to achieve religious uniformity had not led to failure of the state. By the time of the American founding, experience had revealed that people of quite different religious beliefs could be loyal citizens or subjects. The claim here is not that religious beliefs are wholly irrelevant to the government; it may be that some religious beliefs are more conducive than others to behaviors the government legitimately seeks to encourage or require. But this indirect and always debatable government interest in religious beliefs will never make religious beliefs as important to the government as to the individual (the second proposition), and experience showed that government could not impose the religious beliefs it wanted anyway (the first proposition).

This third proposition was the most controversial of the three, and some in the founding generation were not sure it applied to Catholics, or to the hypothetical atheists that occasionally appeared in their rhetoric. Some citizens today continue to believe that atheists are unreliable citizens and that decent government cannot survive without a critical mass of believers. But with increasing religious pluralism, longer experience, and the universalizing logic of legal principle, the law at least has made the point general. It is enough for the state to regulate behavior, not belief; to regulate conduct, not theology or liturgy or church governance. The state could enforce the murder laws in 1791 without agreeing on the proper mode of worship or the proper form of church governance; it can enforce the murder laws today without agreeing on the Ten Commandments, the Sermon on the Mount, the Kantian imperative, or the utilitarian calculus as the best explanation for those laws. It is a sufficient explanation that the People have enacted such a law through constitutional processes and that it violates no limitation on governmental authority enacted by the People through a more authoritative process.

These three propositions are readily inferable from the history of failed governmental attempts to achieve religious uniformity. They are in no sense religious claims; they are testable against the facts of history and the experience of governments and citizens. They are equally accessible to believers and nonbelievers; they are consistent with the most profound belief and with the most profound skepticism.

These three propositions are entirely neutral about the truth or value of any religious belief save one: the third proposition necessarily rejects any belief that the State should or must support religion. But that belief is rejected in the Establishment Clause itself, so it must necessarily be rejected in any justification for the Establishment Clause. Those who believe that religious exercise requires the instruments of government, or that state support is essential or important to continued religious belief, are really arguing for repeal of the Establishment Clause or for its minimalist interpretation.

These three propositions are entirely adequate to explain a special guarantee of religious liberty, in which religion is to be left as wholly to private choice and private commitment as anything can be.[2] Once it is understood that government efforts to control religious belief create conflict and suffering, and that they cannot succeed without the most extraordinary tyranny (and often not even then), any government will abandon such attempts if it is committed to liberty or even if it is committed only to utilitarian avoidance of human suffering. Once it is understood that religion is far more important to individuals than to the government, the same considerations of liberty and utility argue for leaving religion entirely to individuals and their voluntary groups.

C. Some Implications of These Reasons

Most obviously and most powerfully, these three propositions argue for separating the coercive power of government from all questions of religion, so that no religion can invoke government's coercive power and no government can coerce any religious act or belief.

These three propositions argue for presumptively extending this protection to religiously motivated behavior, because attempts to suppress religious behavior will lead to all the problems of conflict and suffering that religious liberty is designed to avoid, and because religious behavior is as likely as religious belief to be of extraordinary importance to individuals. This protection can be only presumptive; sometimes religiously motivated behavior will be sufficiently important to the government to justify suppression. But that is a reason for something like the compelling interest exception; it is not a reason to tell people that they are free to believe their religions but not to practice them....

The principle that government should not coerce religious beliefs or behaviors necessarily entails the proposition that government should not create incentives to change religious beliefs or behaviors—that government should be neutral with respect to religion in all its regulation, taxation, and spending. I have argued elsewhere that this goal is best achieved by substantive neutrality, defined in terms of reducing government incentives to change religious behavior, and not by formal neutrality, defined as the mere absence of religious classifications:

> The religion clauses require government to minimize the extent to which it either encourages or discourages religious belief or disbelief, practice or nonpractice, observance or nonobservance. In this formulation, autonomy and neutrality are mutually reinforcing elements of religious liberty: Government must be neutral so that religious belief and practice can be free. The autonomy of religious belief and disbelief is maximized when government encouragement and discouragement are minimized.[3]...

Secular intellectuals skeptical of religious liberty may argue that other strong personal commitments should have been protected as well. But they were not, for the sufficient reason that other strong personal commitments had not produced the same history. The protected liberty is religious liberty, and although the word "religion" must be construed in light of continuing developments in beliefs about religion, we cannot rewrite the Constitution to say that religious liberty should not receive special protection.

THE PRINCIPAL CONTEMPORARY ISSUES

A. Exemptions for Religious Conduct and Religious Organizations

Laws that restrict religiously motivated conduct or interfere with the autonomy of religious organizations prima facie violate the Free Exercise Clause. The Religious Freedom Restoration Act was an appropriate response to the Supreme Court's unwillingness to enforce the clause [as shown in *Employment Division v. Smith*].

It is common ground that exemptions expand religious liberty. Exemptions are also consistent with substantive neutrality so long as they do not encourage religious belief or practice. Refusal to exempt is not consistent with neutrality, because government regulation is a powerful incentive not to practice one's religion, or to conform it to the government's preferences. Claims for exemptions that align with self-interest are problematic because they create incentives to join the exempted faith, and in practice such claims have not been recognized.

If religious objectors to paying taxes do not have to pay, there is an incentive to adopt the faith that gives rise to the objection. . . .

But with respect to most exemptions, exemptions minimize the incentive effects. Most religious behavior is meaningless or burdensome to nonbelievers. I do not want to have a driver's license without a picture; I would have a harder time cashing checks or proving my identity in other contexts. I do not want to refrain from work on the Sabbath; I am too far behind as it is. I do not want to eat peyote; I would almost certainly throw up. Most exemptions do very little to draw adherents to a faith. But criminal liability or loss of government benefits is a powerful incentive to abandon a faith. Exemptions—treating religion differently—are generally more neutral because they generally minimize government influence on religion.*

---

*The previous two paragraphs were relocated from pp. 350–51 of the original.

NOTES

As a result of editing, the notes for this essay have been renumbered. The note number from the original essay or article is shown in parentheses at the end of each citation.

1. James Madison, *Memorial and Remonstrance Against Religious Establishments* (1785), par. 11, reprinted in *Everson v. Board of Education*, 330 U.S. 1, 69 (1947) (appendix to opinion of Rutledge, J., dissenting). (21)

2. Douglas Laycock, "Formal, Substantive, and Disaggregated Neutrality Toward Religion," *DePaul Law Review* 39 (1990): 993, 1002. (26)

3. Ibid., pp. 1001–1002. (28)

THE VULNERABILITY OF CONSCIENCE: THE CONSTITUTIONAL BASIS FOR PROTECTING RELIGIOUS CONDUCT

CHRISTOPHER L. EISGRUBER AND LAWRENCE G. SAGER

[M]ost modern commentary has proceeded on the assumption that the constitutional status of religious exemptions rises or falls on the degree to which religious practices are constitutionally privileged.... If religiously motivated people are to be exempt from the application of laws that they would otherwise be required to obey, it is assumed, this must be because religion is esteemed by the Constitution in a way that most other human commitments, however intense or laudable, are not....

[But] the paradigm of privilege [i]s deeply misdirecting as a guide to religious liberty in general, and to the problem of religious exemptions in particular....

Christopher L. Eisgruber and Lawrence G. Sager, "The Vulnerability of Conscience: The Constitutional Basis for Protecting Religious Conduct," *University of Chicago Law Review* 61 (1994): 1245, 1252–59, 1262–66, 1282–93, 1296–97.

151

THE CASE AGAINST THE PRIVILEGING VIEW
OF RELIGIOUS EXEMPTIONS

A. The Privileging of Religion Made More Precise: Unimpaired Flourishing

The underlying logic of the privileging view of religious exemptions is this: It is a matter of constitutional regret whenever government prevents or discourages persons from honoring their religious commitments; accordingly, government should act so as to avoid placing religious believers at a substantial disadvantage by virtue of their efforts to conform their conduct to their beliefs. This is the principle of unimpaired flourishing.

The principle of unimpaired flourishing is at the heart of the minority Justices' view in *Smith*, where it sponsored Justice O'Connor's ringing announcement that only governmental interests "of the highest order" could justify interference with religiously motivated conduct.[1] It is also common to the discourse of those commentators who argue for generous religious exemptions. Michael McConnell, for example, holds that "[t]he purpose of free exercise exemptions is to ensure that incentives to practice a religion are not adversely affected by government action."[2]

Unimpaired flourishing...privileges religious commitments over other deep commitments that persons have. Members of our political community are not generally entitled to governmental arrangements that enable them to honor their important commitments without being placed at a substantial disadvantage. If somebody—say, Vincent—is above all committed to his art, and consumes his waking hours in devoted concentration to creating art, he is behaving in a manner that many would approve. Vincent is not, however, entitled in principle to arrangements that spare him the diverse costs of this behavior: Vincent is not entitled to an economic structure that permits him to prosper; Vincent is not entitled to collect unemployment insurance if he is by virtue of his passion unavailable for work; Vincent is not entitled to consume peyote even if, like Coleridge, he does his best work in an altered state of consciousness; Vincent is not entitled to bring toxic paints vital to the full realization of his artistic vision into his locality in the face of local environmental laws prohibiting their possession and use....

[In other words, most theories of religious exemptions rest on the idea of] unimpaired flourishing: they regard state interference with the observance of religious commandments as a constitutional vice that the state must avoid whenever it can do so without imperiling its most basic goals and obligations....

B. Unimpaired Flourishing Applied

As a conception of religious freedom, unimpaired flourishing presents a [serious] normative difficulty. Religious belief need not be founded in reason, guided by reason, or governed in any way by the reasonable. Accordingly, the demands that religions place on the faithful, and the demands that the faithful can in turn place on society in the name of unimpaired flourishing, are potentially extravagant.

Religious belief can direct parents to withhold medical assistance from their children, or adults to withhold such assistance from one another or to refuse such assistance for themselves. It can direct believers to maintain great caches of weapons against Armageddon; to give over their underage children for the sexual gratification of their religious leaders in the meantime; to spend all of their waking hours in arcane study, eschewing all other occupations; to follow dietary regimes that call for refined and expensive foods; or to ingest substances plausibly regarded by secular society as radically poisonous, dangerous, and habituating. Religion can demand sacrifices that range from vows of abject poverty, to the regular undertaking of expensive pilgrimages, to the ritual slaughter of species protected on grounds of civility or threatened extinction. It can underwrite employment practices that secular judgment would regard as grossly exploitative and dictate the subordination of women, persons in particular racial or ethnic groups, or homosexuals. To be at peace with their religious consciences, the faithful may require that public streets be closed to vehicular traffic on the Sabbath; that particular sites be preserved and freely accessible for their holy worship; and even that the basic institutions of their society be pervasively arranged in conformity with their religious precepts.

The potential of religious beliefs to be arbitrarily demanding, to be greedy in their demands on both the individual and the society committed to the unimpaired flourishing of its religiously faithful, is compounded by the possible all-or-nothing quality of religious dictates. In other domains, well-being is generally incremental—having the requirements of well-being partially satisfied is a benefit. But religious demands can be absolute or categorical. They can assume the form: "A, B, and C must all be fully in place or you are condemned to eternal damnation."

The principle of unimpaired flourishing, as a result, commends a vision of a world that is unrecognizable, unattractive, and ultimately incoherent. In this world, the faithful would be licensed to do as their faith requires, with little regard for the consequences as seen from the vantage of secular society. . . .

But, of course, no proponent of the constitutional privileging of religion actually means to take us into this ungainly world. Significantly, almost all judges and commentators who urge something like the principle of unimpaired flourishing nevertheless want collective authority in the United States to remain pretty much as it is; they merely want to find a haven for religiously motivated conduct at the margins of state authority. This produces incoherence of a much more immediate and troubling sort: proponents of unimpaired flourishing are in the unhappy position of offering an unexplainably selective, comparatively modest, practical agenda for reform, on the basis of a sweeping and deeply radical principle of political justice. The result is an analytical scramble. Various limitations are offered, often in combination.[3] Religiously motivated acts that harm others, it is sometimes suggested, may be curtailed by state law, but the state may not interfere with religious believers on paternalistic grounds. . . . Or, it is suggested, secular needs must be balanced against religious needs.

These attempts to rescue unimpaired flourishing from its own logic are unsatisfying. . . .

To this point, we have focused on the unattractive consequences that would follow were we to take the principle of unimpaired flourishing to heart. The difficulty with that principle only deepens when we consider what drives the impulse to treat religious practice in this special and favored way in the first place.

C. The Normative Difficulties of Unimpaired Flourishing

1. The sectarian defect.

In a liberal democracy, the claim that one particular set of practices or one particular set of commitments ought to be privileged (as we have used that term) bears a substantial burden of justification. . . .

Religious believers have available to them one particular justification along these lines: "Our God's commands," they might say, "are the highest commands; we must answer to them in priority to the mundane commands of the State." This is straightforward enough, and might be a good reason for privileging religion in a monistic society of shared religious belief. Note, though, that the constitution would privilege only "our" religion, not religion generally. Our God speaks to (the hypothetical) us with binding normative authority, and nothing more need be said. Our God's authority does not give us a reason for privileging anyone else's religious commitments. Indeed, the sorry world history of religious conflict suggests that one religion's belief system might give it a singularly ferocious reason to impeach the authority of another religion's belief system. Certainly there is nothing in this line of speculation that resonates with the themes of diversity and tolerance that are integral to our constitutional tradition generally and our tradition of religious liberty in particular.

We can remake the religious believer's claim, to turn outward in a reciprocal spirit more suitable to liberal constitutionalism in a plural society: "God's commands are the highest commands. We should recognize that there are other religious groups who believe that their 'God' is the true God, and who take themselves to be bound to the word of their 'God' as we are in fact bound to God's." ...

[But in] a nation with many groups, many values, and many views of the commitments by which a good life is shaped, the shared understanding among some groups that they are each bound by the commandments of a (different) god they believe deserves/demands obeisance is unacceptably sectarian as a basis for the constitutional privileging of religion. Their claim, as a union of groups within a broader, pluralistic society is no different in principle than the sectarian claim of the religious believer we first considered, who reasoned, wholly from within his own religious tradition, that his God was the true, supreme god, and thus the state must permit each believer in the true God to subordinate the state's commands to those of God. As against the artist for whom art is the highest command of life, the activist to whom the pursuit of racial justice is all, or any of us who happen not to be members of the union of the deeply religious, the members of the union have no reason to offer, from within their own beliefs, for the privileging of their commitments that the rest of us lack with regard to our deep commitments.

2. Two nonsectarian strategies.

There are, however, two arguments for the constitutional privileging of religion that do not suffer from this sectarian defect. The first appeals to persons within our political community to recognize—from the outside, in effect—the anguished state of the religious believer who is under state fiat to behave in a way that flatly contradicts the demands of her religion. The second suggests that organized religion enables our society to maintain an important place for the moral, non-self-regarding aspects of life.

One version of the first argument asks us to consider the potential stakes for the religious believer of disobeying her God's commandments. They may be such that it is an understatement to speak of them as matters of life and death; they may be no less than eternal paradise or damnation. We cannot be expected to act as though those are the stakes, of course, but we can appreciate the unhappy state of someone who regards them as the stakes. This seems an unpromising way to put the case. It asks us to assume—in a way that seems especially inappropriate when it comes to matters spiritual—that self-interest rather than conscience is the stronger human drive. It expects us to treat the religious believer's very long-term (possibly abstract, metaphorical) self-interested reasons for obedience as motivationally more powerful than other persons' immediate self-interest and driving passions—the deeply devoted artist, the parent with a hungry child, or the lover overwrought with love, who are driven to disobey the law. Furthermore, it asks us either to treat all religions as having the structure of eternal reward/punishment because some do, or to parse among religions on this peculiar ground....

The better version of this first argument for privileging religion emphasizes mortal conscience rather than eternal consequences. It encourages us to see that the religious believer is in the grip of conscience—a motivation that is at once powerful and laudable—and to regard that circumstance as grounds for excusing her from obedience to laws that force her to choose between her conscience and her well-being at the hands of the state. But while conscience is the better motivational grounds for privileging religion, there remain persuasive objections to the claim. Again, religious conscience is just one of many very strong motivations in human life, and there is no particular reason to suppose that it is likely to matter more in the run of religious lives generally than will other very powerful forces in the lives of both the nonreligious and the religious.

This is not to trivialize religious interests. We have no trouble agreeing with Douglas Laycock when he argues that it would be an error to maintain that "(a) soldier who believes he must cover his head before an omnipresent God is constitutionally indistinguishable from a soldier who wants to wear a Budweiser gimme cap."[4] Likewise, we agree with Michael McConnell that a Saturday work schedule imposes qualitatively different burdens on those who "like to go sailing on Saturdays" and those who "observe the Sabbath" on that day.[5] But these comparisons largely beg the question. Of course, burdens upon religious practice differ from burdens upon tastes in fashion and recreation. Do they also differ from the considerably more weighty burdens imposed by secular commitments to one's family, or by secular moral obligations, or by physical disabilities?

Consider two cases:

(1) Goldman is an army officer. His faith requires him to wear a yarmulke. The yarmulke is inconsistent with the Army uniform. The Army insists that Goldman must resign his commission or comply with the uniform regulation. The Army relies entirely on its interest in uniform appearance; it does not contend that Goldman's obligation to wear the yarmulke will in any other way impair his performance.[6]

(2) Collar is an army officer. He has a rare skin disorder on his neck that prevents him from wearing a tie. Army uniform regulations require that all officers wear ties on certain occasions. The Army insists that Collar must resign his commission or comply with the regulation. The Army relies entirely on its interest in uniform appearance; it does not contend that Collar's disability will in any other way impair his performance.

Should we regard Goldman's interests as more weighty than Collar's? Does the Army have a constitutional obligation to accommodate Goldman's religious burden if it accommodates Collar's disability, or vice-versa? To maintain that the Constitution privileges religion, we would have to uncover some ground for constitutionally favoring Goldman's interests over Collar's, a ground that is not impermissibly sectarian or partisan; and that is precisely what is lacking in the case for privileging religion.

The second nonsectarian argument for the constitutional privileging of religion appeals to our desire as a society to remain alive to the moral, non-self-regarding aspects of life, and sees organized religion as a taproot of this vital aspect of human flourishing. But while religion sponsors the highest forms of community, compassion, love, and sacrifice, one need only look around the world, or probe our own history, to recognize that it also sponsors discord, hate, intolerance, and violence. Religion is enormously varied in the demands it places on the faithful....

We must remember that the claim for the laudability of religious commitment is offered as a reason for exempting behavior that defies otherwise valid general laws. This simple fact is prejudicial to abstract arguments for the virtues of religious conscience. If we believe in a given case that the polity's decision to enact a law was sound, the claim that a conscientious defiance of this same law is virtuous requires some moral gymnastics. There are situations in which our own ambivalence or distaste toward the necessary makes it possible to hold these two views simultaneously. The draft is a good example. We go to war with great moral unease. At best, the intentional killing of soldiers and civilians seems justified rather than just. In such a case, we can sensibly believe that the conscientious dissenter is a morally attractive figure, [exemplify]ing the moral regret that we ourselves feel and hope not to lose, even as we conscript thousands and calculate how to destroy our enemy. But this is a special case, and we would be mistaken to extrapolate from it to a general view about religious conscience.

Religions, of course, are by no means the only sources of moral reflection and impulse; nor are moral reflection and impulse the only forms of elevated human activity. These are not small quibbles to be worked out empirically. They go very much to the heart of the objection to privileging religion. A plural democratic society like ours must develop constitutional principles that recognize that a citizen's ability to contribute to the regime does not depend upon membership in any particular religion, or, indeed, upon religiosity at all. To hold otherwise would simply be another way to insist upon the truth of a particular religion, or to deny the truth of secular ethics....

[Such a holding is] inconsistent with our constitutional tradition, which contemplates a modern, pluralistic society, whose members find their identities, shape their values, and live the most valuable moments of their lives in a grand diversity of relationships, affiliations, activities, and passions that share a constitutional presumption of legitimacy....

THE PROTECTION OF MINORITY BELIEF AS A RATIONALE FOR RELIGIOUS EXEMPTIONS

A. A New Approach: Equal Regard

We advocate a new approach to religious exemptions, founded on protection rather than privilege. Protection can explain and justify the distinct status of religion in our constitutional tradition, offer a workable and attractive approach to religious exemptions, and—surprisingly—make some sense out of the patchwork of precedent regarding religious exemptions.

History provides ample evidence that religious distinctions inspire the worst sorts of political oppression. Post-Reformation religious strife and the religious persecution from which many colonial settlers fled come immediately to our minds. But we should not imagine that we need to look that far; within the memory of many adults, anti-Catholicism and anti-Semitism were rampant in many parts of the United States. The sad history of religious intolerance and the unfortunate sociological truths upon which it rests invite and demand the constitutional protection of minority religious beliefs.

In place of the mistaken claim that religion is uniquely valued by the Constitution, an approach based on protection depends upon the special vulnerability of minority religious beliefs to hostility or indifference. Where privilege sponsored the principle of unimpaired flourishing, protection offers the principle of equal regard. Equal regard requires simply that government treat the deep, religiously inspired concerns of minority religious believers with the same regard as that enjoyed by the deep concerns of citizens generally.

Equal regard needs to be on the active agenda of the judiciary because of the confluence of two circumstances. First, for many religious believers, being able to conform their conduct to the dictates of their beliefs is a matter of deep concern. Second, the religious provenance of these strong behavioral impulses makes them highly vulnerable to discrimination by official decision makers. Both of these propositions are widely acknowledged and do not require detailed support here. But the second bears elaboration.

Religious commandments are not necessarily founded on or limited by reasons accessible to nonbelievers; often they are understood to depend on at or covenant and to implicate forces or beings beyond human challenge or comprehension. Religion is often the hub of tightly knit communities, whose habits, rituals, and values are deeply alien to outsiders. At best, this is likely to produce a chronic interfaith "tone deafness," in which the persons of one faith do not easily empathize with the concerns of persons in other faiths. At worst, it may produce hostility, even murderous hatred, among different religious groups.

The axis of antagonism—even with its broad range from indifference to hostility—does not fully capture the subtle pattern of religious vulnerability. From the perspective of some faiths, it is desirable to convert nonbelievers rather than to injure them. Such messianic faiths may have the welfare of the nonbelievers genuinely and fully in mind as they zealously seek converts to the true faith; they may even have the welfare of the nonbelievers fully in mind as they seek to shape the legal regime to discourage or prevent the non-believers from pursuing their own beliefs. Even when conversion is not their aim, dominant faiths (or clusters of faiths) that recognize the value and con-cerns of others may nevertheless use political power to favor themselves....

These nonantagonist variations may be "kinder, gentler" forms of dis-crimination, but they remain stark failures of equal regard. The possibility of nonantagonistic disregard of minority concerns makes religious discrimina-tion particularly subtle and complex. This will be important to bear in mind as we turn to the task of sketching a jurisprudence of equal regard.

B. The General Methodology of a Jurisprudence of Equal Regard

As we shall see, the complexity of religious discrimination calls forth a some-what complex jurisprudential project in the name of equal regard. One conclusion, however, is easily drawn. Wherever else it may lead, equal regard prohibits the state from singling out the practices of minority religions for distinct and disfavored treatment. Cases like *Church of the Lukumi Babalu Aye v. City of Hialeah*[7] are thus easy under an equal-regard regime. [*Lukumi*, which will be discussed throughout the materials, struck down a set of ordinances that forbade Santeria, an Afro-Caribbean sect in Florida, from engaging in its ritual of sacrificing chickens, but allowed animals to be killed in many other situations and manners, including kosher slaughtering practices.] The Hialeah statute's obvious failure of the equal regard test explains why the same Court that divided deeply in *Smith* could readily find the Hialeah statute—which by its terms targeted the ritual slaughter of animals—unconstitutional. But the transparency of the Hialeah case should not mislead us into thinking that more opaque failures of equal regard are somehow acceptable. When the state fails—whether through hate, habit, a misguided impulse to lead others to the true way, or an indifference born of a lack of empathy—to treat the deep concerns of minority believers with the same solicitude as those of mainstream citizens, the judiciary ought to intervene....

Let us consider the general pattern of claims for religious exemptions where the law is not overtly or facially hostile to a particular religious faith. Such claims can arise in many circumstances, but two recurring prototypes are instructive. In the first, the state has a law of general application in place, but has carved out exemptions for those able to claim personal hardship or some other particularized qualification. These special exemption statutes include laws that designate formal categories of beneficiaries and others that invoke functional categories. An example of a formal special exemption is a law prohibiting the consumption of alcohol but permitting the sacramental ingestion of wine; an example of a functional special exemption is the requirement of "good cause" in unemployment compensation regimes for persons who are unable to accept or continue in a particular job.

In the second prototype for constitutional claims, the challenged state law has no provision for exemptions. It is easy to find examples of this flat rule type: the familiar peyote ban in *Smith* is one.

Equal regard requires that the state treat the deep, religiously inspired concerns of minority religious believers with the same regard as that enjoyed by the deep concerns of citizens generally. In either a special exemption or a flat rule case, the equal regard exemption claimant must demonstrate (a) that a general law significantly interferes with some actions motivated by her deep religious commitment; and (b) that had her deep, religiously inspired concerns been treated with the same regard as that enjoyed by the fundamental concerns of citizens generally, she would have been exempted from the reach of the general law. Proposition (b), in turn, can be supported by one of two claims. Either (1) the state has failed to appreciate the gravity of her interest in complying with the commands of her faith; or (2) the state has appreciated the gravity of her interest, but nevertheless has played favorites among different belief systems on sectarian grounds. Each of these last charges requires some elaboration.

To appreciate the gravity of a religious believer's interest in complying with the commands of her faith, the state must adopt the perspective of the believer; it is not at liberty to judge that interest. Equal regard bars the state from disparaging religious interests that seem unreasonable from a secular perspective. So, for example, the state may not defend its refusal to accommodate a religious interest in animal sacrifice by arguing that it is silly or disgusting for people to take a deep interest in slaughtering chickens.

This establishes a limited kind of deference to religious perspectives. The state is further obliged to defer to the perspective of a religious believer with regard to the existence of an interest of great weight within the life of a believer. The state is obliged to treat these deep interests as equal in importance and dignity to the deep religious or secular interests of other persons. The state is not obliged, however, to accept a religious believer's judgment about the importance of her religious interests as compared to the legitimate secular interests of the state. This distinction is crucial to the idea of equal regard: outside religion, the deep interests of individuals figure into but do not override the secular concerns of the state, as we saw with Vincent the artist, whose artistic passions could not override environmental or drug laws. Equal regard insists on parity for religious belief, not privilege. If religious believers could enforce their priorities over the secular concerns of the state, we would be back to unimpaired flourishing in all of its unacceptable extremity.

The state's obligation to avoid sectarian favoritism among the holders of different belief systems bars it from preferring the deep interests of persons of one faith over those of another. The state cannot act on the perception that one faith is true, ennobling, attractive, or somehow congenial, or that another faith is false, debasing, repulsive, or somehow uncongenial. As with the obligation of the state to appreciate the gravity of a religious believer's interests, however, the obligation to avoid favoritism does not prevent the state from acting on its secular interests. So a decision, for example, to bar the importation of a particular animal on the grounds that it is a notorious carrier of a dangerous disease, does not suffer from the vice of favoritism, even though a particular faith regards the animal as sacred and an important part of its religious ceremonies.

To this point, we have been describing the conceptual entailments of equal regard, entailments that address both special exemption and flat rule cases. We now need to explore more concrete, hands-on judicial approaches to religious exemption claims. Here the difference between flat rule and special exemption cases becomes important.

We can begin with special exemption cases and the curious status of *Sherbert* [*v. Verner*[8]] and its progeny. Equal regard offers a principled basis for a distinction the Court has long since backed into but has not fully elaborated; namely, the distinction between flat rule cases like *Smith*, and special exemption cases, at least functional special exemption cases, like *Sherbert*.

State unemployment benefit regimes understandably require that persons be available for work in order to qualify. Inevitably, cases will arise in which putative beneficiaries are unable to accept or continue in a particular job because of special circumstances. [Consider] a worker who develops a nasty allergy to the material she must handle in her job.... So each state, we can imagine, must develop a mechanism for determining whether a disabling circumstance is weighty enough to justify the worker's refusal to accept or continue in a job, yet narrow enough to leave the applicant generally available for work.

Now, we know this about the facts in *Sherbert* and its progeny: the applicants in each of these cases (in three of the cases the applicant observed the Saturday Sabbath, and in one the applicant took himself to be religiously barred from manufacturing munitions) fit the general profile of persons who would be approved for benefits under administrative regimes of the sort we have sketched. That is, they were generally available for work, they had powerful reasons to decline particular jobs, and the range of employment opportunities they had to decline was comparatively narrow. Under these circumstances... it seems perfectly appropriate to worry that ad hoc administrative refusals to treat such religiously motivated applicants as entitled to unemployment benefits represent a failure of equal regard. It also seems appropriate to protect against such failures by applying the compelling state interest test.

The unemployment benefits cases are not unique in this respect. Not terribly long ago, Jewish synagogues and Catholic churches were often denied planning permission in Protestant suburbs. We can well expect that Muslims, some orthodox Jewish groups, and various other sects will encounter comparable difficulties in locating places of worship and schools. The processing of applications for special use permits and other comparable interactions between municipalities and nonmainstream religious groups may well lend themselves to the *Sherbert* approach.

In all the cases just discussed, the state has defined a functional exemption category: the exemption is available to claimants who meet certain requirements (in the unemployment cases, persons generally available for work but unable to take a particular job for personal reasons; in the zoning cases, noncommercial educational and civic institutions with a reason for wishing to build in a residential neighborhood). In principle, the exemption embraces religious interests along with secular ones. Once we know that a particular claimant fits the relevant profile but has nevertheless been denied accommodation, we may appropriately insist that the state prove that it has honored the principle of equal regard.

Matters are even simpler if a religious claimant demands the benefit of a formal, rather than functional, exemption. At best, the formal category would be a proxy for an unarticulated functional category. At worst, the category would reflect an objectionable discrimination like that rejected by the Santeria case [(*Lukumi*)]. If, for example, a state liquor control ordinance were to exempt the sacramental use of liquor by some sects but not others, the Constitution would require generalizing the exemption.

Less easy to resolve are flat-rule cases, of which *Smith* is a good example. In *Smith*, Oregon's prohibition on the use of peyote was a flat ban, applicable to everyone; there was no exemption procedure and hence no [c]ircumstance that presumptively qualified for exemption. The question posed by equal regard is whether the state's refusal to accommodate the sacramental needs of the Native American Church represented a failure to take the deep interests of the members of the church as seriously as well-recognized secular interests or the interests of adherents to mainstream religions. The question can be posed counterfactually: if strong secular needs (medical uses, for example) or mainstream religious needs had required exception to the peyote ban, would Oregon have made such exceptions?...

Smith and like cases will require exactly this sort of a case-by-case approach, in which evidence of the failure of equal regard is laid on the table and evaluated. In *Smith* itself, the evidence was cloudy at best. Oregon, like many states, made exceptions to its alcohol laws for the sacramental use of wine, but the social implications of sacramental wine and sacramental peyote may be very different. Nine other states and the federal government have made exceptions for the sacramental use of peyote, however, and we are a sufficiently national culture to see in this fact some evidence that such an exception would be reasonable in Oregon as well. That reasonability, coupled with the latitude mainstream religions enjoy to consummate their sacraments, argues for finding a failure of equal regard. *Smith*, we believe, could have plausibly come out either way on a case-by-case equal regard inquiry....

C. Equal Regard and the Special Case of Secular Claimants

A special case that fits imperfectly with our analysis thus far is that of secular claims of conscience.... For our purposes, a person is in the grip of conscience when an ethical tug toward doing the right thing becomes a central, dominating feature of her motivation and self-identity. And, for our purposes, the line between secular and religious conscience is roughly this: religious conscience is crucially dependent on schemes of fact and value (epistemologies) that are private in the sense that they do not depend upon their conformity to generally accepted tests of truth or widely shared perceptions of value; secular conscience, in contrast, appeals to a public epistemology that depends on generally accepted tests of truth and widely shared perceptions of value.

Equal regard, of course, is a symmetrical principle, and applies to secular as well as sectarian concerns. But it does not follow that the enforcement of equal regard as it applies to secular conscience is appropriately on the agenda of the judiciary. After all, in principle, Vincent the artist is entitled to have his deep, artistically inspired concerns treated by the state with the same regard as that enjoyed by the deep concerns of citizens generally; but it does not follow that his entitlement should be judicially enforced as an element of constitutional doctrine. As a judicially enforced constitutional principle, equal regard must be justified by vulnerability to discrimination.

Although our focus thus far has been on the vulnerability of minority religious faiths to discrimination, secular beliefs that take the form of deep commitments of conscience are also distinctly vulnerable to discrimination. Our society is sufficiently religious to make the irreligious themselves targets of discrimination, either by those offended by atheism or by those who sympathize only with religious claims of conscience. Understandably, it is easier for some to associate a passionate conscientious commitment that is markedly out of step with general sentiments in the society—as a claim for exemption from an otherwise valid law would entail—with an eccentric religious command than with a moral claim purporting to apply to all right-thinking persons. The conscientious-objection cases from the Vietnam War era illustrate this sort of discrimination: Congress legislated an exemption that, until modified by the Supreme Court's therapeutic construction, accommodated religious pacifists but not secular ones.[9]

There is an additional reason for including the enforcement of equal regard toward secular commitments of conscience within the domain of judicial responsibility. Once we have placed the protection of religious conscience within that domain, the constitutional demand that diverse belief systems be treated even-handedly makes it inappropriate for the judiciary to parse among claimants on the basis of their metaphysics. Imagine two versions of *Thomas* [a case in which the applicant was denied unemployment benefits for refusing a job]. The first involves Thomas himself, a Jehovah's Witness whose religious scruples make it impossible for him to manufacture tank turrets. The second involves "Secular Thomas," a pacifist who is in all respects identical to the real Thomas, except that his pacifism is secular in character. A constitutional jurisprudence that permitted intervention on behalf of one Thomas but not the other would be unacceptable.

While the judicial protection of conscience appropriately extends to secular as well as religious claimants, the picture changes in one important respect with the move to secular claimants. The protection of religious conscience requires that the state treat religious belief as a "black box"; for purposes of assessing the impact of a sincerely held scheme of religious belief upon the believer, the ultimate truth or the reasonability of the scheme is beyond the constitutional competence of the state. This is implicit in the requirement of equal regard that the state defer to the perspective of a religious believer as to the existence of an interest of great weight within her life; it is a function of the epistemically distinct, closed logic of religious belief.

With secular claims of conscience, however, the believer and the state in principle share a common epistemic foundation. For that reason, the state may legitimately reflect upon and respond to the reasonability of the secular claimant's conscientious commitments. Reasonability here speaks not so much to the plausibility of a given belief, as to the elevation of that belief to a dominant position with regard to motivation and self-identity.

The importance of this becomes clear if we consider two hypothetical cases that might arise under Indiana's unemployment compensation scheme. The first case involves "Secular Thomas," whom we met three paragraphs back. The second case involves claimants who are members of a union. After being laid off work at a factory, both Secular Thomas and the union members are offered jobs as replacement workers when their former colleagues go on strike. The union workers refuse the jobs because they believe, on secular grounds, that it would be immoral to cross the picket lines established by their friends. Secular Thomas refuses the job due to his conscientious objection to the production of armaments. Indiana review officers determine that "Secular Thomas" and the union sympathizers refused work without good cause. Can these claimants invoke the theory proposed here to challenge Indiana's decision?

"Secular Thomas" has the stronger case. Even those who justify military action usually do so only in the face of great anguish and regret. The idea of a just war involves high moral stakes and many imponderables. We may accordingly think it reasonable for "Secular Thomas" to build his moral life around absolute pacifist principles, even if we disagree with those principles and even if by doing so Thomas renders himself incapable of complying with certain public norms (such as those that support the defense industry). Labor law issues have, by contrast, a more economic focus and a less immediate connection to matters of life and death. The stakes are lower and the imponderables less profound. It is possible, but not likely, that we would deem union sympathy to be reasonably constitutive of moral identity in the same way that pacifism is....

From this perspective, the question is not whether the union workers are right about their moral obligations. The question is instead the character of the injury that reasonable workers strongly committed to union solidarity would suffer if they were to defer to society's contrary assessment of those obligations. If the state were to conclude that the quality of this injury does not rise to that of a serious medical allergy, it is not clear that a court should overturn that judgment....

The openness of claims of secular conscience to a public standard of reasonableness is an important gloss on our earlier observations about ... Secular Thomas.... [I]t would indeed be inappropriate for a court to protect the real Thomas and not Secular Thomas. But these observations cannot be generalized to the full run of conscientious secular claimants; they are specific to the (presumably substantial) subset of claimants whose conscientious commitments are reasonable.

NOTES

As a result of editing, the notes for this essay have been renumbered. The note number from the original essay or article is shown in parentheses at the end of each citation.

1. *Smith*, 494 U.S. 895 (O'Connor, J., concurring). (28)

2. [See McConnell excerpt in this book, p. 66.] (29)

3. [Quoting various articles by Professor McConnell.] (31)

4. Douglas Laycock, "The Remnants of Free Exercise," *Supreme Court Review* (1990): 1, 11. (34)

5. Michael W. McConnell, "Religious Freedom at the Crossroads," *University of Chicago Law Review* (1992): 115, 125. (35)

[6. See *Goldman v. Weinberger*, 475 U.S. 503 (1986) (rejecting Capt. Goldman's free exercise claim).]

7. 508 U.S. 520 (1993). (75)

[8. 374 U.S. 398 (1963).]

9. See *United States v. Seeger*, 380 U.S. 163 (1965). (89)

Chapter 5

DEFINING "RELIGION"

EDITOR'S INTRODUCTION: DEFINITIONS IN THE CASE LAW

Closely related to the question whether religious conduct should be exempt from law, when secular-motivated conduct is not, is the question whether the definition of "religion" in the First Amendment might extend beyond traditional theistic beliefs to encompass nontheistic, or secular, forms of conscience. For decades the Supreme Court defined religion in terms of theistic beliefs and duties. In 1890, it spoke of "one's views of his relations to his Creator, and to the obligations they impose of reverence for his being and character, and of obedience to his will." *Davis v. Beason*, 133 U.S. 333, 342. In a dissent in *Macintosh v. United States*, 283 U.S. 605, 633–34 (1931), Chief Justice Hughes defined religion as "belief in a relation to God involving duties superior to those arising from any human relation."

Later, however, the Court responded to the increase in nontheistic world views by broadening the definition. In *Torcaso v. Watkins*, 367 U.S. 488 (1961), it struck down a state law requiring officeholders to declare belief in God. The Court reasoned that the law unconstitutionally favored religions believing in a deity over religions that that did not, including Buddhism, Taoism, Ethical Culture, and Secular Humanism.

The Court also broadened the definition of religion in the statute exempting objectors to military service, in response to nontheistic objectors to the Vietnam War. The statutory exemption, which Congress had already expanded in 1940 beyond familiar pacifist denominations, protected those conscientiously opposed to participation in war "by reason of religious training and belief." 50 U.S.C. § 456(j). Religious belief was still defined in apparently theistic terms, however: "an individual's belief in a relation to a Supreme Being involving duties superior to those arising from any human relation, but not including essentially political, sociological, or philosophical views or a merely personal moral code." But in 1965, in *United States v. Seeger*, 380 U.S. 163, the Court held that this definition covered an objector who rejected dependence on a Creator for a guide to morality and who had a "belief in and devotion to goodness and virtue for their own sakes, and a religious faith in a purely ethical creed." Quoting expansive modern conceptions of religion like that of theologian Paul Tillich—who defined religion in terms of one's "ultimate concern" or "source of being"—the Court held that the exemption encompassed "a sincere and meaningful belief which occupies in the life of its possessor a place parallel to that filled by the God of those admittedly qualifying for the exemption 380 U.S. 176, 187 (quoting Paul Tillich, *The Shaking of the Foundations* [1948], p. 57).

Next, in *Welsh v. United States*, 398 U.S. 333 (1970), a four-member plurality of the Court stretched the language further to protect a claimant who had crossed the word "religious" from his application, had formed his beliefs through readings in "history and sociology," and grounded his objection substantially on "public policy considerations" such as the wastefulness of human and material resources from military endeavors. Nevertheless, four Justices found him to be religious, since his beliefs "function as a religion in his life." The exemption of section 6(j) was held to extend to "those whose consciences, spurred by deeply held moral, ethical, or religious beliefs, would give them no rest or peace if they allowed themselves to become a part of an instrument of war." Ibid., p. 340, 344.

Justice Harlan joined the result in *Welsh*, but argued that the plurality had over-stretched the statutory definition. Instead, he said, the reason to exempt Welsh was that it would violate the Establishment Clause to differentiate religious objectors from nonreligious objectors guided by "an inner ethical voice" that generated the same "intensity of moral conviction" against war. Ibid., pp. 357–58 (concurring in the judgment). Harlan's opinion, and the breadth of the plurality's definition, led many commentators to conclude that the Court was really driven by concerns that it would be constitutionally improper to treat religion differently from deeply held secular moral views (see Chapter 4 for discussion).

The *Seeger-Welsh* definition technically applied only to the draft statute, not the First Amendment, and since then the Court has not revisited the issue. But in a more recent case, a federal appeals judge, Arlin Adams, set forth a three indicia of whether a set of ideas are sufficiently analogous to familiar faiths to be defined as religious:

1. First, do the ideas deal with "ultimate" question such as the "meaning of life and death, [or] man's role in the Universe"?
2. Are the ideas "comprehensive," rather than "confined to one question or one moral teaching"?
3. Are there "formal, external, or surface signs" such as "formal services, ceremonial functions, the existence of clergy, structure and organization, efforts at propagation, observation of holidays," or other features associated with traditional religions? (Such signs, Adams emphasized, are "not determinative...by their absence" but may support a conclusion of religious status.) *Malnak v. Yogi*, 592 F. 3d U.S. 197, 207–10 (3d Cir. 1979) (concurring opinion).

RELIGIOUS LIBERTY AS LIBERTY

DOUGLAS LAYCOCK

DEFINING "RELIGION"

What is "religion" within the meaning of the Religion Clauses? To avoid incoherence the answer must be that "religion" is any set of answers to religious questions, including the negative and skeptical answers of atheists, agnostics, and secularists.

I have argued that the most fundamental reason for religious liberty is to avoid conflict over the answers to religious questions, to enable people of fundamentally different views about religion to live together in peace and self-governance. It is utterly irrelevant to that purpose which answers to religious questions are in conflict. "What is the nature of God and what does He/She want for us?" is the fundamental religious question, and any answer to that question is inherently a religious proposition. "No God exists and this imaginary construct

Douglas Laycock, "Religious Liberty as Liberty," *Journal of Contemporary Legal Issues* 7 (1996): 313, 326–33, 335–37.

wants nothing for us" is a belief about religion. It is not merely a descriptive statement about religion, such as an anthropologist might make, or a scholar of comparative religion. Rather, it is an affirmation of belief, capable of generating commitment and even lifelong activism on behalf of the cause.

The emergence of a vocal nontheistic minority in a predominantly theistic society causes serious social conflict. If the government is allowed to take sides, the two sides will fight to control the government, and the government will disapprove of, discriminate against, or suppress the losers. The most fundamental religious conflict in the United States today is between those who have abandoned theistic belief or accommodated their theism to contemporary secular values, and those who have not....

Each side has its passionate advocates. Many traditional theists genuinely believe that morality can have no secure basis unless founded on God's law; many nontheists are equally certain that religious faith is like reading entrails or denying the Holocaust and that morality can have no secure basis unless founded on reason.... These are the sides in the much discussed culture wars. Any interpretation is wrong if it amounts to a claim that the Religion Clauses award victory to one side or the other.

The second and third [purposes of religious freedom] are also applicable to nontheists. Atheistic and agnostic beliefs will be very important to many individuals who hold such beliefs; these people will define themselves partly in reaction to the strongly held theistic beliefs of others. And these beliefs are of little importance to government if both theists and nontheists can be loyal citizens....

The resistance to this conclusion seems to me partly linguistic and partly strategic. The linguistic argument is that the word "religion" has traditionally been used to refer only to affirmative answers to the great religious questions; atheism, agnosticism, and secularism have been thought of not as religion, but as the opposite of religion. This description of usage is accurate as far as I know in the Founders' time, when the question could hardly have arisen; this description of usage is mostly accurate in this century, but not entirely so.

John Dewey and the first Humanist Manifesto presented humanism as a new religion to supersede traditional religions thought to have become unconvincing. The [Manifesto] warned that "There is a great danger of a final, and we believe fatal, identification of the word religion with doctrines and methods which have lost their significance and which are powerless to solve the problem of human living in the Twentieth Century."[1] [It] then set out fifteen "theses of religious humanism"; these theses included explicit rejection of creation, theism, and "supernatural guarantees of human values." Searching for a new definition of religion, the drafters came up with the wholly unworkable proposition that "Religion consists of those actions, purposes, and experiences which are humanly significant."... [Similarly, the] Encyclopedia of American Religion lists a "liberal family" of religions that includes the Unitarian Universalist Association, the American Humanist Association, the American Ethical Union, American Atheists, and others.

Eventually the religious right began to argue that secular humanism is a religion and that it is established in the schools, and the organized humanist movement began to respond that it is not a religion after all....

[I] do not believe that secular humanism has been established in the schools. Secular humanism offers explicit negative answers to the basic theological questions, but I know of no case in which schools have taught those answers. But certainly we can imagine a school that did teach those answers. We can imagine a government that established atheism, and even think of real examples; the Soviet Union did it.

If atheism is not a religion for constitutional purposes, such an establishment would be perfectly constitutional.... [T]here is no Establishment Clause with respect to secular ideas. If atheism is just a secular idea, government would be free to promote atheism to the same extent that it has ever promoted any other secular idea—say the war effort in World War II, or civil rights during the [1960s]. Government could teach atheism in the schools, promote atheism in the mass media, subsidize the American Atheists and a network of local chapters, and ridicule God as the opiate of the masses. The only sensible interpretation is that this would be an establishment of religion—an establishment of a certain set of views about religion, of a certain set of answers to the fundamental religious questions....

[Turning from establishment to free exercise issues:] The law should recognize nontheistic answers to religious questions as religion for constitutional purposes and for RFRA purposes. And the law should provide parallel protections for theistic and nontheistic beliefs about religion for as far as the parallels can be reasonably extended. Government should be neutral among these beliefs, endorsing none of them and taking no position on the truth or value of any of them.... The Constitution and RFRA should protect the autonomy of atheist, agnostic, and humanist organizations, just as they protect the autonomy of churches; they should protect conduct motivated by disbelief in

God, if any there be, just as they protect conduct motivated by more traditional religious beliefs.

Most controversial, but essential to the pursuit of religious neutrality, the
law should protect nontheists' deeply held conscientious objection to compliance with civil law to the same extent that it protects the theistically motivated conscientious objection of traditional believers. *United States v. Seeger*
and *Welsh v. United States* were rightly decided; they implement policies at the
core of religious liberty. The law cannot protect the pursuit of all personal
commitments or obligations, or all disagreements with the policy or prudence
of political decisions.... What the law can do is protect those moral obligations of nontheists that are functionally equivalent to the protected moral
obligations of theists....

[Laycock then criticizes] the argument that nontheistic objectors cannot
be protected [because nontheism is not "religion"] and so it is discriminatory
to protect theistic objectors [i.e., religious exemptions are improper]. This
argument accepts my claim that neutrality is a central purpose of the Religion
Clauses, and it accepts my claim that theistic and nontheistic answers to religious questions are essentially parallel and entitled to equal treatment. But it
pursues neutrality at the expense of liberty; it repudiates everyone's substantive liberty to exercise a religion rather than extend that liberty from the more
familiar case of theistic conscientious objectors to the parallel case of nontheistic conscientious objectors.

This repudiation of the substantive right to exercise a religion is perverse
in terms of liberty and perverse in terms of human suffering. A principal
argument for the repudiation is to avoid the intangible indignity to nontheists
of knowing that they are ineligible for exemptions available to some theists.
...If exemptions were eliminated, the nontheistic conscientious objectors
would still have to comply with the laws to which they object. They would be
no better off, except that they would no longer feel slighted. The proposed
cost of eliminating this intangible indignity is tangible and vastly disproportionate to the gain: believers whose religion forbids compliance with certain
laws would have to abandon religious behaviors of profound importance to
them, or go to jail, or expatriate, or rebel against the government—even if the
burdensome law serves no particularly important government interest. On the
free exercise side, the argument that nontheistic answers to religious questions
are not religion sacrifices liberty in pursuit of a dog-in-the-manger version of
neutrality....

This perverse combination of results cannot be justified on the mere ground that the Founders did not think to consider atheism a religion. We do know that in the case where they thought most explicitly about disbelief, they protected it—in the Test Oath Clause. This protection did not go unnoticed; it was a point of some controversy in the state ratifying conventions. Other models were available in state constitutions; South Carolina provided that there could be no oaths except for monotheism and belief in a future state of rewards and punishments. But the federal Constitution's prohibition on test oaths is absolute.

More fundamentally, the Founders knew that the principal antagonists in religious conflicts varied from time to time and place to place. They knew about Christians and Muslims in the Crusades, Christians and Jews in the Spanish Inquisition, Catholics and Protestants in Reformation Europe, Anglicans and Puritans in the English Civil War, Episcopalians and Baptists in Virginia, Congregationalists and Baptists in Massachusetts. They knew that the immediate combatants were typically a religious movement on one side and a government on the other.... The identity of the factions did not change the central problem; the Founders' principle had to cover future religious conflicts whatever the factional alignment....

The Founders undoubtedly did not anticipate the current alignment of forces, in which traditional Protestants, Catholics, and Jews maintain their distinct traditions while making common cause against the forces of secularism. But the Religion Clauses speak to this conflict and can still serve to mediate it, helping these antagonists like others before them to live together in a peaceful and self-governing society. The clauses cannot serve this function if one side in the central conflict is defined as a religion and the other side is not....

With respect to the nontheistic objector, the challenge is to identify that cluster of beliefs that are analogous to the cluster of beliefs we recognize as religious in the case of adherents to traditions that we can all agree are religions. Beliefs about the nonexistence of God are plainly analogous to the theist's belief in God's existence....

The nontheist's belief in transcendent moral obligations—in obligations that transcend his self-interest and his personal preferences and which he experiences as so strong that he has no choice but to comply—is analogous to the transcendent moral obligations that are part of the cluster of theistic beliefs that we recognize as religious. The derivation of these beliefs may be murky,... but these beliefs and the sources from which the nontheist derived them are serving the same functions in his life as the equivalent moral beliefs and sources of derivation serve for theists. The nontheist may experience natural law or the equality of all humans as "a transcendent authority prior to and beyond the authority of civil government,"[2] just as the theist experiences divine command or religious tradition. An individual's religious beliefs may evolve from theism to deism to modernism to resymbolized Christianity to humanism to agnosticism to atheism. This evolution is itself an exercise of religion; it is a series of religious choices or of shifting religious commitments. The state should not draw a line across this evolutionary path; it should not decree that anyone who crosses the line forfeits his right to conscientious objection and loses protection for his deepest moral commitments. Such a line would not be consistent with either liberty or neutrality.

Of course judges may draw such a line despite its incoherence. All that should follow is that nontheism would be outside the Religion Clauses and outside RFRA. The scope of protection for religions inside the Clauses and inside RFRA should not be changed, lest the core of religious liberty be determined by anomalous cases at the margin.

Consistently for decades, 95 percent of Americans have said they believe in God or a Universal Spirit. This number includes people whose beliefs are modernist, attenuated, or unconventional; it includes most people on both sides of the culture wars.... These 95 percent will be able to state any conscientious objection to government policy in theistic terms, so their moral beliefs will qualify as religious under theistic definitions.

The problem of avowed nontheists is statistically marginal; judicial refusal to protect the 5 percent should not become the excuse for withdrawing protection from the 95 percent. A judge who says that "religion" in the First Amendment means theism cannot then say that special protection for theism violates the Establishment Clause because it discriminates against the 5 percent he refuses to protect. I would prefer liberty and neutrality for all, but if forced to choose between liberty and neutrality for 95 percent, or liberty for none and neutrality for all, the constitutional choice is easy. The neutrality of universal suppression is not the constitutional vision.

NOTES

As a result of editing, the notes for this essay have been renumbered. The note number from the original essay or article is shown in parentheses at the end of each citation.

1. "Humanist Manifesto I," *New Humanist* 6, no. 3 (1933), reprinted in Corliss Lamont, *The Philosophy of Humanism*, 7th ed. (1990), p. 285. (64)

2. The phrase is from McConnell [see excerpt, p. 66 of this book]. But he would reject the application. (100)

GOD IS GREAT, GARVEY IS GOOD: MAKING SENSE OF RELIGIOUS FREEDOM

MICHAEL S. PAULSEN

[Professor Paulsen bases his definition of religion on John Garvey's thesis (see pp. 121–34 of this book)]: that religious liberty exists to protect religion, and that the reason religion is protected is because it was understood (by the founding generation, at least—and their understanding should control interpretation of the texts they wrote and enacted) to be something uniquely important and valuable in its own right, not merely one instantiation of personal autonomy. Religion was understood to be intrinsically important and valuable in a way distinct from mere secular claims to nonreligious personal ethics.

Constitutional law theorists have made a cottage industry out of trying to craft a constitutional definition of religion that would validate the liberal idea. None has improved on the operational definition supplied by the Virginia Declaration of Rights (and borrowed by Madison in the *Memorial and Remon-*

Michael S. Paulsen, "God is Great, Garvey is Good: Making Sense of Religious Freedom," *Notre Dame Law Review* 72 (1997): 1597, 1620–23.

strance Against Religious Assessments): religion refers to "the duty which we owe to our Creator and the manner of discharging it."[1]

This definition has a good originalist claim to superiority over the various modern ones offered by legal scholars (and by the Supreme Court, as a matter of statutory construction, in *Seeger* [the first Vietnam draft case]). It is simple and straightforward. It makes sense. In all likelihood it closely mirrors the common understanding of religion at the time the First Amendment was adopted. Indeed, it probably mirrors the ordinary understanding of religion today. It includes more than just Christianity, Judaism, and Islam, but it is probably closely tied to theism of some sort (including deism). Most clearly, it involves some notion of an extra-human, transcendent being, entity, or force that is responsible for the world's existence and human existence, that created the world by conscious design, and that may impose duties and responsibilities on humankind. Religion, in the constitutional sense of the word (and in the ordinary sense of the word), is something more than just the projection of an individual's inner sense of self, value, ethics, or morals, or of a social, political, or moral philosophy that involves no such transcendent reality or creative force. Religion, in short, involves some conception of God.

There is only one thing wrong with this definition: it is illiberal. It sacrifices progressive inclusivity for historical fidelity. The "just war" Roman Catholic has a prima facie claim to conscientious objector status, but the agnostic secular humanist does not get in the door. Welsh certainly loses, and Seeger probably loses too. Most Native American religious practices qualify and nearly all traditional Western religious traditions do as well, but Buddhism is a tough case. In this sense, the originalist definition may be (despite its other obvious advantages) too much for liberal society to bear.

There are three responses. The first is that religious obligation is qualitatively different from spiritual or philosophical systems that involve no conception of a transcendent Creator, God. For the believer, the nature of the obligation is stronger. At the risk of being reductionist: the personal ethical individual who objects to war but is forced to bear arms has not been true to his own principles; the religious believer who has been forbidden by God to bear arms against his fellow man, but does so anyway, risks eternal damnation and the fires of hell. That is a big difference. To the committed atheist or dogmatic relativist who then counters that the religious believer's convictions are "all in his head" (as if to imply either that they are made-up or evidence of psychological disease), the rejoinder is that that is exactly the sort of judgment the religion clauses forbid government to make. If government is to be truly neutral as between these two systems of belief, it must take each on its own terms. And taken on their own terms, religion is qualitatively different from secular conscience. [W]e must assume that this claim is every bit as real for the believer as it is crazy in the mind of the secularist. To deny that religion is qualitatively different, and that the burden on sincere religious adherents of being compelled to act contrary to their faith is different and more severe than that imposed on individuals compelled to act contrary to their personal, non-religious conscience, is to stand the First Amendment on its head.

The above provides context for the second response to the liberal objection, which otherwise might seem wooden and harsh. That is, that the text, interpreted according to its original, common, public meaning, protects religion and not secular conscience. Historical evidence shows that this was either the product of a deliberate choice to exclude secular conscience or because of a general understanding that "conscience" meant an objection based upon religious doctrine or discipline. [Citing McConnell's evidence, pp. 95–96 of this book.] Text and historical evidence of original meaning should settle the matter. If this seems illiberal today, that is unfortunate, but irrelevant to the task of textual interpretation of the constitutional provision the framers wrote.

It is true that this approach does not allow for the meaning of the word "religion" in the First Amendment to "grow." But if the words of the Constitution are permitted to change with the circumstances, the word "religion" legitimately may shrink (as "free exercise" has) with the times. Once text and original meaning are abandoned as constraints on constitutional interpretation, all bets are off. *Employment Division v. Smith* is as good an interpretation as any other.

For many, textual arguments are never satisfactory. But there is a third rejoinder to the liberal objection, namely, the practical argument that "freedom" cannot sustain as its object all possible claims of human conscience. Claims of secular conscience only have the result of dragging down claims of religious conscience. That may indeed be the objective, when all is said and done. Loading up the Free Exercise Clause with the poison pill of equal accommodation of nonreligious claims may be designed to tear down genuine free exercise of religion claims, because nontheists find such claims an affront to their sensibilities. But that should give away the game: the effort to append nonreligious conscience to religious claims is an effort (deliberate or not) to water down the Free Exercise Clause, not to enforce it.

NOTE

As a result of editing, the note for this essay has been renumbered. The note number from the original essay or article is shown in parentheses at the end of each citation.

1. Virginia Declaration of Rights, art. 16, quoted in *Everson v. Board of Education*, 330 U.S. 1, 64 (1947) (in case appendix). (58)

Chapter 6

FREE EXERCISE UNDER CURRENT DOCTRINE

FREE EXERCISE IS DEAD, LONG LIVE FREE EXERCISE! *SMITH, LUKUMI,* AND THE GENERAL APPLICABILITY REQUIREMENT

Richard F. Duncan

I. Introduction

The Free Exercise Clause is the Mark Twain of Constitutional Law, because the recent report of its death "was an exaggeration." According to the conventional wisdom in the community of First Amendment scholars, in *Employment Division v. Smith* the Supreme Court "abandoned" its longstanding commitment to protecting the free exercise of religion and "created a legal framework for persecution"[1] of religious dissenters. It is certainly true that under *Smith* the general rule seems to be that government may prohibit what religion requires or require what religion prohibits....

Richard F. Duncan, "Free Exercise is Dead, Long Live Free Exercise! *Smith, Lukumi,* and the General Applicability Requirement," *University of Pennsylvania Journal of Constitutional Law* 3 (2001): 850, 853–56, 859–66, 869, 872–74, 876–81.

Although the general rule of *Smith* thus permits government to prohibit the free exercise of religion, the Court has recognized a number of exceptions that continue to protect religious dissenters under a compelling interest test. Most significantly, *Smith* applies only when government incidentally burdens religiously motivated behavior by means of "a 'valid and neutral law of general applicability.'" As the Court subsequently emphasized in *Church of the Lukumi Babalu Aye v. Hialeah*, "a law burdening religious practice that is not neutral or not of general application must undergo the most rigorous of scrutiny."[2] Thus, the key to understanding the Constitution's protection of religious liberty in the post-*Smith* world is to locate the boundary line between neutral laws of general applicability and those that fall short of this standard.

The purpose of this article is to analyze and theorize about the general applicability standard and its impact on the free exercise of religion. At the end of the day, I will argue that free exercise is alive and well in the wake of *Smith* and (particularly) *Lukumi.*

II. FREE EXERCISE AT THE MILLENNIUM: *SMITH* AND *LUKUMI*

The Doctrine And Reasoning of *Smith*

In *Smith*, the Supreme Court held that the Free Exercise Clause "does not relieve an individual of the obligation to comply with a 'valid and neutral law of general applicability'" even if the law prohibits conduct that his religion requires or requires conduct that his religion forbids....

[The *Smith* opinion by Justice Scalia] appears to have been determined by a formula that can be stated as follows: Religious Pluralism plus Religious Liberty equals Anarchy. As Scalia explicitly put it, any society that protects religiously motivated conduct under a compelling interest test is "courting anarchy, [and] that danger increases in direct proportion to the society's diversity of religious beliefs, and its determination to coerce or suppress none of them." ... This free-exercise-phobia that animates Scalia's opinion in *Smith* has been described eloquently by Ira Lupu: Behind every free exercise claim is a spectral march; grant this one, a voice whispers to each judge, and you will be confronted with an endless chain of exemption demands from religious deviants of every stripe.[3]

In *Smith*, the voice whispering in Justice Scalia's ear warned him that a strongly protective free exercise doctrine would place at risk not only drug laws but also laws dealing with compulsory military service, payment of taxes, manslaughter, child neglect, compulsory vaccination, traffic regulation, minimum wages, child labor, animal cruelty, environmental protection, and racial equality. In short, the social contract itself might not survive a constitutional rule protecting religiously motivated conduct from governmental restrictions.

William Marshall argues that the results in *Smith* should be applauded because free exercise exemptions for religiously motivated conduct promote "inequality" by creating "a constitutional preference for religious over nonreligious belief systems."[4] According to Marshall, when a court grants a free exercise claim, the effect is to unfairly "insulate religious beliefs from social forces" while "competing secular beliefs...must stand or fall on their own accord."

Both Scalia and Marshall raise legitimate concerns....

[At the same time, though,] a rigid application of the doctrine of *Smith* exposes religious minorities to a substantial risk of persecution and unleashes "the forces of homogenization." In 1791, when the First Amendment was ratified, the size of government was minimal and religious diversity "consisted mostly of Protestant pluralism." Today, however, "the scope of pluralism and the scope of government are both vastly greater." If the Free Exercise Clause is viewed as enacting a zero-sum game between democracy and religious pluralism, we will all lose something of inestimable value. However, there is no reason to think that the lion of democracy cannot lie down in peace with the lamb of religious liberty. The best reading of the free exercise doctrine of *Smith* and its progeny recognizes that a democratic society can indeed coexist with a strong commitment to religious pluralism and tolerance.

Although the general rule of *Smith* allowing government to restrict religious exercise has received much more attention, the most important parts of the decision's doctrine are those creating a number of potentially broad exceptions that explicitly provide the highest degree of protection for religious liberty. These exceptions are now the principal source of constitutional protection for religious liberty, and understanding their existence and development in the post-*Smith* caselaw is therefore of critical importance to the religious freedom community.

The *Smith* Exceptions

Laws that are not Neutral or Generally Applicable

[T]he key issue in religious liberty litigation has become locating the borders of neutrality and general applicability....

There is an infinity of hard cases that lies between an "across-the-board criminal prohibition" [which *Smith* approves] and a law that "specifically directs" a restriction only at religiously motivated behavior [which *Smith* disapproves]. Imagine, for example, three states with different approaches to the prohibition of alcoholic beverages. State A enacts a total prohibition of possession and distribution of alcoholic beverages. State B prohibits only the sacramental use of alcoholic beverages. Finally, the prohibition law enacted in State C is widely applicable, but contains an exception that permits alcoholic beverages to be served with meals at restaurants. How does the opinion in *Smith* inform our analysis when these laws are enforced against churches that use alcoholic wine for the Lord's Supper?

The prohibition laws in State A and State B are easy cases. State A has enacted a neutral and generally applicable law—an "across-the-board" prohibition of alcoholic beverages. Under *Smith*, there is no free exercise claim; Christians are free to believe in the sacrament of Holy Communion, but they may not perform the act of drinking sacramental wine from the cup. State B's prohibition law, however, is unconstitutional because it prohibits alcoholic beverages only when they are used in religious rituals.

Although the first two prohibition laws are thus clearly controlled by *Smith*, the opinion has little to say about laws like State C's prohibition statute.... The law is not specifically directed at sacramental wine, but it is discriminatory in the sense that it permits alcoholic beverages to be served in restaurants but not in churches or anywhere else. Ironically, whenever the law is enforced against a church for providing Communion wine to worshipers, elsewhere in State C gourmands will be permitted to enjoy a carafe of wine with brunch at their favorite local bistro. If State C's prohibition law is constitutional, *Smith's* critics are correct when they lament about the end of religious liberty in America.

Sherbert *Transformed:*
Laws with *"A System of Individual Exemptions"*

Although *Smith* is widely understood as having rejected the free exercise doctrine established in *Sherbert* [*v. Verner*], it is important to remember that *Smith* did not overrule *Sherbert....*

[Instead], *Smith* reclassified *Sherbert* as a case in which strict scrutiny was properly applied because free exercise was unequally burdened by South Carolina's individualized—and thus non-generally-applicable—unemployment compensation process. The South Carolina law was not generally applicable, because an applicant was ineligible for unemployment benefits if the Employment Security Commission made a finding that the applicant had failed without "good cause" to accept "suitable work." Since the Commission was empowered to grant "good cause" or "suitability" exemptions to those who had refused work for certain secular reasons, such as an applicant's physical fitness, prior earnings, and prospects for securing local work in his or her customary occupation, but refused to grant a similar exemption to Mrs. Sherbert when she declined employment for religious reasons, the law was tainted by a selective process and, therefore, was not generally applicable. Such an individualized exemption process "provides ample opportunity for discrimination against religion in general or unpopular faiths in particular." Therefore, any refusal to extend discretionary exemptions to claims of religious hardship must be strictly scrutinized....

Notice that the employment compensation scheme in *Sherbert* did not recognize all secular reasons for refusing work as qualifying for the "good cause" or "suitability" exemptions. Some secular reasons, such as the applicant's prior earnings or customary occupation, were considered good reasons for refusing work, while other secular reasons were not considered acceptable. *Smith's* reconceptualization of *Sherbert* states that when the government has in place a system of individual exemptions, it must treat religious exemption claims as well as the most favored secular exemption claims, even if this means that religious claims are treated better than the disfavored subset of secular exemption claims....

This is potentially a very significant free exercise rule, because whenever you are dealing with burdensome regulations administered by governmental departments, public schools, state universities, or similar bureaucracies, there will often be some process for requesting an exemption, waiver, or variance. Even if the regulation or restrictive policy is generally applicable on its face, if a state agency grants ad hoc exemptions, waivers, or variances in even a few cases involving secular claims, it may not refuse to grant similar exemptions, waivers, or variances in cases of "religious hardship" without satisfying strict scrutiny.…

Lukumi, Religious Gerrymanders and Underinclusiveness

As previously discussed, laws such as the hypothetical prohibition statute of State C, which exempts alcoholic beverages served with meals at restaurants from an otherwise across-the-board prohibition, raise interesting questions concerning the meaning of the general applicability requirement mandated by *Smith*. When *Smith* and *Lukumi* are read together, a persuasive argument can be made that laws such as State C's are not generally applicable and may not be enforced against religiously motivated dissenters absent a compelling justification. Indeed, under *Lukumi* religious liberty will often receive greater protection than under pre-*Smith* law, because the Court has made clear that it will no longer apply a "watered down" version of the compelling interest test for free exercise claims that meet *Smith's* requirements.

   Lukumi concerned a regulatory scheme that had been gerrymandered to prohibit the killing of animals only when done as part of a religious ritual. The Court held that this enactment was neither neutral nor generally applicable. Therefore, when the Church of the Lukumi Babalu Aye challenged the law as a violation of its right to practice a religious ritual of animal sacrifice, the Court applied authentic strict scrutiny and held that the law violated the "fundamental nonpersecution principle of the First Amendment."[5] …

The Neutrality Requirement

Although neutrality and general applicability are "interrelated" concepts[,][6] *Lukumi* recognized that these requirements are not identical. The neutrality requirement mandates formal as opposed to substantive neutrality and generally will be satisfied if the law in question neither targets religious practices for special burdens nor adopts classifications that discriminate on the basis of religion. The requirement of general applicability, however, is concerned with laws that are underinclusive in the sense of failing "to prohibit nonreligious conduct that endangers [state] … interests in a similar or greater degree" than the restricted religious conduct that is the subject of the free exercise claim.[7]

Only in rare instances will strict scrutiny be triggered by the neutrality requirement, because it forbids only the most direct forms of religious persecution....

Although the neutrality requirement is an important component of free exercise doctrine under *Smith* and *Lukumi*, it is dwarfed by the potential significance of the general applicability requirement....

The General Applicability Requirement

[I]magine a law that does not target a particular religious practice or classify on the basis of religion, [and thus is neutral,] but which does contain one or a few exceptions for favored secular interests. Suppose a state enacts a (nearly) across-the-board prohibition law that contains a single exception permitting alcoholic beverages to be served with meals at restaurants. This law is certainly widely applicable, but is it generally applicable? If this law is enforced against sacramental uses of alcoholic wine, is the Free Exercise Clause irrelevant under *Smith*, or should rigorous strict scrutiny be applied under *Lukumi*?...

[*Lukumi* indicates that a] law that is underinclusive in the sense of failing to restrict certain "nonreligious conduct that endangers" state interests, "in a similar or greater degree" than the restricted religious conduct is not generally applicable, at least when the "underinclusion is substantial, not inconsequential." For example, the city ordinances struck down in *Lukumi* were designed to promote the city's interest in protecting the public health, which was said to be threatened by the improper disposal of animal carcasses and the consumption of uninspected meat. However, the city did not prohibit hunting and certain other secular activities that equally endangered these public health concerns. These ordinances were thus substantially underinclusive and therefore failed the test of general applicability....

III. BEYOND THE MILLENNIUM: UNDERINCLUSIVE LAWS AND EQUAL REGARD FOR RELIGIOUS EXERCISE

In order to determine if a law restricting religious exercise is underinclusive, one must ask two questions. First, what governmental purposes are being served by the restrictive law at issue? Second, does the law exempt or otherwise leave unrestricted secular conduct that endangers those governmental purposes in a similar or greater degree than the prohibited or restricted conduct of the party seeking the protection of the Free Exercise Clause? In other words, a law burdening religious conduct is underinclusive, with respect to any particular government interest, if the law fails to pursue that interest uniformly against other conduct that causes similar damage to that government interest....

The Newark Police Case

Perhaps the most thoughtful judicial analysis of the general applicability requirement can be found in Judge [now Supreme Court Justice] Alito's opinion in the Newark Police Case, *Fraternal Order of Police v. Newark*[8] (hereinafter "*Newark Police*"). The Newark, New Jersey Police Department had adopted a policy prohibiting police officers from wearing beards. Although this proscription was labeled a "Zero Tolerance" policy by the Chief of Police, exemptions were made for medical reasons and for "undercover officers whose 'assignments or duties permit a departure from the requirements.'" However, the Department refused to grant an exemption to two Sunni Muslim officers who were compelled by their religious beliefs to grow beards.

The Third Circuit held that the Department's decision to allow exemptions for medical beards but not for religious beards took the case out of *Smith* and triggered heightened scrutiny under *Lukumi*. Judge Alito's excellent opinion closely tracked the reasoning of *Lukumi* regarding underinclusiveness as the key to locating the boundary between general applicability and non-general applicability. The no-beard policy was underinclusive because beards grown for medical reasons undermined the Department's interest in uniformity and in fostering "public confidence" in the police force no less than beards grown for religious reasons. The court said that "the medical exemption raises concern because it indicates that the Department has made a value judgment that secular (i.e. medical) motivations for wearing a beard are important enough to overcome its general interest in uniformity but that religious motivations are not." This underinclusiveness was "sufficiently suggestive of discriminatory intent so as to trigger heightened scrutiny under *Smith* and *Lukumi*." The fact that the exception for medical beards was enacted to address a perfectly legitimate governmental interest—accommodating the medical needs of certain police officers—was irrelevant to the court's analysis of the general applicability requirement. Although it is perfectly proper for the state to accommodate secular hardships, religious hardships are entitled to equal consideration under *Smith* and *Lukumi*.

Circuit Judge Alito's opinion in *Newark Police* demonstrates a sophisticated

understanding of the general applicability requirement and the related concept of underinclusiveness. He understands the subtle but important point that
not every exception renders a law underinclusive (and thus non-generally
applicable) under *Lukumi*. A law will be deemed underinclusive only when it
exempts (or otherwise leaves unrestricted) secular conduct that endangers or
undermines the state interests served by the restriction in a similar or greater
degree than religious conduct that is subject to the law's restrictions.

In *Newark Police*, Alito understood that the exemption for medical beards
rendered the grooming policy underinclusive, but the exemption for beards
worn by undercover police officers did not. He recognized that beards grown
for medical purposes undermine the uniform appearance policy in exactly the
same way as beards grown for religious purposes. The exception for beards
worn by undercover officers does not undermine the Department's interest in
uniformity, however, because undercover officers are not held out to the
public as law enforcement personnel. Thus, the exemption for medical beards
rendered the policy non-generally applicable and triggered heightened
scrutiny under the Free Exercise Clause. However, a "no beard" policy that
exempted undercover officers and no one else would satisfy the requirement
of general applicability and would be valid under *Smith*.

Some Additional "Test Suites"[9] for Evaluating the General Applicability Requirement

[W]hen the legislature enacts underinclusive laws and thereby chooses to
accommodate certain "harmful" secular conduct but not "harmful" religious
conduct, it is the duty of courts to intervene and protect the free exercise of
religion. The decision of the legislature to value secular conduct that is not
expressly protected by the Constitution more than analogous religiously motivated conduct is precisely the kind of unequal treatment that should be the
minimum standard for constitutional protection of the free exercise of religion.

[To see how this approach works, c]onsider the following situations:

A person claims an exemption from trespass law to view an apparition of
the Virgin Mary (or other sacred subject) on private land. Assume trespass law
"has exceptions for adverse possession, necessity, [and] law enforcement."[10]

A person claims an exemption to use marijuana as part of a religious
ritual in a state that prohibits possession of marijuana but which exempts the
medical use of the drug when prescribed by a physician.

A person claims a religious exemption from a housing discrimination law that prohibits discrimination on the basis of sexual orientation but which exempts owner-occupied dwellings containing four apartments or less....

The Trespass Test Suite

The first test suite, involving a free exercise claim to trespass on private property to view a sacred apparition, probably involves a law that satisfies the requirement of general applicability. The three exceptions cited by [Professor Eugene] Volokh—adverse possession, necessity, and law enforcement—probably do not render the law of trespass non-generally applicable under *Smith* and *Lukumi*, because the degree of underinclusion does not appear to be substantial. The doctrine of adverse possession is not an exception to the law of trespass, but rather a "strange and wonderful" means of acquiring title by operation of the statute of limitations. The doctrine of adverse possession does not permit anyone to trespass on the property of another; it merely recognizes that once the statute of limitations to recover land from a wrongful possessor has run, the original owner's right to recover the land is barred and the adverse possessor thereby acquires "as perfect title [to the land] as if there had been a conveyance by deed."[11] The law enforcement exception, which allows a public official to commit a trespass when "acting in a lawful manner within the scope of official authority," and the necessity exception, which allows a person to claim "that a trespass was justified or excused by either public or private necessity," are extraordinary and inconsequential exceptions to the general primacy of the sanctity of private property....

[In contrast, suppose] that a legislature enacts an exception to trespass law allowing persons to enter the private property of another for the purpose of playing frisbee, touch football, or other athletic activities. What does this amended test suite tell us about the relative desirability of the competing tests for the general applicability requirement?

This additional exception would almost certainly render the law of trespass substantially underinclusive and thus not generally applicable under my reading of *Smith* and *Lukumi*. Since the legislature has decided to permit a substantial class of secular activities that endangers the right of exclusive possession of private property at least as much (and probably much more) than religiously motivated trespassers, religious defendants should receive strict scrutiny when they assert free exercise claims against enforcement of the highly selective trespass law....

The Marijuana Test Suite

The second test suite, involving a free exercise claim to use the illegal drug marijuana as part of a religious ritual, also appears to concern a law that satisfies the requirement of general applicability. Remember, the law was an across-the-board prohibition of the possession of marijuana with a single exemption for medical use of the drug when prescribed by a physician.

Presumably, the purpose for prohibiting marijuana is to protect citizens against the harmful effects of a dangerous drug. The exception does not render the marijuana law underinclusive with respect to this purpose, because it allows the drug to be used by a patient only when a doctor has prescribed the drug as medically beneficial. Thus, the prescription exception "do[es] not trigger heightened scrutiny [when the law is enforced against religious uses of marijuana] because the Free Exercise Clause does not require the government to apply its laws to activities that it does not have an interest in preventing."[12] In other words, the law satisfies the general applicability requirement because the state's legitimate interest in public health is pursued uniformly against all medically harmful uses of marijuana.

Of course, protecting the health of citizens against a harmful drug may not be the sole purpose of the marijuana prohibition. The law may also be intended to protect innocent third parties against the harmful consequences of the use of marijuana by others, such as risks resulting from persons driving under the influence of the drug, lost productivity caused by use of the drug, or other real or perceived consequences of marijuana use. But even if the law is found to be underinclusive for these purposes, it will still satisfy the test of general applicability so long as the law addresses at least one legitimate governmental purpose and is not underinclusive with respect to that purpose. Thus, the marijuana law in our test suite is generally applicable, even if it is designed to serve multiple purposes, because it is not underinclusive with respect to at least one such purpose: the government's legitimate interest in protecting the health of persons against the unregulated use of a dangerous drug.

But now allow me to suggest a modification to our test suite that may deepen our inquiry. Imagine, for example, that the California legislature prohibits the use of marijuana, but carves out a special interest exception permitting the recreational use of marijuana at rock concerts and alumni receptions at Cal-Berkeley. Surely, this law is substantially underinclusive and its enforcement against religious users of the drug will trigger strict scrutiny under *Lukumi*....

The Housing Discrimination Test Suite

The final test suite, involving a statute that prohibits discrimination in housing on the basis of sexual orientation and exempts owner-occupied dwellings with four units or less, concerns a law that appears to fail the requirement of general applicability. The exception for owner-occupied duplexes, triplexes, and four-plexes undoubtedly removes a significant number of rental units from the law's regulatory restrictions. Thus, the law appears to be substantially underinclusive, because the exception for owner-occupied buildings threatens the state's purpose in protecting tenants against discrimination on the basis of sexual orientation at least as much as discrimination by religiously motivated landlords.

For example, suppose this fair housing law is enforced against a Christian landlady, say Mrs. Murphy, when she refuses to rent a unit in her (non-owner-occupied) five-plex to a homosexual couple because she believes it would be sinful for her to facilitate homosexual conduct. Mrs. Murphy's free exercise claim should be entitled to strict scrutiny under *Lukumi*, because the fair housing law is not a law of general application.

This is so even if we accept that Mrs. Murphy's religiously motivated decision "imposes some real harm on the tenants" who are excluded from residing on her property. Tenants are "harmed" no more by religious exemptions under the Free Exercise Clause than by the analogous secular exemptions approved by the legislature. They have a "right" to be protected against the "harm" of housing discrimination only because the legislature decided to create such a "right" when it enacted the fair housing law. As I read the doctrine of *Lukumi*, when the legislature enacts underinclusive laws and thereby chooses to permit certain secular "harms" but not similar religious "harms," the Free Exercise Clause operates to protect the free exercise of religion. Perhaps the legislature has decided wisely that the associational interests of certain landlords outweigh the "right" of tenants to equal housing opportunities. However, *Lukumi* requires that the free exercise claims of religious landlords receive equal accommodation under the law, unless the state has a compelling justification for its highly selective fair housing law. Moreover, the underinclusiveness of the statute should make it almost impossible for the state to justify the law, because the allowance of secular exemptions "is substantial evidence that religious exemptions would not threaten the statutory scheme."

Free Exercise As Equal Regard: A Unifying Theory and a Reasonable Compromise

Smith and *Lukumi* have transformed the Free Exercise Clause from a liberty rule, under which religiously motivated conduct was protected—at least in theory—against any substantial governmental burden, to an equality rule, under which religious practice is entitled to a kind of most-favored-nation status. In other words, an across-the-board prohibition of some class of behavior may be enforced against religiously motivated conduct, but when the government pursues underinclusive restrictions against religious practices, the Free Exercise Clause is triggered and the selective regulatory scheme will be reviewed under a compelling interest test that is strict in theory and usually fatal in fact. This is an equality rule not a liberty rule, because religious exercise is protected, not as an end in itself, but only to the extent that analogous secular conduct is protected.

Smith and *Lukumi* strike a reasonable compromise between the concerns of those who fear religious liberty as a strain on the social contract and of those who believe that religious freedom is an essential component of ordered liberty, between the concerns of those who fear anarchy and of those who fear religious persecution, between the concerns of those who believe that free exercise exemptions create an unfair constitutional preference for religion over non-religion and of those who believe that the absence of free exercise exemptions in a modern secular state unfairly exposes religious individuals and subgroups to the powerful forces of assimilation and secularization. Under *Smith* and *Lukumi*, the majority may rule without any fear of religious anarchy, so long as the burdens it creates are not imposed selectively. However, if the majority decides to impose civic obligations or restrictions selectively by enacting underinclusive laws, the Free Exercise Clause requires strict scrutiny when the government seeks to enforce these non-generally-applicable burdens against religiously motivated practices....

The reports of the death of free exercise in the wake of *Smith* were more than premature, they were seriously mistaken. Under *Smith* and (especially) *Lukumi*, religious liberty will often prevail against burdens imposed by underinclusive (and thus, non-generally applicable) laws and governmental policies.

NOTES

As a result of editing, the notes for this essay have been renumbered. The note number from the original essay or article is shown in parentheses at the end of each citation.

1. Douglas Laycock, "The Remnants of Free Exercise," *Supreme Court Review* (1990): 1, 4. (5)

2. 508 U.S. 520, 546 (1993). (12)

3. [See Lupu excerpt, pp. 207, 209–11 of this book.] (35)

4. [See Marshall excerpt, p. 77 of this book.] (38)

5. *Lukumi*, 508 U.S. 523. (100)

6. Ibid., p. 531. (105)

7. Ibid., p. 543. (108)

8. 170 F.3d 359 (3d Cir. 1999). (147)

9. [Relocated note:] A "test suite" is a term used by computer programmers to refer to tests designed to determine whether a software program works properly. Eugene Volokh, "Intermediate Questions of Religious Exemptions—A Research Agenda with Test Suites," *Cardozo Law Review* 21 (1999): 595, 599. (125)

10. Ibid., p. 632. (168)

11. Ralph E. Boyer, et al., *The Law of Property: An Introductory Survey*, 4th ed. (1991), p. 49. (173)

12. *Fraternal Order of Police*, 170 F.3d 366. (182)

TOWARD A DEFENSIBLE FREE EXERCISE DOCTRINE

Frederick M. Gedicks

I. Introduction: The Implausibility of Religious Exemptions

What many proponents of religious exemptions do not want to admit is that
they no longer hold the high ground in the battle over religious liberty. During
the nineteenth and early twentieth centuries, American society viewed the
practice of religion—mostly "Judeo-Christian" religion—as an especially good
activity entitled to special privileges. [But this] understanding of religious practice as a uniquely valuable social activity to be encouraged by government has
been displaced by an understanding that reduces religious practice to a personal
preference that is to be neither encouraged nor discouraged by government....

   In this cultural environment, it is difficult to justify giving religious practices special constitutional protection that is not afforded to secular activities
that appear to be just as morally serious and socially valuable as religion....

Frederick M. Gedicks, "Toward a Defensible Free Exercise Doctrine," *George Washington Law Review* 68 (2000): 925, 927–29, 935–45.

How, then, might religious liberty be protected, if not by exemptions? More precisely, how can those concerned about religious liberty argue for a meaningful level of constitutional protection for religious exercise without elevating it above comparable activities motivated by secular morality? [M]y thesis is that religious practices should receive the same kind of constitutional protection afforded to expression and association under the Speech and Equal Protection Clauses. In other words, incidental restriction, time, place, and manner regulation, and prior restraint of religious activity, should be handled doctrinally in the same way that such restrictions, regulations, and restraints of expression are dealt with under the Speech Clause, and burdens imposed on religious practices by underinclusive but nonsuspect classifications should be handled doctrinally in the same way that burdens imposed by such classifications on speech and other fundamental rights and interests are dealt with under the Equal Protection Clause...

II. AN INDEPENDENT MEANING FOR THE FREE EXERCISE CLAUSE

A. Protecting Religious Exercise as Religion

Professor [Robert] Tuttle's discussion of Speech Clause doctrine appears to assume that in the absence of religious exemptions, religious exercise would be protected as a constitutional liberty only to the extent that it can be characterized as speech or association.[1] This doctrinal position constitutes an unwarranted and premature abandonment of the Free Exercise Clause that leaves religious activity with no protection other than a superfluous guarantee against religious discrimination [because flat-out discrimination based on religion is already presumptively unconstitutional under the Equal Protection and Establishment Clauses]....

Accordingly, although religious exercise often manifests itself as speech or association, I take the continuing presence of the Free Exercise Clause in the text of the First Amendment as a warrant to provide religious exercise with doctrinal protection irrespective of whether such exercise might also qualify for protection under the Speech Clause. In short, religious exercise should not be protected as speech, but rather like speech....

[A]s a working hypothesis, I believe the Speech Clause is the best template to use for the development of a newer free exercise doctrine, for three reasons. First, both the Speech Clause and the Free Exercise Clause have the same textual roots, both being located in the First Amendment, literally right next to each other. Second, *Smith* itself invited the Speech Clause analogy, having expressly invoked Speech Clause doctrine as a constitutional norm that the religious exemption doctrine violated.

Finally, and most important, the Free Exercise and Speech Clauses both deal with a conceptually similar problem: they both extend constitutional protection to those whose personal beliefs constrain them to oppose the government or its laws. The Free Exercise Clause extends constitutional protection to those whose religious beliefs constrain them to act in opposition to government; the Speech Clause extends constitutional protection to those whose personal beliefs constrain them to speak in opposition to government....

Speech Clause protections are more broadly developed, however, [than free exercise doctrines and thus can serve as helpful analogies].

Protecting religious activity by analogy to Equal Protection and Speech Clause doctrines does not assume that religious activity is like any other activity, but rather like any other constitutionally preferred activity. What I advocate is not a formal equality among constitutionally preferred and non-preferred activities, but rather a formal equality among constitutionally preferred activities, which as a group are elevated above other activities by virtue of their constitutional preference. If we are to treat constitutional "likes" alike, religious exercise should generally be treated like other fundamental constitutional rights, and in particular like that fundamental right which I maintain it most closely resembles—namely, speech....

B. An Analogical Sketch of a Defensible Free Exercise Doctrine

My proposed free exercise doctrine would generally seek to protect religious activity under the Free Exercise Clause in the same manner and to the same extent that speech and association are protected under the Speech and Equal Protection Clauses. [In other words,] analogous doctrinal protections [to free speech and equal protection] should apply to protect religious exercise even when the activity at issue cannot plausibly be characterized as expression or association for expressive purposes....I summarize below some of the issues relating to each of these doctrinal analogies.

1. Incidental and Time, Place, or Manner Regulation of Religious Activity

[I]t is well-established that incidental and time, place, or manner regulation of speech is subject to intermediate scrutiny under the Speech Clause: such regulation is upheld if it (i) is content-neutral, (ii) is narrowly tailored to serve a significant government interest, and (iii) leaves open adequate alternative channels of expression. Intermediate scrutiny of incidental and time, place, or manner regulation of expression serves at least two purposes. With respect to incidental restrictions, it ensures that government activity that burdens speech is the result of the government's genuine pursuit of legitimate goals, and not a covert attempt to engage in content-based regulation. Second, with respect to both incidental and time, place, or manner restrictions, intermediate scrutiny ensures that government officials engage in a constitutionally acceptable balancing of government and individual interests, not sacrificing fundamental speech rights at the altar of relatively unimportant government goals.

Both purposes are implicated by incidental and time, place, or manner regulation of religious exercise. Laws that incidentally burden religious activity are conceptually analogous to laws that incidentally burden expression or association. Such laws present the danger...that facially neutral laws passed for legitimate purposes may be applied so as to disadvantage unconventional or unpopular religious activity, in the same way that government authorities often use facially neutral laws to disadvantage speech on the basis of its controversial content or unpopular viewpoint.[2] Similarly, many laws that directly burden religious exercise, in particular land-use and zoning regulations, are precisely analogous to time, place, or manner regulation of expression under the Speech Clause. [T]he application of land use and zoning regulations to religious activity frequently dictates whether particular locations may be used for religious worship, the extent to which a religious group may alter the characteristics of the location where it worships, and what kinds of faith-based activities in addition to actual worship may take place at the location. Such laws thus directly control where, when, and under what circumstances religious activity may take place, in the same way that parade permits, sound ordinances, and other such restrictions directly regulate where, when, and under what circumstances otherwise protected expression may occur.

Thus, in the case of both incidental and time, place, or manner restriction of religious activity, judicial review should ensure both that government officials are not seeking to suppress religious activity because of its strangeness or lack of popularity, and that officials are not burdening religious activity out of excessive concern for less weighty government goals. *Smith*, however, subjects such regulations only to minimal scrutiny [i.e., virtually automatic approval]. If religious exercise has the same fundamental constitutional status as speech, it should receive the same level of protection. By analogy to the Speech Clause cases, then, incidental burdens and time, place, or manner restrictions on religious activity should be upheld only if they (i) are religiously neutral, (ii) are narrowly tailored to serve a significant government interest, and (iii) leave open ample alternative means of engaging in the restricted religious activity.

The alternatives analysis dictated by the foregoing test could prove to be especially protective of religious exercise, particularly in cases of incidental burdens. It is not common for the Supreme Court to invalidate a content-neutral law that incidentally burdens protected expression, because alternative means of communicating the speaker's message are almost always left open by incidental burdens on speech. When such alternatives are not available, however, courts have not hesitated to exempt speakers from the incidental burdens of general laws.[3] ... By contrast, alternatives do not usually exist for engaging in religious worship or otherwise satisfying religious obligations when the government incidentally burdens religious practices. As a general matter, then, the inquiry into whether the religious claimant has "ample alternative means" of practicing her religion could result in more frequent invalidation of government action that incidentally burdens a claimant's religious exercise....

In cases involving "high-value" speech, ... the Supreme Court has held that the excessive expense of alternative channels of communication is a sufficient reason for invalidating time, place, or manner regulations, even when the regulation is content-neutral and serves non-trivial regulatory interests. In *City of Ladue v. Gilleo*,[4] for example, the Court invalidated a ban on home-based signs because they are a common, inexpensive, convenient, and effective means of political communication that has no comparable alternative. Similarly, in *Martin v. City of Struthers*,[5] the Court struck down a flat ban on door-to-door distribution of pamphlets and literature, in part because of its widespread use in poorly financed political causes, even though the ban protected a person's interest in remaining undisturbed in his or her home.

Martin is especially important in this context because it was brought by a minority religious group [the Jehovah's Witnesses] punished for proselytizing door-to-door....

2. Standardless Licensing of Religious Activity

[M]ost zoning and land use schemes give to local government officials and administrators broad discretion to prohibit or to permit religious land uses. Under the Speech Clause, licensing and other regulatory schemes that grant government discretion to prevent speech ex ante (as opposed to punishing it ex post) are subject to significant substantive and procedural restraints. Unless such discretion is controlled or limited by substantive standards governing the issuance of a license, it is presumptively unconstitutional as a prior restraint. Limiting standards must be both content-neutral and "narrow, objective, and definite"; broad appeals to a state's police power do not pass muster. Procedurally, licensing schemes must provide that the government shoulder the burden of proving that the proposed speech is not constitutionally protected, that the government either issue the license for the speech or seek judicial review of its refusal to issue it within a specified and brief period of time, that any restraint on the expression in advance of a final judicial determination be limited to "preservation of the status quo," and that the final judicial decision on the restraint be rendered promptly.

By analogy to the standardless licensing cases, then, the exercise of government discretion to deny religious uses of property functions as a "prior restraint" of religious activity that should be subject to safeguards analogous to those set against prior restraint of speech—that is, the exercise of government discretion in applying zoning and other land use regulations to determine whether religious uses shall be permitted should be constrained by definite, objective, religion-neutral criteria, and the government should bear the burdens of (i) proving that the religious land use is not protected by the Free Exercise Clause; (ii) making a prompt decision about the use within a specified period of time; and (iii) seeking immediate judicial review and a prompt final judicial decision whenever it refuses to permit a religious land use.

The standardless licensing decisions reflect the reality that government discretion is frequently exercised to disadvantage controversial or unpopular speech. They resonate with *Smith*'s requirement [citing *Sherbert v. Verner*] that strict scrutiny be applied to government decisions that deny religious exemptions within the context of a system providing for individualized assessment of and exemption from a law's burdens on secular conduct. [T]his portion of *Smith* is best understood as a determination that discretionary exemption schemes are not laws of general applicability, and thus present the risk that government might pursue legitimate goals by focusing the cost of such goals on unpopular, unusual, or obscure religions.... [L]ocal government discretion is frequently exercised to deny or otherwise to penalize uses sought by unpopular or unfamiliar minority religions, often at the same time that similar and even identical uses are approved for larger, more established religions.

Thus, applying the substantive and procedural principles of the standardless licensing cases to religious zoning and land use decisions—again, irrespective of whether the activity associated with the use might also be characterized as speech—would seem to be a rich source of potential doctrinal protection for the free exercise of religion in the context of land use decisions. Requiring that government rely on neutral definitive standards, for example, placing the burden of proving the inappropriateness of religious land use on the government and requiring that the government initiate immediate judicial review of any denial of an application for a religious land use, would make it significantly more difficult for government officials to cover anti-religious animus with the cloak of administrative discretion.

3. Religious Association

[In addition,] a doctrine of religious association under the Free Exercise Clause could be developed by analogy to the freedom of association under the Speech Clause. The Supreme Court has long recognized that meaningful protection of the freedom of speech also requires protection of a freedom to associate with others for expressive purposes. The freedom of speech, in other words, includes the freedom to join with others to exchange ideas and pursue expressive goals.[6] Accordingly, the Court has held that incidental and time, place, or manner burdens on the freedom of association are subject to heightened scrutiny under the Speech Clause: government action that threatens to change the content or character of an association's message must be narrowly tailored to protect a compelling or substantial government interest unrelated to the suppression of ideas.

[It is true,] of course, that many of the most important dimensions of religious exercise do not constitute the communication of ideas, and thus are not protected by the freedom of association. An analogous freedom of religious association under the Free Exercise Clause, however, could protect group religious exercise directly: meaningful protection of the individual right to practice one's religion would also require protection of the right to associate with like-minded others to enhance spiritual experience through joint worship and other communal activities, even if such activities cannot plausibly be characterized as expressive. Accordingly, incidental government action that would change significantly the content or character of a religious association's beliefs, values, or activities would have to be narrowly tailored to a substantial government interest.

A doctrine of freedom of religious association under the Free Exercise Clause would protect many of the same interests now ostensibly protected by the church autonomy cases.[7] These cases involved disputes within a denomination over ownership of church property or appointment to an ecclesiastical office that found their way into a secular court. The cases generally hold that a court may not adjudicate controversies between religious claimants when doing so would require judicial interpretation of the content or merits of a religious belief or practice. Theological questions, in other words, are not justiciable by secular courts.[8] When adjudication calls for judicial interpretation of religious doctrine, the church autonomy cases call on the court to defer to the interpretation advanced by the denomination's internal governing structure or, if no such interpretation is forthcoming, to abstain altogether from adjudicating the case.

Since 1979, however, the abstention rule of the church autonomy cases has been subject to a serious qualification. In *Jones v. Wolf*, the Supreme Court held that a secular court properly adjudicates internal denominational disputes if it does so by reference to "'neutral principles of law,'" without resort to interpreting religious doctrine.[9] ... Since *Smith*, some courts have understood "neutral, general laws" from that decision as being synonymous with "neutral legal principles" in *Jones*, thereby expanding the neutral principles exception to apply to virtually any secular law that does not facially classify on the basis of religion.

When read with *Smith*, the neutral principles exception of *Jones* seriously undercuts the protection from government intrusion that the church autonomy cases once afforded to religious groups. After all, when neutral legal principles suggest how a denominational dispute should be decided, the independence and autonomy of the church is irrelevant, and a court may proceed to resolve the dispute in accordance with such principles even if the resolution ignores or contradicts the result indicated by the church's own governing structure. This means that the church autonomy cases provide no obstacle to a court that wishes to intervene in a denominational dispute, as long as the court can identify (as it nearly always can) a secular law whose application would resolve the dispute without resort to interpretation of religious doctrine.

Anchoring the church autonomy principle in a Free Exercise Clause analogy to freedom of association under the Speech Clause might actually provide more reliable protection for religious group activity than that afforded by existing doctrine under the church autonomy cases. Under a right of religious association analogous to freedom of association under the Speech Clause, the justification for a court's refraining from adjudicating an internal dispute of a religious group would not be the nonjusticiability of theological questions, and religious groups would not be vulnerable to court adjudication of their internal disputes whenever a court can identify an applicable secular law, as they currently are under the expanding neutral principles exception of *Jones* and *Smith*. Rather, the internal affairs of religious groups would be protected from government regulation whenever such regulation would restrict or alter the group's beliefs and practices, unless the government could articulate a compelling justification. That government regulation or court intervention might be on the basis of neutral principles would be irrelevant.

Additionally, protecting church autonomy by a right of religious association rather than by a rule of religious nonjusticiability would not extend to religious groups any greater protection than the freedom of association extends to advocacy groups founded on secular morality. In that respect, a right of religious association is more in tune than the church autonomy cases with a contemporary culture that is no longer able to distinguish religiously motivated activity from activity motivated by secular commitments of comparable moral seriousness.

4. Underinclusive Classifications that Burden Religious Activity

One of the murkier aspects of *Smith* is the constitutional effect of exemptions for secular conduct from laws that do not exempt religious exercise....

The difficult case is ... where a law exempts some secular conduct while leaving substantial amounts of secular conduct and all religious exercise subject to the law—say, a statute prohibiting the use of marijuana that exempts medicinal use of the drug, but not religious sacramental use, or a law enforcement dress code prohibiting beards that exempts those with certain skin conditions, but not those whose religious beliefs require them to wear beards. I [maintain] that such a law is not "generally applicable," and that, therefore, a government refusal to exempt religious conduct that is incidentally burdened by such a law should be subject to strict scrutiny under *Smith* and *Lukumi*. [Gedicks' conclusion here parallels that of Duncan in the preceding excerpt.]

NOTES

As a result of editing, the notes for this essay have been renumbered. The note number from the original essay or article is shown in parentheses at the end of each citation.

1. [An example may be found in the Marshall excerpt, p. 77 of this book.] (24)

2. The pervasive discrimination experienced by unpopular religions under the guise of land use and zoning regulation is [d]ocumented in W. Cole Durham Jr., "Discrimination Against Minority Churches in Zoning Cases," Appendix to *Brief of the Church of Jesus Christ of Latter-day Saints as Amicus Curiae for Respondents*, pp. A-1–A-23; *City of Boerne v. Flores*, 521 U.S. 507 (1997); and Douglas Laycock, "State RFRAs and Land Use Regulation," *UC Davis Law Review* 32 (1997): 755. (61)

3. See, e.g., *Hustler Magazine v. Falwell*, 485 U.S. 46 (1988) (tort of intentional infliction of emotional distress without required showing of New York Times malice held unconstitutional as applied to parodies of public figures and public officials because of potential chilling effect on political criticism); *New York Times v. Sullivan*, 376 U.S. 254 (1964) (tort of libel per se without required showing of malice held unconstitutional as applied to criticism of government officials because of potential chilling effect on such criticism); *NAACP v. Button*, 371 U.S. 415 (1963) (regulation barring solicitation of legal business held unconstitutional as applied to NAACP because of potential chilling effect on discussion and institution of expressive litigation). (65)

4. 512 U.S. 43 (1994). (68)

5. 319 U.S. 141 (1943). (70)

6. See, e.g., *Boy Scouts v. Dale*, 530 U.S. 640 (2000) [(holding that antidiscrimination law could not be applied to prevent Boys Scouts from refusing openly gay scoutmaster whose activities conflicted with Scouts' organizational messages)]. (87)

[7. Several of these cases, running from 1872 to 1979, are discussed in greater detail in Chapter 7 of this book.]

8. [See, e.g., Laurence H. Tribe,] *American Constitutional Law*, 2nd ed. (1988), p. 1232, § 14-11. ("[L]aw in a nontheocratic state cannot measure religious truth.... [I]t is now settled that the resolution of religious questions can play no role in the civil adjudication of such disputes—that ecclesiastical doctrines cannot be used to measure right or wrong under civil law.") (94)

9. 443 U.S. 595, 602–03 (1979). (96)

Chapter 7

JUDICIAL EXEMPTIONS
Balancing Harms to Religion
Against Harms to Society

A. BURDENS ON THE SINCERE EXERCISE OF RELIGION

WHERE RIGHTS BEGIN: THE PROBLEM OF
BURDENS ON THE FREE EXERCISE OF RELIGION

IRA C. LUPU

One question upon which little attention has been focused [in free exercise of religion cases] is the character of government activity necessary to constitute a "burden." Before courts ever reach the rigorous standard of review appropriate to free exercise cases, they must be satisfied that the harm complained of falls within the boundaries of the clause. These boundaries could be constructed quite narrowly; for example, the ambit of the clause might be limited to criminal prohibitions on actions required by religious belief, and government-created compulsions to take actions forbidden by religious norms. At

---

Ira C. Lupu, "Where Rights Begin: The Problem of Burdens on the Free Exercise of Religion," *Harvard Law Review* 102 (1989): 933, 933–36, 943–48, 953–54, 957–59, 961–68, 97–81.

the other extreme, the scope of free exercise could be understood in the broadest possible sense, encompassing any government action that increases the expense, discomfort, or difficulty of religious life. Deciding what constitutes a burden on the free exercise of religion—that is, deciding where rights under the clause begin—will inevitably have profound consequences for other aspects of free exercise doctrine, and thus for the regime of religious liberty itself.

Two recent controversies [have] highlighted the significance and difficulty of defining a constitutionally cognizable burden upon free exercise. In *Lyng v. Northwest Indian Cemetery Protective Association*,[1] a 5–3 majority of the Supreme Court relied entirely upon the burden concept in holding that the Free Exercise Clause did not bar government construction of a road upon public lands long used for purposes of religious ritual by several Native American tribes. Not long before, in *Mozert v. Hawkins County Board of Education*,[2] the Sixth Circuit invoked a similar analysis in ruling against a group of parents who claimed that the reading requirements in the Tennessee public schools violated their free exercise rights and those of their children. Thus, the government victories in *Lyng* and *Mozert* were not the result of judicial application of the review standard for free exercise cases. Rather, the courts in those cases avoided applying that standard by holding that the harms inflicted by the challenged government policies were not of the sort that would trigger the protections of the free exercise clause [in the first place].

The concept of burden is thus emerging as crucial in free exercise law. It serves as the latest in a series of gatekeeper doctrines, which function to increase the likelihood of failure at the prima facie stage, and thereby to reduce the number of claims that must be afforded the searching inquiry demanded by the free exercise clause....

Unfortunately,... the law that has emerged thus far creates an intolerable risk of discrimination against unconventional religious practices and beliefs, and threatens to narrow the protection of religious liberty overall....

I. The Evolution of the Burden Requirement in Free Exercise Adjudication

[Professor Lupu begins by tracing the expansion of free exercise rights to 1989, from *Reynolds* (only religious beliefs protected, not conduct) to *Sherbert* and *Yoder* (conduct protected, even against a generally applicable law, unless the government had a compelling interest).] As the scope of protected exercise has expanded, and the requirement of justification has increased in severity, pressure has mounted to map manageable boundaries to the set of claims that courts would seriously entertain. The burden concept arose, at least in part, in response to that pressure....

The Contemporary Emergence of the Burden Concept

Mozert involved complaints by schoolchildren and their parents that the public school reading curriculum to which the children were exposed impermissibly burdened religious belief. After some preliminary skirmishing, the district court held that the reading program in the county's public schools did offend the free exercise rights of the complainants. On the burden question, the court concluded that a cognizable harm had been inflicted because the "plaintiffs' religious beliefs compel them to refrain from exposure" to the required reading materials,[3] and the school board had "required that the student-plaintiffs either read the offensive texts or give up their free public education."

The Sixth Circuit reversed. Chief Judge Lively's opinion for the panel rested explicitly on a finding that the reading requirements did not amount to a burden sufficient to trigger scrutiny under free exercise standards.[4] Because the children were obliged only to read the challenged material, and not to affirm the truth of what they read, the court concluded that neither their interests in free exercise nor those of their parents had been affected in a legally cognizable fashion. *Mozert* thus stands for the unattractive principle that compulsory exposure to ideas from which an individual is obliged by religion to dissociate does not even implicate the Free Exercise Clause, much less violate it.

The Supreme Court has contributed to this development [especially in the *Lyng* case, suggesting that it] may be prepared to narrow the set of conflicts that will produce injury cognizable under the Free Exercise Clause....

The *Lyng* litigation challenged the decision of the United States Forest Service to construct a six-mile roadway, adjacent to Indian holy places, in a federally owned California forest.... [F]ive members of the Supreme Court... found no legally cognizable burden on the Indians' free exercise interests, and held for the government. Moreover, the Court reached this conclusion despite substantial and uncontroverted evidence that the road construction would cause significant and irreparable harm to several tribes' religious practices. Justice O'Connor's opinion announced that burdens on free exercise could not result from acts of government "which have no tendency to coerce individuals into acting contrary to their religious beliefs";[5] in her view, the challenged road-building had no such tendency. Justice Brennan's dissent rejected the "coercion" test in favor of an inquiry into whether the challenged action "posed a substantial and realistic threat" to "central" aspects of the claimant's religion, an approach that he found easily satisfied by the record in this case.[6]

The implications of *Lyng* are numerous and disturbing. One need not be an ardent champion of American Indian rights to see in it a distressing insensitivity to Indian spiritual patterns. *Lyng* blocks at the threshold all Indian free exercise claims involving tribal use of public lands for ritual observance. Because it thus spares the government from any obligation to justify its policies, *Lyng* generates a sweeping license for the government to approve of and engage in land development no matter how severely such development affects the religious practices of American Indians.

On a broader level, *Lyng* has highlighted what may become a significant threshold inquiry in Free Exercise Clause adjudication. The *Mozert* court's use of the burden concept, as noted earlier, suggests that it is not simply Native American claims, or land-use claims, or some combination of the two, that will be denied the protective standard of review appropriate to free exercise claims. Indeed, as Justice Brennan suggested in his *Lyng* dissent, individuals and groups whose lives are pervasively religious will frequently experience the impact of government policy and practice in a wide variety of ways. Substantial questions concerning the scope of religious freedom are thus at stake in the content supplied by courts to the concept of burden.

II. BURDENS AND THE STRUCTURE OF FREE EXERCISE ADJUDICATION

One might expect free exercise claims to arrive in court with great momentum on their side. Such claims are presented in the fancy pedigree of constitutional right, not as claims of lesser magnitude or as appeals to discretion. Moreover, they are grounded in concern for religious liberty, a principle to which we as a society have long been rhetorically committed.

For several reasons, however, these claims are often deeply troubling. First and foremost, they typically require exemption from or cessation of some government policy that the political branches have ratified and that has legitimate, secular justification. Behind every free exercise claim is a spectral march; grant this one, a voice whispers to each judge, and you will be confronted with an endless chain of exemption demands from religious deviants of every stripe. Second, an affirmative response to free exercise claims is sometimes thought to collide with establishment clause limitations on the state's power to favor religion.

To the extent that free exercise claims create discomfort, pressure mounts to find techniques and doctrines for rejecting such claims without seeming unreasonable or unsympathetic to values of religious liberty. When the burden concept is compared to the inquiries into sincerity, religiosity, and state interest frequently demanded by current free exercise norms, one can readily understand the attraction of courts to a restrictive doctrine at the threshold of claims....

The Components of the Claim

[Certain threshold] elements of the prima facie case furnish opportunities for the government to oppose, and courts to reject, free exercise claims. In addition to the required showing of burden, claimants must persuade the decision maker that the burden (whatever it is) falls on sincerely held religious convictions. [But the requirements of sincerity and religiosity cannot dispose of many claims.]

To focus on the sincerity with which convictions are held by claimants appears at first glance to be the most promising approach for separating bona fide claims from spurious ones. Sincerity seems akin to good faith and other mental states that the law has for years made relevant to a wide variety of questions. Moreover, sincerity will be evaluated on the basis of extrinsic and objective evidence concerning the claimant's actions, statements, and demeanor. Judges, juries, and other legal decision makers thus can determine sincerity by examining whether the religious views the claimant offers in support of the claim are consistent with other manifestations of the claimant's beliefs. Moreover, a finding of insincerity would presumably make decision makers quite comfortable with rejecting a free exercise claim; such a finding would mark the claimant as one who fraudulently invokes religion and the Constitution in order to further some form of nonreligious self-interest.

From the decision maker's perspective, however, the strengths of a focus on claimant sincerity turn out to be its weaknesses as well. First, the inquiry into sincerity cannot completely escape the distinctly bad aroma of an inquisition. The decision maker can rarely be morally certain that the claimant is not sincere in his professed religious commitments, especially if all of the evidence supporting a finding of insincerity predates the asserted time of the religious commitment. True conversions are possible, however rare they may be. Errors are thus likely to arise in the application of a sincerity standard, and false negatives will result in both inflictions of moral suffering and violations of the Constitution.

Second, the questioning of sincerity may operate invisibly and subconsciously against unknown or unpopular religions. The more unusual a claimant's religion, the easier it will be for decision makers to conclude, on the basis of an unarticulated view that "no one could really believe this," that the claimant's beliefs are not sincerely held. If the errors that arise in the application of a sincerity standard are biased in this direction, those who most need the protection of the Constitution will be those least likely to enjoy it....

The question of what counts as religiosity for purposes of free exercise disputes fares little better as a reliable device for assessing the merits. Theologians, sociologists, and others have struggled mightily with definitional questions, but have hardly approached anything resembling agreement on what constitutes religion or religious belief. Although courts and legal commentators have themselves wrestled, often admirably and instructively, with approaches to the problem of definition, the human capacity for variation in matters of spirituality suggests little reason to believe that lawyers will improve the situation.

The definitional problem is compounded by its relation to the likelihood of discrimination against unusual spiritual claims. In the absence of objective criteria, decision makers tend to fall back on the familiar experience or the romantic ideal. The result is, at best, reasoning by induction from conventional Western patterns of religion and, at worst, simple equations of religion with Christianity. When narrow, ethnocentric models of religion are employed by decision makers, free exercise adjudication may readily become a vehicle for judicial violations of the Establishment Clause. Although courts may occasionally have reasonable success in distinguishing the commercial from the religious aspects of concededly religious enterprise, separating the truly religious from what is "merely" moral, ethical, or natural hardly appears to be a promising across-the-board strategy for judges and other decision makers.

One additional factor, usually termed "centrality," occasionally surfaces in judicial and scholarly analysis of what constitutes a prima facie free exercise claim. It is sometimes said that government-created burdens on more central aspects of a religion constitute greater intrusions, and therefore require a higher degree of justification, than burdens on more peripheral features. Indeed, Justice Brennan advanced a version of this approach in his dissent in *Lyng*; he contended that the burden of the road being built by the United States government fell upon matters at the heart of the religion practiced by Indian tribes in the vicinity.

By now the difficulties of centrality as an operative legal concept will sound familiar. The idea cannot be employed without judicial standards concerning the meaning and significance of religious behavior, teachings, and phenomena. Any attempt to declare such standards, however, runs the usual and grave risk of bias toward Western, monotheistic religions, which have a recognized center in worship of a single Supreme Being. Moreover, any imaginable process for resolving disputes over centrality creates the spectre of religious experts giving conflicting testimony about the significance of a religious practice, with the state's decision maker authoritatively choosing among them. A horary and well-respected line of cases, concerning disputes over property between warring factions within a church, strongly suggests that judicial resolution of theological controversy is both beyond judicial competence and out of constitutional bounds....

What exists in common in the concepts of sincerity, religiosity, and centrality are questions of spiritual meaning and significance. We are understandably suspicious of judicial responses to such questions, and some believe deeply that we cannot be legitimately and meaningfully bound by judicial answers. Hence the attraction to the threshold concept of burden; it offers, in terms known to and resonant within the legal system, another way of weeding out certain free exercise claims without forcing judges to enter the thicket of theology....

III. SHAPING THE CONTOURS OF THE BURDEN REQUIREMENT

The Inadequacy of Existing Principles

Judges have developed two basic approaches to the burden problem—the coercion theory articulated [in] *Lyng*, and the substantial impact theory developed by Justice Brennan in his *Lyng* dissent. Although either can coexist comfortably with the constitutional text, neither is sufficiently sensitive to the full range of constitutional functions that must be served.

One can hardly deny that coercion plays a crucial conceptual part in defining what constitutes a burden on religious liberty. The most severe burdens—torture and execution of religious dissidents—involve coercion in its ugliest and most violent form. Indeed, a wide range of punitive legal measures can be destructive to the free exercise of religion; the use of imprisonment, fines, and seizure of property are potent enough to discourage all but the most ardent religious adherents.

In cases of psychological or emotional coercion, however, the concept becomes so riddled with conceptual and philosophical difficulty that it becomes entirely inadequate as a source of governing norms in the free exercise context. Philosophers and legal scholars have long been vexed by questions concerning the voluntariness and causation of behavior, such as the extent to which those in dire need are coerced by what may seem to be exploitative offers of exchange. The crucial questions here usually concern the distinctions between threats and offers; the former entail the possibility of one being made worse off, and so are coercive, whereas the latter offer a choice that might make one better off, and therefore are not coercive. The distinction cannot be employed, however, without agreement on the appropriate way to measure one's situation in the absence of the choice. Because assumptions about one's legitimate legal and moral expectations are frequently controversial, the usefulness of the threat/offer distinction in defining coercion is distinctly limited.

The limitations associated with a focus on coercion have significant implications for current law. A coercion-based test could easily undermine a settled line of free exercise cases involving conditions on statutorily created benefits.[7] To be sure, these cases can be viewed as involving threats—for example, if you are unavailable for work on your Sabbath, you will forfeit unemployment benefits to which you are otherwise entitled. If one takes a narrow view of entitlements, however, these cases can be seen as involving only non-coercive offers—if you will make yourself sufficiently available for work, we (the state) will provide you with cash benefits when you are thrown out of your job.

Moreover, the outcome of a coercion test can easily be manipulated by shifting the locus of inquiry. By breaking down the particular context in which a free exercise claim arises and focusing only on the relatively less coercive aspects of the government's conduct, rather than on the preceding compulsion, a court can avoid a finding of coercion altogether. In *Mozert*, for example, the appeals court emphasized that schoolchildren are merely asked to read and discuss certain material and are under no compulsion to affirm or believe what they read. This argument entirely ignores the coercive quality of both compulsory school laws and the social settings in which children are placed as a result of those laws.

If the current conception of coercion is both murky at its edges and dangerously narrow, an approach focused on impact is likely to be no clearer and both under- and over-inclusive in application. Indeed, a doctrine that would trigger active free exercise review whenever government activity had any impact whatsoever upon religion would have an immense sweep. The adherents of many religions that call for strict adherence to a behavioral code—for example, Orthodox Judaism, various fundamentalist sects of Christianity, and conservative Islam sects—may find themselves in constant conflict with the changing norms and practices advanced by government. Consider government pronouncements concerning civil rights, or government advancement of a Middle East foreign policy that is either hostile or conciliatory toward the PLO, or promotion by government of education for a technologically complex modern world. All of these represent instances of government activity that falls short of coercive regulation, but is likely to impede adherence to religious norms by making them seem antiquated, silly, or radically deviant.

More generally, government is often engaged in value promotion, efforts which inevitably compete with religious norms. A standard that focuses on effects would presumably encompass these conflicts, which could create real consequences for religions whose teachings strayed widely from the government-reinforced mainstream. Judicial application of free exercise standards to such conflicts—for example, to complaints by religiously motivated anti-abortionists against the operation of state-subsidized clinics in which abortions are performed—could have radical repercussions for a wide variety of government programs.

If such burdens were to pass the free exercise threshold, courts would frequently face painful all-or-nothing choices. Unlike regulation, from which government can exempt religious actors and leave the regulatory policy otherwise intact, a violation premised on cultural impact can only be remedied by an order that the offending activity cease. Lawsuits of this character thus present the danger of general and well-supported government policies being undermined solely because they create psychic pressure on a religious minority to conform to or believe in general community norms. Most such suits would presumably fail at the standard-of-review stage; it is difficult to imagine a judge ordering the Pentagon closed because of a lawsuit by a group of pacifist Quakers. Yet the tendency for absurd disproportion between intrusion and remedy is so great that courts are best kept free of such disputes altogether.

In his *Lyng* dissent, Justice Brennan attempted to steer clear of the sweeping implications of an impact-based theory by imposing a requirement that the challenged action have "substantial external effects." This suggestion, like the coercion approach, contains a certain amount of wisdom. The proposed test of substantiality appears initially to be a reasonable method of excluding de minimis cases and unacceptably thin-skinned plaintiffs.

Even if limited by a test of substantiality, however, an impact-based approach would be difficult to maintain in a coherent fashion.... Does the maintenance of a huge defense establishment by the federal government of the United States generate "substantial external effects" on the [pacifist] Society of Friends?... Thus, judging burdensomeness by impact-focused theories, even if limited by tests of "substantiality," is unlikely to produce any more defensible results than employing coercion-based theories.

Prevailing judicial approaches to defining what constitutes a legally cognizable burden on religious exercise thus leave much to be desired....

Religious Liberty and the Common Law Principle

The current approaches to defining cognizable burdens for the purpose of free exercise adjudication are unable to avoid conceptual indefiniteness, to constrain the discrimination made possible by broad judicial discretion, or to erect prudential limits on coverage. These defects in existing standards, however, suggest a general direction in which analysis of the burden problem should proceed. Instead of viewing the problems of law and religion as divorced from the ordinary concerns of the legal system, one may draw creatively on the entire Anglo-American legal tradition in service of the Free Exercise Clause.

In particular, the common law—or what might better be called the general principles of our law—might serve as a source from which useful and sensible judgments may be derived concerning what constitutes a burden on the free exercise of religion. If this idea were to be put in "rule" form, the first approximation of it would be something like this: Whenever religious activity is met by intentional government action analogous to that which, if committed by a private party, would be actionable under general principles of law, a legally cognizable burden on religion is present. For reasons of national uniformity in the identification of federal rights, application of the common law principle would require courts to look to generally prevailing categories of legal duties, rather than to the law of any particular state....

1. Justifications for the Common Law Principle—Much can be said, beginning with the claims of history, in support of the common law approach suggested here. The approach has eminently respectable antecedents. The Statute of Virginia for Religious Freedom, enacted in 1786, was an important forerunner of the Free Exercise Clause. The Virginia statute was well known to Madison, who participated in the struggle for its enactment, and, only three years later, was a principal draftsman of the first amendment religion clauses. The Virginia statute provides in pertinent part: "Be it enacted by the General Assembly, That no man shall...be enforced, restrained, molested or burthened, in his body or goods, nor shall otherwise suffer on account of his religious opinions or belief...."[8] The reference to being "burthened in his body or goods" resonates with the common law principle proposed here. At the very least, it reveals that eighteenth-century statesmen understood the relationship between security of person and property, on one hand, and religious liberty on the other....

2. Application of the Common Law Principle—The applications at the core of the common law principle will be entirely unsurprising and uncontroversial. Without doubt, all cases in which allegedly religious activity is met by the threat of imprisonment or fine, whether criminal or civil, would fall within the common law principle, because such cases involve physical restraints or seizures of property of the sort that the common law has long made actionable between private parties. The prohibition on polygamous marriage at issue in *Reynolds* [*v. United States*], for instance, would present a clear case of free exercise burden, because the federal government prosecuted, tried, and sought to imprison Reynolds as a response to his religious choice to be married to more than one woman at a time.

In cases closer to the margin of the common law approach, however, the outcome of the burden inquiry might well be different from that of the current law. Reconsider *Lyng*. The doctrine of easement by prescription, designed to "stabiliz[e] long continued property uses,"[9] seems especially well tailored to the problem in *Lyng*, and indeed to the general problem of Indians' use of land for religious purposes. The Restatement of Property [section 457] provides that "an easement is created by such use of land, for the period of prescription, as would be privileged if an easement existed, provided the use is (a) adverse, and (b) for the period of prescription, continuous and uninterrupted." The undisputed facts and the government's own investigation in *Lyng* strongly support the conclusion that the Indian tribes and their members would have had a strong easement claim against a private landowner under this standard. The tribes had used the land in question for religious purposes for at least two hundred years, and thus would have had little trouble satisfying the relevant requirements for the prescription period....

[Moreover, the] tribal use of the land at issue in *Lyng*, as the district court found and Justice Brennan's dissent emphasized, had for many generations flowed from a deep concern for the spiritual properties associated with the land. Of course the complex tribal attitudes embodied in this concern may not easily translate into Western legal notions of adversity and claim of right. Nevertheless, the longstanding spiritual commitments and accompanying land uses documented in the case would be sufficient to satisfy a court that for two hundred years the tribes would not have conceded the authority of the United States to evict them, constructively or otherwise, from this land. Indeed, this and other Indian land-use claims might fit the ancient English common law formula of use continuing for so long that "the memory of man runneth not to the contrary."[10] The common law approach, as I would apply it, would thus support a finding of burden on the facts of *Lyng*.

Burdens on Free Exercise and the Problem of Conditional Benefits

When government provides a constitutionally gratuitous benefit, it typically acts in ways that exceed any duties imposed upon private persons by the common law. If I promise a gift of money to help out my unemployed neighbor, for example, I incur no liability if I break my promise. Similarly, if I condition the promise on my neighbor's willingness to accept work if offered, I incur no liability if my neighbor's refusal of work that must be performed on her Sabbath causes me to decline to make the gift. Nevertheless, the cases from *Sherbert v. Verner* in 1963 through [others] all hold that conditions of precisely this sort are sufficient to trigger the Free Exercise Clause.

These cases can be squared with the common law approach to defining free exercise burdens by supplementing the traditional common law conception of property with the concept of "entitlement." "Entitlements," which qualify as property for procedural due process purposes, are benefits that are universal, and held or expected under objective criteria, or scarce, and terminable only for substantive cause when persons possess them. The entitlement concept finds its roots in a legal theory in which property interests, protected by the Constitution, arise from other legal sources that establish them. However formal the concept may be, it serves to protect the security of vulnerable individuals against the loss of government benefits upon which they legitimately depend....

Sherbert and the other unemployment compensation cases are easy to explain when entitlement analysis is considered. Indeed, the unemployment compensation cases might fall into either of the two entitlement categories. Unemployment benefits are universally available to the involuntarily unemployed, and availability for Saturday work might be viewed as a limiting condition on a universal entitlement. Alternatively, under a view of the benefits as scarce and subject to forfeiture only for good cause, a termination of benefits for refusing a position requiring Saturday work is a loss of property and hence a burden in the conventional, common law sense. Either way, if the limiting condition affects behavior that meets the other threshold requirements of religiosity and sincerity, the condition should be subject to free exercise review....

Application of the entitlement strand of the common law principle also leads to a more thorough analysis of *Mozert*. Chief Judge Lively argued that the reading requirements imposed by the school system did not rise to the burden level because students were not required to affirm the content of what they read. A more precise view of the problem, however, would include the observation that public schools are a state-provided benefit to which school-age children are typically entitled by law. As a matter of state policy, reading requirements may be conditions of continued access to the entitlement. If failure to comply with the condition—in this case, for religious reasons—results in forfeiture of a universally available entitlement, the reading requirements may be viewed as burdensome under the common law principle.

NOTES

As a result of editing, the notes for this essay have been renumbered. The note number from the original essay or article is shown in parentheses at the end of each citation.

1. 485 U.S. 439, 108 S. Ct. 1319 (1988). (7)

2. 827 U.S. 1058 (6th Cir. 1987). (8)

3. *Mozert v. Hawkins County Public Schools*, 647 F. Supp. 1194, 1200 (E.D. Tenn. 1986). (98)

4. 827 F.2d at 1070. (44)

5. 108 S. Ct. at 1326. (53)

6. Ibid., p. 1334–36, 1339 (Brennan, J., dissenting). (54)

[7. See, e.g., *Sherbert v. Verner* and later cases involving unemployment compensation payments.]

8. Va. Code. Ann. § 57–1 (1986). (126)

9. R. Powell and P. Rohan, *The Law of Real Property*, vol. 3 (1987), pp. 34–105, 413. (139)

10. See, e.g., *Mounsey v. Ismay*, 1 Hurl. & Colt. 729, 729, 158 Eng. Rep. 1077, 1077 (Q.B. 1863). (149)

B. MEASURING GOVERNMENTAL INTERESTS

TAKING THE FREE EXERCISE CLAUSE SERIOUSLY

STEPHEN PEPPER

SOME PROBLEMS WITH TAKING FREEDOM OF RELIGION SERIOUSLY

Sincerity

In a world in which many people wish to engage in racial discrimination in private school admissions, granting a religious exemption from the otherwise applicable denial of tax-exempt status will provide a significant incentive to strategic claims of religious scruples. The government is then put to the uncomfortable choice either of allowing itself to be lied to or of setting up a process to assay the sincerity of religious claims.

Stephen Pepper, "Taking the Free Exercise Clause Seriously," *Brigham Young University Law Review* (1986): 323–24, 325–28, 332–36

[Pepper notes the same problems of second-guessing claimants' sincerity described by Lupu in the previous excerpt and argues:]

Taking the Free Exercise Clause seriously means coming to terms with the sincerity issue rather than avoiding it. Two major possibilities present themselves. First, one can attempt to distinguish between situations in which "strategic behavior" is likely to occur and those in which it is less likely, and allow substantial free exercise protection only in the latter. As noted above, the Supreme Court's recent decisions could be explained in this manner, although it is not the reason articulated by the Court. This can only be done by degree, however. While few of us desire to educate our children at home, there are some who wish to do so. Under the *Yoder* opinion, only a religious motivation will protect such conduct, and those whose motivation is secular may feign a religious mandate to come under the protection of the Free Exercise Clause. Similarly, while most of us prefer not to lose our jobs, many do at one time or another want to quit. Under *Sherbert*, only a religious basis for voluntarily quitting will provide unemployment insurance benefits. On the other side of the spectrum, avoiding taxes appeals to almost all of us. Free exercise protection would be much more limited on this latter side of the spectrum. This "likelihood of strategic behavior" criterion would protect a meaningful amount of religious conduct and at the same time avoid large-scale determinations of sincerity. A great deal of religious conduct would nonetheless remain unprotected. The observation above about taxes suggests a narrower version of this alternative which would leave more conduct protected. Taxation may simply be a singular area in regard to the probability of insincere claims. Taxation may therefore be an area where the Free Exercise Clause simply must be circumscribed to a far greater extent than in other areas such as employment or social welfare legislation. The [*United States v.*] *Lee* case might be justifiable on this basis.[1] ...

Limits

Absolute freedom cannot be tolerated, even in the name of religion, even if the text of the free exercise clause has no qualifiers.... Freedom of speech doctrine has been struggling for sixty years to determine the limits of the unqualified freedom granted in the First Amendment. Taking the Free Exercise Clause seriously requires that limits be determined and articulated.

1. *The rights of others*

A promising starting point is Madison's early formulation placing the limits of religious conduct at "the preservation of equal liberty" or the "existence of the state." The latter phrase I shall equate with "compelling" or "overriding" interests, and discuss below. The former, "equal liberty," I take to mean the rights of others. The Free Exercise Clause is written to limit governmental conduct and to give shelter from governmental impingement; it is not a license to impinge on private third parties. For example, if your religious shrine is in my backyard, your free exercise right does not trump my property right and allow you to trespass. On the other hand, if your religious shrine is on government property, the Free Exercise Clause may well give you a preferential right of access that others do not share and that the government must recognize. Another example is suggested by the *Lee* case. If Lee had refused to make social security tax contributions for employees who did not share his conscientious objection to the social security system, then his conduct would not be between just himself and the government, but would also invade the private rights of third parties....

Such a private/public dichotomy is important because it narrows the scope of religious freedom to a manageable size. Damage to governmental interests may damage others. For example, my child's ignorance may make the economy less productive (*Yoder*), or my refusal to pay a tax may make your contribution greater (*Lee*). But these harms are indirect and partial—they are general harms, and hence their effect on any individual is diluted. In *Sherbert*, *Yoder*, *Lee*, [and several other cases,] granting the claimed exemption does no direct harm to any identifiable third party. My religious obligation to trespass on your backyard or my religious obligation to indoctrinate your child are quite different. The Free Exercise Clause is written in terms of a right as against the collective, not against individuals. This line may not be as clear or automatic as one would like, but it is an important line that can be drawn.... ([W]hen I call on the government to enforce my property right in my backyard against your use of a religious shrine, there ought not be a balancing process between property rights and religious liberty; it must be seen as my private right, not a governmental interest, at issue.)

2. Governmental interests

Leaving aside "compelling" and "overriding" interest rhetoric, it is worth noting that the actual harm threatened in the *Yoder* and *Sherbert* cases was entirely speculative and abstract. The state would have to pay Adel[e] Sherbert's twenty-six weeks of benefits, but that is all. The children not going to school in *Yoder* were not being harmed in any concrete, measurable way.... [S]ignificant protection for religious conduct would be provided merely by requiring...that government show a non-speculative, identifiable, measurable, non-trivial injury to a legitimate interest.[2]

In *Bob Jones University v. United States*,[3] the Court affirmed IRS denial of the University's tax exempt status resulting from religiously based racial discrimination.... The Court recognized the "compelling" and "overriding" nature of the government's general interest "in eradicating racial discrimination in education,"[4] but never narrowed that general governmental interest as it did in *Yoder.* No effort was made to measure the likely effect of exemption for religious dissenters on the government's generally very strong interest. Certainly Bob Jones University itself continuing as tax exempt would have no generalized devastating effect on racial integration in education. How many similarly situated institutions are there? More important, how many institutions would make insincere claims of a religious basis for racial discrimination if an exemption were recognized? And would it be possible (and at what expense) to limit an exemption to that very small group with a genuinely religious basis for racial discrimination? The *Bob Jones* case is extraordinarily difficult; two constitutional interests of the highest order clash. It is difficult to discern what result taking the Free Exercise Clause seriously in *Bob Jones* would lead to, but it would lead to a quite different opinion. The *Sherbert-Yoder* doctrine involves a careful narrowing and weighing of interests, as exemplified by the *Yoder* opinion itself, not the conclusory work exhibited in *Bob Jones.**

A second step would be to rule out administrative inconvenience and administrative costs as interests sufficient to justify impingement on religious conduct unless they are substantial in proportion to the overall administrative costs of the governmental program or conduct at issue.... [P]rimarily bureaucratic values—such as uniformity, routinization, and mechanization—ought

---

*This paragraph has been relocated from pp. 323–24 of the original.

to be viewed with skepticism as justifications for impingement on the constitutional right of religious liberty.

If the line is merely drawn here and goes no further, freedom of religion will be given substantial protection from governmental impingement. Where to draw the line beyond this modest point is a complex question.

NOTES

As a result of editing, the notes for this essay have been renumbered. The note number from the original essay or article is shown in parentheses at the end of each citation.

1. [In *United States v. Lee*, 455 U.S. 252 (1982), the Court refused to exempt Amish carpenters and artisans from paying social security taxes for their Amish employees, even though the sect objected to Social Security on the ground that caring for those in need was the responsibility of the religious community not the government.] (115)

2. One such governmental interest, of course, is the "equal rights of others," discussed in the immediately preceding sub-section. "Non-trivial, non-speculative, direct injury to third parties resulting from religious conduct may be a useful criterion for removing free exercise clause protection." (155)

3. 461 U.S. 574 (1983). (102)

4. Ibid., p. 604. (104)

THE NEW ATTACKS ON RELIGIOUS FREEDOM LEGISLATION, AND WHY THEY ARE WRONG

Thomas C. Berg

If the proper standard for evaluating claims to religious exemptions is something significant but moderate, is it appropriate to use the compelling interest test, which stands for the strictest form of judicial scrutiny possible? The critics of RFRA-type legislation say that the compelling interest language does not accurately describe the review that courts have given or should give to religious accommodation claims. They argue that the use of a weakened form of review under this name will "subvert [the test's] rigor in the other fields" where it should remain the most stringent—for example, cases involving state discrimination against religion, against a disfavored racial group, or against the expression of a political or ideological viewpoint.[1] I have some sympathy with these contentions. Arguably, given the percentage of religious exemption claims that has been rejected in the past, language

Thomas C. Berg, "The New Attacks on Religious Freedom Legislation, and Why They Are Wrong," *Cardozo Law Review* 21 (1999): 415, 425–32.

reflecting an intermediate standard of review would more accurately describe the kind of analysis that courts will inevitably apply in exemption cases.

However, there are also good reasons to use the compelling interest language, and the problems with its use are not as severe as the critics claim. The compelling interest standard, even if not perfect, communicates the notion that only a set of basic, important social duties can justify the substantial restriction of religiously motivated conduct. In addition, because judges often under-enforce even strong claims for exemption of religious conduct, intermediate scrutiny would probably produce even weaker results. The compelling interest test is probably necessary in order to secure even moderate protection in religious exemption cases.

Moreover, the criticisms of the compelling interest test rest on a misunderstanding of the test's practical workings. Whether the case involves a discriminatory law or a generally applicable one, the Court is often willing to accept that the law in question serves a compelling purpose in the abstract. Often the reason a discriminatory law flunks the compelling interest test is that the law, while sounding important in the abstract, is less so in the concrete situation. There is no compelling justification for the discriminatory treatment of one form of expression as opposed to another, or the discriminatory treatment of religion as opposed to non-religion. To put it another way, the law is not precisely drawn to achieve the compelling interest asserted.

For example, in [the *Lukumi* case], the set of city ordinances invalidated under the compelling interest test prohibited the killing of animals but allowed a host of exceptions including food consumption and licensed slaughterhouse use, leaving the ritual sacrifices by members of the Santeria religion as virtually the only activity prohibited. The city relied on its interests in public health and preventing cruelty to animals, and the Court did not deny that those interests could be compelling in the abstract. Instead it said only that the interests were not compelling "in the context of these ordinances," and that even if they were compelling, they were not "drawn in narrow terms."[2] The suppression of religious conduct went beyond what was required by health and safety interests (for example, the city could have just required sanitary conditions and disposal of the animals); by prohibiting the Santeria practices alone, the ordinances left out a substantial amount of conduct that would cause the same problems, thereby showing that the goal being served was not really compelling. Again, the discriminatory nature of the restrictions undercut the assertion of any compelling need in the specific case....

Because the discriminatory nature of a law typically undercuts the goals it purports to serve, discriminatory laws almost always fail strict scrutiny. There is seldom, if ever, a strong reason to legislate only on the problems caused by either religious activity, a particular racial group, or political viewpoint; such legislation almost always reflects prejudice and not a significant societal interest. But the matter differs somewhat for generally applicable laws restricting conduct. The more broadly the government applies a restriction, the more credible is its assertion of social need.... Thus, it is not surprising that even the compelling interest test would give religious conduct less than an absolute right to exemption from generally applicable laws, while effectively giving per se protection against laws discriminating against religion or against particular forms of speech. The fact that some claims for conduct exemptions fail shows not that a different test is being applied, but simply that the compelling interest test produces mixed results in that category of cases.

[Nevertheless,] the compelling interest analysis should remain a significant hurdle for the government to clear even in cases involving truly general restrictions on conduct. The key is that the religious claimant seeks not to strike down the law altogether, but only to secure an exemption or other form of accommodation from its terms. Once again, therefore, the threat is not to the government's underlying interest in the abstract. Rather, the only consequence is that this particular believer or group will be exempted, which is generally far less disruptive to the government's regulatory purposes. Unless the government can show a serious harm from the exemption itself, then it must follow the "less restrictive means" of exempting the religious believer while continuing to enforce the law in general.[3] This structure of analysis makes it possible to avoid many conflicts between religion and government; the believer can practice her faith, and the government can achieve its goal in the other 99 percent of cases....

One function of the compelling interest test is that certain kinds of governmental interests are categorically insufficient to justify substantial restrictions on religious freedom. The law in question must at least relate to "public safety, peace, and order," in the words of *Yoder* and *Sherbert*.[4] Preservation ordinances [which forbid changes to historic buildings], and some zoning ordinances, reflect only aesthetic interests and thus are not sufficient.

In addition, the exemption analysis can take into account whether the religious claimant's conduct, even if exempted from the specific terms of the law, will nevertheless be consistent with the general societal interest that underlies the law. If it will, then there is certainly no compelling interest in denying the exemption. The prime example is *Yoder* [see p. 59], where the Amish system of informal vocational education for their teenagers served "precisely those overall interests" in self-reliance and intelligence that the state asserted in support of requiring children to attend formal schooling. Likewise, the fact that Sikh boys are disciplined in the use of their ceremonial knives supports the ruling that those knives, if securely sewn shut, should be permitted in school.[5] Native Americans, whose claim of a right to ingest peyote in their worship services is strongly supported by the church's own restrictions on peyote use outside the context of worship and who have demonstrated success in attacking the problem of alcohol abuse in their community, should be permitted to ingest peyote within the context of a worship service. Finally, [in *Lee*] the Amish record of caring for their own members and refusing social security benefits should have led to exempting them from compulsory social security taxes.

This principle is not simply a function of whether the government's interest is being served. It stems from one of the theoretical premises for protecting religious freedom. The framing generation believed that religious groups were likely to have their own communal norms that would restrain their members' behavior and direct it in a productive fashion. The Framers believed, therefore, that respecting those norms played a crucial role in fostering virtue among the citizenry without excessive governmental regulation of behavior.[6] Although this outlook does not constitute the only justification for protecting religious freedom, and therefore should not exhaust the scope of a religious freedom statute, it remains an important factor today.

In some cases, however, it is unwarranted even to grant a single exemption for a religious claim. First, it may be that any individual instance of particular religious activity imposes on the basic rights of another person: for example, a religiously motivated human sacrifice, or a religiously motivated trespass on another's backyard. Religious freedom does not include the right to commit direct invasions of another person's life, liberty, or property—the historic framework of criminal or tortious acts. This generally libertarian framework is an attractive starting point for religious freedom disputes. First, such a libertarian framework provided the legal background against which the Framers drafted religious freedom rights, and provided a structure that the Framers would largely have assumed in defining those rights.[7] Second, the libertarian framework of bodily, property, and contractual rights must be respected, at least to a significant extent, if religious freedom is to mean very much. The libertarian framework specifically aims to recognize a considerable scope of freedom for the actor—by giving her control over her own body and property—while at the same time defining limits on that freedom in order to protect the bodily and property rights of others. If the government can choose to define any action as a violation of another's rights, then religious freedom will mean little. If the government has carte blanche to define a religious landlord's refusal to rent to an unmarried couple as a violation of their rights, then the religious landlord will lose a crucial space—her property—in which to exercise her religious beliefs. If the government has carte blanche to define a religious organization's refusal to hire a person as a violation of her rights, then religious organizations will lose the ability to control who carries out their mission and how. Thus, antidiscrimination laws should be subjected to close scrutiny to the extent that they conflict with religious conscience....

Alternatively, granting even one exemption may logically entail granting a host of others, thus undermining a law not just at the margin, but in its basic purposes. This result will be more likely when the exemption strongly coincides with secular self-interest—thus creating a strong incentive to assert the claim—and when it is difficult to separate sincere from insincere claims. On such grounds, the Supreme Court refused to require draft exemptions for conscientious objectors to particular wars,[8] and courts have refused to exempt sacramental users of marijuana even though sacramental users of peyote are exempt.[9] Moreover, if an exemption strongly coincides with secular self-interest, granting it may go beyond protecting religious conscience and may primarily create an affirmative incentive to practice religion. It was likely on this ground that the Supreme Court refused to recognize tax exemptions limited to religious claims, at least where no strong claim of conscience underlay the objection to paying taxes.[10] But such arguments against exemption must rest on specific evidence, not on mere speculation.

NOTES

As a result of editing, the notes for this essay have been renumbered. The note number from the original essay or article is shown in parentheses at the end of each citation.

1. See, e.g., *Employment Division v. Smith*, 494 U.S. 872, 888 (1990). (50)

2. *Lukumi*, 508 U.S. 546. (53)

3. See, e.g., Religious Freedom Restoration Act of 1993, 42 U.S.C. § 2000bb–3 (1994) (requiring the government to show that "application of the burden to the person" is the least restrictive means to a compelling interest); *Wisconsin v. Yoder*, 406 U.S. 205, 221 (1972) (stating that despite validity of state's interest "in the generality of cases, we must searchingly examine the interests that the State seeks to promote" in the particular case). (60)

4. *Yoder*, 406 U.S. 230; *Sherbert*, 374 U.S. 400, 403. (62)

5. See *Cheema v. Thompson*, 67 F.3d 883 (9th Cir. 1995) (as held under RFRA). (65)

6. For support and discussion, see Mark Tushnet, *Red, White, and Blue: A Critical Analysis of Constitutional Law* (1988), p. 274 (noting that founding generation saw religious groups as places where citizens could learn the habit of recognizing the common good). See also Timothy L. Hall, "Religion and Civic Virtue: A Justification of Free Exercise," *Tulane Law Review* 67 (1992): 87, 106–07 ("Eighteenth-century Americans generally agreed that religion was a principal social actor in the formation of civic virtue"); Michael W. McConnell, "Accommodation of Religion," *Supreme Court Review* (1985): 1, 19–20 (noting that founding generation guaranteed religious liberty "in the hope and expectation that religious observance would flourish, and with it morality and self-restraint among the people"). (68)

7. As Madison put it, religious exercise should be free up to the point where it "trespass[es] on private rights or the public peace." "Letter from James Madison to Edward Livingston" (July 10, 1822), reprinted in Gaillard Hunt, ed., *The Writings of James Madison*, vol. 9 (1910), pp. 98, 100. (69)

8. See *Gillette v. United States*, 401 U.S. 437 (1971). (72)

9. See *Olsen v. Drug Enforcement Administration*, 878 F.2d 1458 (D.C. Cir. 1989). (73)

10. See *Jimmy Swaggart Ministries v. Board of Equalization*, 493 U.S. 378 (1990). (74)

A COMMON-LAW MODEL FOR RELIGIOUS EXEMPTIONS

EUGENE VOLOKH

A General Regime of Exemptions for Conduct Even When It Harms Others

[One] possible kind of free exercise claim is a broad right to do whatever your religion motivates (or, in some formulations of the theory, compels) you to do, simply because of your religious motivation. Taken literally, such a claim is clearly too broad. Surely no court would immunize, for instance, murder or rape simply because the perpetrator acted out of religious conviction.

Nonetheless, one might argue, while the right to life or to bodily integrity is more important than religious freedom, the right to religious freedom is more important than some other rights. Thus, the argument might go, religious conduct might be protected even when it harms others in certain ways, perhaps even when it constitutes, for instance, assault, breach of contract, copyright infringement, libel, trespass on private property, or negligent

Eugene Volokh, "A Common-Law Model for Religious Exemptions," *UCLA Law Review* 46 (1999): 1465, 1469–70, 1510–13, 1515–23, 1525–29.

infliction of physical injury. One formulation I have sometimes heard is that religious conduct should be constitutionally protected even when it harms others so long as the harm to others is outweighed by the importance of the conduct to the religious observer.

But such a claim is normatively unappealing. My relationship with my God may be important to me, but how can it by itself—setting aside any special, narrower justification[s]—be a constitutionally sufficient justification for my harming you, even slightly? From your perspective and the legal system's perspective (even if not from my own), my God is my God, not yours, and the Constitution doesn't give those acting in His name sovereignty over your legally recognized rights and interests....

A General Regime of Exemptions for Conduct That Does Not Harm Others

The most common claim for a constitutional exemption regime is [different]—a broad right to do what your religion motivates you to do, simply because of your religious motivation, but only so long as it doesn't harm others. Jefferson's defense of religious freedom, for instance, was justified by the argument that someone's "say[ing] there are twenty gods, or no God... neither picks my pocket nor breaks my leg."[1] Madison wrote that religion should be "immun[e] ... from civil jurisdiction, in every case where it does not trespass on private rights or the public peace."[2] Similarly, Michael McConnell, one of the leading authors on free exercise law, argues that we should be "free to practice our religions so long as we do not injure others."[3] ...

[W]hen exemption proposals are limited to conduct that doesn't harm others—that doesn't invade their rights or impose improper externalities on them—they they seem quite appealing. After all, if my religiously motivated actions genuinely harm no one, why shouldn't I be allowed to engage in them?

The Private Rights and Interests of Others

The Debates About What Constitutes the Private Rights and Interests of Others

The difficulty is that what constitutes "invading the rights of others" and "imposing improper externalities on others" are hotly contested questions. Do people have a right not to be economically pressured into working at exploitative wages? Do people have a right to be free from various kinds of discrimination in private commercial transactions? Do children have a right—unwaivable by them because of their immaturity—to be educated until age sixteen?[4] Do litigants have a right to require a reluctant witness to testify?[5]

Do householders have a right to be free from the intrusion and annoyance created by certain kinds of land use by their neighbors? Do businesspeople have the right to be free from various forms of unfair competition—unfair because it's monopolistic or potentially involves misleading consumers, or because it takes advantage of certain cost savings? Does a person's failure to report for the draft impose unjustified externalities on other draft-eligible people? Do creditors have a right to repayment by a bankrupt debtor that precludes the debtor from giving away his property as he sees fit [for example, in tithes to a church]? The answers to these questions can't be deduced through pure logic or traditional constitutional analysis.

Similarly, there are lively debates about when the likelihood of violation of others' rights by some justifies a restraint on the liberty of all. Most agree that some such prophylactic rules are proper: Consider bans on drunk driving, which are justified by the possibility that a drunk driver might cause injury to another, even though most instances of drunk driving do not actually cause such injury. May the law likewise ban other driving practices—such as driving a horse and buggy without an orange reflector—that foreseeably pose a risk to others, but that need not necessarily cause injury?[6] What about possession and use of alcohol or drugs, which lead some people to act criminally or tortiously, but which others use quite safely?[7] What about possession or carrying of certain weapons, which some people use to violate others' rights but which others use for innocent, even laudable, purposes?

Neither is there a consensus about whether certain externalities actually flow from certain kinds of behavior, or which of those externalities are improper. Is an employer imposing an improper externality on taxpayers when, by paying employees a lower wage, it "casts a direct burden for [the employees'] support upon the community," on the theory that "[w]hat these workers lose in wages the taxpayers are called upon to pay"?[8] Is an employment agency imposing an improper externality when, through its actions, it increases unemployment, and do such agencies' actions in fact tend to increase unemployment? Is a motorcyclist acting improperly when he rides his motorcycle without a helmet, thus increasing his chances of suffering an injury for which the taxpayers will have to pay? Does drug use really lead to more street crime than would the less restrictive alternative of decriminalization?

Thus, the debate is not really about whether people should be able to do what they please so long as they don't harm others. The reason for most restrictions on conduct is precisely that people think the conduct does harm others. In my experience, for instance, when people have defended the religious landlady's claimed right to discriminate against unmarried couples in housing rentals, they have rarely claimed that, just because the landlady's beliefs are religious, she is entitled to deny to tenants their private right to equal treatment (the second kind of claim I outlined above). Nor have they generally admitted that the landlady's conduct imposes some real harm on the tenants while arguing that the harm is outweighed by the benefit to the landlady's religious practice. After all, when conduct genuinely causes harm to another—as for instance when the conduct is a trespass on the other's property, a breach of contract, or an infringement of the other's copyright—such a harm, even if relatively modest, can't be justified on the grounds that the person inflicting the harm might get a tremendous spiritual benefit from acting this way.

Rather, supporters of the landlady's right usually make the [different] claim—that the landlady's religiously motivated decision should be immune because it doesn't really harm the tenants, since the tenants don't really have a true private right to equal treatment. The debate is thus about who ultimately defines what constitutes "infringement of the private rights of others" or "imposition of improper externalities on others"—the legislature or the courts.

The Connection to the Early 1900s
Substantive Due Process Debates

The power to define, as a final, constitutional matter, the limits of another's lawful private rights or to decide what constitutes an unjustified externality is the very power that proved so troubling in the early 1900s substantive due process cases [such as the famous case of *Lochner v. New York*[9]]. Those cases, after all, didn't purport to reject the government's right to protect people against injuries inflicted by others, but they did claim for courts the power to finally define what was an injury and what was not. A minimum-wage law was unconstitutional [in *Adkins v. Children's Hospital*] because the employer wasn't hurting the employee by paying him too little.[10] A ban on employers' requiring employees to agree not to join a union was unconstitutional because it didn't violate anyone's rights for an employer to discriminate based on a person's union membership. A law allowing certain kinds of picketing was unconstitutional because union members had no right, and could be given no right, to engage in "palpable wrongs" such as "libelous attacks," "abusive epithets," and "unlawful annoyance and...hurtful nuisance."[11] A maximum-hours law was unconstitutional [in *Lochner* itself] because there was no legally cognizable harm, the Court assumed, in a bakery owner's bargaining with employees for a work week longer than sixty hours.

On the other hand, a requirement that an employer issues a discharged employee a letter "setting forth the nature and character of his service [rendered] and its duration, and truly stating what cause, if any, led him to quit such service" was upheld because it helped preserve the employee's reputation, which "is an essential part of his personal rights—of his right of personal security."[12] A zoning law prohibiting apartment buildings in a certain residential area was upheld because the buildings, with their tendency to create various externalities for neighbors—"street accidents," "noise," "interfer[ence]... with the free circulation of air and monopoliz[ation of] the rays of the sun"— "come very near to being nuisances."[13] An alcohol ban was upheld because "the general use of intoxicating drinks" leads (albeit indirectly) to "idleness, disorder, pauperism, and crime."[14] Some claims of externalities and countervailing private rights won and some lost, with little to explain the distinction beyond the moral and practical senses of the judges, and perhaps the degree to which the claims fit with traditional common-law rules.

The Court ultimately repudiated this substantive due process jurisprudence, because it concluded that the legislature may redefine private rights by, for instance, deciding that people had a right to "protection from unscrupulous and overreaching employers," or to be free from being "exploit[ed]...at wages so low as to be insufficient to meet the bare cost of living."[15] Likewise, the legislature may try to prevent more indirect externalities, such as the "burden [imposed] upon the community" for the support of workers who are being paid less than "[t]he bare cost of living."[16] The legislature wasn't limited to protecting private rights akin to those traditionally secured by the common law, such as reputation or freedom from nuisance. It could also recognize new private rights, even controversial ones, and protect them even though this meant limiting the liberty of people to infringe those new rights.

A constitutional religious exemption regime would either return courts to identifying their own favored view of what really constitutes others' private rights and interests, and enforcing it contrary to the political branches' views, or would require them to rule that certain violations of others' private rights and interests must be permitted just because the violator acted for religious reasons....

[For example,] say a landlady believes it would be sinful for her to rent an apartment to an unmarried couple. Again, if she makes a substantive due process challenge to a law banning marital-status discrimination in housing, she will lose (assuming she falls outside the narrow zone of constitutional protection provided by the right of intimate association). Sure, she might claim she isn't violating anyone's rights by her decision, and again libertarians may agree. No one, they will argue, has a right to rent another's property over the owner's objections. But the legislature has taken a different view—unlike the libertarians, it believes everyone has a right to be treated equally, even in the opportunities to use another's property. And it is not for courts to decide whether the legislature's or the libertarians' moral vision is correct.

[In contrast,] a constitutional religious exemption regime would require courts to decide the questions that substantive due process jurisprudence suggests they ought not decide. The law commands the landlady to do something she thinks is religiously prohibited, so the landlady would have to be exempted unless the law passes strict scrutiny. Whether there is a compelling government interest in prohibiting discrimination rests—[j]ust as with prohibiting trespass, copyright infringement, or assault—on whether a person has the right to be free of such discrimination.

A court applying a constitutional exemption regime of the "so long as it doesn't interfere with the rights of others" variety will have to resolve this difficult moral question itself, perhaps trumping the legislative decision. "While there is a private right to be free from race or sex discrimination," the court may say, as some courts have indeed said, "there's really no private right to be free from marital status discrimination, no matter what the legislature might conclude." A court applying a constitutional exemption regime of the "even if it does interfere with the rights of others" stripe may have to go further: "Even if there is a private right to be free from marital status discrimination, a landlady who wants to violate this right for religious reasons must be free to violate it, simply because she's religiously motivated." Again, the first of these seems unjustified, and the second seems normatively unattractive.

[Professor Volokh contrasts the constitutional exemption regime with a "common-law exemption regime." Under the latter, courts could issue rulings defining and limiting those rights and interests that override religious freedom—just as courts issue rulings in cases involving torts, contracts, and other common-law subjects—but, as in these other areas, the legislature could then override the court's judgment.]

[A] court applying a common-law exemption regime may actually give the [religious] landlady what she wants. The principle of the common-law regime is that there is nothing wrong with the court's saying "While there is a private right to be free from race or sex discrimination, there really is no private right to be free from marital status discrimination"—so long as the court doesn't add "no matter what the legislature might say." In fact, this distinction between different kinds of discrimination may be quite reasonable, and is akin to the distinctions courts have traditionally drawn in exercising the moral and practical judgment involved in creating the common law.

If the legislature agrees with the court that there is no private right to be free from marital-status discrimination, then the court decision will stand. This might happen if, for instance, that particular discrimination ban was aimed more at relieving a broader economic problem of occasional shortages of housing for particular groups (a problem that a narrow religious exemption probably wouldn't exacerbate) than at securing perceived private rights to be free from individual instances of discrimination. But if the legislature takes a different view of private rights, its view could prevail, just as the legislature's view of countervailing private rights prevails over the courts' when the question is the scope of one's right to act free of tort liability.

Finally, consider the right-to-assisted-suicide cases. In *Washington v. Glucksberg*,[17] the Court concluded that this claimed right does not fall within the narrow "right of privacy," in which judicial, rather than legislative, judgment is paramount. Given this conclusion, it was easy to defend bans on assisted suicide against substantive due process claims. "Whom do I hurt by assisting a suicide?" Dr. Kevorkian asks. Well, the government might say, allowing assisted suicide by some will create an improper externality for others: It will lead to their being pressured—by greedy or distraught family members, or by greedy or uncaring doctors—into choosing suicide. And because the court can't tell whether such a prediction would be right or wrong, the matter is left to the legislature.

But say a doctor claims a religious obligation to assist the suicide of someone whose life has lost what the doctor considers to be the proper dignity; or say a patient claims a religious obligation to end his life with a doctor's help. (Some have in fact asserted such obligations.) Under a constitutional religious exemption regime, just as under the substantive due process regime rejected in *Glucksberg*, the court would have to do what *Glucksberg* correctly concluded courts shouldn't do.

One constitutional exemption model would require that the court decide whether, as a moral matter, the supposed externality—pressure on others to commit suicide even when they wouldn't otherwise choose it—is improper, and whether, as a practical matter, the supposed externality is indeed likely to materialize (a hotly contested question). Under the other constitutional exemption model, the court would have to decide whether, even if letting people commit assisted suicide does impose an improper externality on others, they should nonetheless be allowed to inflict this externality simply because their motivations are religious. Neither of these approaches seems sound, and both seem inconsistent with the reasoning of *Glucksberg* and more generally with the rejection of the early 1900s substantive due process claims.

Again, a common-law exemption regime would actually let a court carve out an exemption here, if the court concludes that such an exemption wouldn't harm other patients—for instance, if the court disagrees with the prediction that recognizing a right to assisted suicide would actually cause improper pressure on patients. But if the legislature disagrees, either immediately or after looking at the results of several years of this experiment, it can reverse this judgment and prevent what it concludes is harm to others....

The above argument thus counsels against a general constitutional exemption regime for religiously motivated action. Such action, when it hurts others, can't be protected just because of its religiosity. And while the notion that "you may do as you please—or as your God pleases—so long as you don't hurt others" is appealing, the ultimate definition of "hurt others" should be made by legislatures (as in the common-law model), not by courts (as in the constitutional model).

[However, Professor Volokh continues, his argument also shows that "*Employment Division v. Smith*'s criticism of the constitutional exemption model does not condemn" religious freedom legislation like the Religious Freedom Restoration Act (RFRA) or state versions of RFRA (discussed in the next part of this book).]

As under the constitutional exemption model, state RFRAs (and the federal RFRA applied to federal laws) let courts decide in the first instance whether an exemption is to be granted. But because RFRAs may be revised by the legislature, the courts' decisions aren't final. Ultimately, the tough calls will be governed by the political process, just as they have been in the common-law system under which American law has generally evolved.

From this observation flow some other conclusions. First, . . . the common-law framework gives exemption supporters some of what they want, despite the possibility of legislative override. By letting courts take the lead in carving out exemptions for conduct that, in the courts' view, doesn't really harm others, the framework shifts the burden of overcoming legislative inertia to favor exemption supporters. Exemptions would thus be rejected only based on a considered judgment, rather than by mechanical application of laws that may have been enacted without any consideration of their possible effect on religious practices. . . . [And] state RFRAs may embolden judges to carve out exemptions that they might not have carved out under the constitutional exemption model.*

NOTES

As a result of editing, the notes for this essay have been renumbered. The note number from the original essay or article is shown in parentheses at the end of each citation.

1. Thomas Jefferson, *Notes on the State of Virginia*, ed. William Peden (1955), p. 159. (150)

2. "Letter from James Madison to Edward Livingston (July 10, 1822)," in Gaillard Hunt, ed., *The Writings of James Madison*, vol. 9 (1901), p. 100. (151)

3. McConnell, ["Free Exercise Revisionism and the Smith Decision," *University of Chicago Law Review* 57 (1990): 1109, 1128; see also [Pepper excerpt, p. 221 in this book]. (152)

4. Compare *Yoder*. (159)

5. Compare [cases and articles involving assertions by some observant Jews that Jewish law forbids one to give testimony against a family member in a legal proceeding]. (160)

6. *Cf. State v. Miller*, 538 N.W.2d 573, 577–79 (Wisc. Ct. App. 1995) [(striking down such a ban as applied to Amish who objected to putting bright reflectors on their buggies)]. (166)

7. . . . As to peyote, [for example,] compare *Smith*, 494 U.S. 905–06 (O'Connor, J.,

---

*The following two paragraphs are relocated from p. 1469 of the original.

concurring) (concluding that a religious exemption for peyote users may lead to serious health effects and to an increase in illegal drug trafficking); ... with, for example, [ibid.] , pp. 913, 916 (Blackmun, J., dissenting) (concluding that peyote is not harmful because of "[t]he Native American Church's internal restrictions on, and supervision of, its members' use of peyote" and that "[t]here is ... practically no illegal traffic in peyote"). ... (167)

8. *West Coast Hotel Co. v. Parrish*, 300 U.S. 379, 399 (1937) (using this argument to uphold a minimum-wage law). (169)

[9. 198 U.S. 45 (1905).]

10. 261 U.S. 525 (1923). (173)

11. *Truax v. Corrigan*, 257 U.S. 312, 327–28 (1921). (175)

12. *Prudential Insurance Co. v. Cheek*, 259 U.S. 530, 545–46 (1922). (177)

13. *Village of Euclod v. Ambler Realty Co.*, 272 U.S. 365, 394–95 (1926). (178)

14. *Mugler v. Kansas*, 123 U.S. 623, 662 (1887). (179)

15. *West Coast Hotel*, 300 U.S. 398–99. (180)

16. Ibid., p. 399. (181)

17. 521 U.S. 702 (1997). (199)

PART III

LEGISLATIVE PROTECTION OF RELIGIOUS FREEDOM

Chapter 8

THE DEBATE OVER THE RELIGIOUS FREEDOM RESTORATION ACT (RFRA)

WHAT HATH CONGRESS WROUGHT?
AN INTERPRETIVE GUIDE TO THE
RELIGIOUS FREEDOM RESTORATION ACT

Thomas C. Berg

The Development and Passage of RFRA

[Because of its broad rejection of free exercise exemptions, the ruling in *Employment Division v.*] *Smith* provoked immediate and widespread surprise and anger. A petition for rehearing was joined by a large number of religious and civil liberties groups and more than fifty law professors. After the denial of the petition, a broad-based coalition of religious and civil liberties groups formed to pursue the next alternative, restoring religious freedom by statute.

The legislative remedy suggested in *Smith* itself—exemptions directed one-by-one at particular instances of conflict—suffered from significant weaknesses. A drafter and leading academic supporter of RFRA, Professor

Thomas C. Berg, "What Hath Congress Wrought? An Interpretive Guide to the Religious Freedom Restoration Act," *Villanova Law Review* 39 (1994): 1, 12–17.

Douglas Laycock, later testified to Congress that such "piecemeal" exemptions, enacted "one statute at a time, are not a workable means of protecting religious liberty." Laycock reasoned that "[n]o church is big enough or tough enough to fight [opposing interests] off, over and over, at every level of government" and that individual believers would face even greater obstacles.[1] Thus, religious freedom advocates quickly settled on an across-the-board approach, announcing a general standard covering all free exercise claims, rather than insisting that exemptions be granted in specific situations.

The coalition behind RFRA included such unlikely allies as the American Civil Liberties Union and the Traditional Values Coalition.[2] Obviously, the partners started from different and often conflicting premises. On the one hand, the secular civil liberties organizations and their members generally advocate keeping religion one step removed from the public square so as to prevent ecclesiastical coercion and facilitate the establishment of a "secular public moral order."[3] They also believe, however, that the free exercise guarantee should continue to shield the rights of minority religions and those "living apart in enclaves demarcated from the civil order."[4] On the other hand, religious groups vary widely in their attitudes toward government support of and involvement with religion—although none could accept *Smith's* proposition that religious conscience must be subordinate even to modest secular interests of government. Thus, the coalition behind RFRA was fragile. Overall, the coalition partners could agree on the general principle of restoring religious freedom, but consensus would evaporate if any of a number of other issues were specifically addressed in the statute.

Maintaining the size and breadth of the coalition was crucial to passing the Act in Congress. In such a religiously pluralistic nation as America, no single group, or even a small cluster of like-minded religious organizations, could pool enough power to enact RFRA. Religious freedom does not generally rank among Congress' most pressing concerns. The statute's breadth would guarantee Congress' support for religious freedom in a wide range of situations, potentially raising the hackles of many interest groups and government agencies. Thus, support for the statute had to be equally broad. Because it enacted a general standard, rather than dictating the result in any particular dispute, the statute did not promise "concentrated benefits."[5] As a result, proponents could not depend on one sufficiently powerful group to push the matter to completion because its very survival depended on it.

To preserve maximum political attractiveness, the RFRA coalition decided that the most promising route was to design and market the statute primarily as a simple restoration of previously existing free exercise rights. The *Smith* decision was a particularly easy target because of the sweeping and contentious way in which it subordinated minority rights to majority rule. But in order to maintain the coalition, RFRA's proponents were largely forced to avoid dealing explicitly with more difficult and controversial questions such as: how to specify the precise level of protection for religious conduct; how to square free exercise exemptions with Establishment Clause limits on favoritism for religion; and how to address all of the pre-*Smith* cases that had likewise contributed to the downfall of free exercise rights. As one leading proponent of the statute explained to Congress, every alternative formulation to the "compelling interest" test "create[d] more problems than it solve[d]."[6]

Because of the necessity for maintaining the broad coalition, a near fatal blow to RFRA was struck when, in early 1991, some anti-abortion groups attacked the bill on the ground that it might create a statutory right to choose abortion as a matter of religious conscience. The National Right to Life Committee and the United States Catholic Conference both complained that, just as the Supreme Court had begun to cut back on the privacy theory of *Roe v. Wade*,[7] RFRA might give abortion-rights litigators a new theory to argue. Both organizations wanted the bill to explicitly reject such claims. The Catholic Church also sought further amendments to prevent anyone from using RFRA to attack either government funding of religious organizations or their tax-exempt status....

These issues, particularly abortion, stalled RFRA in Congress for almost two years. The defection of some Catholic and anti-abortion legislators reduced the voting bloc. Moreover, President [George H.W.] Bush signaled that he would oppose RFRA unless it contained anti-abortion language, and the bill's supporters lacked the votes to overcome presidential opposition. Alternatively, inserting the anti-abortion and other amendments would certainly drive away liberal coalition members like the ACLU, forfeit the votes of liberal members of Congress and doom the proposed statute. The internecine dispute also drained whatever energy RFRA's proponents might have had for undertaking a substantial alteration of the categories of free exercise jurisprudence. The distraction helped ensure that the statute would not go far beyond the simple notion of restoring a "compelling interest" standard for "burdens" on religion.

In the last half of 1992, however, a combination of developments concerning abortion removed RFRA's major impediments. Free exercise arguments for abortion were made redundant by the revival of other bases for abortion rights—including the surprising reaffirmation of substantive due process rights in *Planned Parenthood v. Casey*[8] and the election of President Bill Clinton, who supported federal abortion rights legislation. Clinton, unlike Bush, was also ready to sign RFRA without anti-abortion amendments. Opposition from religious groups faded away, and they settled for language in the statute and committee reports that left undisturbed previous law on abortion, funding and tax exemptions.

Thus, RFRA was reintroduced in March 1993 and, having already been thoroughly examined and debated, passed and became law in a few months.

NOTES

As a result of editing, the notes for this essay have been renumbered. The note number from the original essay or article is shown in parentheses at the end of each citation.

1. Religious Freedom Restoration Act of 1991: Hearings on H.R. 2797 Before the Subcommittee on Civil and Constitutional Rights of the House Committee on the Judiciary, 102nd Congress, 2nd Session 10–11 (1992) (testimony of Douglas Laycock) [hereinafter "Hearings"]. (48)

2. Among the other liberal religious and civil liberties organizations in the coalition were the American Humanist Association, Americans United for Separation of Church and State, the Anti-Defamation League of B'nai B'rith, the People for the American Way, and the Unitarian Universalist Association. Conservative religious groups included Agudath Israel, Concerned Women for America, the Home School Legal Defense Association, the Mormon Church, the National Association of Evangelicals, and the Southern Baptist Convention's Christian Life Commission. (49)

3. Kathleen M. Sullivan, "Religion and Liberal Democracy," *University of Chicago Law Review* 59 (1992): 195, 198. (50)

4. Ibid., p. 219. (51)

5. See James Q. Wilson , *The Politics of Regulation* (1980), pp. 366–70. (52)

6. "Hearings," p. 29 (statement of Dean M. Kelley). (54)

7. 413 U.S. 110 (1973). *Webster v. Reproductive Health Services*, 492 U.S. 490 (1989), at the time the latest pronouncement from the Court on abortion, had upheld regulations previously struck down under *Roe*'s framework, and seemed to foretell *Roe*'s imminent demise. (55)

8. 505 U.S. 833 (1992) (modifying *Roe* but retaining the basic right to abortion). (62)

RFRA, CONGRESS, AND THE RATCHET

Douglas Laycock

The Reason for the Act

The debate over RFRA is not about something abstruse. If it sometimes seems abstruse, that is the fault of those who are debating. RFRA is about human liberty and the alleviation of human suffering. It is about people who are told to abandon the mode of worship that they have experienced all their lives, and that their faith group has experienced through generations. Abandon your mode of worship or go to jail.

That was the artificially posed issue in *Employment Division v. Smith*, as the Court treated that case, it was about the criminal prohibition of a worship service. That was the issue in *Church of the Lukumi Babalu Aye, Inc. v. City of Hialeah*, which was in fact about the criminal prohibition of a worship service [where animals were sacrificed]. That was the issue in an unreported case

Douglas Laycock, "RFRA, Congress, and the Ratchet," *Montana Law Review* 56 (1995): 145, 145–48, 152–63.

called *McClellan v. Zavaris*. McClellan was an Episcopalian in the Colorado prison system on a work release program. On Sunday mornings, prison authorities let him out to go to Mass. But they said that if he took Communion at the Mass, he would be put back in the general prison population....

[Moreover,] RFRA is about occasional outbreaks of real persecution that are based on or implemented through statutes that are facially neutral and generally applicable within the meaning of *Smith*. The Mormon persecution in the nineteenth century—in which hundreds of church leaders were imprisoned, the Church lost its legal existence, its corporate charter was revoked, and all its property was forfeited to the government—grew out of persistent efforts to enforce a facially neutral law against polygamy [upheld in *Reynolds v. United States*]. The efforts to suppress Jehovah's Witness proselytizing in small towns all over America in the 1930s and 1940s were mostly based on facially neutral ordinances taxing or regulating solicitation. The Ku Klux Klan used a facially neutral statute [in the 1920s] in its attempt to shut down all the Catholic schools in Oregon.[1] The current attempts by the Cult Awareness Network and others to suppress the Hare Krishnas, the Scientologists, the Unification Church, and other such groups are based on general principles of tort law—principles that at least the plaintiffs claim are facially neutral and generally applicable. If you want to think about bitter contemporary conflicts that pose the risk of future waves of persecutions if either side persuades a large majority that it is entirely right, consider the growing conflict between gay rights groups and conservative religious traditions.

Exemptions make it possible to compromise conflicts like these. Without the possibility of exemptions, then either you can not have a gay rights law, or the gay rights law has to apply to the appointment of the Catholic clergy and to everything else that goes on within conscientiously objecting churches. Exemptions make possible a world in which the gay citizens of America can live their life, and in which those who have conscientious objections to gay sex can have a private enclave in which they can live their faith and do not have to fully conform to the rules that have freed gays from discrimination in secular society.

Now, it is true that the Supreme Court did not announce an explicit constitutional right to such exemptions until 1963, [in *Sherbert v. Verner*,] but that does not mean that there was steady regulation of acts based on religious faith before 1963. In fact the issue rarely arose. In an era of much smaller government, much less regulation, and much greater willingness to defer to religious traditions, there was not much square conflict between government regulation and the consciences of various religious groups. All of that has changed. Regulation is much more pervasive, and regulators are much less willing to defer to religious claims.

Therefore, RFRA is an important statute. It is not a technical statute or a minor adjustment to arcane constitutional doctrine. The central argument for the Act is that exemptions increase the scope of human liberty for believers and non-believers alike....

CONSTITUTIONALITY

Congress has the power to enact RFRA under Section 5 of the Fourteenth Amendment. Repeated majorities of the Supreme Court have acknowledged congressional power to go beyond judicial interpretation of the Reconstruction Amendments. Much of the law of private racial discrimination depends on Congress' analogous powers under Section 2 of the Thirteenth Amendment [which prohibits slavery and its "badges or incidents"]. The most familiar and most directly analogous exercises of this power are the various Voting Rights Acts,[2] in which Congress has forbidden practices with disparate impact on minority voters—practices that the Supreme Court had expressly upheld.[3]

The structure of RFRA is entirely parallel to the structure of the Voting Rights Acts. In each context, the Supreme Court requires plaintiffs to prove facial discrimination or actual discriminatory motive to show a constitutional violation. And in each context, Congress created a statutory right in which plaintiffs show a significant burden on their voting rights, but no bad motive and no facial discrimination, and this shifts the burden of justification back to the government. If Congress has power to dispense with proof of bad motive or facial discrimination in voting cases, I think it has power to do so in religion cases.

Despite these precedents, several of the contributors to this symposium find federalism and separation of powers problems with RFRA. [Among other things, they] say that Congress cannot enforce its own understanding of the Free Exercise Clause because that would interfere with the Supreme Court's role as authoritative interpreter of the Constitution....

The Supreme Court's interpretive role includes multiple functions that apply in many contexts; I wish to begin by making some distinctions. "It is emphatically the province and duty of the judicial department to say what the law is" [as the Court said in *Marbury v. Madison*];[4] in case of square conflict, the Supreme Court is the ultimate interpreter of the Constitution. I do not think that the Supreme Court is the exclusive interpreter of the Constitution, but that claim depends on definitional disputes about the meaning of interpretation, and it is not essential to my argument. What is necessary and sufficient to my argument is a less ambiguous formulation: the Court does not have exclusive power to protect our liberties or define their scope. In the absence of a court order or opinion expressly constraining the behavior of the other branches, they can act on their own view of liberty or of the Constitution, and it matters little whether we think of such action as constitutional interpretation or as something else.

The claim that the judiciary is the exclusive or even dominant protector of our liberties is a very recent and mistaken idea, one that has arisen principally in the civil liberties community in the last generation. This view of constitutional structure comes from the experience of *Brown v. Board of Education*[5] and the moral authority of that decision. It comes from the experience of defending the Court against attacks on its legitimacy, and from the debate over *Brown* and the debate over *Roe v. Wade*, from the debate over the legacy of the Warren Court.

Perhaps more than anything, it comes from *Cooper v. Aaron*.[6] *Cooper* was the Little Rock school desegregation case, in which the State of Arkansas attempted to interpose its sovereign authority between the people and the Supreme Court's allegedly unconstitutional decision in *Brown v. Board of Education*. The state said that *Brown* could not be enforced in Arkansas; the school board said that at least it could not be enforced until the threat of mob violence subsided. The Court rejected these arguments in an opinion signed by all nine Justices. The Court said that "the federal judiciary is supreme in the exposition of the law of the Constitution." ... [It] said that if state legislatures could "annul the judgments of the courts of the United States, and destroy the rights acquired under those judgments, the constitution itself becomes a solemn mockery." The President sent federal troops to Little Rock to get a handful of black students into Central High School, ensuring that *Cooper* would not be soon forgotten.

Cooper [is correct for the facts involved there]. Judgments must be obeyed or constitutional rights become merely precatory. When the Supreme Court enforces a right that it finds in the Constitution, the states and the other branches must obey. In that context, the states and the other branches must comply with the Court's interpretation of the Constitution.

But the issue presented by RFRA is quite different[.] Here the question is whether the powers of the other branches are limited by the Court's interpretation when the Court finds no constitutional right and issues no order against the other branches. Can the other branches then protect liberty on their own?

It seems to me clear that they can. This is the Supreme Court's ratchet theory in *Katzenbach v. Morgan*.[7] *Katzenbach* says that Congress cannot in any way reduce the protection for civil liberties that is provided by the Court, but Congress can increase the protection provided by the Court.... The Section 5 power goes in only one direction; Congress can add protection, but it can never take away protection. I think that a substantive understanding of the ratchet theory is squarely based in the historical context of the Fourteenth Amendment and separation of powers.

First consider the federal government, where the issues are much easier. Congress may legislate or refuse to legislate on grounds of its view of liberty or its view of the Constitution. For example, the Court may say that Congress has the power to ban obscene books from interstate commerce. Congress does not have to exercise that power; it can choose not to ban obscene books. Congress may think that banning books would be bad policy, or that it would unnecessarily restrict liberty, or that it would be unconstitutional. Congress may reject a book-banning bill based on its own judgment of the constitutional question presented, even if it knows the Supreme Court would uphold the bill if it were passed. Indeed, some commentators insist that a conscientious legislator must make an independent judgment about constitutional questions.

Similarly, the President may use his veto power and his executive order power on the basis of his judgment about what the Constitution requires. Thus, the President might veto a book-banning bill on the ground that he thinks it is unconstitutional. Presidents Madison and Jackson issued famous vetoes based on constitutional grounds; Ronald Reagan vetoed a legislative re-enactment of the FCC's Fairness Doctrine on constitutional [free speech] grounds. President Truman integrated the military by executive order. President Clinton tried to protect gays in the military by executive order, and wound up with "Don't ask, don't tell."...

The only real issue about the validity of RFRA is a federalism issue. The federalism issue is whether Congress can restrain the states more than the

Supreme Court says the states should be restrained. Federalism in the protection of liberty was what the Civil War and the Fourteenth Amendment were all about. And with respect to that period, our modern view of the Court as the dominant or sole protector of liberty and interpreter of the Constitution is wildly anachronistic. Congress in 1866 did not view the Supreme Court as a reliable protector of liberty. The paradigm cases of what the Supreme Court does in our time are *Brown v. Board* and *Roe v. Wade.* But the paradigm case in 1866 was *Dred Scott v. Sandford.*[8]

We all know that *Dred Scott* somehow upheld slavery, but let me remind you of some of its more specific holdings. *Dred Scott* held that congressional power to regulate the territories did not apply to territories acquired after 1787, and that Congress was wholly without power to stop the spread of human slavery throughout the West. *Dred Scott* held that the right to buy, own, and sell another human being was a fundamental right of property and that Congress had no power to interfere. *Dred Scott* held that the right to carry that human being across state lines and into new territories, and there to create new state governments that would forever protect one's right to buy, own, and sell him, was part of the fundamental right with which Congress had no power to interfere. *Dred Scott* held that a black person could not be a citizen of the United States, and that he "had no rights which the white man was bound to respect." The plain implication was that Congress had no power to do anything about that either. *Dred Scott* invalidated the Missouri Compromise, and thus deprived Congress of any effective power to compromise the great issue that divided the nation and threatened civil war. Thus, *Dred Scott* was one of the proximate causes of a war in which 600,000 Americans died for their conflicting views of federalism and human liberty.

Congress proposed the Reconstruction Amendments and coerced their ratification to secure the fruits of victory, or as Lincoln said at Gettysburg, "To the end that these honored dead shall not have died in vain." Taking no chances, Congress denied the seceded states representation in Congress until the Fourteenth Amendment was ratified. I do not believe that the Congress that lived through *Dred Scott* and the War, and that used such extraordinary means to get the amendment ratified, would rely solely on the Court that decided *Dred Scott* for the amendment's efficacy. To put it the other way, I do not believe that that Congress would give that Court a wholly unreviewable power to refuse to enforce the amendment or to interpret it into meaninglessness. In that historical context, it would make no sense for Congress to have intended that if the Supreme Court interpreted the majestic generalities of the Reconstruction Amendments in a narrow and hostile way that failed to accomplish their purpose, then the Congress would have no power to give more specific instructions, no power to attempt to say, "That is not what we meant; here is what you have to do to protect human liberty." ...

Dred Scott and the reaction to *Dred Scott* are not the only evidence of how Congress viewed the Supreme Court in that period. We also know that Congress repealed the Court's jurisdiction to review a constitutional challenge to Reconstruction.[9] Reconstruction was undoubtedly the most important federal program of the time, a congressional and military effort to protect the liberties of the freedmen. Congress did not trust the Supreme Court to pass on Reconstruction, for fear the Supreme Court might give the wrong answer.

We also know that Congress in that period added an extra Justice to the Court, expanding the Court to ten to give Lincoln an extra vote when he needed it. We know that Congress then reduced the number of Justices to seven to make sure Andrew Johnson got no appointments, and then expanded it back to nine to let Ulysses S. Grant fill the seats. These were Congresses acutely aware of the risk that a president might be hostile to the congressional conception of human liberty, and that he might appoint Justices who were hostile to that conception and who would defeat the purposes of legislation and amendments designed to protect liberty. It is hard to imagine that a Congress with such views would leave itself without power to protect human liberty when the Court refused to do so.

Of course these same Congresses continued and expanded on the founders' practice of looking to an independent judiciary as one key protector of our liberties. Congressional legislation in this period included creation of a federal cause of action for all violations of federal law under color of state law,[10] and four great grants of federal jurisdiction: original civil rights jurisdiction, civil rights removal jurisdiction, modern habeas corpus jurisdiction, and finally, general federal question jurisdiction.... But [these] are not at odds with my thesis.

A unifying principle underlies both Section 5 and the grants of federal jurisdiction. The principle was to multiply the institutions capable of protecting federal rights because it was not safe to rely exclusively on any single institution... [T]he federal courts were charged with interpreting and enforcing the new constitutional rights, but the amendments also conferred on Congress alternate powers of enforcement....

Indeed, early drafts of the Fourteenth Amendment were merely a grant of power to Congress; judicially enforceable substantive provisions were added later. Substantive constitutional provisions were necessary to avoid the risk that a subsequent Congress controlled by readmitted Southerners and Northern Democrats would repeal enforcement legislation. But many participants in the debate seem to have assumed that the congressional role would be dominant and that the judicial role would be much more modest. History has not worked out that way; the judicial role has been quite large and generally quite beneficial. The judicial role has been so large that we in our time have come to think of the judiciary as the principal (or the only) protector of our liberties. But that was not how Congress thought of it in 1866....

This inferred congressional understanding fits squarely with the theory of separation of powers adopted by the first generation of founders. We have separation of powers because no human being can be trusted with all the powers of government. We have separation of powers so that if one branch tries to abuse our liberties, there are two other branches that might step in to do something about it. Separation of powers makes it difficult to sustain a campaign of repressing liberty unless all three branches at least acquiesce. So when the Court fails to protect our liberties, it is perfectly consistent with the original theory of separation of powers that Congress can step in. It is not inconsistent; it is not odd; it is not an anomaly; it is why powers are separated. The ratchet theory is a simple function of the Constitution's bias in favor of protecting liberty against the abuses of government.

At times in the past—Reconstruction and the Civil War being the most dramatic examples—the Executive and the Congress were the active, aggressive, and dominant protectors of liberty, and the Court was dragging its feet. At other times, it has been Congress or the Executive that was hostile to liberty, and the Court that was doing something about it. Both patterns are right. Both patterns are how separation of powers is supposed to work.

The ratchet theory breaks down when constitutional rights conflict. Congress has power to expand the Court's definition of constitutional rights into what the Court says is the discretionary authority of the states, but Congress does not have power to expand one constitutional right into space that the Court says is protected by a different constitutional right. For example, if the Court says that affirmative action violates a white worker's right to equal protection of the laws, then Congress cannot require affirmative action as a means of enforcing the equal protection of the laws....

If the Court were willing to say that RFRA violates the Establishment Clause in some of its applications, then those applications would be unconstitutional and Congress would be bound by the Court's judgment. [But RFRA does not violate the Establishment Clause.]

NOTES

As a result of editing, the notes for this essay have been renumbered. The note number from the original essay or article is shown in parentheses at the end of each citation.

1. See *Pierce v. Society of Sisters*, 268 U.S. 510 (1926) (striking down the law).

2. 42 U.S.C. §§ 1973 to 1973gg–10. (33)

3. Compare [e.g.,] *Thornburg v. Gingles*, 478 U.S. 30 (1986) (invalidating, under Voting Rights Act, multi-member districts that dilute minority influence in jurisdictions with history of racially polarized voting) with *City of Mobile v. Borden*, 446 U.S. 55, 61–65 (1980) (upholding multi-member districts under the Constitution in absence of showing that districts were created for discriminatory purposes). (34)

4. 5 U.S. (1 Cranch) 137, 177 (1803). (37)

5. 347 U.S. 483 (1954). (38)

6. 358 U.S. 1 (1958). (40)

7. 384 U.S. 641, 651 n.10 (1966). (44)

8. 60 U.S. (19 How.) 393 (1857). (54)

9. See Ex parte McCardle, 74 U.S. (7 Wall.) 506 (1869) (upholding repeal of jurisdiction). (64)

10. 42 U.S.C. § 1983. (69)

CITY OF BOERNE V. FLORES:
A LANDMARK FOR STRUCTURAL ANALYSIS

MARCI A. HAMILTON

I. INTRODUCTION

The Court's decision [in *City of Boerne v. Flores*[1]] invalidating [RFRA as applied to state laws] is a sterling example of the sturdiness of the Constitution's structure and, indeed, of the Court in the face of immense and impressive political pressure....

This Essay is an analytical exegesis of the Court's opinion from the perspective of the Constitution's structure of government, with special emphasis on the principles that encourage legislative responsibility and accountability. The following discussion delineates three characteristics of an accountable and responsible Congress that are central to the Framers' vision and that were reaffirmed in the *Flores* opinion. First, Congress is given enumerated, limited powers. This simultaneous provision and limitation of power is intended to

Marci A. Hamilton, "*City of Boerne v. Flores*: A Landmark for Structural Analysis," *William and Mary Law Review* 39 (1998): 699, 704–707, 709–15, 717–22.

ensure a separation of powers among the federal branches and a system of dual sovereignty between the states and the federal government.... Second, Congress must perform those tasks assigned to it reasonably well in order to avoid other constitutional pitfalls. This is the proportionality or means-end fit requirement. Third, Congress cannot unilaterally define its constitutional role. This is the principle of popular sovereignty, wherein government power is derived from the people rather than inherent in any institution....

II. THE FEDERAL GOVERNMENT IS A GOVERNMENT OF ENUMERATED AND LIMITED POWERS

From many perspectives, the legislative process employed in RFRA is a prescription for constitutional disaster. Congress rubber-stamped the views of a powerful interest group, rather than engage its independent judgment; it addressed an asserted social problem without ascertaining whether the problem in fact existed; it imposed a legalistic formula to be applied to the imagined problem without serious inquiry into the impact of such a formula; it attempted to redress the imagined problem in every forum and arena imaginable; and it failed to inquire adequately into the constitutionality of its own actions....

One message of the *Flores* decision is that Congress should treat structural constitutional issues as threshold issues. Moreover, it ought to take the utmost care when it considers the constitutionality of its actions when it is tempted, as it was with RFRA, to abdicate its constitutional obligation to exercise its independent decision-making authority and to simply follow the lead of a powerful interest group. The near unanimous vote in Congress, combined with the strength of the Coalition for the Free Exercise of Religion, which drafted and lobbied for RFRA, are no excuse to attenuate constitutional examination, but to the contrary should have sent constitutional warning bells pealing through Congress. Especially when a bill touches upon central First Amendment values and when the people cannot grasp its content because it is written in legalese, members of Congress are obligated to investigate with care their motivations in the context of independent consideration of the Constitution's requirement and the public's interest.

The advice rendered to Congress on the constitutionality of RFRA was fleeting and incomplete, leaving the structural questions all but unanswered. The [Congressional Research Service] rendered its verdict on Congress's power under Section 5 of the Fourteenth Amendment ("Section 5") in a mere paragraph, with the most erroneous clause being: "[T]he Supreme Court has repeatedly held that Congress may use [Section 5] power to define and protect rights that are more expansive than what the Court has held to be constitutionally protected." Despite the separation-of-powers and federalism issues raised by this sentence, the CRS did not consider these issues important. It is not as though there was no legal precedent that might have prompted such concerns.... For example, Justice Harlan's powerful dissent in *Katzenbach v. Morgan*[2] should have raised some concern....

The enumerated powers doctrine has been at the heart of the Court's structural jurisprudence. A line of modern Supreme Court cases has emphasized the central importance of the enumerated powers doctrine, that is, the rule that the "Constitution creates a Federal Government of enumerated powers. As James Madison wrote, '[t]he powers delegated by the proposed Constitution to the federal government are few and defined.'"[3] Most recently, in *Printz v. United States*,[4] issued two days after the *Flores* decision, the Court reaffirmed that the Constitution confers "upon Congress...not all governmental powers, but only discrete, enumerated ones."

The enumerated powers doctrine is crucial to keeping in equipoise the various societal powers set in motion by the Constitution—the federal branches, the states, and the people. When Congress fails to abide by its enumerated powers, it transgresses important boundaries between the federal branches and between the federal government and the states. There is no vacuum of power outside Congress's limited powers. Rather, when it exceeds its limited powers, it strays into domains reserved for other branches, the states, or the people....

With RFRA, Congress misjudged the scope of its power under Section 5 and therefore [as *Flores* held] simultaneously "contradict[ed] vital principles necessary to maintain separation of powers and the federal balance." In other words, by failing to hew to its demarcated enumerated powers, Congress overtook federal duties more properly reposed in the Court and transgressed the line that separates federal from state power....

In response to those defenders of RFRA who claimed that Section 5 permitted Congress to alter constitutional rights, the Court frankly acknowledged that congressional authority under Section 5 is broad, but "[a]s broad as the congressional enforcement power is, it is not unlimited." This statement is not qualified by an exception for near unanimous votes in Congress or legislation urged by respectable and powerful groups. Rather, even when both houses of Congress act in unison in response to a legitimate and respected group, limits on federal power remain firm.

Federalism operates as a barrier to the congressional temptation to wander into general-unenumerated-lawmaking authority. Echoing the Supreme Court's earlier statement in *United States v. Lopez*[5] that "the Constitution... [withholds] from Congress a plenary police power that would authorize enactment of every type of legislation," the *Flores* decision stated that the Fourteenth Amendment does not grant Congress the authority to "legislate generally upon life, liberty, and property," but rather limits Congress's power to remedying "offensive state action, [that is] 'repugnant' to the Constitution."[6] The Religious Freedom Restoration Act offends federalism because it "is a considerable congressional intrusion into the States' traditional prerogatives and general authority to regulate for the health and welfare of their citizens."[7] In other words, the enumerated powers doctrine is intended to prevent incursions on federalism and to force Congress to account for its actions in the text and design of the Constitution....

The majority opinion's final and summarizing paragraph reinforced the theme of meaningful limits on congressional power with the observation that deference is due Congress, especially when it engages its Section 5 powers, but its "discretion is not unlimited,... and the courts retain the power, as they have since *Marbury v. Madison*, to determine if Congress has exceeded its authority under the Constitution."

III. Congress's Assigned Tasks Must Be Performed Reasonably Well

Under the Court's structural examination of Congress's exercises of power, Congress is not only constrained to act within an identified, enumerated power, but also must enact law that is reasonably well suited to its ends. This proportionality requirement is especially important when Congress is not in fact remedying an existing constitutional violation, but rather attempting to prevent a nascent constitutional violation. The Court stated, "[w]hile preventive rules are sometimes appropriate remedial measures, there must be a congruence between the means used and the ends to be achieved. The appropriateness of remedial measures must be considered in light of the evil presented." RFRA was dramatically out of proportion to its alleged justifications. As the Court noted, this wholesale alteration in free exercise jurisprudence, which applied to every law passed at any time, was erected on the flimsiest of foundations: a handful of anecdotes and dated stories of religious persecution. This disproportion signified that Congress had passed beyond its constitutional boundaries....

The means-end requirement is a mechanism that operates to keep an overeager Congress from transgressing the lines of power drawn by the Constitution and is especially important in the Section 5 context. As the *Flores* case illustrates, the Fourteenth Amendment invites Congress to enforce constitutionally protected liberties, but that invitation creates tremendous temptation to define those liberties. When Congress reaches beyond its power to enforce and, instead, embraces the power to define, it collides with both the federalism and separation-of-powers limitations on the congressional exercise of power. The proportionality requirement brings Congress back down to earth and its essential institutional competence, directing it to examine real social problems and to construct "appropriate" solutions.

IV. Congress Is Not Permitted to Engage in Self-Definition

The Constitution is the source of each federal branch's parameters, which is to say that the branches may not independently define their powers. In *Flores*, the Court stated this principle, drawing upon its holding in *Marbury v. Madison*, parts of which I quoted in my opening statement before the Court: "If Congress could define its own powers by altering the Fourteenth Amendment's meaning, no longer would the Constitution be 'superior paramount law, unchangeable by ordinary means.' It would be 'on a level with ordinary legislative acts, and, like other acts,...alterable when the legislature shall please to alter it.'"[8] The Court illustrated this point with the statement that Congress's attempt to redefine the meaning of the Free Exercise Clause in RFRA was aimed at "circumvent[ing] the difficult and detailed amendment process contained in Article V."

Before *Flores*, many in the legal world overread the Court's Section 5 jurisprudence to permit Congress to revise the meaning of the Constitution, effectively giving itself the power to define its powers vis-à-vis the states on an ad hoc basis. As the Court stated quite clearly in *Flores*, this is a principle that pits the Fourteenth Amendment squarely against *Marbury v. Madison*. Indeed, Justice Harlan more than once had warned that Section 5 was on a collision course with settled separation-of-powers concepts....

With its decision in *Flores*, the Court elucidated the suppressed issue in Section 5 discussions—whether the Fourteenth Amendment vitiates or attenuates *Marbury* when Congress acts pursuant to its Section 5 authority. The Court rightly concluded that *Marbury* was not trumped by the Fourteenth Amendment. *Flores* bore out Harlan's reading of the relationship between Section 5 and the separation of powers and fully vindicated his vision of the Fourteenth Amendment as providing ample remedial power [i.e., the power to devise remedies for violations of constitutional principles announced by the Court], but not amendment power [i.e., the power to interpret the Constitution differently from the Court and thus enforce stronger constitutional principles]....

Interestingly, the Court, in its analysis of a law that implicated both separation-of-powers and federalism principles simultaneously, did not fall into the contentious 5-4 split that has characterized its federalism decisions in the Commerce Clause arena. When federalism concerns were joined to the sort of blatant separation-of-powers problem posed by RFRA, the Justices joined forces in a no-nonsense way. In other words, one structural problem engenders more soul-searching and closer votes, but two structural problems engender certitude and confidence in a decision to invalidate an act of Congress.

The proponents of broad federal power under Section 5 have been wearing structural blinders in the RFRA debate. Even after *Flores* taught us that *Marbury* remained good law despite the enactment of the Fourteenth Amendment, many argued that *Marbury* did not provide a stronghold against congressional exercise of power under the enumerated powers doctrine, and therefore RFRA is likely still constitutional when applied to federal law. This contention was and remains unsupported.

RFRA exhibits its structural weaknesses even when one looks at its application to federal law. The law is a slap in the face of the Court, crossing separation-of-powers boundaries in an unapologetic fashion. Indeed, the vast majority of the *Flores* decision, as a matter of rhetoric and logic, applies as persuasively to federal as to state law.

Section 5 was the constitutional hook on which Congress and its advisors hung the Act. Congressional interpretation of Section 5 transformed it into a general lawmaking power so vast that it would have permitted Congress, in effect, to define and implement its unilateral interpretation of the Constitution. The same tactic has been attempted with respect to RFRA's application to federal law. In answer to the question of RFRA's validity as applied to federal law, some have claimed that it is "obviously" an application of the

Necessary and Proper Clause[9] as though that clause gives Congress unnamed powers in addition to its enumerated powers. There is nothing obvious about it....

The text of the Constitution makes clear that the Necessary and Proper Clause is not an independent power inserted for the purpose of vitiating the enumerated powers doctrine. Rather, it is a clause that limits Congress to its enumerated powers and elaborates on that enumeration by explaining that Congress should have a fair amount of latitude to execute those enumerated powers. RFRA's breathtaking scope—its application to every law, every government, and every time period in American history—precludes straight-faced arguments that it could have been grounded in any specific enumerated power, such as the commerce, tax, or spending power. If Congress is going to enact a law regulating religious liberty, then it cannot act in this essentially abstract, across-the-board manner, but rather must ground the regulation in one of the existing enumerated powers. The structure, text, and history of the First Amendment teaches that it is not an enumerated power, and thus the Necessary and Proper Clause cannot be linked to the First Amendment to justify congressional power to enact RFRA.

If RFRA's record supporting its Section 5 authority was weak, then its record applying RFRA to federal law is virtually blank....

In effect, *Marbury* and *Flores*, taken together, constrain Congress to solve social problems within the parameters set by the Constitution, to treat discrete problems discretely, and not to paint with the big brush the Framers wielded in their efforts to redraft the structure of government and society. The institutional competence of Congress demands focus on concrete problems and concrete solutions, something sorely lacking in RFRA.

As the decision in *Flores* pointed out: Article V precludes Congress from single-handedly amending the Constitution. Congress, which has no constitutional obligation to include everyone—or anyone—in its deliberative processes, is prohibited from amending the Constitution by itself. The amendment procedures are structured to alert the people and to slow the pace of amendment. The crucial constitutional value of accountability is exercised through the tandem operation of Article V and the First Amendment's speech and press clauses. If the dramatic change in the law signaled by RFRA is to be accomplished, then it cannot happen in the backroom of a legislature but rather must survive the crucible of public and press scrutiny. RFRA was not subjected to ratification procedures, and its legalistic formulation was impenetrable to all but an elite group. The Constitution's formalistic structure prevents Congress from shifting the balance of power between church and state in every circumstance, in the absence of public awareness and debate. For that reason, RFRA's invalidation is a victory for the people.

NOTES

As a result of editing, the notes for this essay have been renumbered. The note number from the original essay or article is shown in parentheses at the end of each citation.

[1. 521 U.S. 507, 117 S. Ct. 2157 (1997).]

2. 384 U.S. 641, 659–71 (1966) (Harlan, J., dissenting) (discussing the federal government's limited powers). (40)

3. *United States v. Lopez*, 514 U.S. 549, 552 (1995) (citations omitted). (47)

4. 117 S. Ct. 2365 (1997). (48)

5. 514 U.S. 549 (1995). (60)

6. *Flores*, 117 S. Ct., p. 2166. (63)

7. Ibid., p. 2171. (64)

8. [Ibid.,] p. 2168 (citing *Marbury v. Madison*). (80)

[9. U.S. Constitution, art. § 8, cl. 18 ("The Congress shall have power...To make all Laws which shall be necessary and proper for carrying into Execution the foregoing Powers.")]

Chapter 9

LEGISLATIVE ACCOMMODATIONS, THE INSTITUTIONAL ROLES OF COURTS AND LEGISLATURES, AND THE ESTABLISHMENT CLAUSE

EDITOR'S INTRODUCTION: SUPREME COURT RULINGS ON LEGISLATIVE ACCOMMODATIONS AND THE ESTABLISHMENT CLAUSE

In addition to considering whether exemptions for religious conduct are ever mandated by the Free Exercise Clause, the Court has also ruled on whether legislative efforts to accommodate religion through statutory exemptions are forbidden by the Establishment Clause as a form of "favoritism" or "subsidy" for religious acts over other deeply held moral views. Such provisions are common; one survey found them in more than two thousand federal and state statutes. James Ryan, "*Smith* and the Religious Freedom Restoration Act: An Iconoclastic Assessment," *Virginia Law Review* 78 (1992): 1407, 1445–47. Challenges to them raise the question whether religion is constitutionally distinctive enough to permit accommodation by elected officials, even if not to require accommodation as a constitutional mandate. Approached from a different perspective, are the problems with treating religion differently from other moral views so great that exemptions limited to religion are not just not required but actually forbidden? The dual question of mandatory and permissive exemptions has generated three common approaches: (1) The pro-accommodation view, under which exemptions (sometimes) are constitutionally required and legislative exemptions certainly are permitted. (2) The anti-exemptions view, under which both legislative and judicial-constitutional exemptions are improper. (3) The legislative-discretion view, under which exemptions may be enacted by legislatures are not declared by courts as constitutional mandates—as the Court held in *Employment Division v. Smith*. (The excerpt from Professor Lupu, p. 276 of this book, advances a fourth position: that exemptions should be declared solely by judges as constitutional mandates.)

The Supreme Court has approved the general concept of legislative exemptions of religion, although it has invalidated some provisions as excessive and impermissible favoritism for religion. The statutory exemptions from military service themselves testify to the tradition of accommodating religious conscience—although the Court's broad definition of "religion" for that statute in *Seeger* and *Welsh* (see Chapter 5) likely reflected discomfort with the differential treatment of religious and deeply held secular objection. In *Corporation of Presiding Bishop v. Amos*, 483 U.S. 327 (1987), the Court unanimously upheld a provision exempting religious organizations from the federal law against religious discrimination in employment for all employees, not just those in "religious" jobs. The Court defended accommodation in broad terms, saying that there is "ample room" between the two religion clauses to permit exemptions that are not required. It said that a law becomes an establishment not when it simply "allows churches to advance religion," but only when "the government itself has advanced religion through its own activities and influence"; and that an exemption removing a legal burden from religion need not come "packaged with benefits to secular entities." Ibid., pp. 336–38 (emphases in original). The broad exemption removed the threat of liability for discrimination in cases where judges or juries failed to sympathize with an organization's claim that a particular job had religious significance. Likewise, in *Employment Division v. Smith* itself, 494 U.S. 890, the Court indicated general approval of "nondiscriminatory religious-practice exemption[s]."

Two other decisions, however, invalidated particular statutory accommodations. In *Estate of Thornton v. Caldor*, 472 U.S. 703 (1985), the Court struck down a state law giving an employee an absolute right to refuse to work on the day he observed as his Sabbath. The statute impermissibly favored religion because of its "unyielding weighting of Sabbath observers over all other interests," including the interests of employers in being able to schedule work at reasonable cost and the interests of other employees in not having to fill in for the religious objector. Ibid., pp. 709–10. And in *Texas Monthly v. Bullock*, 489

U.S. 1 (1989), the Court struck down a state sales-tax exemption limited to religious publications, including periodicals or books "consist[ing] wholly of writings promulgating the teachings of," or "sacred to," "a religious faith." A three-justice plurality opinion found that the exemption gave an "unjustifiable awar[d] of assistance to religious" and "convey[ed] a message of endorsement" as against publications not exempted. Ibid., p. 15. Although the plurality did not disapprove all exemptions limited to religion, it said an exemption was impermissible if it "either burdens nonbeneficiaries markedly"—and a tax exemption forced other taxpayers to make up the lost revenue—"or cannot reasonably be seen as removing a significant state-imposed deterrent to the free exercise of religion"—and a sales tax imposes only a minimal marginal cost on religious publications. Ibid., pp. 14–15. The other justices joining the result qualified this analysis some. Justices Blackmun and O'Connor, concurring in the judgment, suggested that the statute would be constitutional if it exempted "the sale of atheistic literature distributed by an atheistic organization." Ibid., p. 29. And Justice White, also concurring in the judgment, emphasized that the First Amendment's Free Press Clause forbids government discrimination based on the content of publications. Ibid., pp. 25–26.

Most recently, in *Cutter v. Wilkinson*, 544 U.S. 709 (2005), the Court distilled its legislative-exemption rulings into a three-part test. Cutter upheld the section of the Religious Land Use and Institutionalized Persons Act of 2000 (RLUIPA)—the successor to RFRA—that prohibited state prison officials from imposing substantial burdens on prisoners' religious exercise unless application of the burden was the least restrictive means of achieving a compelling governmental interest. 42 U.S.C. § 2000cc. The prison provision passed the test because (1) "it alleviates exceptional government-created burdens on private religious exercise"; (2) under the provision, "courts must take adequate account of the burdens a requested accommodation may impose on nonbeneficiaries"; and (3) it requires courts to ensure that "[its] prescriptions are and will be administered neutrally among different faiths." Ibid., p. 720. On the first point, the Court emphasized that RLUIPA removes exceptional burdens because in prisons, government asserts "a degree of control unparalleled in civilian society and severely disabling to private religious exercise" such as prisoners' worship, dress or dietary requirements, or receipt of religious literature. Ibid., pp. 720–21. On the second point, the Court noted that the compelling interest standard—unlike the absolute accommodation requirement in *Caldor*—allowed consideration of the burdens on others and on the prison system, because RLUIPA's background indicated that courts should "apply the [s]tandard with 'due deference to the experience and expertise of prison and jail administrators in establishing necessary regulations and procedures to maintain good order, security and discipline, consistent with consideration of costs and limited resources'" Ibid., p. 723 (quoting statement of legislative sponsors). Finally, because it required a compelling interest for all substantial burdens, the provision did not differentiate among bona fide faiths.

RELIGIOUS INSTITUTIONS, THE NO-HARM DOCTRINE, AND THE PUBLIC GOOD

MARCI A. HAMILTON

The principle at issue is whether the courts are institutionally competent to craft free exercise exemptions. Under the reasoning of [*Smith, City of Boerne v. Flores*, and other] cases, courts are not competent to carve out individual exemptions from generally applicable laws; that is the province of the legislature. That is the explicit holding in *Smith*. This is not to say that the state or federal legislatures could not craft a statute that would do the work of the ministerial exception [i.e., the judicial rule exempting churches from the federal antidiscrimination laws as to their hiring of clergy]. They could. When the legislature does so, it brings better tools to assess the exemption options than a court has available. It can study the issue from many angles, from listening to constituents to using hearings, experts, and appointed commissions to assess the issue. The legislature is in a strong position to make a judgment

Marci A. Hamilton, "Religious Institutions, The No-Harm Doctrine, and the Public Good," *Brigham Young University Law Review* (2004): 1099, 1195–1202.

regarding what degree of harm will result from permitting a religious institution to discriminate "because of such individual's race, color,...sex, or national origin."[1] In sharp contrast, a court has only the evidence in one case and the views of two parties before it, and there is no guarantee that the facts before it or the parties' positions are representative of such disputes. Nor does a court have the capacity to independently investigate the issue. Indeed, its lack of investigative power makes it all too likely that its determinations will be based on opinion and personal views, rather than factors relevant to the public good. To be sure, legislatures are not perfect institutions; the point here is simply that they are comparatively better than courts in choosing which exemptions to carve out of a law and which to reject....

According to the [*Smith*] Court, legislatures are in the most appropriate position to determine whether harm needs be prevented, and so long as the legislature regulates to rid society of a particular harm, and does not single out a religious institution or individual in the process, the law is presumptively constitutional. In other words, the proper focus of the legislature is the public good, the needs of society. The same public good horizon can then be applied by a legislature to create exemptions from neutral, generally applicable laws, but the exemption is driven by a full consideration of the public good, not constitutional necessity....

The question is left where to draw the line between legitimate exemptions and those that are illegitimate. There are two scenarios that raise questions: exemptions that involve laws making harmless conduct illegal and those exemptions that are not lifting a burden on religiously motivated conduct, but rather granting religious entities special privileges simply because they are religious. The first should raise red flags of potential discrimination, while the second is in violation of the Establishment Clause.

1. Exemptions that make harmless conduct illegal

Where the legislature addresses only actions by individuals that do not impact and harm others, there is a good question whether the public good has been or can be served. Laws outlawing harmless behavior are hard to justify in light of the public good....

The slipperiness in this approach lies in the definition of harm. Some philosophers have abandoned the [concept of "harm to others" as a limiting principle] because it does not lead to concrete conclusions about certain moral issues facing the society.... This is a legitimate philosophical concern, but it need not deter its application in the legal-political arena.

The representative form of government assigns to the legislature the task of assessing the public good in light of all the circumstances and facts. In fact, the legislative task at its very core is to weigh competing social goods and harms. In this context, the task is no different. When considering whether to relieve a religious entity of a legal duty, the legislature should weigh on the one hand the importance of respect and tolerance for a wide panoply of religious faiths, and on the other whether the harm that the law was intended to prevent can be tolerated in a just society. For the philosophers, the problem with this approach is that it could result in endless cycling of the harm concept because there is no logical or hermeneutical principle that will finally determine actual harm. The finality problem is solved in the republican form of government, however, because a determination of harm can be made final. When the legislature determines that there should be no exemption or that there should be one, and enacts a law reflecting its judgment, it renders the final word on the balance of harms. The law reflects no more than contemporary understandings and need make no claims to transcendent value, but it is final for contemporary purposes.

The utility of employing legislative judgment here (as opposed to judicial judgment) is that the legislature has tremendous power to repeal the laws that it finds are noxious in practice. Precedent has not nearly the pull that it has in the judicial arena. Thus, judgments about relative harm can be revisited and reweighed. The repealability of the harm analysis takes into account the human nature of regulation—it is always based on imperfect understanding and always capable of being viewed through different lenses at a later time....

A good example of this phenomenon can be found in the exemptions for the religious use of peyote,[2] which appear to be harmless to society. The drug, unlike heroin, is not quickly addictive or part of a worldwide illegal market. It is also unattractive to recreational users because it often leads to nausea and headaches and in a significant number of instances yields no result. Moreover, those who use it tend to stay in the place of worship well beyond its effectiveness and therefore do not drive impaired or engage in any other harmful behavior that could affect others following its use. Thus, the Church's use of peyote is harmless to society and therefore worthy of an exemption.

That does not mean, however, that its use should be legalized for all users. A recreational user (if one is inclined to take it despite its recreational defects) is likely to be more inclined to drive or otherwise harm others under the influence, because the use would not be limited to a religious ceremony that lasts longer than the effects of the hallucinogen. The harm calculus thus weighs in favor of a religious exemption but not in favor of outright legalization.

2. Exemptions that do more than lift a burden on religiously motivated conduct

The *Smith* Court implied that there are some legislative exemptions that may violate the Establishment Clause. Legislative exemptions that only lift the burden placed on the religiously motivated because the conduct when done by the religious entity will not harm individuals or society, and do no more, have followed the Court's doctrine. The open question is what happens when a legislature grants an exemption for religious institutions that provides more than is needed to lift the burden. For example, the peyote exemptions for religious use are constitutional, but an exemption for any use by religious entities would not be. The latter gives religious entities the right to use peyote in all circumstances, not only in religious ceremonies, and therefore provides a benefit to religious entities solely because of their religious status, not because their religious conduct has been burdened. That is a violation of the Establishment Clause.[3]

The RFRAs violate the Establishment Clause in a different way, by flaunting the republican government principle. They make all or most of the federal or relevant state laws presumptively illegal. Justice Stevens referred to this as "a legal weapon that no atheist or agnostic can obtain."[4] The process of enactment is the precise opposite of what should occur in a legitimate legislative determination of exemptions. It is blind accommodation, where the legislature has given religious entities across the board power to trump thousands of laws. These across-the-board approaches make it impossible for any legislature to make the public good determination that legitimates an exemption. The legislature is handing religious entities a power to battle generally applicable, neutral laws, without taking upon itself the necessity of determining whether voiding the law for some is in the public's interest. It is a benefit without consideration of the public good and therefore is a subsidy as opposed to a legitimate exemption.

NOTES

As a result of editing, the notes for this essay have been renumbered. The note number from the original essay or article is shown in parentheses at the end of each citation.

1. 42 U.S.C. § 2000e-2(a)(1) (2000). (418)

2. The federal government and a majority of states exempt the religious use of peyote.... (438)

3. See *Lemon v. Kurtzman*, 403 U.S. 602, 612–13 (1971) (noting that to avoid violating the Establishment Clause, a statute's "principal or primary effect must be one that neither advances nor inhibits religion"). (440)

4. *City of Boerne v. Flores*, 521 U.S. 507, 537 (Stevens, J., concurring). (441)

THE TROUBLE WITH ACCOMMODATION

IRA C. LUPU

[A] distinction is often drawn by courts and commentators between mandatory accommodation—that required by force of the Free Exercise Clause—and permissive accommodation—exercises of political discretion that benefit religion, and that the Constitution neither requires nor forbids. Claims to mandatory accommodations always present free exercise questions, because their underlying theory is that the Free Exercise Clause is violated if the accommodation is not provided. Claims to permissive accommodations always raise Establishment Clause questions, because their underlying theory is that government is free to respond beneficially to religion-specific concerns....

[I]mportant institutional differences attend the distinction between mandatory and permissive accommodations. The judiciary may respond to mandatory accommodation claims, either by adjudicating them outright or relying on their premises as a background norm in statutory interpretation.

Ira C. Lupu, "The Trouble with Accommodation," *George Washington Law Review* 60 (1992): 743, 751, 753, 768, 771–72, 776–78.

Under our system of government, however, courts have no authority to accommodate permissively; the political discretion of courts extends no farther than the interpretive margin in adjudicating claims of right. In contrast, the political branches—legislators, executives, bureaucrats—may engage in any form of accommodation, up to the Establishment Clause limit....

THE POSITIVE LAW OF ACCOMMODATION

The Special Problem of Permissive Accommodations

[Whether one interprets the Establishment Clause broadly or narrowly,] permissive accommodations present their own unique difficulties. Many policies challenged under the Establishment Clause at least arguably involve some rough parity for religious and nonreligious counterpart activities. For example, states may undertake to aid all private schools, religious or not. In such circumstances, omission of the religious variant may seem like discrimination against, or hostility towards, religion.

In contrast, permissive accommodation policies almost always are religion-specific. Such policies always prefer religion to their non-religious counterparts, and sometimes prefer named sects to others. [In Supreme Court cases, permissive] accommodations have not fared very well of late. [Discussion of *Estate of Thornton v. Caldor* and *Texas Monthly v. Bullock* omitted (see pp. 268–69 above).]

Moreover, *Smith* undercuts permissive accommodation even as it pretends to encourage it. One of the strongest arguments for permissive accommodations is that they might be mandatory after all. In a world with no mandatory accommodations, this argument disappears. Government may burden religion incidentally, and may, by way of exemptions, seek to lift such a burden; as long as such burdens do not violate the Constitution, however, the case for lifting them from religious entities but not from those engaged in counterpart secular activity remains hard to fathom.

TOWARD A BODY OF ACCOMMODATION PRINCIPLES

I want to sketch briefly the kind of accommodation principles I find normatively attractive, institutionally defensible, and constitutionally sound.

These principles track the distinction offered above between mandatory and permissive accommodations. The Free Exercise Clause sometimes obligates government to afford special treatment to religion, and courts should be prepared to honor that obligation on appropriate occasions. I therefore reject *Smith* on every level. Second, permissive accommodations should be eliminated. Government may aid religion as part of a program broad enough to include both religious and nonreligious counterparts, but may not aid religion otherwise unless the Constitution so requires. In short, I would assign strong, judicially enforceable content to both the Free Exercise Clause as a platform for mandatory accommodations and the Establishment Clause as a barrier to permissive accommodations, and leave little room between them for the exercise of political discretion. . . .

Permissive Accommodations, Equal Liberty, and the Establishment Clause

Two substantive vices, both connected with the overarching constitutional principle of equal liberty, attend permissive accommodation. The first is the problem of religious favoritism. The forms such favoritism are likely to take may differ, depending upon whether legislators or administrators are the decision makers, and whether the accommodation is pro-majoritarian or not.

When legislators accommodate religion, the action is likely to fall into one of two categories. First, legislative politics most probably will favor dominant religious traditions. Thus, legislatures are more likely to make a public holiday of Christmas than any other day of sectarian religious celebration, or to make special provisions for Sunday Sabbath observance, or to make fund-raising easier for familiar religious institutions than novel and threatening ones.[1]

In those cases in which legislatures explicitly accommodate religious minorities, there is a very strong tendency to be sect-oriented and sect-specific. For example, Congress has carefully designed an exemption from the self-employment tax imposed by the Social Security Act; the Amish will qualify for the exemption, but other persons who are self-reliant as a matter of religious conviction will not. A number of states and the federal government exempt members of the Native American Church from restrictions on peyote use and possession, but do not similarly exempt other religious groups and individuals who make ritual use of peyote. The federal government exempts from the obligation to support workplace labor organizations employees who belong to and adhere to the tenets of a "bona fide religion" historically and conscientiously opposed to such support.[2] The peyote provision discriminates unreasonably against less well-known or influential sects. The peyote exemption, the self-employment tax exemption, and the labor-support exemption all disfavor individuals, acting independently of sects, with comparable religious practices and principles.

Administrative accommodations are typically ad hoc and less visible, and thus tend to suffer even more from the likelihood of invidious religious favoritism and discrimination....

The second vice associated with permissive accommodation is its tendency to discriminate against nonreligious association. As I have argued elsewhere, the Establishment Clause protects equal religious liberty, [which is] a subprinciple in the larger category of equal liberty of association. What is unique to religion are the special protections—the noncomparative rights—protected by the Free Exercise Clause. This latter set of mandatory protections exhausts all the religion-specific actions that government may take.

NOTES

As a result of editing, the notes for this essay have been renumbered. The note number from the original essay or article is shown in parentheses at the end of each citation.

1. See *Larson v. Valente*, 456 U.S. 228, 244–46 (1982) (invalidating state fundraising regulation containing an exemption designed to favor mainstream churches). (168)

2. 29 U.S.C. § 169 (1988). (171)

WHY IS RELIGION SPECIAL?
RECONSIDERING THE ACCOMMODATION OF RELIGION UNDER THE RELIGION CLAUSES

STEVEN G. GEY

[Professor Gey offers a "narrow" definition of religion that includes "three key aspects":] [1] religion's guiding principles are derived from a source beyond human control; [2] religious principles are immutable and absolutely authoritative; [3] religious principles are not based on logic or reason, and therefore may not be proved or disproved. Each of these three characteristics is incompatible with any democratic theory of the modern state....

First, popular control of government and law is the essence of democracy in any form. By definition, democratic theory views all government actions as reflections of temporal human authority. This authority may be channeled through representative agencies and mediated by constitutional processes, but

Steven G. Gey, "Why Is Religion Special? Reconsidering the Accommodation of Religion Under the Religion Clauses," *University of Pittsburgh Law Review* 52 (1990): 75, 173–74, 176–77, 179–84.

a democratic government's ultimate claim to legitimacy must be that those subject to the dictates of the system acquiesce to the system's exercise of power. Conversely, when a government places its imprimatur on principles derived from an extra-human source, or uses its resources to cultivate allegiance to an extra-human authority, it implicitly places certain political questions beyond human control. Democracy depends on the perpetuation of a healthy anti-authoritarian mindset among the citizenry; religion cultivates deference to some authority or power that cannot be questioned or changed, or even fully comprehended by the human mind.

Likewise, whereas religion asserts that its principles are immutable and absolutely authoritative, democratic theory asserts just the opposite. The sine qua non of any democratic state is that everything political is open to question; not only specific policies and programs, but the very structure of the state itself must always be subject to challenge. Democracies are by nature inhospitable to political or intellectual stasis or certainty. Religion is fundamentally incompatible with this intellectual cornerstone of the modern democratic state. The irreconcilable distinction between democracy and religion is that, although there can be no sacrosanct principles or unquestioned truths in a democracy, no religion can exist without sacrosanct principles and unquestioned truths.

The third characteristic identified by the narrow definition of religion reinforces these tendencies. Because religious principles are essentially non-rational and unprovable, they are insulated from many ordinary forms of political critique. Because religion concedes at the outset that it reaches policy conclusions by other means, empirical and utilitarian challenges to these policies are foreclosed. For example, it is fruitless to dispute the veracity of creationism within the intellectual framework of the scientific method if adherents of creationism believe in the inviolability of the story of creation set forth in Genesis. It is also impossible to critique the inegalitarian implications of social or economic policies if the state may respond that it is obligated by God to enact into law the untestable commands and principles of theological doctrine....

As such, religion is fundamentally incompatible with the critical rationality on which democracy depends. In a proper democracy, political truth is developed, not discovered, and it may change over time as the individual components of political truth lose their usefulness or become counterproductive to the larger social undertaking. In a religious context, on the other hand, truth is discovered, not developed, and its essential verities cannot be challenged or disproved. The adherent's disapproval of received truth in a religious scheme is an indication of the adherent's inadequate faith or devotion, rather than an indication of flaws in the governing religious concepts. A democratic system should be structured in a way that encourages the development and application of critical reason. A government that places itself in the service of nonrational and unquestionable religious principles, therefore, loses its claim to democratic legitimacy....

I should emphasize that none of the above is a criticism of religion itself, the views of particular religious faiths, or the internal operation of religious orders. The arguments above relate only to extending the influence of religion and religious organizations into the political sphere. The very characteristics that define modern religion—its reliance on faith in what is unknowable, unprovable, but absolutely true—provide a recipe for oppression when transferred to the political sphere and enshrined into law. Faith ultimately may be rewarded, but it should not be rewarded with political power.

[This understanding of religion] places the establishment clause in its proper context, as an expression of the Enlightenment movement away from political theory's prior reliance on political certainty and immutable hierarchy, and toward a concept of the political structure that is fluid and (at least in theory) responsive to democratically determined decisions about the temporal needs of society. In other words, the Establishment Clause removed from political discourse the final resort to the Almighty that had previously characterized determinations of political truth, and simultaneously severed the state's tie with an unelected and very powerful clergy. The Establishment Clause is itself a value choice in favor of collective relativism and uncertainty about everlasting political truth. Religious values (and the expression of such values) that conflict with these themes of rationality and skepticism are protected, but because of their undemocratic nature, these values cannot be written into law, nor may the state use the adherence to these values as the basis for granting specific legal or political advantages....

The above discussion indicates that a proper interpretation of the First Amendment precludes the extension of a broad form of the accommodation principle into Establishment Clause jurisprudence. Under this interpretation of the Establishment Clause, a democratic government may not subscribe to the dictates of a higher authority than that of the secular democratic process itself, nor may the government be the agency of such an authority. Application of the above analysis to the free exercise clause reveals that the accommodation principle also should be excised from free exercise jurisprudence....

Accommodation problems arise in the free exercise context when a religious adherent seeks to avoid general social obligations imposed by secular authorities on the ground that such behavior violates a duty imposed by the higher, transcendental authority. In the accommodation cases, [both mandatory accommodation as in *Sherbert* and *Yoder*, and permissive accommodation,] the Court has interpreted the Free Exercise Clause to mean that the state usually may, and sometimes must, respect such transcendental obligations. In all such cases, one of the following scenarios occurs: the state subordinates its legitimate secular objectives to the religious principles relied upon by the adherent, the state subsidizes the religiously motivated behavior, or the state shifts some social burden from the adherent to a nonadherent. Each of these consequences conflicts with the interpretation of the Establishment Clause set forth above....

[A]ll religion contains an ineffable transcendental core that cannot be explained to or experienced by outsiders to the religion. Combining this with the acknowledgement that the Establishment Clause embodies a fundamental value choice in favor of the secular uncertainties of the Enlightenment leads to the conclusion that government has fulfilled its duty under the Free Exercise Clause when it refrains from taking action that impugns the transcendental core of religion, and from forcing religious adherents to renounce the theological principles of their faith. Government has no free exercise obligation beyond protecting religious belief, and the verbal or symbolic expression of religious belief. With regard to behavior motivated by religion, the state's obligations are no more substantial than its obligations to those exercising other rights under the First Amendment.

This interpretation would continue to provide substantial protection to religion. Under a broad and uniform protection of expression, religion would undoubtedly be placed at the highest level in the first amendment hierarchy. Therefore, religious beliefs, verbal expression such as prayer, proselytizing, worship services, and the symbolic representation of faith through religious iconography, would all receive virtually unlimited protection, subject only to traditional time, place, and manner regulation that is already permitted under the Court's present free exercise interpretation....

An example of religious accommodation suggested by Jesse Choper illustrates the rationale for prohibiting accommodation of religiously mandated behavior beyond the scope of religious expression.[1] "Suppose that a school regulation requires pupils to wear shorts during gym class for the aesthetic effect of uniform dress and that one child requests an exemption because her religious scruples forbid her to bare her legs." Choper notes that a "religion-blind" accommodation for all students who object to the dress regulation would protect the religious student, but would destroy the state's aesthetic goal of uniformity. Granting the exemption only to a few religious objectors, however, would substantially preserve the state's objective of aesthetic uniformity. Choper argues that, in this case, the school should be permitted to accommodate the religious objector, while refusing to accommodate nonreligious objectors, because the accommodation would not "coerce, compromise, nor influence the religious beliefs of any school children."

Under the view of the Establishment and Free Exercise Clauses I have set forth in this section, the accommodation suggested by Dean Choper would not be permissible. The school board's decision to accommodate the religious objector can be explained in one of two ways: The school board is either certifying the validity of the religious student's views, or it is deferring to a superior authority over which the state has no control. The first explanation is clearly incorrect; if the school board accepted the religious student's views concerning the need for personal modesty as religiously correct, the board would cease requiring any students to dress immodestly. In Establishment Clause terms, however, the alternative explanation of the school board's behavior is equally unsatisfactory. By ceding authority over the objecting student to the higher religious authority, the school board subjugates democratic control over a particular policy area to a nondemocratic, extrahuman force.

Dean Choper's example seems like a difficult case because the secular policy involved—the desire to create an undifferentiated mass of identically attired gym students—is trivial, if not downright silly. Imposing a silly policy on a sincere religious objector compounds the silliness. But this argument proves too much. If it is silly for the school board to be concerned with something as trivial as students' attire in gym class, why is the religious objection to that attire not equally trivial and silly? If the answer to that question is that the mode of dress required by the school board implicates the religious student's fundamental decision to lead a conservative lifestyle, which requires extreme modesty in all forms of personal behavior including dress in gym class, then the objection to the school's regulation seems more consistent with broad protection of expression generally (or with some version of the privacy right) than with religion. That the student's objections to the dress code arise from lifestyle decisions derived from a belief in a transcendent authority adds nothing to the claim unless the state is permitted to grant such authorities special deference. Once the state openly defers to an unquestionable and absolute religious authority, we are once again confronted with the problem that the authoritarian and undemocratic nature of religion is inconsistent with the anti-authoritarian and democratic biases of the Constitution.

For the same reasons, each of the Supreme Court's mandatory accommodation decisions [such as *Sherbert* and *Yoder*] should be overruled.... Under the approach I have recommended, accommodations [are] offensive because they forge an alliance between the state and religion, and are based on assumptions about the relative strength of secular and transcendental duties that the state should not be permitted to make. Without resorting to these impermissible assumptions, it is impossible to grant an accommodation to the likes of Ms. Sherbert or Mr. Thomas without extending the same protection to everyone else in society who believes sincerely (but for secular reasons) that she must observe a day of rest every week, or must refuse to work on armaments production.

NOTE

As a result of editing, the note for this essay has been renumbered. The note number from the original essay or article is shown in parentheses at the end of each citation.

1. See Jesse Choper, "The Religion Clauses of the First Amendment: Reconciling the Conflict," *University of Pittsburgh Law Review* 41 (1980): 673. (502)

ACCOMMODATION OF RELIGION:
AN UPDATE AND A RESPONSE TO THE CRITICS

MICHAEL W. MCCONNELL

I consider the argument that accommodations of religion are by their very nature unconstitutional in purpose and effect extremely weak. By this I do not mean that all government benefits to religion called "accommodations" are constitutional, but that accommodations that [remove a burden from a religious practice that the individual has voluntarily, independently chosen, and that do not impose "disproportionate" costs on others] are constitutional.

To begin with, there is no ambiguity with regard to the historical record: Accommodations of religion in the years up to the framing of the First Amendment were frequent and well known, and no one took the position that they constituted an establishment of religion. For the most part, the largely Protestant population of the states as of 1789 entertained few religious tenets in conflict with the civil law; but where there were conflicts, accommodations

---

Michael W. McConnell, "Accommodation of Religion: An Update and a Response to the Critics," *George Washington Law Review* 60 (1992): 685, 713–19, 739–40.

were a frequent solution. [See the colonial and founding-era legislative exemptions discussed in the McConnell and Hamburger excerpts, Chapter 3 of this book.] Although the existence of these exemptions does not necessarily establish that accommodations were mandatory, it at least demonstrates that they were permitted....

The argument that accommodations are unconstitutional turns out to be predicated, almost exclusively, on the claim that accommodations are a form of "subsidy" or "favoritism" toward religion.... This can mean only one of two things. Either accommodations "favor religion" in the sense that they reward and encourage religious behavior, or they "favor religion" in the sense that they protect religion from interference even though nonreligious individuals and institutions would not receive the same degree of protection.

If the first meaning is adopted, the charge that accommodations "favor" religion is simply inaccurate. Under the Supreme Court's analysis of accommodation, ... government action that rewards or encourages religion is unconstitutional. Accommodation is legitimate only to the point that it facilitates or removes obstacles to independent religious decisions; any supposed "accommodation" that induces or "aggressively encourages" a religious practice should be invalidated. There are many examples of accommodations that permit the religious observer to engage in a practice but create no incentive to do so: to wear a turban or a yarmulke, to say prayers at designated times, to limit one's diet, to attend religious services on particular occasions, to avoid personal photographs, to prevent an autopsy on the body of a loved one, to refuse to display an orange warning triangle on the back of one's buggy, to decline the benefits of ninth and tenth grade, to ingest a bitter and unpleasant drug, to decline medical care, or to refuse to participate in Social Security—just to mention a few examples from recent free exercise controversies. It is absurd to say that the government "promotes" these practices when it decides not to penalize them....

It is particularly peculiar to say that accommodations "promote" religion in view of the fact that accommodations in the government sector arise, by definition, only when religious practices and government policy are in conflict. Far from "enacting into law the religious preferences of the political majority," or bringing about an "alliance between church and state,"[1] accommodations reflect a decision to tolerate dissent from the policies adopted by the political majority. Accommodations are forbearance, not alliance. They do not reflect agreement with the minority, but respect for the conflict between temporal and spiritual authority in which the minority finds itself.

The second possible interpretation of the charge that accommodations "favor religion" is that they protect religious freedom more than the freedom to conduct oneself in accordance with nonreligious norms. This kind of "favoritism toward religion," however, is inherent in the very text of the First Amendment. The government must refrain from actions that officially prefer one religion over another, or religion over nonreligion—even though it is free to embrace certain secular ideologies and organizations and to oppose others. The government must also refrain from actions that punish or penalize the practice of religion—though it is free to punish or penalize other forms of human conduct. How could the First Amendment forbid the establishment or protect the exercise of "religion," if religion cannot receive protection not accorded secular individuals or institutions? ...

[A]nti-accommodationists [f]ail to appreciate the significance of the Establishment Clause for the accommodation question. Anti-accommodationists object to "singling out" religion for special protection under the Free Exercise Clause, but they typically have no qualms about "singling" out religion for special prohibitions under the Establishment Clause. Government may advance secular causes such as feminism or capitalism, subsidize controversial private organizations such as Planned Parenthood or the Republican Party, and issue government propaganda about improper private habits such as smoking or teenage sex; but it may not identify itself officially with Christianity, subsidize churches as such, or propagandize for religious views. This half of the Religion Clauses suits the anti-accommodationists just fine. But when religion is singled out for protection, this strikes them as terribly unfair. My position is that the government must "single out" religion in both free exercise and establishment contexts, with the goal of approximating a substantive neutrality in a religiously pluralistic culture....

A final argument against accommodation of religion is that religious commitments—at least those most likely to give rise to claims of accommodation—are inconsistent with the democratic order. [McConnell quotes, among others, Gey's argument (p. 281) that religion contravenes democracy's premise] that "there can be no sacrosanct principles or unquestioned truths." ...

Is it necessary to respond [to such arguments]? Is it necessary to point out that the great attacks on the democratic ideal and the most intense demands for obedience in this century have come from those for whom no extraworldly source of decent limits exists? Or that their prison camps were filled with brave individuals who claimed divine inspiration for their adherence to principle? Is it not obvious that intolerance and ideological blindness come in secular as well as religious hues? That persons of varying faiths can be equal citizens in a pluralistic republic? Indeed, that the wellsprings of religious experience have made a certain contribution to the development of the democratic spirit? ...

The view that religion "undermines" the democratic spirit certainly played no part in this country's adoption of the First Amendment. The Founders were far more likely to assume, as did Washington, that religion is the "indispensable support[t]" for republican government.[2] The reaction of the Founders to the subgroups among them whose religious convictions conflicted with the needs of the civil order was not to accuse them of undemocratic tendencies, but to protect their sincere claims of conscience.

NOTES

As a result of editing, the notes for this essay have been renumbered. The note number from the original essay or article is shown in parentheses at the end of each citation.

1. [Gey excerpt, p. 280 of this book.] (141)

2. President George Washington, "Washington's Farewell Address" (Sept. 17, 1796), in Henry S. Commager, ed., *Documents of American History*, vol. 1 (1973), pp. 169, 173. (250)

PART IV
OTHER
FREE EXERCISE ISSUES

Chapter 10

RELIGIOUS INSTITUTIONS' FREE EXERCISE

TOWARDS A GENERAL THEORY OF THE RELIGION CLAUSES: THE CASE OF CHURCH LABOR RELATIONS AND THE RIGHT TO CHURCH AUTONOMY

Douglas Laycock

Free Exercise and the Right to Church Autonomy

A. The Three Faces of Free Exercise

The Free Exercise Clause protection for religious activity includes at least three rather different kinds of rights. In each category, some claims have been accepted and others rejected; none of these rights is protected absolutely.

One category is the bare freedom to carry on religious activities: to build churches and schools, conduct worship services, pray, proselytize, and teach moral values. This is the exercise of religion in its most obvious sense.

Douglas Laycock, "Towards a General Theory of the Religion Clauses: The Case of Church Labor Relations and the Right to Church Autonomy," *Columbia Law Review* 81 (1981): 1373, 1389–92, 1394–96, 1398–1400.

Second, and closely related, is the right of churches to conduct these activities autonomously: to select their own leaders, define their own doctrines, resolve their own disputes, and run their own institutions. Religion includes important communal elements for most believers. They exercise their religion through religious organizations, and these organizations must be protected by the clause.

Third is the right of conscientious objection to government policy. The phrase is most prominently associated with the military draft, but there has also been conscientious objector litigation with respect to war taxes, compulsory education [*Yoder*], and other requirements that conflict with the moral scruples of certain sects or individual believers....

Each of these rights has solid support in the case law, but many courts and commentators think only in terms of conscientious objection. One of the most common errors in free exercise analysis is to try to fit all free exercise claims into the conscientious objector category and reject the ones that do not fit. Under this approach, every free exercise claim requires an elaborate judicial inquiry into the conscience or doctrines of the claimant. If he is not compelled by religion to engage in the disputed conduct, he is not entitled to free exercise protection. Thus, courts have tried to decide whether activities of organized churches were required by church doctrine or were something that the churches did for nonreligious reasons....

This approach reflects a rigid, simplistic, and erroneous view of religion. Many activities that obviously are exercises of religion are not required by conscience or doctrine. Singing in the church choir and saying the Roman Catholic rosary are two common examples. Any activity engaged in by a church as a body is an exercise of religion. This is not to say that all such activities are immune from regulation: there may be a sufficiently strong governmental interest to justify the intrusion. But neither are these activities wholly without constitutional protection. It is not dispositive that an activity is not compelled by the official doctrine of a church or the religious conscience of an individual believer. Indeed, many would say that an emphasis on rules and obligations misconceives the essential nature of some religions.

Moreover, emphasis on doctrine and requirements ignores the fluidity of doctrine and the many factors that can contribute to doctrinal change. A church is a complex and dynamic organization, often including believers with a variety of views on important questions of faith, morals, and spirituality. The dominant view of what is central to the religion, and of what practices are required by the religion, may gradually change. Today's pious custom may be tomorrow's moral obligation, and vice versa....

[Thus when] the state interferes with the autonomy of a church, and particularly when it interferes with the allocation of authority and influence within a church, it interferes with the very process of forming the religion as it will exist in the future.... In the labor relations context, it is impossible to predict the long-term effect of forcing religious leaders to share authority with a secular union, or of substituting one employee for another as a result of a discrimination charge or a union grievance. A number of such substitutions may have a cumulative effect, especially if, as seems likely, there is some bias in the process making them. Employees who are more aggressive and less deferential to authority, and therefore more litigious, are more likely to invoke remedies that result in compulsory replacement of one employee with another. Thus, any interference with church affairs may disrupt "the free development of religious doctrine."[1]

Such government-induced changes in religion are too unpredictable to be avoided on a case-by-case basis. They can be minimized only by a strong rule of church autonomy. The Free Exercise Clause therefore forbids government interference with church operations unless there is, to use the conventional phrase, a compelling governmental interest to justify the interference. Identifying those governmental interests that are sufficient is a complex task that requires further exploration.

B. Church Autonomy and Entanglement

Anything that I would describe as an interference with church autonomy the Supreme Court might describe as an [impermissible] entanglement [between church and state, forbidden by the Establishment Clause]....

C. The Church Autonomy Precedents

The Supreme Court has not yet passed on a claim to church autonomy in the broad terms proposed here. But, as noted, church autonomy is a component of entanglement doctrine. More importantly, the Court has recognized a right to church autonomy in a series of cases involving disputes over control of church property, church organization, and entitlement to ecclesiastical office. All but one of these cases arose out of church schisms; the exception involved a claim to have inherited an endowed chaplaincy.

The doctrinal details of this right to autonomy are in flux and not entirely clear. In [cases involving disputes over] ecclesiastical appointment and church organization[,] the Court has uniformly held that secular courts are bound by the decision of the highest church authority recognized by both sides before the dispute began.[2] In property disputes, the Court announced a similar rule [in 1872] as a matter of federal common law.[3] ...

But the Court has not required states to follow the federal rule in property cases; it recently said [in the case of *Jones v. Wolf*] that states are free to use any approach that does not require secular courts to determine questions of church doctrine or the allocation of church authority.[4] State courts may construe deeds, contracts, church constitutions, and similar documents that indicate property ownership, but only if these documents are construed under "neutral principles of law," i.e., as ordinary legal instruments and without regard to questions of religious doctrine. This "neutral principles" approach was approved by a sharply divided Court. But the Court agreed unanimously on the goal of church autonomy. The argument turned on whether the dissenters' approach would better implement the decision of the church itself with less secular interference....

[The right of church autonomy is supported by] both the Free Exercise and Establishment Clauses in these schism cases. When a secular court awards property or an ecclesiastical post on the basis of its resolution of a question of religious doctrine, it establishes the winning faction. But this is merely a consequence of the primary constitutional violation—interfering with the right of the original church, which included both factions, to resolve the controversy itself. [This is] a free exercise right, a right to church autonomy....

D. Autonomy and Church Labor Relations

Church labor relations rather plainly fall within the right of church autonomy. Deciding who will conduct the work of the church and how that work will be conducted is an essential part of the exercise of religion. In the language of the Supreme Court's autonomy cases, labor relations are matters of "church administration"; undoubtedly, they affect "the operation of churches."[5]

Occasionally, a labor relations law requires a church to violate its official doctrine or collective conscience. These cases present conscientious objection claims as well as church autonomy claims. But it is worth repeating that the right of church autonomy does not depend on conscientious objection.

Churches may object to regulation on church autonomy grounds even when their official doctrine seems to support the regulation. Two examples from the recent church labor relations cases illustrate the point. The Roman Catholic Church has long supported the moral right of workers to organize and bargain collectively, and the moral duty of employers to bargain. Yet most local bishops resisted NLRB jurisdiction over teachers in parochial schools. Similarly, the Seventh Day Adventists resisted the Secretary of Labor's authority to enforce the Equal Pay Act in their schools, even though official church doctrine endorsed equal pay.

There are a variety of possible reasons, all constitutionally legitimate, for these examples of resistance to regulation that arguably reinforces church teaching. These churches may have been hypocritically seeking to exempt themselves from a moral duty they preach to others. Such conduct is not very admirable, but free exercise protection is not limited to churches the government admires. Alternatively, these churches may have resisted government regulation on principle, to avoid creating an adverse precedent that might support some more objectionable regulation in the future.

There is a third possible reason, and it casts further light on the nature of the right to autonomy. Even if government policy and church doctrine endorse the same broad goal, the church has a legitimate claim to autonomy in the elaboration and pursuit of that goal. Regulation may be thought of as taking the power to decide a matter away from the church and either prescribing a particular decision or vesting it elsewhere—in the executive, a court, an agency, an arbitrator, or a union. And regulation takes away not only a decision of general policy when it is imposed, but many more decisions of implementation when it is enforced.

For example, the NLRA initially takes away the decision whether to recognize a union. But once there is a union and a duty to bargain, a vast array of decisions that the church could once make autonomously must be shared with the union, and in the event of disagreement, with arbitrators, the NLRB, and the courts. A church might be willing to bargain with an uncertified union over wages and a few key working conditions, but resist NLRB jurisdiction to avoid the Board's expansive list of mandatory bargaining subjects. Forcing church authorities to share control of religious institutions with a labor union may not stir quite the same emotions as forcing them to relinquish control to schismatics. But a common principle is at stake in both cases: each is an interference with church control of church affairs.

Similarly, antidiscrimination laws initially prevent the church from deciding whether to discriminate among its employees and applicants. Many churches may wish to discriminate on the basis of religion, and some on the basis of race, sex, or national origin. Equally important, churches that do not want to discriminate at all are deprived of the chance to define discrimination. Some may oppose unequal treatment of individuals because of race, sex, or national origin, but want to be free to act on any facially neutral basis even if it has disparate impact on racial, sexual, or ethnic groups. Even churches that accept the full scope of collective bargaining and the government's definition of discrimination may be seriously alarmed at the prospect of secular enforcement. This requires secular tribunals to review the church's comparisons of the responsibility and difficulty of jobs and of the skills, qualifications, and performance of workers; its motives for personnel decisions and the credibility of its claims to have acted for religious reasons; the religious or other necessity for employment practices that have disparate impact; even the effect on workers of its bishops' prayers and Bible readings.

NOTES

As a result of editing, the notes for this essay have been renumbered. The note number from the original essay or article is shown in parentheses at the end of each citation.

1. *Presbyterian Church v. Hull Church*, 393 U.S. 440, 449 (1969). (150)
2. E.g., *Serbian E. Orthodox Diocese v. Milivojevich*, 426 U.S. 696 (1976) [(holding that state court could not overturn hierarchically organized church's defrocking of bishop and reorganization of diocese)]. (169)
3. *Watson v. Jones*, 80 U.S. (13 Wall.) 679 (1872). (170)
4. *Jones v. Wolf*, 443 U.S. 595, 602 (1979). (172)
5. *Kedroff v. St. Nicholas Cathedral*, 344 U.S. 94, 107 (1952). (200)

FREE EXERCISE EXEMPTIONS AND RELIGIOUS INSTITUTIONS: THE CASE OF EMPLOYMENT DISCRIMINATION

IRA C. LUPU

THEORIES OF FREE EXERCISE AND IMMUNITY FROM ANTI-DISCRIMINATION LAW

A. Church Autonomy

Professor Laycock's version of church autonomy is the most expansive of those yet advanced. Laycock, who would cloak all church activities in a protective mantle of legal autonomy, focuses particularly on issues of church labor relations. While he concedes that church autonomy might have to give way to state interests of extraordinary importance, he argues that "alleged

Ira C. Lupu, "Free Exercise Exemptions and Religious Institutions: The Case of Employment Discrimination," *Boston University Law Review* 67 (1987): 391, 399–401, 406–409, 419–20, 422–26.

state interests in...protection of...church workers from exploitation...are usually illegitimate."[1] ...

[H]owever, the concept of church autonomy is not a defensible one.... [A]utonomy theories tend to shield undesirable behavior without producing any guarantee of a commensurate return of constitutional value.

1. Institutional Autonomy and Constitutional Law

Churches, of course, are not the only private institutions through which individuals exercise First Amendment rights. Rights of political participation are exercised through the vehicle of political parties. Rights of speech and press are often exercised by corporate entities, including newspaper companies, television stations with corporate owners, and publishing houses that produce books or magazines. Universities are a form of organizational arrangement through which scholars pursue academic inquiry, another activity of First Amendment concern.

In all these instances, the institutions engaged in constitutionally protected activities are entitled to no special autonomy rights by virtue of their function.... [For example, f]ew would deny that the position of editor-in-chief of a major newspaper, or the job of head of the news division of one of the major television networks, are occupational opportunities of substantial significance to the system of free expression. A claim of "press autonomy" akin to that of "church autonomy" would insulate press institutions from civil rights suit[s] if they decided to limit these positions to white males. The precise arguments made by [Laycock]—that permitting such suits would expose "internal" matters of the institution to public, judicial review—are equally available in press cases as in church cases [yet the newspaper is not exempt from the law].

Recognizing such claims of autonomy [is unsound because it] will, by definition, insulate from regulation behavior that the political branches have decided needs regulating. As the autonomy cloak spreads, the quantity of such otherwise illegal behavior, and the harms it causes, will presumably increase. And as the scope of autonomy moves farther away from the special activities that legitimate the autonomy claim, tolerance of those harms becomes increasingly difficult to justify.

Moreover, assertions of autonomy may be as likely to cloak economically self-interested behavior as they are to protect ideological purity. Because institutional autonomy claims will provide this cloak for behavior that is self-interested and otherwise unlawful behavior, their availability will create incentives for organizations to hide a variety of non-religious or non-speech activity behind the cloak. This, in turn, will tend to debase activities which we have come to respect as constitutionally special, turning them into easily accessible havens for economic and social outlaws....

2. Church Autonomy and Supreme Court Precedent

a. The "Internal Dispute Cases." [In arguing for church autonomy rights, Laycock relies] upon a series of cases limiting judicial power to resolve disputes internal to a particular church. Typically, the intra-church dispute cases involve controversies over the ownership and possession of real property, or the question of who is entitled to make appointments to positions of church leadership....

[But] the Supreme Court's 1979 decision in *Jones v. Wolf* has seriously undermined any support for church autonomy in the strong sense put forward by Laycock. In *Jones v. Wolf*, the majority of a local Presbyterian congregation, located in Georgia, had elected to withdraw its affiliation with the Presbyterian Council of the United States. A minority faction within the congregation remained loyal to the national council, and the two factions contested control over the real property of the church....

In a landmark opinion, the Supreme Court approved of what it described as the "neutral principles of law"[2] approach to resolving church disputes. This approach "requires a civil court to examine certain religious documents...for language of trust in favor of the general church." So long as that inquiry can be made without requiring the court "to resolve a religious controversy," state courts are free to substitute this conventional dispute-resolution methodology in place of deference to "the authoritative ecclesiastical body."

The Court made clear that the constitutional evil to be avoided in all cases is judicial resolution of questions of religious doctrine and practice and that, in making efforts to so avoid, states may choose between deference and "neutral principles" as methodological approaches....

Jones v. Wolf undercuts the premises of Laycock's theory of church autonomy. In one sense, of course, church bodies remain autonomous even after *Jones v. Wolf*. They can structure their legal transactions, including the secular documents which evidence them, in whatever way they choose. Moreover, from this same ex ante perspective, whoever is in control of the church can create a church government that reinforces the decision-making power of particular officers or agencies. By doing both of these things—carefully structuring its political arrangements and its property transactions—a church can minimize the likelihood of judicial intrusion in subsequent disputes.

This, however, is a kind of contractual and organizational freedom that is in no way unique to churches. Subject to the requirements of law, other corporate bodies can similarly insulate their internal decisions from judicial nullification.

The kind of autonomy for which Laycock contends, however, is not of this ex ante, planning variety. It is rather of the ex post variety: in a conflict between the church and any of its members or employees, says Laycock, courts are precluded from taking any side other than that of the church.

The grant of authority to state courts in *Jones v. Wolf* to use "neutral principles of law" in resolving intra-church disputes is antithetical to Laycock's claim. It may be quite clear that a church is hierarchical, and it may be equally clear who speaks for the top of the hierarchy. Nevertheless, a court is free to examine relevant documents and rule against the hierarchical authority, if it can avoid resolving disputes concerning the content of religious doctrines.

On this understanding, no doctrine of church autonomy exists to bar employment discrimination suits arising out of non-religious discrimination. Such suits do not necessarily require any determination of disputed questions of faith within a church. It might well be that all church documents and all church officials declare, for example, that only Caucasians may be church ministers. In such a case, there is no question, in Laycock's terms, of identifying who speaks for the church or of the content of the church's position. Rather, the only question would be whether the church position should control, or whether it must yield to the dictates of civil rights law....

There is yet another reason why the intra-church dispute cases do not immunize churches from civil rights actions. Employment discrimination cases are simply not "internal" matters. The plaintiff herself may never have been a member of the church. More fundamentally, the interests being protected and enforced in civil rights actions are not only the interests of the parties; substantial public and third-party interests are present as well. Religious institutions, like other important social institutions, are influential in shaping behavior and moral convictions. The way in which such institutions treat women or racial minorities is likely to have significant consequences in other spheres of life. Those who may suffer these consequences thus have a vital interest in the behavior of religious institutions. In the face of these interests, these disputes cannot reasonably be perceived as "internal." By contrast, the public interest tends to be much smaller in the typical dispute involving church members' competing claims to church property or church office, in which there is little external concern other than that the dispute be settled peacefully. If *Jones* undercuts ex post church autonomy in disputes that are substantially "internal," there can be no case left for such autonomy when external interests mount....

B. Employment Discrimination Law and Free Exercise: The Case Against Institutional Exemptions

1. *Autonomy, Free Exercise, and Organizations*

Rights of free exercise are quintessentially rights of autonomy. The right of religious liberty embraced by the clause protects interests in making and maintaining spiritual commitments, and in living in accord with one's deepest presuppositions about humankind and nature. Pursuant to free exercise principles, the state may be obliged to relieve the conscientious suffering inflicted on individuals for whom obedience to secular law causes violation of religious duty. Moreover, individuals, not institutions, are always the ultimate source of religious conviction. Free exercise decisions establish that individuals can assert these claims even if agents of the religious organizations to which they belong take a wholly different view of the faith. And, [for several reasons,] free exercise principles demand, quite properly, a showing that claimants are proceeding from sincere conviction.

All of these attributes of free exercise claims—religious commitment, the urge to relieve religious suffering, free and private choice of conviction, and sincere embrace of such conviction—can only be understood as reflecting qualities of autonomous human beings. But if free exercise exemption rights are thus rights of autonomy, organizations may not possess them. Organizations qua organizations are incapable of emotion and self-consciousness. Organizations cannot experience the indignity or shame associated with a loss of autonomy. Most importantly, organizations cannot hold convictions or make spiritual commitments, and they cannot demonstrate the sincerity with which organizational positions are held. Recognizing organizational claims to free exercise exemptions from secular law thus tends to undermine the entire structure and legitimacy of free exercise law....

2. Organizations, Aggregated Rights, and Derivative Free Exercise Rights

Even if organizations lack autonomy rights under the Free Exercise Clause, individuals have them. Moreover, the individual claim to choose one's own "priest," without substantive interference from the government, is a very strong one. The personal choice of spiritual confidante and leader may be tied up quite intimately with the manner of exercising one's religious conviction.

Assuming, arguendo, that individuals have an autonomy right to choose a priest, we must confront the question of organizational exercise, as distinguished from possession, of such a right. The organization might plausibly be viewed as exercising the aggregate rights of its congregants, or as exercising a derivative right to make choices that will enhance the free exercise rights of its members. Any attempt to disable religious organizations from claiming free exercise immunity from employment discrimination law must inevitably respond to arguments of these types.

a. Aggregated Rights. One might think of a religious organization as being a simple conduit for the exercise of the aggregated rights of its members. So viewed, the organization does not have a voice of its own; rather, it amplifies the voices of its members. On such a theory, an organizational claim to be free of employment discrimination laws in hiring would be understood as an aggregation of the individual rights of its members to be similarly free.

The aggregated rights view is substantially undermined by insights derived from contemporary organization theory. This work has identified and elaborated the ways in which bureaucratic managers develop their own interests in organizational structure, and how they operate the organization in ways that advance those interests. Moreover, as organizations grow larger and more complex, various constituent interests develop within them, and various intensities of interest appear within particular constituencies. These observations have led theorists to conclude that organizations cannot be understood simply as devices for aggregation of preferences or interests of those who hold a stake in the organization.

[These concerns apply to religious organizations, too.] Interests are frequently divided among professional clergy, other professional employees, non-professional employees, lay leadership, active congregants, and more passive or wholly inactive congregants. There is no reason to think that the legal voice of the religious body will somehow fully and correctly transmit all the congregants' preferences and spiritual needs. The likelihood that religious leadership will be a reliable transmitter of preferences is undermined still further in cases concerning large state-wide, regional, or national religious organizations. When the issues are day-to-day discretionary choices, the legal system quite sensibly permits the organization to speak through an agent's voice. The gravity of a decision regarding an organizational free exercise right to exemption from general law, however, demands a stronger and more unified aggregate voice than the agency relationships in large organizations will allow.

The aggregated rights theory is undermined yet further by the strong possibility of divided views within the organizational membership, and the implications of that division for the ultimate aggregated view. On matters as volatile and controversial as the exclusion of females from positions of leadership, it is hard to imagine the absence of disagreement on the subject among church members. For groups that are large in number and noninsular, unanimity on such issues is virtually impossible. Moreover, in those organizations lacking the absence of electoral or other forms of direct control by the congregation over its spiritual leaders, the likelihood that the leaders speak accurately over time for the aggregated views of their congregants is even smaller....

Finally, a theory of aggregation ignores the crucial, constitutional interest in the sincerity of individual convictions....

b. Derivative Rights. [The "derivative rights" theory argues] that organizations are the most efficient mechanisms for religious people to utilize in the selection of spiritual leaders, and that affording organizations broad discretion in doing so will enhance and secure the personal rights of members to select ministers of their own. Although the derivative rights claim is the strongest one available to the organizational claimant, the position is ultimately unpersuasive....

Up to a point, permitting derivative rights in religious organizations [makes sense]. It is efficient, and in no way troublesome, to permit such organizations to enter into employment contracts, for example. But the points of legitimacy and efficiency in recognizing derivative rights end where free exercise exemption claims begin. As the preceding discussion develops, the overwhelming character of both the history and doctrinal development of free exercise is focused upon protecting intrinsic and internal rights of individual religious conscience, rather than instrumental rights of religious organization.

Recognition of derivative rights, like recognition of direct organizational rights or recognition of the organization as an aggregating device, effectively eliminates the requirement that free exercise claims proceed from conscientious and heartfelt concerns. Elimination of this requirement might permit the successful assertion of bad faith exemption claims. In this context, bad faith claims include those driven wholly or in large part by non-religious prejudice against women or members of other groups protected by the civil rights laws. If employment decisions rest on such prejudice, rather than on conscientious religious commitments, there is no constitutionally cognizable reason to immunize them from regulation. Allowing organizations to assert derivative free exercise rights, however, would subvert the process of inquiry into sincerity, and would thereby impede careful sorting of the possible mixture of motivations that led to discriminatory employment decisions.

NOTES

As a result of editing, the notes for this essay have been renumbered. The note number from the original essay or article is shown in parentheses at the end of each citation.

1 Douglas Laycock, "Towards a General Theory of the Religion Clauses: The Case of Church Labor Relations and the Right to Church Autonomy," *Columbia Law Review* 81 (1981): 1374. (31)

2. *Jones v. Wolf,* 443 U.S. 595, 602 (1979). (60)

RELIGIOUS ORGANIZATIONS AND FREE EXERCISE: THE SURPRISING LESSONS OF *SMITH*

KATHLEEN A. BRADY

LESSONS FROM *SMITH*

I will [use *Employment Division v. Smith*] as a prism through which to analyze the rights of religious organizations under the Free Exercise Clause.... *Smith* raises a number of issues that help to clarify [whether and how strongly to protect group autonomy]. When these issues are examined closely, the results are surprising. *Smith* supports a broad right of autonomy for religious groups that extends to internal matters with clear religious significance as well as activities that appear more mundane or secular.

Kathleen A. Brady, "Religious Organizations and Free Exercise: The Surprising Lessons of *Smith*," *Brigham Young University Law Review* (2004):1633, 1672–77, 1683–86, 1689–90, 1694–95, 1699–1704.

A. Religious Groups and Freedom of Belief

The first guidepost that *Smith* provides lies in the first few lines of the Court's analysis where the Court draws a distinction between protections for religious beliefs and protections for religious action. According to *Smith*, the "free exercise of religion means, first and foremost, the right to believe and profess whatever religious doctrine one desires."[1] *Watson v. Jones* expressed a similar view. In America, the "law knows no heresy, and is committed to the support of no dogma, the establishment of no sect."[2] Action receives less protection. While an individual is free to believe whatever he or she chooses, the Free Exercise Clause does not guarantee the right to act on these beliefs where neutral laws of general applicability stand in the way. An individual's religious beliefs [*Smith* says] do not "excuse him from compliance with an otherwise valid law prohibiting conduct that the State is free to regulate." ...

Thus, in the world that *Smith* envisions, the beliefs and actions of religious individuals are treated very differently. In the realm of ideas, *Smith* envisions unrestricted freedom. The Free Exercise Clause entitles individuals to believe and profess whatever doctrines they desire, and *Smith* expects that individuals will hold a wide range of different religious views, orthodox as well as unorthodox, popular and unpopular. Restrictions on religious practice are, by contrast, unavoidable, but *Smith* hopes that legislatures will make accommodations where reasonable. Moreover, *Smith* does not expect restrictions on action to affect the complexity and diversity of opinion. Religious individuals will continue to hold whatever religious beliefs they desire even if the beliefs are not actionable....

The *Smith* Court says little about the conditions that would be necessary to maintain the type of unrestricted freedom of belief that it envisions.... [But r]eligious groups play an indispensable role in shaping and fostering the freedom of belief that *Smith* envisions and is committed to.

Numerous scholars have observed the connection between religious groups and individual religious convictions. Individuals express and exercise their beliefs in religious communities, and religious organizations also play an essential role in shaping the beliefs that individuals hold. As Frederick Gedicks has written, "[g]roups are ongoing and independent entities that influence in their own right how individuals think, express themselves, and act."[3] Thus, "[a]lthough in some respects groups are aggregations of their individual members, in other respects, groups are prior to and independent of their members." Justice Brennan draws the same connection between individual religious belief and group activity.... According to Justice Brennan, "[f]or many individuals, religious activity derives meaning in large measure from participation in a larger religious community."[4] These religious groups do not simply express individual religious beliefs, but the "community represents an ongoing tradition of shared beliefs, an organic entity not reducible to a mere aggregation of individuals."

Groups play yet another important role in the formation of individual belief. Religious communities are the vehicle for the development of doctrine. It is through religious communities that individuals jointly develop religious ideas and beliefs. Thus, the very formulation of religious opinions takes place within religious groups, as does the transmission and exercise of beliefs....

Nor is the development of religious ideas and doctrine an abstract affair. Religious organizations do not simply teach or formulate doctrine in the abstract. They also seek to live out their beliefs in their relationships with fellow communicants. They seek to put their beliefs into action in shaping organizational structure, developing rules for church discipline, clarifying the rights and duties of members and employees, and fostering more informal social expectations and standards. Indeed, it is through this process of living beliefs in community that ideas are tested and, again, refined and reformed. It is also through this process that beliefs are preserved. Without the ability to put ideas into practice within the community, it would be difficult for the group to maintain its commitments and convictions. Indeed, without the opportunity to practice their convictions in community life, church members may not be able to fully understand what their beliefs mean and require. Restrictions on individual action outside the community may not undermine religious belief if these opportunities are present, but restrictions on internal group life could be devastating.

If religious groups play an essential role in shaping individual religious belief and, indeed, in the very formulation of religious ideas, the freedom of belief that *Smith* envisions requires protections for religious organizations. If religious communities are not able to teach, develop, and live out their ideas free from state interference, individual belief will also be suppressed. The diversity of religious beliefs that *Smith* envisions presupposes a diversity of religious communities, each of which is able to structure its own internal life according to its own unique religious views and perspectives....

B. Misunderstandings and Temptations

If special protections for religious groups are necessary to preserve the freedom of belief that *Smith* envisions, the next step is to determine how far these protections should extend. Does *Smith* call for a broad right of church autonomy, or should protections be limited to situations in which [a particular] religious belief or practice is actually burdened [or the activity is deemed "quintessentially" religious]? ...

To answer these questions, one must look at another issue raised in *Smith*. One of the reasons given by the *Smith* majority for its rule regarding individual religious practice is the difficulty that judges would have in identifying which beliefs are central in different religious traditions. Providing relief whenever a believer's religious conduct is burdened by government action would produce chaos, but limiting exemptions to situations involving practices central to the individual's faith is unworkable. Judges do not have the ability to make such determinations: "[i]t is not within the judicial ken to question the centrality of particular beliefs or practices to a faith, or the validity of particular litigants' interpretations of those creeds."[5] If this concern is explored further in the group context, it becomes clear that limiting judicial relief to actual burdens on group belief or practice may be preferable in theory, but it is unworkable in fact. Judges are no more fit to make the types of inquiries required under such an approach than they are to identify which beliefs are central in different religious traditions.... The only reliable way to protect the religious beliefs and activities of religious groups is a broad right of church autonomy that extends to all aspects of church affairs, even the most routine and mundane.

[In some cases courts improperly second-guess a religious group's assertion of doctrine.] In other cases, failure of courts to identify burdens on group practices and belief results from an unfamiliarity with church doctrines. The complexity of church doctrine and its development over time often makes ascertaining conflicts between government regulation and church doctrine particularly difficult. State and lower federal court cases upholding the application of labor statutes to church institutions illustrate these problems.

Many of these cases have involved social services organizations or schools operated by the Catholic Church, and courts have repeatedly found that collective bargaining is consistent with Church doctrine. Indeed, in several cases, the courts have observed that the Catholic Church has long supported unionization and collective bargaining. According to the Second Circuit in *Catholic High School Association v. Culvert*, "the Encyclicals and other Papal Messages make clear that the Catholic Church has for nearly a century been among the staunchest supporters of the rights of employees to organize and engage in collective bargaining."[6] However, a more thorough analysis of the Catholic Church's social teaching reveals that the Church's views are far more complicated than these courts assume. While the Catholic Church strongly supports worker rights and collective bargaining, the Church's vision of collective bargaining is very different from the framework established in the NLRA and state labor laws that resemble the federal statute.

While secular statutes presuppose and entrench an adversarial relationship between management and labor, the Catholic Church's goal is a cooperative relationship based on charity, mutual respect and concern, and the common good.[7] ... For example, whereas the availability, threat, and actual use of economic weapons such as strikes and lockouts is "part and parcel" of the system that the NLRA sets up, the Church envisions a process of reasoned discussion and cooperation based upon a desire for mutual understanding, reconciliation, and achievement of the common good.... Thus, while the Church clearly supports collective bargaining and worker rights, courts upholding the application of secular labor statutes to Catholic institutions have not recognized the deep differences between the Church's vision and the legal frameworks that these courts have imposed....

Church institutions [generally] have not argued that the Catholic vision of collective bargaining is incompatible with secular regimes. Indeed, in a few cases, Catholic institutions had been voluntarily bargaining with unions under secular law for years....

Thus, courts may have difficulty determining whether government regulations burden group beliefs or practices because the religious group itself may be unaware of potential conflicts. Conflicts between religious doctrine and secular law may exist, but they may not be visible at the outset to either the church or the courts. In other cases, courts may be stymied by multiple interpretations of church doctrine. There are, for example, Catholic scholars who genuinely believe that collective bargaining under federal and state law is compatible with the Church's vision for labor relations. They and I disagree about the proper interpretation of Catholic social teaching. Sometimes multiple interpretations of church doctrine are a sign that the group's beliefs are changing or developing. In either case, there may be no single authoritative

view but many legitimate positions, all of which represent permissible interpretations of existing beliefs. Where multiple interpretations of church doctrine exist, any choice among them will entangle the courts in religious questions and interfere with the free development of doctrine. Indeed, the fact that
religious doctrine is not static but develops over time means that government
regulation which imposes no burden today may do so tomorrow, and views
which are unorthodox today or even barely articulable may be authoritative
tomorrow. It will be difficult for courts to recognize and keep up with such
changes particularly where new doctrines are in the early stages of development or adoption....

These examples from cases involving labor and employment regulation
illustrate a basic lesson that is repeated over and over again in the Supreme
Court's intrachurch dispute decisions and yet again in *Smith*. Courts are not fit
to interpret religious doctrine and engage in religious questions. As the Court
in *Watson v. Jones* observed, where civil courts resolve religious questions, the
appeal is "from the more learned tribunal... to one which is less so."[8] Thus,
whether mandatory collective bargaining conflicts with Catholic doctrine is
not a question that the Second Circuit or any other court is competent to
answer. Nor are courts competent to measure the burden on religious doctrine when federal antidiscrimination laws are applied to the employment
policies of conservative Christian schools. Judicial inquiry into the centrality
of religious beliefs as prohibited in *Smith* is just one impermissible form of
entanglement in church doctrine. The determination of whether government
regulation places a burden on organizational belief and practice is another....

Efforts by courts and scholars to carve out special areas of protection for
quintessentially religious matters are no less problematic. [For example,]
courts addressing the application of antidiscrimination statutes to religious
organizations have developed a ministerial exception that protects the
church-minister relationship from state interference regardless of whether
the organization has a religious basis for its actions. The church-minister relationship is an area of "prime ecclesiastical concern"[9] so "close to the heart of
the church"[10] that the state may not interfere even if there is no doctrinal
reason for the discrimination. Interference in the church-minister relationship, by definition, burdens religious practice....

[But quintessential or core "employees" cannot be limited to clergy.]
While the Catholic Church is one of the most hierarchical of all Christian
denominations, the Catholic Church does not limit essential religious func-

tions to ordained clergy or those with similar leadership, teaching, or worship roles. For example, in the Catholic Church's social mission, those who feed and counsel the needy also proclaim the Church's message just as much as do preachers from the pulpit. For many scholars, the social services activities of religious organizations are viewed as less purely or quintessentially religious than teaching and worship. For example, [Carl] Esbeck has [d]escribed social services activities as a "second tier of religious ministry" that is "more the outgrowth of truths held by religious faiths than they are centrally dealing with the particulars of one's perception of ultimate truth."[11] For the Catholic Church, this is a misunderstanding of the Christian message. When Christ reveals God's love for humanity on the cross, he invites others to share in his life by imitating this love. Serving the poor and needy is not a second tier expression of one's faith. It is part and parcel of the Gospel message. Indeed, it is the Christian message in deed as well as word. When church members serve their neighbors in need, they follow, model, and witness the love of God. Thus, within the work of the counselor, the administrator, and even the cook there is the essence of the Catholic Church's teaching....

Thus, while the operations of Catholic social services organizations may appear to be essentially secular, they are, in fact, suffused with religious significance.... For the Catholic Church, social services activities are no more secular than worship and preaching....

[Because of these problems in defining limited autonomy rights], the only effective and workable protection for the ability of religious groups to preserve, transmit, and develop their beliefs free from government interference is a broad right of church autonomy that extends to all aspects of church affairs....

C. Religious Belief and Democratic Government

At this point, the reader might object to the direction of my argument. If limiting relief to identifiable burdens on religious belief and practice is not possible and no line can be drawn between quintessentially religious matters and less significant practices, the lesson of *Smith* is to abandon special protections for religious groups altogether. The *Smith* Court reached that conclusion in the context of individual religious exercise when it found that judges were unfit to determine when government action burdens practices central to individual believers. Why should the outcome be different with respect to religious groups?... Moreover, while it might be desirable, in the abstract, to provide strong protections for religious belief and the groups that shape and sustain belief, there are countervailing state policies at stake when neutral laws of general applicability are involved. [Moreover,] the internal affairs of religious groups can have substantial effects upon the larger society, sometimes quite negative, and, thus, the state has important interests in extending neutral regulation to religious groups....

On this question as well, *Smith* provides important guidance. In the framework that *Smith* establishes for individual religious exercise, democratic processes play the central role in protecting religious liberty. The Free Exercise Clause does not guarantee relief where individual practice is burdened by neutral state action, but citizens can and, when reasonable, should extend such protection through legislative accommodations.

The faith that *Smith* places in democratic government invites consideration of the conditions that are necessary for its flourishing. If strong protections for individual religious belief and the groups that nurture and sustain belief are critical for successful democratic government, a broad right of church autonomy should certainly be preferred over the alternative of no special protections at all. Many scholars in recent years have emphasized the importance of religious groups and other voluntary associations for sustaining a well-functioning democratic order. Religious groups are among the "mediating structures" or institutions of "civil society" that stand between the individual and the state and transmit the values, skills, and attitudes necessary for self-government. As the source of moral values, they function as "seedbeds of civic virtue."[12] As training grounds for the exercise of democratic skills and responsibilities, they are "schools for democracy."[13] However, for many scholars who have emphasized the importance of associational life in the democratic order, this critical role does not call for strong protections against state interference. To the contrary, the state has an important role in shaping the internal affairs of religious and other civic groups so that they are congruent with democratic norms and shared public values. These scholars fear minority groups who teach "illiberal" values that will destabilize rather than strengthen democratic government. Too much diversity in associational life is not a good thing when this diversity undermines our common civic culture.

For those who desire congruence between the internal affairs of civil society institutions and shared public values, full freedom of religious belief is not desirable nor are strong protections for religious group autonomy....

Pointing to the role that religious groups play in shaping culture and transmitting values, these scholars have argued that employment discrimination within religious organizations threatens a "culture of subordination" that harms outsiders as well as members.[14] Discrimination by religious institutions "send[s] a powerful social message" and "imbeds...prejudice in American culture."[15]...

[These views] misunderstand the proper relationship between religious groups and democratic government. Democratic government is not supported best by homogeneity of beliefs and values, even beliefs whose correctness seems unassailable and values that seem essential for democratic life. Shaping associational life so that the internal practices and values of religious groups and other mediating institutions match shared public norms stifles new ideas that could challenge prevailing perspectives in progressive directions. Where government regulation inhibits the preservation, transmission, and development of minority beliefs within religious communities and other civic groups, it disserves democracy, not serves it.... The dangers are especially grave when democratic majorities are given primary responsibility for protecting individual liberties as they are in *Smith*. While it may be preferable in theory to protect only positive alternatives and new ideas that are helpful rather than harmful, humility requires us to admit that we do not always know where today's errors lie or where tomorrow's advances are hidden....

Religious groups and other civic associations [also] are buffers against overweening state power. Religious groups enhance individual autonomy by providing the context for personal development and expression. Religious groups can also provide a realm of privacy, intimacy, and supportive social bonds. In addition, religious groups mark the limits of state jurisdiction by addressing spiritual matters that lie beyond the temporal concerns of government.

[Religious groups serve yet another function:] [F]or many religious groups, spiritual matters have much to say about the shape of the temporal order. Religious communities with prophetic traditions speak to the state and its citizens about the content of laws, the distribution of wealth and power, and the requirements of justice.... [F]or many religious traditions, including the Catholic tradition discussed above, the norms of the church are viewed as a guide for the norms of politics....

Indeed, it is activist religious traditions such as these that have contributed much to the development of America's political culture over the course of its history. Judge John Noonan has observed that religious "crusades" played an indispensable role in ending slavery and in the fight for civil rights a century later.[16] Nothing guarantees that religious crusades will be for the good, writes Judge Noonan. Nor have any succeeded without conflict. However, much would have been lost without their contributions to the formation of American civic culture and political values. Though the ideals of religious crusades were at one time unpopular and unorthodox, and even abhorrent to many, many were, in fact, seeds of progress. . . .

At this point the reader might raise a further concern. I may have demonstrated that strong protections for religious belief and the groups that nourish these beliefs are important for democratic self-government, but my argument applies equally well to nonreligious associations. Just like religious groups, nonreligious organizations may advocate and model new perspectives for social and political life. Why, then, the reader may ask, should religious groups receive greater protection from government interference than nonreligious groups enjoy? . . .

The proper response to this concern is not to diminish protections for religious organizations but to expand them for secular associations that play similar roles in the lives of individuals and the larger community.

NOTES

As a result of editing, the notes for this essay have been renumbered. The note number from the original essay or article is shown in parentheses at the end of each citation.

1. 494 U.S. 877. (253)

2. 80 U.S. (13 Wall.) 679, 728 (1872). (254)

3. Frederick Mark Gedicks, "Toward a Constitutional Jurisprudence of Religious Group Rights," *Wisconsin Law Review* (1989): 99, 107. (271)

4. *Corporation of Presiding Bishop v. Amos*, 483 U.S. 327, 342 (1987) (Brennan, J., concurring in the judgment). (274)

5. *Smith*, 494 U.S. 887. (286)

6. 753 F.2d 1161, 1170 (2d Cir. 1985). (305)

7. See Kathleen A. Brady, "Religious Organizations and Mandatory Collective Bargaining Under Federal and State Labor Laws: Freedom From and Freedom For," *Villanova Law Review* 49 (2004): 77. (308)

8. 80 U.S. (13 Wall.) 729. (324)

9. *Minker v. Baltimore Annual Conference of United Methodist Church*, 894 F.2d 1354, 1357 (D.C. Cir. 1990). (327)

10. *Bollard v. Cal. Province of the Society of Jesus*, 196 F.3d 940, 946 (9th Cir. 1999). (328)

11. Carl H. Esbeck, "Establishment Clause Limits on Governmental Interference with Religious Organizations," *Washington & Lee Law Review* 41 (1984): 347, 377. (360)

12. See, e.g., Mary Ann Glendon, *Rights Talk: The Impoverishment of Political Discourse* (1991), p. 109[.] (386)

13. Peter L. Berger and Richard John Neuhaus, *To Empower People: From State to Civil Society*, ed. Michael Novak (1996), p. 194.... (387)

14. Jane Rutherford, "Equality as the Primary Constitutional Value: The Case for Applying Employment Discrimination Laws to Religion," *Cornell Law Review* 81 (1996): 1049, 1114, 1123. (394)

15. Joanne C. Brant, "Our Shield Belongs to the Lord: Religious Employers and a Constitutional Right to Discriminate," *Hastings Constitutional Law Quarterly* (1994): 275, 277; Rutherford, [*Cornell Law Review* 81:]1091. (396)

16. See John T. Noonan Jr., *The Lustre of Our Country: The American Experience of Religious Freedom* (1998), 250–52, 256–58. (413)

THOUGHTS ON *SMITH* AND
RELIGIOUS-GROUP AUTONOMY

Laura S. Underkuffler

INTRODUCTION

[I]f religious individuals are precluded by *Smith* from claiming broad immunity from civil laws and civil courts, can religious groups and institutions continue to claim that immunity, under the doctrine of religious-group autonomy?...

[Professor Underkuffler answers that] there is no convincing basis for distinguishing individual religious exemptions, struck down in *Smith*, from aggressive forms of religious-group autonomy. Nor is the ideal of individual religious freedom necessarily furthered by the broad immunity of religious groups from civil laws. While religious groups may be places that nurture and sustain individual religious belief, they may also be hostile, bitter places, which wield coercive and oppressive power.

Laura S. Underkuffler, "Thoughts on Smith and Religious-Group Autonomy," *Brigham Young University Law Review* (2004): 1773, 1774, 1782–86.

I have never been a fan of the *Smith* opinion. It is my view that freedom of religion—or freedom of conscience, as I have defined it—has very distinct value, which is recognized in our constitutional scheme. By affording individual religious exercise no special protection, *Smith* denies this principle. However, frustration with *Smith* should not blind us to the deep problems that an aggressive vision of religious-group autonomy presents. The prospect of religious groups with broad, autonomous power poses special dangers, both to dissenting individuals and to the goals of government, which should impel us to view it cautiously. Indeed, our reservations about the supremacy of religious claims should, if anything, be stronger when we consider the claims of religious groups....

RELIGIOUS-GROUP AUTONOMY: MORE VALUABLE, OR MORE DANGEROUS?

[P]rofessor Brady argues that the doctrine of religious-group autonomy survives *Smith* because it furthers one of the very important principles that *Smith* upholds. Professor Brady begins with the observation that the Supreme Court has long upheld [and reaffirmed in *Smith*] the value of religious belief and its protection by the First Amendment. [Thus, she argues,]

> If religious groups play an essential role in shaping individual religious belief and indeed in the very formulation of religious ideas, [then] the freedom of belief that *Smith* envisions requires protections for religious organizations.... Full freedom of belief is not possible without a corresponding right of religious groups to teach, develop, and practice their doctrines and ideas.[1]

It is the doctrine of religious-group autonomy that affords religious groups this freedom. And because of the inherent difficulties involved in any secular inquiry into what religious beliefs are, or the extent to which they are sustained by groups, the "only effective and workable" solution is to grant a broad right of autonomy to religious groups that extends to all aspects of their affairs.

Professor Brady candidly acknowledges that this approach will have costs. Granting religious groups autonomy will have costs in terms of the other, contrasting values and actions that the wider community wishes to promote. However, she argues that the opposition between religious-group autonomy and the implementation of democratic government is overdrawn. Religious groups, like all citizens' groups, are important "for sustaining a well-functioning democratic order." They are sources for moral values and recognition of responsibilities. They may act "[a]s training grounds for the exercise of democratic skills."

It is undoubtedly true that religious groups and institutions are important expressions of religious belief, and that they may add to the vibrancy of a liberal democratic society. However, in the particular context that we are considering, there are other, darker realities with which we must reckon.

First, let us consider Professor Brady's foundational assumption that religious groups "nurture and sustain" individual religious belief, making these groups deserving of protection from civil law. This case for religious-group autonomy is grounded in the idea that such groups are supportive and positive places for the expression and growth of individuals' religious faith.

Invoking this model, in this context, raises an immediate objection. The cases in which religious groups seek freedom from secular norms—for instance, the employment and labor relations cases that are Professor Brady's focus—involve not support, but conflict. In these cases, the religious group is not experienced by the aggrieved person as a warm, positive, nurturing place; it is experienced as a negative, hostile place, in which the religious group attempts to exert, on the individual, oppressive and coercive power. These situations involve disputes—bitter disputes; so bitter, in fact, that individuals seek recourse in civil laws and civil courts. In these situations, it is difficult to say that "vindicating individual religious beliefs" is obviously achieved by granting the religious groups complete, autonomous, and despotic power. What we have here is the clash of individual religious beliefs, the clash of individual religious values.

We might well believe that when the "nurturing" model applies, our commitment to religious-group autonomy is justified. However, when this model does not apply, should we continue, blindly, to grant religious groups that status? Put another way, if nurturing individual religious belief is our goal, is there a reason why the religious beliefs and values of the many should necessarily prevail (in effect) over the religious beliefs and values of dissenters? There is a tendency, by those who advocate religious-group autonomy, to focus on the needs of the target group and its members. What about the needs of the complainants?

There are certain situations, of course, when an aggrieved individual's recourse to civil laws and civil courts might—for other reasons—quite reasonably be denied. For instance, if the individual has voluntarily adopted the religious group's understandings, values, and authority, it is reasonable to expect that those understandings, values, and authority will govern the dispute, to the exclusion of the civil courts. As the Supreme Court has stated, "decisions of proper church tribunals on matters purely ecclesiastical, although affecting civil rights, are accepted in litigation before the secular courts as conclusive, because the parties in interest made them so by contract or otherwise."[2] This is no different from the effect given by civil courts to the determinations made by judicatory bodies established by clubs, civic associations, and other private consensual agreements. Indeed, this "contractarian" understanding of religious-group autonomy explains judicial deference in many intragroup disputes, such as those involving "ministerial," "church property," and other purely ecclesiastical matters. However, neither this contractarian theory nor the ideal of the "nurturing" group supports a broad, across-the-board presumption of religious-group autonomy in individual-recourse cases.

Thus, the idea of individual benefit as the reason for an aggressive vision of religious-group autonomy is questionable at best. In addition, religious-group autonomy involves obvious costs for societal goals and values. We must remember the range of situations in which claims of religious-group autonomy can arise, even under more conservative formulations. For instance, it is often suggested that religious-group autonomy should be granted for the groups' "internal operations." Although this might seem like a limited grant, it could include fund-raising activities, the treatment of employees or prospective employees, the operation of religious schools, and more. Such "internal operations" of religious groups have frequent, serious, external effects on critically important societal goals and values. With the enforceability of civil rights laws, education standards, workplace safety rules, and other laws at issue, it is difficult to maintain that the secular state has no vital interests at stake, or that religious groups should, in their internal operations, be "islands of autonomy."

For those who would go farther—and grant religious groups autonomy for all operations and all affairs—the list is even more daunting. For instance, a religious group could claim autonomy for its land-use decisions, or conflicts with zoning, environmental, and historic preservation laws; its commercial dealings with outside parties (for example, contractual disputes and antifraud laws); its political/lobbying activities, and conflicts with election laws and anticorruption laws; and more. The list is endless....

Indeed, when we think positively of the prospect of religious groups as exempt from civil laws, we tend to imagine this power as exercised by traditional religious groups, whose activities we admire. What of the harder cases? What of groups who espouse and implement religious hatred, racial hatred, the subordination of women, the persecution of gay men and lesbians, or other beliefs abhorrent to civil society? If autonomy is given to some religious groups, it must, perforce, be given to all. Yet, we would hardly want the activities of all such groups to be protected, untouchable, "islands of autonomy."

Professor Brady acknowledges that even the "internal affairs" of religious groups can have substantial impacts upon the larger society—some quite negative—giving the state important regulatory interests. She argues, however, that "[f]ull freedom of belief, even unpopular and unorthodox belief, is essential to the health of democratic society[,] as are the groups that make such beliefs possible." If—by this—she means freedom of belief, and the right to associate with like believers, I concur wholeheartedly. In those limited areas, the democratic value of religious freedom clearly outweighs the discomfort experienced by others, which the existence of those beliefs may engender. Indeed, even when we consider exemptions for individual free exercise claims, under pre-*Smith* law, my sympathy with her position (on balance) continues. However, when we consider the question of religiously motivated conduct by religious groups, the stakes are much higher. With the religious strife and oppression that currently engulfs vast parts of the world, the view that religious groups should simply be left alone to do good works seems alarmingly inadequate.

[I] do not believe that religion is simply another philosophical or personal belief system that should, as a constitutional matter, be treated "equally" in the name of "equality." I believe that religion is different, both in its unique power and value to individual lives and in its special dangers, when mixed with government. Those of us who believe in religion's special value might not like *Smith* and thus [might] be tempted to view any broadening of religious freedom, for individuals or groups, as some kind of victory. However, individual religious freedom under pre-*Smith* doctrine was a far more limited and benign construct than a sweeping idea of religious-group autonomy. Religion, when "combined" in groups and institutions, wields tremendous social, economic, and political power. It carries far more dangers of oppression, coercion, and the assumption of governmental power than does individual free exercise. This does not mean that government should have the power to crush religious groups, or to dictate their truly internal affairs. But neither does it mean that we should grant these groups carte blanche, as societal actors, by granting them sweeping autonomy.

NOTES

As a result of editing, the notes for this essay have been renumbered. The note number from the original essay or article is shown in parentheses at the end of each citation.

1. [Brady excerpted article, *Brigham Young University Law Review* (2004):] 1677. (32)

2. *Gonzalez v. Roman Catholic Archbishop*, 280 U.S. 1, 16 (1929). (38)

Chapter 11

FREE EXERCISE AND GOVERNMENT FUNDING

THE MISTAKES IN *LOCKE V. DAVEY* AND THE FUTURE OF STATE PAYMENTS FOR SERVICES BY RELIGIOUS INSTITUTIONS

Thomas C. Berg and Douglas Laycock

In the last twenty years, the ground has shifted dramatically in the federal constitutional disputes over the provision of government funds to religious schools and social services. Once the question was which few funding programs would be permitted to include religious schools under the Burger Court's demanding Establishment Clause rules.[1] But the Rehnquist Court changed direction and permitted the inclusion of religious institutions in more and more funding programs. Under the new approach, the pressing constitutional question became whether the Free Exercise and Free Speech Clauses permit government to exclude religious institutions from programs that fund private secular institutions providing the same services. The new

Thomas C. Berg and Douglas Laycock, "The Mistakes in *Locke v. Davey* and the Future of State Payments for Services by Religious Institutions," *Tulsa Law Journal* 40 (2004): 227, 227–35, 237–39, 242–50.

question arose because many states are likely to exclude religious schools because of political opposition or because of state constitutional restrictions on providing funds to "sectarian" institutions or instruction.

In *Locke v. Davey*,[2] the Supreme Court confronted the new question: whether singling out religious education for exclusion from generally available education benefits violates the Free Exercise Clause by discriminating against religious choice. The Court rejected the free exercise challenge by a strong 7-2 vote, on a set of facts seemingly sympathetic to the challenger. The State of Washington provides high-achieving students of modest family incomes with scholarships usable at any of the dozens of colleges in the state, for any of scores of majors, but denies scholarships to those few students who choose to major in theology taught from a devotional perspective. By upholding the Washington exclusion, the Court may have signaled that states will have broad discretion in all their funding programs to discriminate against religious educational choices. The free exercise claim for equal funding may have been strangled in its infancy.

In our view, it would be unfortunate if *Davey* ended the entire debate. We think that the majority opinion does not go nearly so far, and that even its narrower holding rests on a series of mistakes, large and small, about the nature and purposes of the Religion Clauses. Most importantly, the Washington exclusion violates the Clauses' central goal by permitting government to distort the individual choice of scholarship recipients about whether to major in a religious subject. After detailing this and other problems with the opinion, we turn to the issues that remain after *Davey*, especially the prime issue of vouchers to fund education from kindergarten through 12th grade ("K–12")....

I. THE COURT'S OPINION

Joshua Davey was eligible for a state Promise Scholarship to attend college on the basis of his academic record and his family's modest income. He was declared ineligible, however, because he decided to major in theology, along with business administration, at Northwest College, an evangelical Protestant school. The disqualifying feature of his theology major was that it would be taught from a standpoint that was "devotional in nature or designed to induce religious faith." If the theology major at Northwest College had reflected a "secular" or "purely academic" approach to religion and the Bible, Davey would have kept his scholarship.

Davey challenged his exclusion from the scholarship on two constitutional grounds. The first was that it violated the Free Exercise Clause, by singling out a religious choice for denial of a government benefit, under decisions such as *Church of the Lukumi v. City of Hialeah*[3] and *McDaniel v. Paty*.[4] The second was that it violated the Free Speech Clause, under decisions such as *Rosenberger v. Rector and Visitors of University of Virginia*,[5] by discriminating against theology programs taught from a religious viewpoint....But the Supreme Court [rejected these claims].

In rejecting Davey's free exercise claim, the majority made two sets of arguments. The first was that denial of funding is not a constitutionally significant burden on religion, or is at most a minimal one. The Court rejected the argument that singling out religion for exclusion from funding was "presumptively unconstitutional" under decisions like *Lukumi*.[6] That case involved criminal prohibition and an attempt "to suppress ritualistic animal sacrifices of the Santeria religion." But the burden on religion from discrimination in funding was "of a far milder kind," because withholding funding "imposes neither criminal nor civil sanctions on any type of religious service or rite," "does not deny to ministers the right to participate in the political affairs of the community," and "does not require students to choose between their religious beliefs and receiving a government benefit."

The majority's second set of arguments was much narrower. The Court cast the case as one about the training of clergy, and it concluded that the state had distinctively strong interests in denying funding for such activity. The majority said that there were "few areas in which a State's antiestablishment interests come more into play" than funding of clergy training, and it offered several reasons why. First, training to join the clergy was unlike "training for secular professions": "[t]raining someone to lead a congregation is an essentially religious endeavor" and is "akin to a religious calling as well as an academic pursuit." The Constitution has "distinct views" about religious activity "that find no counterpart with respect to other callings or professions." "That a State would deal differently with religious education for the ministry than with education for other callings is a product of these views, not evidence of hostility toward religion." In addition, "[s]ince the founding of our country, there have been popular uprisings against procuring taxpayer funds to support church leaders, which was one of the hallmarks of an 'established' religion."

This second set of arguments is limited to the funding of clergy and does not necessarily validate the denial of funding for other religious choices or activities. Indeed, the majority noted that Washington allowed recipients to use Promise Scholarships for religious instruction—to attend pervasively religious colleges like Northwest, and to take devotional theology classes as long as that was not their major. The majority went so far as to say, in response to Justice Scalia's warning that the decision would authorize states to exclude religion from all public services, that "the only interest at issue here is the State's interest in not funding the religious training of clergy."

II. DAVEY'S MISTAKES

The *Davey* decision rests on a series of mistakes about the nature and purpose of the Religion Clauses. Some of these mistakes concern the basic standard that should apply to free exercise claims challenging the exclusion of religion from funding programs. Others concern the state interests that might justify the exclusion of devotional-theology majors from generally available state college scholarships.

A. Confusion about Neutrality: Formal Nondiscrimination Versus Substantive Religious Choice

Davey argued that the state's exclusion of theology majors is "presumptively unconstitutional because it is not facially neutral with respect to religion." The argument...sounded in nondiscrimination: Davey relied on the "fundamental" and "minimum" requirement of the Free Exercise Clause [set forth in *Lukumi*] that a law may not single out religiously motivated activity for unfavorable treatment.[7]...The "unique disability" imposed in *McDaniel v. Paty* was denying to members of the clergy a generally available opportunity—the right to serve in the state legislature if elected by the voters.[8] In *Davey*, the "unique disability" imposed on devotional theology majors was to deny them a generally available financial benefit solely because they chose a particular religious course of study....

The Court rejected the argument that this facially discriminatory treatment of religion violated the Free Exercise Clause. One of its key premises was that the First Amendment treats religion differently from other activities....

We wholeheartedly agree that the Constitution often requires distinctive treatment of religion. But in cases such as *Davey*, the proper principle is nondiscrimination against religion. Both nondiscrimination in Davey's case

and distinctive treatment in other situations ultimately serve a more fundamental goal: that government should avoid interfering with the voluntary
choices of private individuals in religious matters.

The ultimate goal of the Constitution's provisions on religion is religious
liberty for all.... The ultimate goal is that every American should be free to
hold his own views on religious questions, and to live the life that those views
direct, with a minimum of government interference or influence.

The fundamental principle to achieve that goal is for the government to
maintain "substantive neutrality" toward religion[:]

> [T]he religion clauses require government to minimize the extent to which
> it either encourages or discourages religious belief or disbelief, practice or
> nonpractice, observance or nonobservance.... [R]eligion [should] be left as
> wholly to private choice as anything can be. It should proceed as unaffected
> by government as possible.[9] ...

Substantive neutrality is not always the same as formal neutrality, [i.e.,] facial
nondiscrimination or the absence of religious classifications. Sometimes the
government may or even must treat religion differently from other ideas and
activities in order to preserve the goal of minimum government interference
in religious choices and commitments. For example, the government may
accommodate private, voluntary religious exercise by exempting it from burdensome regulation, even if the exemption does not "come packaged with
benefits to secular entities."[10] Even though such an exemption gives religion
distinctive treatment, it is constitutionally legitimate if it "does not have the
effect of 'inducing' religious belief, but instead merely 'accommodates' or
implements an independent religious choice."[11]

When the government itself speaks, it must also treat religion distinctively. Neutrality usually requires that the government not express religious
views itself or take a position on religious questions, even though it may
express views on a host of nonreligious questions and even seek to lead public
opinion concerning them. But restrictions on the government's own religious
speech do not authorize government to discriminate against the voluntary
religious speech or activity of private individuals....

As everyone concedes, the instruction at private colleges where Washington's scholarships could be used was private speech and private activity, not
government speech. The scholarships could be applied to a broad variety of

educational choices, including any accredited college and any major except theology from a religious viewpoint. These wide ranging courses taught by varying faculty are bound to include conflicting perspectives, and thus—like the long list of student publications funded in *Rosenberger*—they cannot logically be called the position of the state....

Denying Davey's scholarship plainly interfered with his individual choice in religious matters. The Court has repeatedly recognized [most recently in *Zelman v. Simmons-Harris*] that providing aid to private individuals under neutral, secular criteria and allowing them to use that aid at either religious or nonreligious schools promotes the "genuine and independent choices of [those] individuals."[12] Conversely, to withdraw aid because a student chooses a religious major interferes with the student's choices. [*Davey*] said that the effect is "mild" when discrimination takes the form of denying a benefit, but there is no basis for that assertion. By declaring a major in pastoral ministries, Davey lost nearly $2,700 in scholarship aid for two years of college. Common sense, precedent, and the record all suggest that the prospect of losing such an amount would often affect a student's choice of major, especially for Promise Scholarship recipients with their modest family incomes.... Northwest College's financial aid officer testified that students consider "changing [their] major to get" or retain the state scholarships.

By excluding theology studies taught from a "devotional" perspective, the state created an incentive for students not to pursue that major and instead to pursue a major less infused with religious teaching.... In addition, because Washington allows scholarships for those pursuing a religion major taught from a secular perspective, it might induce some students committed to a religion major to choose a college whose approach to the study of religion is more secular and less devotional. At the margin, it might induce some colleges to tip their religion courses from the devotional toward the secular in order that their religion majors may receive Promise Scholarships.

These distortions of private choice should have been held to violate the First Amendment. State interference with private religious choice is minimized when the state funds nothing, or when it funds everything within a neutrally defined category. Discriminatory funding is always the worst policy, because it pressures citizens to adapt their own religious choices to the state's favored categories....

B. Unconstitutional Penalty on Religious Choice

[Moreover, by] excluding Davey from a scholarship, the state did not merely decline to fund religious instruction as the Court claimed. The state went further and imposed an independent penalty on Davey's religious choice, by denying him aid for secular courses—aid to which he would otherwise be entitled—because he chose to pursue a theology major taught from a religious perspective. The state subjected Davey to an unconstitutional condition.

The Court's case law distinguishes unconstitutional conditions from mere refusals to fund. "Our 'unconstitutional conditions' cases involve situations in which the Government has placed a condition on the recipient of the subsidy rather than on a particular program or service, thus effectively prohibiting the recipient from engaging in the protected conduct outside the scope of the federally funded program."[13] Put differently, the cases distinguish between government "merely refus[ing] to pay" for an activity, and government "deny[ing] ... any independent benefit" because the beneficiary engages in the activity.[14] ...

[W]ithdrawing Davey's scholarship went beyond "refus[ing] to pay for" religion; it "den[ied an] independent benefit" by withdrawing aid for his entire education. Davey took numerous courses for which he would have received scholarship support had he not declared theology as a major. All Northwest College theology majors took core courses in subjects such as English and math. But the penalty for choosing a theology major was particularly clear in Davey's case. He proposed to double major in business administration and theology. He lost funding for his business administration degree solely because he also chose to major in theology at Northwest. The Washington exclusion is so broad—covering the entire "school where the scholarship is used"—that Davey could not pursue a secular degree at Northwest College even in an entirely separate program from his theology degree, with no overlap in faculty, classroom space, or other features.

The Court answered that the scholarship exclusion did not "require students to choose between their religious beliefs and receiving a government benefit," assertedly because "Promise Scholars may still use their scholarship to pursue a secular degree at a different institution from where they are studying devotional theology." As the state put it, Davey could use the Promise Scholarship for the non-theology major at Northwest, and then "simultaneously us[e] his own money to pursue a theology degree in a separate program at a second school."

This answer is no solution whatsoever. The Court implicitly suggests that the student pay close to two full-time tuitions simultaneously and bear the serious inconvenience of attending two full-time programs at potentially distant campuses. The state alternatively suggested that a student pursue each degree half-time—and therefore, of course, take twice as long to finish college. Either course is so "unduly burdensome" that the condition "effectively prohibit[s] the recipient from engaging in [a theology degree] outside the scope of the [state] funded program." ...

It was absurd for the Court to say that Davey would not be significantly burdened by undertaking, and paying for, two college educations instead of one. The Court came to this result because of a separate principle—that government can require physical separation of funded and unfunded activities. The Court has allowed governments to carry this principle to extreme lengths. If government is willing to pay for most college educations but not for theology majors, it can require rigorous separation of the two to avoid any indirect subsidy to theology majors. Taken to its logical conclusion, this approach authorizes government to ban any activity it chooses on any premises where government funds are spent, to ensure that the government funds do not inadvertently subsidize the banned activity. This rule of physical separation threatens to completely swallow the rule against unconstitutional conditions....

C. Denying Scholarships Served None of the Purposes of the Religion Clauses

Refraining from state funding of private religious education can, in some situations, serve the Religion Clauses' goals of liberty and religious autonomy. Government money is a powerful source of government influence; government expenditures on religion generally expand government influence in a field where that influence should be minimized.

Describing the same point from the private perspective, voluntary funding of religious instruction often maximizes individual liberty and the influence of private choice. Each individual can decide when, how, and how much to contribute to whom, and whether to contribute at all. Voluntary funding of religious organizations protects individual conscience and keeps government out of religion.

But Washington's exclusion of theology majors like Davey served none of these goals. Indeed, it transgressed a number of them. Government funding decisions have the least impact on private religious choice when government funds nothing, or when it funds everything within a neutrally defined category. Government does maximum harm to free choice when it funds some choices and refuses to fund their directly competing alternatives. The Court claimed that *Davey* was a strong case for refusing state aid. In reality, the case was very weak....

The Founding-Era History

We can review the weakness of the state's interests in *Davey* by comparing modern education funding like Promise Scholarships with the funding of religion that the Founders rejected and the *Davey* majority cites. As the Court noted, "[p]erhaps the most famous example of public backlash" against funding of clergy was Virginia's rejection of the general assessment to support clergy in 1785. The Court relied on the rejection of the general assessment as a reason to resist nondiscriminatory funding of scholarships for higher education. But the two programs are fundamentally different....

As is made clear by its full title—A Bill Establishing a Provision for Teachers of the Christian Religion—the essence of the general assessment was a massive discrimination in favor of religious viewpoints. In a time of minimal government, Christian clergy and Christian places of worship were to be singled out for special subsidy. Supporters of the measure did all they could to make it nonpreferential as among Christian denominations.... But there was no attempt to make the general assessment neutral as between religion and nonreligion. No one claimed, or could have claimed, that clergy and church buildings fell within the neutrally drawn boundaries of some larger category of state-funded activities. And no one claimed, or could have claimed, that the state would receive any secular service or benefit not derived from the religious functions of the churches. The argument for the general assessment was the familiar argument for other forms of establishment—that the state would benefit from having a more Christian population....

All modern funding cases, including *Davey*, are fundamentally different from the general assessment. No one proposes to fund the inherently religious functions of churches. No one proposes the funding on the ground that religion alone provides a unique or greater social benefit than do secular ideas; and no one proposes to fund religious organizations preferentially over secular organizations providing the same service. Instead, the state funds a service—in this case, higher education—that is offered by both secular and religious providers. Higher education at religious colleges like Northwest College met all the state's accreditation requirements and offered a wide range of courses less infused with religion than those in the theology department.

The broad neutral category of higher education includes, as one of its many applications, the training of clergy, and the training of clergy is a core religious function. But for multiple reasons, *Davey* is still like the modern funding cases and unlike the general assessment. The training of clergy is clearly an incidental application of a vastly broader program; the training of clergy also serves the state's goal of educating its citizenry; and the decision to direct the money to religious uses is made by private citizens with no encouragement from the state. [Moreover, the state's scholarship program—unlike some other aid schemes—does not involve any conditions interfering in the curriculum of the participating college.] Discriminatory exclusion of theology majors powerfully interferes with private religious choice, but treating them identically with all other majors does not influence anyone's choice. Excluding theology majors from a generally applicable program is a far greater departure from religious neutrality than including them....

D. State Discretion to Choose a Church-State Policy

Given the effect of Washington's exclusion on religious choice and the weakness of the asserted justifications, the Court's ruling ultimately rests on giving the states wide discretion in making policy toward religion. The majority led off by saying that "[t]hese two Clauses, the Establishment Clause and the Free Exercise Clause, are frequently in tension," but that "'there is room for play in the joints' between them. In other words, there are some state actions permitted by the Establishment Clause but not required by the Free Exercise Clause." By emphasizing the state's discretion, the majority was able to find that the discrimination against theology majors was permitted even though the unanimous Court in *Witters* [*v. Department of Services*[15]] had found that it was not required by Establishment Clause values. In our view, the argument for discretion here rests on the final deep misconception of the Religion Clauses.

It is no accident that the Court's formulation ties the need for "play in the joints" between the clauses to the idea that they are "in tension." If the Free Exercise and Establishment Clauses conflict or push in opposite directions, then indeed the reach of one clause or both needs to be cut down; otherwise, anything the state did concerning religion in a given situation would run into a constitutional barrier on one side or the other. But the matter is different if the two clauses are not conflicting, but complementary—if they constitute two aspects of a single statement or principle about religion and the government. If both clauses together serve the goal of protecting individual religious choice, then it makes perfect sense to say that a policy—like Washington's—that distorts religious choice is both unsupported by the Establishment Clause and violative of the Free Exercise Clause.... Indeed, if the two clauses work together, one would expect that a policy that serves no Establishment Clause values would also conflict with Free Exercise Clause values.

The Religion Clauses should be read as complementary aspects of a single principle. To interpret them as conflicting is, as one of us has previously argued, "a mistake at the most fundamental level."[16] It "imputes incoherence to the Founders," and it ignores the historical record: "The Religion Clauses were no compromise of conflicting interests, but the unified demand of the most vigorous advocates of religious liberty."

Certainly the state needs some discretion to choose among different policies that affect religion. There should be discretion when the state's interest in acting is strong—as the "compelling interest" test in free exercise law tries to ascertain—and perhaps when the constitutional principles at stake in a case are ambiguous or conflicting, so that either course of action may affect religious freedom.

But in *Davey*, as we have argued, there was little argument that constitutional principles were in tension, or that the denial of funds would serve certain religion clause principles. The exclusion of students like Davey violates the core principles of religious choice and serves none of the salutary purposes that rules against discretionary state funding of religious education might serve....

III. *DAVEY*, VOUCHERS, AND OTHER AID CASES

Before the Court's decision, observers generally saw the *Davey* case as simply the first Supreme Court skirmish in the war over whether funding programs may include religious institutions such as schools and social services. The main battle is not over college scholarships for religious majors, but over the inclusion of church-affiliated K–12 schools in programs of vouchers given to families to use at the school of their choice. Including religious schools in voucher programs is permissible under *Zelman* [cited above], but many states and cities might exclude religious schools for political and policy reasons or because of state constitutional provisions that bar aid to "sectarian" or religious institutions or instruction....

Davey can be read to allow states to exclude religious schools from K–12 voucher programs. But it can easily be read much more narrowly, and in view of our criticisms of the decision, we think the narrow reading is much to be preferred. The key question is which of the two bases for *Davey* set out in part I is most fundamental. The first basis—that the denial of funding is not a constitutionally significant burden on religion—broadly applies to the funding of K–12 education and likely dooms any free exercise challenge to the exclusion of religious schools from vouchers. If withholding a $2,700 two-year college scholarship is only a "mil[d]" burden on religion because "[i]t imposes neither criminal nor civil sanctions," then neither is it a real burden to withhold a K–12 voucher, typically worth only a little more per year....

But the second, narrower basis for *Davey*—that the state has a particular "historic and substantial" interest in denying funds for clergy training—does not apply to K–12 vouchers, by its terms or its reasoning.... Recall first that the Court treated training of clergy as a "distinct category of instruction": it differs from "training for secular professions" in that it "resembles worship'" and is "akin to a religious calling as well as an academic pursuit." [By contrast, K–12 religious] schools pursue not only religious instruction but also secular education. They train students for the same secular professions and careers that secular schools do; in the Court's words, they "pla[y] a significant and valuable role in raising national levels of knowledge, competence, and experience."[17] The schools teach the same "common subjects like math, English, social studies, and science, that all accredited schools provide," and "a decent elementary or secondary school education in English, math, and science provides secular educational value, even if it takes place in a thoroughly religious setting."[18]

Religious K–12 schools, then, do not provide "a distinct category of instruction": excluding them excludes instruction that falls within the same category as secular schools but is done from a religious viewpoint. It is a pure case of discrimination against an activity solely because of its religious motivation or viewpoint—the core forms of discrimination impermissible under the Free Exercise and Free Speech Clauses, respectively. Core discrimination against religious motivation or viewpoint also strengthens the inference for the anti-religious animus that the Court said was absent in *Davey*. In concluding that Washington had no such animus, the Court relied heavily on the fact that scholarship students could take non-theology majors and classes taught from a pervasively religious perspective. But in a K–12 program, this would be the very option that excluding religious schools would forbid. The Court in *Davey* thought it important that "the entirety of the Promise Scholarship Program goes a long way toward including religion in its benefits," which cannot be said when religious K–12 schools are excluded from voucher programs.

In addition, the history of opposition to funding clergy that *Davey* cites is not relevant to the inclusion of religious K–12 schools in vouchers and other general programs of education funding....

Opposition to funding K–12 religious schools dates not to the founding era, but to the mid-nineteenth century and the Protestant campaign to expand public schools and deny support to the newly forming Catholic school systems. The opposition to supporting Catholic schools contained a significant strain of anti-Catholic bigotry, as numerous studies have shown. The opponents pushed for Protestant-style prayers and Bible readings in the public schools, while blocking funding to "sectarian" (a code word for Catholic) schools on the ground that they would educate their students in religious "superstitions" and anti-democratic habits. The opponents failed to enact a federal constitutional ban on aid to sectarian schools through the Blaine Amendment of 1876, but they succeeded in inserting similar bans—"little Blaine Amendments"—into nearly forty state constitutions between the mid-1800s and the early 1900s.

The elements of religious prejudice behind the nineteenth-century state bans on funding have generated arguments that those provisions are unconstitutionally tainted and cannot be applied today under the Free Exercise and Equal Protection Clauses. In *Davey*, the Court sidestepped this argument on the ground that the Washington constitutional provision at issue—which barred state funds from being "appropriated for or applied to religious worship, exercise or instruction"[19]—was not based on or associated with the Blaine Amendment....

However, *Davey* clearly does not foreclose challenges to other state constitutional provisions more directly tied to state or federal Blaine amendments. The Court noted that another, broader Washington provision—requiring that schools "supported wholly or in part by the public funds shall be forever free from sectarian control or influence"[20]—was a descendant of the federal Blaine Amendment but was not at issue in the case. When a state exclusion of religion rests on such a provision, it is still open to challenge on the ground that it reflects anti-Catholic animus.

NOTES

As a result of editing, the notes for this essay have been renumbered. The note number from the original essay or article is shown in parentheses at the end of each citation.

1. See, e.g., ... *Lemon v. Kurtzman*, 403 U.S. 602 (1971). (1)

2. 540 U.S. 712 (2004). (3)

3. 508 U.S. 520 (1993). (7)

4. 435 U.S. 618 (1978). (8)

5. 515 U.S. 819 (1995). (9)

6. *Davey*, 540 U.S. 720. (13)

7. *Lukumi*, 508 U.S. 523, 532. (28)

8. 435 U.S. 632 (Brennan and Marshall, JJ., concurring). (31)

9. Douglas Laycock, "Formal, Substantive, and Disaggregated Neutrality Toward Religion," *DePaul Law Review* 39 (1990): 993, 1001–1002 (footnotes omitted). (37)

10. *Corporation of Presiding Bishop v. Amos*, 483 U.S. 327, 338 (1987). (39)

11. *Thomas v. Review Board*, 450 U.S. 707, 727 (1981) (Rehnquist, J., dissenting on other grounds). (40)

12. *Zelman*, 536 U.S. 639, 649 (2002) [(upholding inclusion of religious schools in voucher program)]. (47)

13. *Rust v. Sullivan*, 500 U.S. 173, 197 (1991). (64)

14. *Regan v. Taxation with Representation*, 461 U.S. 540, 546 (1983). (65)

[15. 474 U.S. 481 (1986).]

16. Douglas Laycock, "Continuity and Change in the Threat to Religious Liberty: The Reformation and Era and the Late Twentieth Century," *Minnesota Law Review* 80 (1996): 1047, 1088. (116)

17. *Board of Education v. Allen*, 392 U.S. 236, 247 (1968). (132)

18. Thomas C. Berg, "Vouchers and Religious Schools: The New Constitutional Questions," *University of Cincinnati Law Review* 72 (2003): 151, 173. (133)

19. Washington Constitution, art. I, § 11. (144)

20. Washington Constitution, art. IX, § 4. (147)

LOCKE V. DAVEY AND THE
LIMITS TO NEUTRALITY THEORY

STEVEN K. GREEN

Government neutrality toward religion has been a touchstone for religion clause jurisprudence since 1947. Only since 1990, however, has neutrality risen to a position of dominance and, some may argue, near exclusivity in church-state analysis. In 1990, [in *Employment Division v. Smith,*] the Supreme Court reversed an almost thirty year approach of applying strict scrutiny to laws of general applicability that burden religion, substituting a more deferential review.... Thus, governments are no longer required to provide exemptions for religiously motivated conduct that violates religion-neutral laws— e.g., states can require Amish horse-drawn buggies, like other slow moving vehicles, to display bright orange warning symbols despite the unique religious offense to Amish theology. Equal treatment, irrespective of a neutral law's resulting impact, is all that the Constitution requires....

Steven C. Green, "*Locke v. Davey* and the Limits to Neutrality Theory," *Temple University Law Review* 77 (2004): 913, 914–17, 921–30, 932–33, 941–48, 950–55.

But neutrality's rise to Establishment Clause dominance was most apparent in an area that had otherwise been the sole purview of that clause: the public funding of private religious schools. Combined with notions of private choice, neutrality commanded the day in a series of cases involving tax deductions, scholarships, and other educational benefits that flowed to students attending religious schools and colleges. Neutrality theory reached its apex and position of dominance in *Mitchell v. Helms*[1] and *Zelman v. Simmons-Harris*, the latter decision upholding publicly funded vouchers for private religious schooling [where the voucher terms were equal or neutral for both secular and religious schools]....

[I]n *Locke v. Davey*, [however,] a surprisingly lop-sided Court majority held that Washington State could deny a public scholarship to an otherwise eligible applicant solely because he planned to use the monies to study for the ministry at a church-related college.... Despite the breadth of the program and the existence of private choice—factors that were determinative in *Zelman* and touted in *Mitchell*—the Court subordinated principles of neutrality to the state's preference for its own vision of separationism as set out in its constitution....

[O]ne would expect that if neutrality allows the extension of generally available benefits to religious school students, it would also prohibit the exclusion of similar benefits, particularly when bolstered by the existence of private choice and supported by free exercise, free speech, and equal protection claims. Only nine years earlier the Court had said as much in *Rosenberger v. Rector & Visitors of the University of Virginia*[2] when it prohibited the University of Virginia from denying generally available benefits to a student-published Christian magazine....

[Thus *Locke v. Davey*] raises questions about the neutrality principle and its limits. This article argues that while the *Locke* decision is correct, it represents a missed opportunity to expound on the limits of neutrality theory and its connection to the philosophical basis underlying the religion clauses. This article argues that the Court's reliance on neutrality has been misplaced in certain contexts—in particular, in funding programs—that the government need not act neutrally toward religion within its own policy choices such that it can (and often should) prefer secular solutions to religious solutions, and that a secular preference is consistent with the purpose and meaning of the Constitution....

I. *Locke v. Davey*

The Holding

The majority opinion [in *Locke*] is correct on one level: [the case] is far different from the situations presented in *Lukumi* and *McDaniel*. Those cases involved the suppression of religion in that one law had the object of religious persecution while the other imposed special disabilities [exclusion from eligibility for the state legislature] on the basis of religious status, disabilities that affected McDaniel's civil and political rights. In *Lukumi*, the ordinance singled out religiously based conduct—animal sacrifice, a ritual central to Santeria worship—for criminal penalty. At the same time, the ordinance allowed for other forms of ritualistic and nonritualistic killings of animals. For the Court, the Hialeah ordinance represented a clear case of legislative gerrymandering to impede the rituals of one religious faith. In addition, there was indisputable evidence of intent to discriminate; the "object" of the ordinance, the Court noted, was to suppress religious practices.

No such "targeting" occurs with the Washington Promise Scholarship. While the statute and regulations exclude only theological degrees from eligibility, the exclusion was not enacted for the purpose of penalizing religion but for the purpose of adhering to Washington's constitutional mandate not to aid or advance religion. This is not mere semantics. The Hialeah city council sought to outlaw a religious practice offensive to a majority of denizens. In contrast, the Washington policy does not regulate or prohibit theological study or training; it merely declines to fund its expression. Davey could still practice his faith unimpeded.... Also, [the] distinction between ritualistic killings (prohibited) and Kosher and other nonritualistic killings in *Lukumi* could only be explained as based on animus, whereas the Washington distinction is consistent with a constitutional principle to avoid state involvement with core religious functions, such as the training of clergy....

Importantly, in so interpreting *Lukumi*, the *Locke* Court cleared up a disagreement among the circuits on whether singling out religion under a statute is per se unconstitutional (as *Davey* and his amici argued) or whether a claimant needs to make an additional showing that the distinction burdens religious practice.... Rehnquist's holding that there is no "presumptive unconstitutionality" is a better reading of *Lukumi*, as the alternative interpretation would call all religious based distinctions—even benign ones—into question.

... [The Court's] holding affirms the ability of states to permissibly accommodate religious practice in order to relieve burdens on religious practice that may fall short of free exercise violations. ... State efforts that target accommodation of religion, such as under so-called state Religious Freedom Restoration Acts ("RFRAs"), are permissible. ...

The *Locke* Court's summary disposal of *McDaniel*, is less convincing, however. ... There, the Court found that [when Tennessee] exclude[d] clergy from holding office, McDaniel was denied the ability to be a minister—a constitutionally protected right—and participate in the political process at the same time, which the Court, quoting James Madison, termed a "privation of a civil right."[3] [T]he law effectively precluded McDaniel from exercising both rights. ... [I]n contrast to the Tennessee law, the Washington law does not turn on anyone's status—all qualified applicants are eligible regardless of their faith. Davey could be a minister and receive the scholarship for non-theological programs; he was not disqualified because of any status or on account of his beliefs, but only because he wished to use the scholarship for an unapproved major. ...

However, this distinction obscures the fact that Davey still could not receive his benefit and pursue his religious calling at the same time. He was effectively forced to choose between exercising his religious beliefs and receiving a government benefit, a choice the Court sometimes terms an "unconstitutional condition." ... *Locke* [thus] called for a more thorough analysis of why the unconstitutional conditions doctrine—if it still exists—does not apply in this context. The quick answer is that ... Washington was not restricting the expression of a grant recipient unrelated to the purposes of the benefit; neither was the exclusion "aimed at the suppression of ideas thought inimical to the Government's own interest."[4] Rather, the condition imposed by Washington—do not spend the scholarship on clergy training—is on the manner in which the benefit is used. ... At a minimum, *Locke* is consistent with the Court's willingness to afford leeway to government grant programs to exact broader rules than necessary to ensure that public funds do not subsidize disfavored activities. ...

Davey and his amici argued that the state burdened his practice by coercing his religious choices, an action presumably inconsistent with government neutrality toward religion. But as already explained, Davey was not required to surrender a constitutional right to receive the benefit, but merely adjust its use. As an initial matter, the Court has held that a state's failure to fund the exercise of a fundamental right does not infringe on that right. The burden placed on Davey's religious practice was no greater than the financial burden placed on low income pregnant women who were denied Medicaid funds to obtain an abortion. As the court declared in *Harris v. McRae*: "A refusal to fund protected activity, without more, cannot be equated with the imposition of a 'penalty' on that activity."[5] Refusal to fund theological training on its own does not infringe on Davey's free exercise rights.

As for the claim that the prohibition burdens Davey's religious choices, not all burdens on religious choices are of equal force or are necessarily forbidden. ... The statutes in issue in *Harris* [and other cases involving denials of abortion funding] also affected people's choices regarding the exercise of constitutional rights. However, the Court held that state spending choices that encourage a person to forgo exercising a protected right is not the same as restricting the exercise of that right. The government can and does create incentives for secular education over religious—it does so all the time by funding public schools over parochial schools. Similarly, the National Institutes of Health can give grants for research that relies on evolutionary theories and prefer such grant applications over research that relies on creationism....

[Apart from whether excluding Davey from the program burdened him,] Rehnquist's discussion of Washington's interest in its exclusion may be the most important part of the opinion. The majority found that "the State's interest in not funding the pursuit of devotional degrees is substantial,"[6] based in large part on the longstanding historical "prohibitions against using tax funds to support the ministry." Washington's prohibition against the funding of clergy training is "scarcely novel," Rehnquist iterated; "[i]n fact, we can think of few areas in which a State's antiestablishment interests come more into play."

Quite clearly, few would contest that the public funding of religious ministries strikes at the heart of the nonestablishment concept. The salient issue is how broadly or narrowly the Court perceived the state's interest.... [Some have argued that] while a prohibition against funding clergy activities is historically supportable, such justifications would not support a broader distinction against use at religious schools generally, or the funding of religiously based social service agencies where the funds do not support inherently religious activities.

This reading of the opinion is supportable.... But then again, clergy training was the issue before the Court, so it was not unusual for Rehnquist's opinion to highlight those particular facts.... In the final analysis, because the majority's discussion of Washington's rationale for the exclusion was unnecessary given the lack of any countervailing free exercise or free speech violation, it would be erroneous to read too much in the Court's emphasis on clergy training. . . .

What is curious about the Court's decision, however, is its willingness to defer to heightened state nonestablishment concerns when the threat comes in the form of a generally available, neutral program coupled with private choice. If a religious use of a benefit obtained under such conditions "is not readily subject to challenge under the Establishment Clause," [as the Court held in approving the voucher program in *Zelman*,][7] then the state concern would seem to represent more of a "mere shadow" than a "real threat."[8] In essence, the *Locke* decision fails to explain adequately why the elements of neutrality, availability, and choice are not sufficiently effective in this context, notwithstanding the state's greater nonestablishment interest. It is to the issue of neutrality that this article now turns.

II. NEUTRALITY THEORY

The Rise of Neutrality Theory

Although the Court's application of neutrality principles in the religion clause context has divided commentators, few would contest that neutrality has become the operative analytical guide for religion clause adjudications. [Professor Green reviews *Rosenberger, Mitchell, Zelman*, and other decisions in detail.] . . .

Neutrality theory does more, however, than remove Establishment Clause bars to permissive funding programs that include religious recipients. . . . In *Rosenberger*, [the Court held not merely that including religious publications in a funding program was permissible under the Establishment Clause, but that excluding religious publications was impermissible discrimination against religious viewpoints under the Free Speech Clause.] . . .

As a result, one could be forgiven for anticipating that principles of evenhanded-neutrality would guide the Court's holding in *Locke*. . . . The failure of the *Locke* majority even to address the issue is therefore remarkable, to say the least.

Neutrality and *Locke*

[T]he [*Locke*] holding can be viewed as being consistent with neutrality principles in one respect.... Because neutrality is not a self-defining concept, it must derive its meaning by looking to other values the religion clauses were designed to protect. The substantive value in Washington's refusal to fund clergy training is to insulate a core religious function from potential government regulation and oversight. A funding ban on clergy training also prevents religious dependence on government largesse while it avoids potential competition among religions for a share of a limited government appropriation. Also, Washington may have been concerned that any funding scheme might prefer some religions over others. After all, most religious denominations educate their clergy at the graduate level, not through undergraduate Bible colleges. Allowing Davey to use an undergraduate scholarship for clergy training would have resulted in disparate treatment of religious groups.... By affirming the ability of Washington to make such distinctions, the Court traded an approach of formal, evenhanded-neutrality for a more flexible concept that emphasizes these substantive religion clause values.

However, neither the Chief Justice nor Justice Souter—the leading advocate of substantive neutrality on the Court—sought to reconcile the *Locke* holding with these values. Thus Justice Scalia is correct in asserting the majority opinion "makes no serious attempt to defend the program's neutrality."[9] By not even responding to Scalia's critique, the *Locke* majority may be telegraphing a message that there are limits to the application of neutrality principles in funding programs....

III. Neutrality and Non-Establishment

The Limitations of Neutrality Theory

Understanding the limits to neutrality theory requires an exploration into the values the Establishment Clause is designed to protect. First and foremost, non-establishment promotes religious liberty by preventing government interference with religious belief, practice, or doctrine. This impulse has two strains, the first to protect individual liberty against government coercion and the second to protect the autonomy and independence of religious bodies. Securing freedom of conscience was paramount to the founding generation. The framers believed the government funding of religious entities was inherently coercive as was the government prescription of any religious exercise. Religion "can be directed only by reason and conviction, not by force or violence," Madison wrote,[10] a sentiment shared by Jefferson who insisted that to require a person to support even his own faith was "sinful and tyrannical" and deprived him of his "comfortable liberty."[11] The framers were also keenly aware of the corrosive effect of government on religious institutions. Establishments "tend[ed] also to corrupt the principles of that very religion it is intended to encourage."[12] ...

Nonestablishment also promotes other important values: ensuring religious equality, preventing the accumulation of power by one religion or a union of religions and any alignment thereof with government, alleviating dissension among religions through competition for benefits or favoritism, and protecting the legitimacy and integrity of both government and religion....

Many have argued that an approach of neutrality addresses these values by minimizing government influences on religious belief and practice. According to Stephen Monsma, a leading proponent of neutrality theory, government "should neither advantage nor disadvantage any particular religion, nor should its actions either advantage or disadvantage religion in general or secularism in general."[13] Such even-handed neutrality may promote equal treatment of religions and therefore diffuse religious factionalism and further government legitimacy in the eyes of religious dissenters, but it will not address most other concerns.... An evenhanded approach does not protect the independence and autonomy of religious institutions from neutral government regulations—in fact, neutrality instructs that religion is not exempt from general government oversight. The corrosive effect of government on religion may occur just as readily when it comes packaged in the form of a grant program available to religious and secular entities alike. Moreover, permitting religious entities to administer programs long associated with government sovereignty—such as operating prisons or juvenile diversion programs—or to make eligibility determinations for public entitlements—comes dangerously close to awarding governmental authority to religion, a leading fear of the framers. Finally, the payment of public funds to religious entities under a neutral program does not address the fundamental concern of coercion posed by religious assessments....

[Moreover, as] Alan Brownstein and Derek Davis have argued, the application of neutrality principles frequently has unintended consequences of favoring some religious groups over others in the receipt of government access and benefits.[14] According to Professor Davis, "rather than achieving their purpose of eliminating discrimination against religious groups, [neutral programs] merely rearrange the nature of discrimination, often in favor of majority religions or those groups predisposed to receiving government subsidy." While I agree with Professors Brownstein and Davis on the likely results of applying neutral principles in most funding programs, such concerns still beg the question of whether the Constitution mandates an approach of religious neutrality in the first instance. In essence, both proponents and critics of neutrality theory have too readily presumed that neutrality toward religion in government funding programs is a fundamental constitutional value. The secular nature of our liberal democracy suggests that it is not.

Neutrality and Secular Government

The overarching problem with applying neutrality principles to the religion clauses is that it presupposes a particular relationship between religion and democratic government under which equal treatment should apply. Here, supporters of neutrality have made claims, to a large degree unchallenged, of government's obligation to treat religion as favorably as non-religion....

This argument is inconsistent with the secular nature of democratic government, under which the government is entitled to privilege secular values over religious ones. The Constitution contemplates a secular public order, one in which government may promote liberal democratic principles to the exclusion of other ideologies, including religious ones. This secular composition reflects the "self-conscious" decision of the nation's founders to base the new republican governments on reason, rather than on faith.[15] Historians generally agree that "the Enlightenment, with its emphasis on rationalism and empiricism and its rejection of religious faith and mysticism, was the primary epistemology of the founding generation."[16] All of the framers were imbued with Enlightenment thought and based their discussions about republican government on rationalism and empiricism. To be sure, other ideological epistemologies informed the thinking of the founding generation: Whig theories; classical republicanism; English common law; and evangelical and covenant theologies. But Enlightenment rationalism dominated the culture and permeated these other epistemologies. Members of the founding generation saw no conflict between Enlightenment and religious principles and viewed rationalism as a means to achieve religious truths.

Enlightenment rationalism, as expressed by the influential John Locke, taught that government would no longer propagate and defend religious truths: "the care of souls is not committed to the civil magistrate."[17] Instead, the purpose of government was to "protect and advance the 'civil goods' of men rather than to make them pious." Such sentiments are reflected in contemporary writings such as the Federalist Papers and in the record of the ratification debates, where the secular nature of the new government was not in dispute....

The "underlying epistemology of the Constitution, then, is reason rather than faith."[18] As such, the government may favor rational approaches to policy formation over alternative epistemologies, including religious systems. The government need not be neutral or evenhanded toward religion in administering its programs; it may prefer rational, empirically based solutions and outcomes over religiously based ones. Importantly, the preference for and advancement of secular policies over religious policies is not the same as discrimination against religion. Where government promotion of secularism crosses the line into coercion is when the government requires private citizens to agree with its positions or policies. Government must also avoid taking sides on matters of contested religious belief. But this on its own does not disable the government from promoting secular policies and perspectives to the exclusion of comparable religious ones.

This is an important distinction that is worth repeating. Government may advance secular ideals without disparaging religion. Contrary to what some may claim, the boundary between secularism and religion is not a zero-sum game, such that every secular value is advanced at the cost of a comparable religious value. Neither government nor society operates in a Manichean framework. While government should not consciously disparage religion or religious choices, it may create incentives for secular ones.

The consequence of this privileging of secularism over religion is that general funding programs may exclude religious applications of a received government benefit. A further consequence of this secular privileging is that some private recipients may be encouraged to make secular choices when they would prefer religious ones. This, of course, is anathema to prevailing neutrality theory, which teaches that government should refrain from influencing people's choices along religious lines. While this is true with respect to coercive government regulations or general government services, this does not hold true when the government engages in discretionary spending programs through which it seeks to advance a concept of the common good. As with Mr. Davey, the denial of a benefit because of potential religious uses may affect one's religious choices and steer one into a secular pursuit, but such encouragement is vastly different from the harsh and corrupting hand of a government regulator. The point is that the government routinely engages in conduct that influences people's choices, some of which may be religiously grounded; for example, mandatory recycling may conflict with a religious belief to "subjugate the world." To do so, however, is not inconsistent with a constitution grounded on rational secular values....

[The government may seek] to promote secular goals that inadvertently influence someone's religious choices. For example, a school district's decision to promote contraceptive use over abstinence in its high school health education classes may encourage some students to reject religious approaches to premarital sexual activity. The school may go the next step and provide a student audience for Planned Parenthood but not the National Right to Life. Provided the school district has not created a speech forum or set out to disparage religious views of premarital sexual activity, it is not barred from providing only a secular perspective on the issue....

As a result, neutrality principles should not govern discretionary spending programs like the Washington Promise Scholarship. The government must act in a religiously neutral fashion when it is providing public services or creating a forum for the expression of diverse ideas. But when it comes to spending programs to promote particular goals, the government can—and usually should—prefer secular solutions and applications over comparable religious ones.

NOTES

As a result of editing, the notes for this essay have been renumbered. The note number from the original essay or article is shown in parentheses at the end of each citation.

1. 530 U.S. 793 (2000). (12)
2. 515 U.S. 819 (1995). (27)
3. *McDaniel*, 435 U.S. 626. (79)
4. *Speiser v. Randall*, 357 U.S. 513, 519 (1958). (84)
5. 448 U.S. 297, 317 n.19 (1980). (92)

6. *Locke*, 540 U.S. 725. (105)

7. *Zelman*, 536 U.S. 652. (132)

8. See *Abington School Dist. v. Schempp*, 374 U.S. 203, 308 (1963) (Goldberg, J., concurring). (133)

9. *Locke*, 540 U.S. 731 [(dissenting opinion)]. (217)

10. James Madison, "Memorial and Remonstrance," in *Church and State in American History*, ed. John F. Wilson and Donald L. Drakeman (2003), pp. 63, 64 . (225)

11. Thomas Jefferson, "Act for Establishing Religious Freedom," in *Church and State in American History* (1779), p. 68. (226)

12. "Letter from Thomas Jefferson to Rev. Samuel Miller" (January 23, 1808), in John Frederick Wilson, *Church and State in American History* (2003), p. 74. (227)

13. Stephen V. Monsma, *When Sacred and Secular Mix: Religious Nonprofit Organizations and Public Money* (1996), p. 178. (238)

14. Alan E. Brownstein, "Interpreting the Religion Clauses in Terms of Liberty, Equality, and Free Speech Values—A Critical Analysis of 'Neutrality Theory' and Charitable Choice," *Notre Dame Journal of Law Ethics and Public Policy* 13 (1999): 243, 247–56; Derek H. Davis, "The Thomas Plurality Opinion: The Subtle Dangers of Neutrality Theory Unleashed," in *Church-State Relations in Crisis: Debating Neutrality*, ed. Stephen V. Monsma (2002), pp. 75, 84–87. (253)

15. See Isaac Kramnick and R. Laurence Moore, *The Godless Constitution* (1996), p. 27. (258)

16. Suzanna Sherry, "Enlightening the Religion Clauses," *Journal of Contemporary Legal Issues* 7 (1996): 473, 477. (259)

17. John Locke, *A Letter Concerning Toleration*, reprinted in *John Locke: A letter Concerning Toleration In Focus*, ed. John Horton and Susan Mendus (1991), p. 18. (263)

18. Sherry, "Enlightening the Religion Clauses," p. 492. (267)

APPENDICES

CONSTITUTION OF THE UNITED STATES OF AMERICA

PREAMBLE

We, the people of the United States, in order to form a more perfect union, establish justice, insure domestic tranquility, provide for the common defense, promote the general welfare, and secure the blessings of liberty to ourselves and our posterity, do ordain and establish this Constitution for the United States of America.

ARTICLE I

Section I

1. All legislative powers herein granted shall be vested in a Congress of the United States, which shall consist of a Senate and House of Representatives.

Section II

1. The House of Representatives shall be composed of members chosen every second year by the people of the several States; and the electors in each

State shall have the qualifications requisite for electors of the most numerous branch of the State Legislature.

2. No person shall be a Representative who shall not have attained to the age of twenty-five years, and been seven years a citizen of the United States, and who shall not, when elected, be an inhabitant of that State in which he shall be chosen.

3. Representatives and direct taxes shall be apportioned among the several States which may be included within this Union, according to their respective numbers, which shall be determined by adding to the whole number of free persons, including those bound to service for a term of years, and excluding Indians not taxed, three-fifths of all other persons. The actual enumeration shall be made within three years after the first meeting of the Congress of the United States, and within every subsequent term of ten years, in such manner as they shall by law direct. The number of Representatives shall not exceed one for every thirty thousand, but each State shall have at least one Representative; and until such enumeration shall be made, the State of New Hampshire shall be entitled to choose three; Massachusetts, eight; Rhode Island and Providence Plantations, one; Connecticut, five; New York, six; New Jersey, four; Pennsylvania, eight; Delaware, one; Maryland, six; Virginia, ten; North Carolina, five; South Carolina, five, and Georgia, three.

4. When vacancies happen in the representation from any State, the executive authority thereof shall issue writs of election to fill such vacancies.

5. The House of Representatives shall choose their speaker and other officers; and shall have the sole power of impeachment.

Section III

1. The Senate of the United States shall be composed of two Senators from each State, chosen by the Legislature thereof for six years; and each Senator shall have one vote.

2. Immediately after they shall be assembled in consequence of the first election, they shall be divided as equally as may be into three classes. The

seats of the Senators of the first class shall be vacated at the expiration of the second year, of the second class at the expiration of the fourth year, and of the third class at the expiration of the sixth year, so that one third may be chosen every second year; and if vacancies happen by resignation, or otherwise, during the recess of the Legislature of any State, the executive thereof may make temporary appointments until the next meeting of the Legislature, which shall then fill such vacancies.

3. No person shall be a Senator who shall not have attained to the age of thirty years, and been nine years a citizen of the United States, and who shall not, when elected, be an inhabitant of that State for which he shall be chosen.

4. The Vice-President of the United States shall be President of the Senate, but shall have no vote unless they be equally divided.

5. The Senate shall choose their other officers, and also a President pro tempore, in the absence of the Vice-President, or when he shall exercise the office of President of the United States.

6. The Senate shall have the sole power to try all impeachments. When sitting for that purpose, they shall all be on oath or affirmation. When the President of the United States is tried, the chief-justice shall preside: and no person shall be convicted without the concurrence of two thirds of the members present.

7. Judgment in cases of impeachment shall not extend further than to removal from office, and disqualification to hold and enjoy any office of honor, trust, or profit under the United States; but the party convicted shall nevertheless be liable and subject to indictment, trial, judgment, and punishment, according to law.

Section IV

1. The times, places and manner of holding elections for Senators and Representatives shall be prescribed in each State by the Legislature thereof; but the Congress may at any time by law make of alter such regulations, except as to the place of choosing Senators.

Section V

1. Each House shall be the judge of the election, returns, and qualifications of its own members, and a majority of each shall constitute a quorum to do business; but a smaller number may adjourn from day to day, and may be authorized to compel the attendance of absent members, in such manner and under such penalties as each House may provide.

2. Each House may determine the rule of its proceedings, punish its members for disorderly behavior, and, with the concurrence of two thirds, expel a member.

3. Each House shall keep a journal of its proceedings, and from time to time publish the same, excepting such parts as may in their judgment require secrecy; and the yeas and nays of the members of either House on any questions shall, at the desire of one fifth of those present, be entered on the journal.

4. Neither House, during the session of Congress, shall, without the consent of the other, adjourn for more than three days, nor to any other place than that in which the two houses shall be sitting.

Section VI

1. The Senators and Representatives shall receive a compensation for their services, to be ascertained by law, and paid out of the treasury of the United States. They shall, in all cases, except treason, felony, and breach of the peace, be privileged from arrest during their attendance at the sessions of their respective houses, and in going to and returning from same; and for any speech or debate in either house, they shall not be questioned in any other place.

2. No Senator or Representative shall, during the time for which he was elected, be appointed to any civil office under the authority of the United States which shall have been created, or the emoluments whereof shall have been increased during such time; and no person holding any office under the United States shall be a member of either House during his continuance in office.

Section VII

1. All bills for raising revenue shall originate in the House of Representatives, but the Senate may propose or concur with amendments, as on other bills.

2. Every bill which shall have passed the House of Representatives and the Senate shall, before it become a law, be presented to the President of the United States; if he approve, he shall sign it, but if not, he shall return it, with his objections, to that House in which it shall have originated, who shall enter the objections at large on their journal, and proceed to reconsider it. If after such reconsideration two thirds of that House shall agree to pass the bill, it shall be sent, together with the objections, to the other House, by which it shall likewise be reconsidered; and if approved by two thirds of that House it shall become a law. But in all such cases the votes of both Houses shall be determined by yeas and nays, and the names of the persons voting for and against the bill shall be entered on the journal of each House respectively. If any bill shall not be returned by the President within ten days (Sundays excepted) after it shall have been presented to him, the same shall be a law in like manner as if he had signed it, unless the Congress by their adjournment, prevent its return; in which case it shall not be a law.

3. Every order, resolution, or vote to which the concurrence of the Senate and House of Representatives may be necessary (except on a question of adjournment) shall be presented to the President of the United States; and before the same shall take effect shall be approved by him, or being disapproved by him, shall be repassed by two thirds of the Senate and the House of Representatives, according to the rules and limitations prescribed in the case of a bill.

Section VIII

1. The Congress shall have power to lay and collect taxes, duties, imposts, and excises, to pay the debts and provide for the common defense and general welfare of the United States; but all duties, imposts, and excises shall be uniform throughout the United States.

2. To borrow money on the credit of the United States.

3. To regulate commerce with foreign nations, and among the several States, and with the Indian tribes.

4. To establish an uniform rule of naturalization and uniform laws on the subject of bankruptcies throughout the United States.

5. To coin money, regulate the value thereof, and of foreign coin, and fix the standard of weights and measures.

6. To provide for the punishment of counterfeiting the securities and current coin of the United States.

7. To establish post offices and post roads.

8. To promote the progress of science and useful arts, by securing for limited times to authors and inventors the exclusive rights to their respective writings and discoveries.

9. To constitute tribunals inferior to the Supreme Court.

10. To define and punish piracies and felonies committed on the high seas, and offenses against the law of nations.

11. To declare war, grant letters of marque and reprisal, and make rules concerning captures on land and water.

12. To raise and support armies, but no appropriation of money to that use shall be for a longer term than two years.

13. To provide and maintain a navy.

14. To make rules for the government and regulation of the land and naval forces.

15. To provide for calling forth the militia to execute the laws of the Union, suppress insurrections, and repel invasions.

16. To provide for organizing, arming, and disciplining the militia, and for governing such part of them as may be employed in the service of the United States, reserving to the States respectively the appointment of the officers, and the authority of training the militia according to the discipline prescribed by Congress.

17. To exercise exclusive legislation in all cases whatsoever over such district (not exceeding ten miles square) as may, by cession of particular States and the acceptance of Congress, become the seat of Government of the United States, and to exercise like authority over all places purchased by the consent of the Legislature of the State in which the same shall be, for the erection of forts, magazines, arsenals, dry docks, and other needful buildings.

18. To make all laws which shall be necessary and proper for carrying into execution the foregoing powers, and all other powers vested by this Constitution in the Government of the United States, or in any department or officer thereof.

Section IX

1. The migration or importation of such persons as any of the States now existing shall think proper to admit shall not be prohibited by the Congress prior to the year one thousand eight hundred and eight, but a tax or duty may be imposed on such importation, not exceeding ten dollars for each person.

2. The privilege of the writ of habeas corpus shall not be suspended, unless when in cases of rebellion or invasion the public safety may require it.

3. No bill of attainder or ex post facto law shall be passed.

4. No capitation or other direct tax shall be laid, unless in proportion to the census or enumeration hereinbefore directed to be taken.

5. No tax or duty shall be laid on articles exported from any State.

6. No preference shall be given by any regulation of commerce or revenue to the ports of one State over those of another, nor shall vessels bound to or from one State be obliged to enter, clear, or pay duties in another.

7. No money shall be drawn from the Treasury but in consequence of appropriations made by law; and a regular statement and account of the receipts and expenditures of all public money shall be published from time to time.

8. No title of nobility shall be granted by the United States. And no person holding any office of profit or trust under them shall, without the consent of the Congress, accept of any present, emolument, office, or title of any kind whatever from any king, prince, or foreign state.

Section X

1. No state shall enter into any treaty, alliance, or confederation, grant letters of marque and reprisal, coin money, emit bills of credit, make anything but gold and silver coin a tender in payment of debts, pass any bill of attainder, ex post facto law, or law impairing the obligation of contracts, or grant any title of nobility.

2. No State shall, without the consent of the Congress, lay any impost or duties on imports or exports, except what may be absolutely necessary for executing its inspection laws, and the net produce of all duties and imposts, laid by any State on imports or exports, shall be for the use of the Treasury of the United States; and all such laws shall be subject to the revision and control of the Congress.

3. No State shall, without the consent of Congress, lay any duty of tonnage, keep troops or ships of war in time of peace, enter into any agreement or compact with another State, or with a foreign power, or engage in war, unless actually invaded, or in such imminent danger as will not admit of delay.

Article II

Section I

1. The Executive power shall be vested in a President of the United States of America. He shall hold his office during the term of four years, and, together with the Vice-President, chosen for the same term, be elected as follows:

2. Each State shall appoint, in such manner as the Legislature thereof may direct, a number of electors, equal to the whole number of Senators and Representatives to which the State may be entitled in the Congress; but no Senator or Representative or person holding an office of trust or profit under the United States shall be appointed an elector.

3. [The electors shall meet in their respective States and vote by ballot for two persons, of whom one at least shall not be an inhabitant of the same State with themselves. And they shall make a list of all the persons voted for, and of the number of votes for each, which list they shall sign and certify and transmit, sealed, to the seat of the government of the United States, directed to the President of the Senate. The President of the Senate shall, in the presence of the Senate and House of Representatives, open all the certificates, and the votes shall then be counted. The person having the greatest number of votes shall be the President, if such number be a majority of the whole number of electors appointed, and if there be more than one who have such majority, and have an equal number of votes, then the House of Representatives shall immediately choose by ballot one of them for President; and if no person have a majority, then from the five highest on the list the said House shall in like manner choose the President. But in choosing the President, the vote shall be taken by States, the representation from each State having one vote. A quorum, for this purpose, shall consist of a member or members from two thirds of the States, and a majority of all the States shall be necessary to a choice. In every case, after the choice of the President, the person having the greatest number of votes of the electors shall be the Vice-President. But if there should remain two or more who have equal votes, the Senate shall choose from them by ballot the Vice-President.]*

---

*This clause is superseded by Article XII.

4. The Congress may determine the time of choosing the electors and the day on which they shall give their votes, which day shall be the same throughout the United States.

5. No person except a natural born citizen, or a citizen of the United States at the time of the adoption of this Constitution, shall be eligible to the office of President; neither shall any person be eligible to that office who shall not have attained to the age of thirty-five years and been fourteen years a resident within the United States.

6. In case of the removal of the President from office, or of his death, resignation, or inability to discharge the powers and duties of the said office, the same shall devolve on the Vice-President, and the Congress may by law provide for the case of removal, death, resignation, or inability, both of the President and Vice-President, declaring what officer shall then act as President, and such officer shall act accordingly until the disability be removed or a President shall be elected.

7. The President shall, at stated times, receive for his services a compensation, which shall neither be increased nor diminished during the period for which he shall have been elected, and he shall not receive within that period any other emolument from the United States, or any of them.

8. Before he enter on the execution of his office he shall take the following oath or affirmation: "I do solemnly swear (or affirm) that I will faithfully execute the office of President of the United States, and will, to the best of my ability, preserve, protect, and defend the Constitution of the United States."

Section II

1. The President shall be Commander-in-Chief of the Army and Navy of the United States, and of the militia of the several States when called into the actual service of the United States; he may require the opinion, in writing, of the principal officer in each of the executive departments upon any subject relating to the duties of their respective offices, and he shall have power to grant reprieves and pardons for offenses against the United States except in cases of impeachment.

2. He shall have power, by and with the advice and consent of the Senate, to make treaties, provided two thirds of the Senators present concur; and he shall nominate, and by and with the advice and consent of the Senate shall appoint ambassadors, other public ministers and consuls, judges of the Supreme Court, and all other officers of the United States whose appointments are not herein otherwise provided for, and which shall be established by law; but the Congress may by law vest the appointment of such inferior officers as they think proper in the President alone, in the courts of law, or in the heads of departments.

3. The President shall have power to fill up all vacancies that may happen during the recess of the Senate by granting commissions, which shall expire at the end of their next session.

Section III

He shall from time to time give to the Congress information of the state of the Union, and recommend to their consideration such measure as he shall judge necessary and expedient; he may, on extraordinary occasions, convene both Houses, or either of them, and in case of disagreement between them with respect to the time of adjournment, he may adjourn them to such time as he shall think proper; he shall receive ambassadors and other public ministers; he shall take care that the laws be faithfully executed, and shall commission all the officers of the United States.

Section IV

The President, Vice-President, and all civil officers of the United States shall be removed from office on impeachment for and conviction of treason, bribery, or other high crimes and misdemeanors.

ARTICLE III

Section I

The judicial power of the United States shall be vested in one Supreme Court, and in such inferior courts as the Congress may from time to time ordain and establish. The judges, both of the Supreme and inferior courts, shall hold their offices during good behavior, and shall at stated times receive for their services a compensation which shall not be diminished during their continuance in office.

Section II

1. The judicial power shall extend to all cases in law and equity arising under this Constitution, the laws of the United States, and treaties made, or which shall be made, under their authority; to all cases affecting ambassadors, other public ministers, and consuls; to all cases of admiralty and maritime jurisdiction; to controversies to which the United States shall be a party; to controversies between two or more States, between a State and citizens of another State, between citizens of different States, between citizens of the same State claiming lands under grants of different States, and between a State, or the citizens thereof, and foreign States, citizens, or subjects.

2. In all cases affecting ambassadors, other public ministers, and consuls, and those in which a State shall be party, the Supreme Court shall have original jurisdiction. In all the other cases before mentioned the Supreme Court shall have appellate jurisdiction both as to law and fact, with such exceptions and under such regulations as the Congress shall make.

3. The trial of all crimes, except in cases of impeachment, shall be by jury, and such trial shall be held in the State where the said crimes shall have been committed; but when not committed within any State the trial shall be at such place or places as the Congress may by law have directed.

Section III

1. Treason against the United States shall consist only in levying war against them, or in adhering to their enemies, giving them aid and comfort. No person shall be convicted of treason unless on the testimony of two witnesses to the same overt act, or on confession in open court.

2. The Congress shall have power to declare the punishment of treason, but no attainder of treason shall work corruption of blood or forfeiture except during the life of the person attained.

ARTICLE IV

Section I

Full faith and credit shall be given in each State to the public acts, records, and judicial preceedings of every other State. And the Congress may by general laws prescribe the manner in which such acts, records and proceedings shall be proved, and the effect thereof.

Section II

1. The citizens of each State shall be entitled to all privileges and immunities of citizens in the several States.

2. A person charged in any State with treason, felony, or other crime, who shall flee from justice, and be found in another State, shall on demand of the Executive authority of the State from which he fled, be delivered up, to be removed to the State having jurisdiction of the crime.

3. No person held to service or labor in one State, under the laws thereof, escaping into another shall, in consequence of any law or regulation therein, be discharged from such service or labor, but shall be delivered up on claim of the party to whom such service or labor may be due.

Section III

1. New States may be admitted by the Congress into this Union; but no new State shall be formed or erected within the jurisdiction of any other State, nor any State be formed by the junction of two or more States, or parts of States, without the consent of the Legislatures of the States concerned, as well as of the Congress.

2. The Congress shall have power to dispose of and make all needful rules and regulations respecting the territory or other property belonging to the United States; and nothing in this Constitution shall be so construed as to prejudice any claims of the United States, or of any particular State.

Section IV

The United States shall guarantee to every State in this Union a republican form of government, and shall protect each of them against invasion, and, on application of the Legislature, or of the Executive (when the Legislature cannot be convened), against domestic violence.

ARTICLE V

The Congress, whenever two thirds of both Houses shall deem it necessary, shall propose amendments to this Constitution, or, on the application of the Legislatures of two thirds of the several States, shall call a convention for proposing amendments, which, in either case, shall be valid to all intents and purposes, as part of this Constitution, when ratified by the Legislatures of three fourths of the several States, or by conventions in three fourths thereof, as the one or the other mode of ratification may be proposed by the Congress; provided that no amendment which may be made prior to the year one thousand eight hundred and eight shall in any manner affect the first and fourth clauses in the Ninth Section of the First Article; and that no State, without its consent, shall be deprived of its equal suffrage in the Senate.

ARTICLE VI

1. All debts contracted and engagements entered into before the adoption of this Constitution shall be as valid against the United States under this Constitution as under the Confederation.

2. This Constitution and the laws of the United States which shall be made in pursuance thereof and all treaties made, or which shall be made, under the authority of the United States, shall be the supreme law of the land, and the judges in every State shall be bound thereby, anything in the Constitution of laws of any State to the contrary notwithstanding.

3. The Senators and Representatives before mentioned, and the members of the several State Legislatures, and all executive and judicial officers, both of the United States and of the several States, shall be bound by oath or affirmation to support this Constitution; but no religious test shall ever be

required as a qualification to any office or public trust under the United States.

ARTICLE VII

The ratification of the Conventions of nine States shall be sufficient for the establishment of this Constitution between the States so ratifying the same.

THE AMENDMENTS
TO THE CONSTITUTION*

The Conventions of a number of the States having, at the time of adopting the Constitution, expressed a desire, in order to prevent misconstruction or abuse of its powers, that further declaratory and restrictive clauses should be added, and as extending the ground of public confidence in the Government will best insure the beneficent ends of its institution;

Resolved, by the Senate and House of Representatives of the United States of America, in Congress assembled, two-thirds of both Houses concurring, that the following articles be proposed to the Legislatures of the several States, as amendments to the Constitution of the United States; all or any of which articles, when ratified by three-fourths of the said Legislatures, to be valid to all intents and purposes as part of the said Constitution, namely:

AMENDMENT I

Congress shall make no law respecting an establishment of religion, or prohibiting the free exercise thereof; or abridging the freedom of speech, or of the press; or the right of the people peaceably to assemble, and to petition the Government for a redress of grievances.

---

*The Bill of Rights consists of the first ten amendments to the Constitution.

AMENDMENT II

A well regulated Militia, being necessary to the security of a free State, the right of the people to keep and bear Arms, shall not be infringed.

AMENDMENT III

No Soldier shall, in time of peace be quartered in any house, without the consent of the Owner, nor in time of war, but in a manner to be prescribed by law.

AMENDMENT IV

The right of the people to be secure in their persons, houses, papers, and effects, against unreasonable searches and seizures, shall not be violated, and no Warrants shall issue, but upon probable cause, supported by Oath or affirmation, and particularly describing the place to be searched, and the persons or things to be seized.

AMENDMENT V

No person shall be held to answer for a capital, or otherwise infamous crime, unless on a presentment or indictment of a Grand Jury, except in cases arising in the land or naval forces, or in the Militia, when in actual service in time of War or public danger; nor shall any person be subject for the same offense to be twice put in jeopardy of life or limb; nor shall be compelled in any criminal case to be a witness against himself, nor be deprived of life, liberty, or property, without due process of law; nor shall private property be taken for public use, without just compensation.

AMENDMENT VI

In all criminal prosecutions, the accused shall enjoy the right to a speedy and public trial, by an impartial jury of the State and district wherein the crime shall have been committed, which district shall have been previously ascertained by law, and to be informed of the nature and cause of the accusation; to be confronted with the witnesses against him; to have compulsory process for obtaining witnesses in his favor, and to have the Assistance of Counsel for his defence.

Amendment VII

In Suits at common law, where the value in controversy shall exceed twenty dollars, the right of trial by jury shall be preserved, and no fact tried by a jury, shall be otherwise re-examined in any Court of the United States, than according to the rules of the common law.

Amendment VIII

Excessive bail shall not be required, nor excessive fines imposed, nor cruel and unusual punishments inflicted.

Amendment IX

The enumeration in the Constitution, of certain rights, shall not be construed to deny or disparage others retained by the people.

Amendment X

The powers not delegated to the United States by the Constitution, nor prohibited by it to the States, are reserved to the States respectively, or to the people.

Amendment XI

The Judicial power of the United States shall not be construed to extend to any suit in law or equity, commenced or prosecuted against one of the United States by Citizens of another State, or by Citizens or Subjects of any Foreign State.

Amendment XII

The Electors shall meet in their respective states, and vote by ballot for President and Vice-President, one of whom, at least, shall not be an inhabitant of the same state with themselves; they shall name in their ballots the person voted for as President, and in distinct ballots the person voted for as Vice-President, and they shall make distinct lists of all persons voted for as President, and of all persons voted for as Vice-President and of the number of votes for each, which lists they shall sign and certify, and transmit sealed to the seat of the government of the United States, directed to the President of the Senate; The President of the Senate shall, in the presence of the Senate and House of Representatives, open all the certificates and the votes shall then be counted; The person having the greatest Number of votes for President, shall be the President, if such number be a majority of the whole number of Electors appointed; and if no person have such majority, then from the persons having the highest numbers not exceeding three on the list of those voted for as President, the House of Representatives shall choose immediately, by ballot, the President. But in choosing the President, the votes shall be taken by states, the representation from each state having one vote; a quorum for this purpose shall consist of a member or members from two-thirds of the states, and a majority of all the states shall be necessary to a choice. And if the House of Representatives shall not choose a President whenever the right of choice shall devolve upon them, before the fourth day of March next following, then the Vice-President shall act as President, as in the case of the death or other constitutional disability of the President. The person having the greatest number of votes as Vice-President, shall be the Vice-President, if such number be a majority of the whole number of Electors appointed, and if no person have a majority, then from the two highest numbers on the list, the Senate shall choose the Vice-President; a quorum for the purpose shall consist of two-thirds of the whole number of Senators, and a majority of the whole number shall be necessary to a choice. But no person constitutionally ineligible to the office of President shall be eligible to that of Vice-President of the United States.

AMENDMENT XIII

1. Neither slavery nor involuntary servitude, except as a punishment for crime whereof the party shall have been duly convicted, shall exist within the United States, or any place subject to their jurisdiction.

2. Congress shall have power to enforce this article by appropriate legislation.

AMENDMENT XIV

1. All persons born or naturalized in the United States, and subject to the jurisdiction thereof, are citizens of the United States and of the State wherein they reside. No State shall make or enforce any law which shall abridge the privileges or immunities of citizens of the United States; nor shall any State deprive any person of life, liberty, or property, without due process of law; nor deny to any person within its jurisdiction the equal protection of the laws.

2. Representatives shall be apportioned among the several States according to their respective numbers, counting the whole number of persons in each State, excluding Indians not taxed. But when the right to vote at any election for the choice of electors for President and Vice-President of the United States, Representatives in Congress, the Executive and Judicial officers of a State, or the members of the Legislature thereof, is denied to any of the male inhabitants of such State, being twenty-one years of age, and citizens of the United States, or in any way abridged, except for participation in rebellion, or other crime, the basis of representation therein shall be reduced in the proportion which the number of such male citizens shall bear to the whole number of male citizens twenty-one years of age in such State.

3. No person shall be a Senator or Representative in Congress, or elector of President and Vice-President, or hold any office, civil or military, under the United States, or under any State, who, having previously taken an oath, as a member of Congress, or as an officer of the United States, or as a member of any State legislature, or as an executive or judicial officer of any State, to support the Constitution of the United States, shall have engaged in insurrection or rebellion against the same, or given aid or comfort to the enemies thereof. But Congress may by a vote of two-thirds of each House, remove such disability.

4. The validity of the public debt of the United States, authorized by law, including debts incurred for payment of pensions and bounties for services in suppressing insurrection or rebellion, shall not be questioned. But neither the United States nor any State shall assume or pay any debt or obligation incurred in aid of insurrection or rebellion against the United States, or any claim for the loss or emancipation of any slave; but all such debts, obligations and claims shall be held illegal and void.

5. The Congress shall have power to enforce, by appropriate legislation, the provisions of this article.

Amendment XV

1. The right of citizens of the United States to vote shall not be denied or abridged by the United States or by any State on account of race, color, or previous condition of servitude.

2. The Congress shall have power to enforce this article by appropriate legislation.

Amendment XVI

The Congress shall have power to lay and collect taxes on incomes, from whatever source derived, without apportionment among the several States, and without regard to any census or enumeration.

Amendment XVII

The Senate of the United States shall be composed of two Senators from each State, elected by the people thereof, for six years; and each Senator shall have one vote. The electors in each State shall have the qualifications requisite for electors of the most numerous branch of the State legislatures. When vacancies happen in the representation of any State in the Senate, the executive authority of such State shall issue writs of election to fill such vacancies: Provided, That the legislature of any State may empower the executive thereof to make temporary appointments until the people fill the vacancies by election as the legislature may direct. This amendment shall not be so construed as to affect the election or term of any Senator chosen before it becomes valid as part of the Constitution.

Amendment XVIII

1. After one year from the ratification of this article the manufacture, sale, or transportation of intoxicating liquors within, the importation thereof into, or the exportation thereof from the United States and all territory subject to the jurisdiction thereof for beverage purposes is hereby prohibited.

2. The Congress and the several States shall have concurrent power to enforce this article by appropriate legislation.

3. This article shall be inoperative unless it shall have been ratified as an

amendment to the Constitution by the legislatures of the several States, as provided in the Constitution, within seven years from the date of the submission hereof to the States by the Congress.

Amendment XIX

The right of citizens of the United States to vote shall not be denied or abridged by the United States or by any State on account of sex. Congress shall have power to enforce this article by appropriate legislation.

Amendment XX

1. The terms of the President and Vice President shall end at noon on the 20th day of January, and the terms of Senators and Representatives at noon on the 3d day of January, of the years in which such terms would have ended if this article had not been ratified; and the terms of their successors shall then begin.

2. The Congress shall assemble at least once in every year, and such meeting shall begin at noon on the 3d day of January, unless they shall by law appoint a different day.

3. If, at the time fixed for the beginning of the term of the President, the President elect shall have died, the Vice President elect shall become President. If a President shall not have been chosen before the time fixed for the beginning of his term, or if the President elect shall have failed to qualify, then the Vice President elect shall act as President until a President shall have qualified; and the Congress may by law provide for the case wherein neither a President elect nor a Vice President elect shall have qualified, declaring who shall then act as President, or the manner in which one who is to act shall be selected, and such person shall act accordingly until a President or Vice President shall have qualified.

4. The Congress may by law provide for the case of the death of any of the persons from whom the House of Representatives may choose a President whenever the right of choice shall have devolved upon them, and for the case of the death of any of the persons from whom the Senate may choose a Vice President whenever the right of choice shall have devolved upon them.

5. Sections 1 and 2 shall take effect on the 15th day of October following the ratification of this article.

6. This article shall be inoperative unless it shall have been ratified as an amendment to the Constitution by the legislatures of three-fourths of the several States within seven years from the date of its submission.

AMENDMENT XXI

1. The eighteenth article of amendment to the Constitution of the United States is hereby repealed.

2. The transportation or importation into any State, Territory, or possession of the United States for delivery or use therein of intoxicating liquors, in violation of the laws thereof, is hereby prohibited.

3. The article shall be inoperative unless it shall have been ratified as an amendment to the Constitution by conventions in the several States, as provided in the Constitution, within seven years from the date of the submission hereof to the States by the Congress.

AMENDMENT XXII

1. No person shall be elected to the office of the President more than twice, and no person who has held the office of President, or acted as President, for more than two years of a term to which some other person was elected President shall be elected to the office of the President more than once. But this Article shall not apply to any person holding the office of President, when this Article was proposed by the Congress, and shall not prevent any person who may be holding the office of President, or acting as President, during the term within which this Article becomes operative from holding the office of President or acting as President during the remainder of such term.

2. This article shall be inoperative unless it shall have been ratified as an amendment to the Constitution by the legislatures of three-fourths of the several States within seven years from the date of its submission to the States by the Congress.

AMENDMENT XXIII

1. The District constituting the seat of Government of the United States shall appoint in such manner as the Congress may direct: A number of electors of President and Vice President equal to the whole number of Senators

and Representatives in Congress to which the District would be entitled if it were a State, but in no event more than the least populous State; they shall be in addition to those appointed by the States, but they shall be considered, for the purposes of the election of President and Vice President, to be electors appointed by a State; and they shall meet in the District and perform such duties as provided by the twelfth article of amendment.

2. The Congress shall have power to enforce this article by appropriate legislation.

AMENDMENT **XXIV**

1. The right of citizens of the United States to vote in any primary or other election for President or Vice President, for electors for President or Vice President, or for Senator or Representative in Congress, shall not be denied or abridged by the United States or any State by reason of failure to pay any poll tax or other tax.

2. The Congress shall have power to enforce this article by appropriate legislation.

AMENDMENT **XXV**

1. In case of the removal of the President from office or of his death or resignation, the Vice President shall become President.

2. Whenever there is a vacancy in the office of the Vice President, the President shall nominate a Vice President who shall take office upon confirmation by a majority vote of both Houses of Congress.

3. Whenever the President transmits to the President pro tempore of the Senate and the Speaker of the House of Representatives his written declaration that he is unable to discharge the powers and duties of his office, and until he transmits to them a written declaration to the contrary, such powers and duties shall be discharged by the Vice President as Acting President.

4. Whenever the Vice President and a majority of either the principal officers of the executive departments or of such other body as Congress may by law provide, transmit to the President pro tempore of the Senate and the Speaker of the House of Representatives their written declaration that the President is unable to discharge the powers and duties of his office, the Vice President shall immediately assume the powers and duties of the office as

Acting President. Thereafter, when the President transmits to the President pro tempore of the Senate and the Speaker of the House of Representatives his written declaration that no inability exists, he shall resume the powers and duties of his office unless the Vice President and a majority of either the principal officers of the executive department or of such other body as Congress may by law provide, transmit within four days to the President pro tempore of the Senate and the Speaker of the House of Representatives their written declaration that the President is unable to discharge the powers and duties of his office. Thereupon Congress shall decide the issue, assembling within forty eight hours for that purpose if not in session. If the Congress, within twenty one days after receipt of the latter written declaration, or, if Congress is not in session, within twenty one days after Congress is required to assemble, determines by two thirds vote of both Houses that the President is unable to discharge the powers and duties of his office, the Vice President shall continue to discharge the same as Acting President; otherwise, the President shall resume the powers and duties of his office.

Amendment XXVI

1. The right of citizens of the United States, who are eighteen years of age or older, to vote shall not be denied or abridged by the United States or by any State on account of age.

2. The Congress shall have power to enforce this article by appropriate legislation.

Amendment XXVII

No law, varying the compensation for the services of the Senators and Representatives, shall take effect, until an election of Representatives shall have intervened.